new media

theories

and

practices

of

digitextuality

edited by

anna everett

and

john t. caldwell

routledge
new york and london

Published in 2003 by
Routledge
29 West 35th Street
New York, NY 10001
www.routledge-ny.com

Published in Great Britain by
Routledge
11 New Fetter Lane
London EC4P 4EE
www.routledge.co.uk

Routledge is an imprint of the Taylor & Francis Group
Copyright © 2003 by Taylor & Francis Books, Inc.

Printed in the United States of America on acid free paper.

10 9 8 7 6 5 4 3 2 1

Library of Congress Cataloging-in-Publication Data

New media : theories and practices of digitextuality / edited by Anna Everett & John T. Caldwell.
   p. cm.
   Includes bibliographical references and index.
   ISBN 0–415–93995-X (HB : alk. paper) — ISBN 0–415–93996–8 (pbk. :alk. paper)
   1. Visual communication. 2. Digital media. I. Everett, Anna, 1954- II. Caldwell, John Thornton, 1954-

P93.5 .N48 2003
302.23—dc21

2002015999

The publishers have generously given permission to reprint material from the following copyrighted works: "The Radio As an Apparatus of Communication," from *Brecht on Theatre*, edited and translated by John Willett. Translation copyright © 1964, renewed 1992 by John Willett. Reprinted by permission of Hill and Wang, a division of Farrar, Straus and Giroux, LLC. "The Radio As an Apparatus of Communication," in Bertolt Brecht, *Grosse Berliner und Frankfurter Ausgabe* (vols. 19, 21, 23, 24) © Suhrkamp Verlag Frankfurt am Main 1988 and translations and Brecht material © Stefan S. Brecht. *For the Birds* (figures 14.2, 14.3, and 14.4) and Luxo Jr. (figure 14.1) courtesy of Pixar Animation Studios; © Pixar Animation Studios. Neuron image (figure 4.1) courtesy of Fromherz/MPI Biochemistry; © Fromherz/ MPI Biochemistry. Oxygen Media Images: Girl at Computer (figures 15.3, 15.4, and 15.5) and "I Am Baby" (figure 15.2) courtesy of Oxygen Media, LLC. © Oxygen Media, LLC. "From Barbie to Mortal Kombat: Further Reflections," by Henry Jenkins, http://culturalpolicy.uchicago.edu/conf2001/papers/jenkins.html. "Too Many Notes: Computers, Complexity and Culture in *Voyager*," by George E. Lewis, copyright © 2000 by the International Society for the Arts, Sciences, and Technology, the owner of *Leonardo Music Journal*; http://muse.jhu.edu/edu/demo/ lmj/10.1lewis.html.

new media

Previously published in the AFI Film Readers series
edited by Charles Wolfe and Edward Branigan

Authorship and Film
David A. Gerstner and Janet Staiger

Westerns
Janet Walker

Masculinity
Peter Lehman

Violence and American Cinema
J. David Slocum

The Persistence of History
Vivian Sobchack

Home, Exile, Homeland
Hamid Naficy

Black Women Film and Video Artists
Jacqueline Bobo

The Revolution Wasn't Televised
Lynn Spigel and Michael Curtin

Classical Hollywood Comedy
Henry Jenkins and Kristine Brunovska Karnick

Disney Discourse
Eric Smoodin

Black American Cinema
Manthia Diawara

Film Theory Goes to the Movies
Jim Collins, Ava Preacher Collins, and Hilary Radner

Theorizing Documentary
Michael Renov

Sound Theory/Sound Practice
Rick Altman

Fabrications
Jane M. Gaines and Charlotte Herzog

Psychoanalysis and Cinema
E. Ann Kaplan

contents

list of illustrations   vii

acknowledgments   ix

introduction   xi

 issues in the theory and practice of media convergence
 anna everett and john t. caldwell

part one: digitextual deconstructions

1. digitextuality and click theory: 3
 theses on convergence media in the digital age
 anna everett

2. the radio as an apparatus of communication   29
 bertolt brecht

3. invisible media   33
 laura u. marks

4. exit meat: 47
 digital bodies in a virtual world
 mischa peters

part two: digitextual aesthetics

5. space invaders: 63
 thoughts on technology and the production of culture
 peter lunenfeld

6. the poetics of augmented space   75
 lev manovich

7. too many notes: 93
 computers, complexity, and culture in *voyager*
 george e. lewis

8. the stories digital tools tell   107
 tarleton gillespie

part three: prefiguring digitextuality

9.   second-shift media aesthetics: 127

programming, interactivity, and user flows
john t. caldwell

10. narrative mapping   145
stephen mamber

11. real-time fairy tales: 159

cinema prefiguring digital anxiety
mark williams

12. tulip theory   179
jeffrey sconce

part four: digitextual practices

13. net ratings: 197

defining a new medium by the old, measuring
internet audiences
karen s. f. buzzard

14. flashing digital animations: 209

pixar's digital aesthetic
katherine sarafian

15. log on: 225

the oxygen media research project
constance penley, lisa parks, and anna everett

16. from barbie to mortal kombat: 243
further reflections
henry jenkins

17. endnotes for a theory of convergence 255
joe amato

notes on contributors   265

index   269

illustrations

Figure 1.1. TiVo's advertising pamphlet. © TiVo.

Figure 1.2. Man watching TV. © Cox Cable.

Figure 1.3. Woman using a laptop computer. © A. Everett.

Figure 4.1. Network of snail neurons on a silicon chip. Courtesy of Fromherz/ MPI Biochemistry. © Fromherz/MPI Biochemistry.

Figure 10.1. Franco Moretti's map of *Bleak House.*

Figure 10.2. Thumbnail images from Alfred Hitchcock's *The Birds.*

Figure 10.3. Etienne-Jules Marey's twenty-four-hour train schedule of all Paris–Lyon trains from *La Methode Graphique.*

Figure 10.4. Author's narrative map of all events on the day when a racetrack robbery occurs in Stanley Kubrick's *The Killing.*

Figure 10.5. Map from the Center for Hidden Camera Research (www.cinema. ucla.edu/Mamber2).

Figure 14.1. Luxo Jr. © Pixar Animation Studios.

Figures 14.2–14.4. Progression of frames from Pixar's animated short film *For the Birds* (dir. Ralph Eggleston, 2000). © Pixar Animation Studios.

Figure 15.1. The Hydrogenmedia website. Design by Jon LaPointe.

Figure 15.2. "I Am Baby" ad. Courtesy of Oxygen Media, LLC. © Oxygen Media, LLC.

Figures 15.3–15.5. Hewlett-Packard commercials for Oxygen. Courtesy of Oxygen Media, LLC. © Oxygen Media, LLC.

acknowledgments

We would like to express our gratitude first to all the contributors for making this project an exciting and rewarding one for us. We also thank AFI Film Reader series editors Charles Wolfe and Edward Branigan for their generous editorial guidance and support of the project. We want to take this opportunity to express our special thanks to Taji Duncombe, Katrin Geller, Marlon Hinner, Stacy Paradise, and Kelley Drukker for their valuable assistance with securing rights and permissions in a timely manner. Our deep appreciation also goes out to Bill Germano for his solid support, patience, and belief in this project. We are grateful as well to Gilad Foss for all his editorial help and diligence. Last, but certainly not least, we thank the rest of the Routledge editorial team who worked so hard on this book.

Anna Everett
First I would like to thank my co-editor, John T. Caldwell, for accepting my invitation to work on this deferred project and for helping to bring it to fruition. This project could not have happened without the generous support of the University of California Office of the President, which secured my research and writing time in the very practical form of the UC President's Fellowship. I also thank my colleagues at the University of California, Santa Barbara: Edward Branigan, Anna Brusutti, Dana Driskel, Lisa Parks, Constance Penley, Bhaskar Sarkar, Janet Walker, and Charles Wolfe for their generosity and enthusiasm for this project. I'd like to give special thanks to Ellen Saal and Pascale Bassan for their assistance with this project. Finally, I thank my husband, Aldon L. Nielsen, for his intellectual support and understanding, but this time I thank him publicly for having never minded my longstanding domination of the remote control device(s) in our home.

John T. Caldwell
I very much appreciate Anna Everett, Edward Branigan, and Charles Wolfe's invitation to be a part of this timely project. I would like to thank my colleagues at UCLA—Janet Bergstrom, Nick Browne, Teshome Gabriel, Stephen Mamber, Chon Noriega, Robert Rosen, Vivian Sobchack, and Peter Wollen—for creating an environment

where ideas like those in this book will always generate extensive dialogue and attention. I am especially grateful to Horace Newcomb, George Lipsitz, and Herman Gray for providing models of scholarship that have greatly influenced my thinking about media and culture.

introduction

issues in the theory and

practice of media

convergence

anna   everett   and   john   t.   caldwell

Digital media technologies and their so-called killer apps, and the popular adoption and acceptance of these computer applications, are revolutionizing our sensory perceptions and cognitive experiences of *being in the world.* In the process, new visual, aural, linguistic, and literary codes and signifiers are emerging that require new hermeneutic responses on our part simply to keep pace. When we consider the far-reaching impact of ascendant digital media systems and what their increasing corporatization augurs for individuals' technology access and technologized social processes alike, then the essential role of media theorists, scholars, and practitioners in helping to ensure that humanistic values prevail in the new digital order is clear. Our project of humanizing technology in what has been called a posthuman age requires a trenchant interrogation of the ideological, political, structural, and representational assumptions underpinning much of the new media hegemony.[1] This includes technology legislation, policies, organizational and corporate patterns of use, and the cacophonous new media rhetoric (including hype and antihype). Alternative forms of digital media hype—more sober, democratizing, adventurous, and creative new media discourses and vision—become more important than ever.

This anthology project thus enters the growing discursive fray over old and new media dialectics or "convergence" (in today's media industry parlance) by outlining some new theses and conceptual frameworks capable of engaging with particular aspects of the nascent digital media rhetorics, ethics, aesthetics, practices, and histories, and their film and television antecedents. These discussions include observations about the growing influence these new media exert on our contemporary social, cultural, political, and economic institutions, imperatives, and values. The significance of this work is its scope and range of discussions and analyses from digital media watchers both within and outside the academy. By bringing together in one volume insider perspectives grounded in traditional film and media scholarship and in influential industrial media art and business practices, *New Media* enacts a mode of intellectual and practical convergence that the new digital media topoi will increasingly demand.

This book also questions the mainstream media's often hyperbolic discourses that construct the new digital media's impact in terms of simplistic utopic/dystopic binary oppositions that foreclose reasoned and sober debate around digital and computing media technologies' actual uses and effects. What this project confronts that bears on film and other media study is the fact that it is not enough merely to accept or reject the idea that digital media are transforming our discipline in varying degrees, either for good or ill. Neither, we recognize, does it suffice simply to glom onto these newer technologies older theoretical and critical methodological approaches and assumptions that fail to take into account what is truly novel and transformative about these digital media advances. Having said that, however, it is important to stress that cinema and television studies scholars and industrial media practitioners are uniquely prepared for the present task of envisioning, theorizing, and articulating issues revolving around the digital media revolution and its impact on and implications for contemporary cultural theory and praxis.

part 1: digitextual deconstructions

To achieve the ends outlined above, the first section of this book will consider some theoretical and philosophical questions posed by digital media technologies' current status, and some familiar claims about their transformative possibilities and capabilities. We are especially interested in the presumed capacities of digital media to deconstruct, recode, reconstruct and re-present formerly neat epistemological categories of, say, real/imaginary, time/space, male/female, self/other, body/mind, analog/digital, art/commerce, and so on. An important goal of the following discussions is to sort out some of the spectacular claims and apocalyptic imaginings of digital technology's sway. At the same time, there is an attempt here to weave an empowering and liberatory speculative counterdiscourse around digital media and those progressive aspects of its mutabilities, in form, utility, expression and aesthetics.

In "Digitextuality and Click Theory: Theses on Convergence Media in the Digital Age," Anna Everett contextualizes the digital media revolution in dialectical terms specific to film and television history and new-media studies. Included here is a reinterpreting of Julia Kristeva's term *intertextuality* conjoined with the overdetermined term *digital*, to yield Everett's neologism *digitextuality*, wherein she asks, Are RealPlayer and QuickTime video digitextual tools for realizing André Bazin's "total cinema" and Rudolf Arnheim's vision of the "complete film"? Such questions, and more, are explored in her alternative digital media hype imagined as "click theory," which includes "new media's lure of a sensory plenitude available simply and ubiquitously with the clicking apparatuses of a mouse, video game joystick, and WebTV remote control device." What motivates Everett's detour through some key classical film theory ideas is the urge to temper the hype of the "new" in digital media aesthetics and formalist structures with a sober reflection on its similarities to discourses and practices of the past. Everett effectively presents digitextuality as a useful heuristic for recognizing the tremendous impact of the digital revolution on nearly all aspects of our everyday lives.

In addition to pointing out the importance of maintaining a proper balance between issues of new-media formalism and aesthetics, practices, and ethics and the new-media rhetorics, Everett is concerned with the potential of America's new media monopolies to displace the Althusserian ideological state apparatuses' function with an even more potent ideological corporate apparatuses' function, as represented by the new-media convergence industries. Along these lines, Everett challenges the hyped discourse of the posthuman and what she sees as digital formalism's decade-long preoccupation with an art-for-art's-sake depoliticization imperative. Instead, she follows Jean-François Lyotard, and his discussion of the inhuman, to revalue discourses of embodiment in the digital age. After all, she argues, we only achieve new media's lure of bodily transcendence and plenitude through the very bodies we attempt to flee. She wants to rethink and recuperate a politics of the body vis-à-vis digitextuality's latent use value.

The second chapter is Bertolt Brecht's 1932 manifesto "The Radio As an Apparatus of Communication." As with any manifesto, Brecht's is a polemic that strives to arouse readers toward an acceptance of a revolutionary vision that in this instance centers on the liberatory potential of the radio as powerful new apparatus for social change. What Brecht laments is the radio's commodification as yet another cultural innovation put in the service of "prettifying public life" instead of serving as a means of transforming it. Despite his fears that "society was not yet advanced enough to accept it," Brecht envisioned the radio as the finest possible communication apparatus in public life that could be made to step out of the program and product-supply business and organize its listeners as suppliers. When we consider that the Internet and other digital technologies appear to fulfill many of the emancipatory promises Brecht and other classical media technology theorists imagined, the need for charting the historical continuities linking the old media to the new becomes readily apparent. Thus, Brecht's essay functions in this volume as an important historical referent and philosophical anchor for many contemporary discussions about the role and impact of new media formations in the practices and politics of our everyday lives.

Laura U. Marks's conceptualization of "Invisible Media" (chapter 3) offers an insightful approach to thinking about the ways that much of new media functions at the level of invisibility. This chapter shifts our attention from present debates about old and new media forms that focus on the visible (or formal) features of the new-media topology and their distinctiveness to the more traditional media approaches. In her discussion of new-media invisibility as practiced by "the military, science, financial institutions, and mass communications," Marks alerts us of the need to study these functions as they pertain to, among other things, chemical and biological warfare, nanotechnology, and "the corporate-driven decoding of the human genome, quantum and other nondigital computing." Her comparison between these mainstream uses of media invisibility and their "rebellious" counterparts suggests an interesting power struggle between these entities that expands on the usual debates concerning the media wars.

Marks's discussion of war and invisibility is salient. By contrasting the mediations of the Vietnam and Persian Gulf Wars—in terms of a visible/invisible discursive binary—Marks's deployment of the "enfolding/unfolding" heuristic is clarified, and we are better informed about what is at stake in the functionings of invisible media strategies. Marks makes effective use of Paul Virilio's familiar Gulf War analyses, and her evocation of Hakim Bey's temporary autonomous zone as an explanatory trope for engaging with the seemingly ever-changing nature and dynamics of new media practices and structures is convincing. Also central in Marks's work is its address to the political economies of new-media representations and ideological suasions, especially as they intersect with user experiences. Marks's observations about and considerations of what she calls "new genres of database art" through the online works of its practitioners (the Giver of Names project, eToys, "e-rational," etc.) are illuminating for what they reveal about unanticipated uses of new media and its powers of invisibility. Her concept of software and viruses as loiterers is a particularly useful idea for thinking about new-media invisibility.

Chapter 4, Mischa Peters's "Exit Meat: Digital Bodies in a Virtual World," brings together two discursive realms of thought about postmodern culture's fixation on the possibilities of a human and machinic convergence, most popularly recognized as the posthuman condition. Through her intertextual reading of the often contradictory ideas contained in the works of such diverse writers as Anne Balsamo, José van Dijck, William Gibson, Donna Haraway, Katherine Hayles, and John Hockenberry, for example, Peters locates some utopic and dystopic contours in their respective views. It is the tensions existing among these writers' figurations of the posthuman idea that leads Peters to formulate a schema to help us better grasp the degree to which our society simultaneously welcomes and eschews scientific modifications of the human body on its path to the posthuman ideal. Peters's four-part construction of the types of bodily images that emerge in these writers' works is broken into "conceptual bodies," "natural bodies," "modified bodies," and "enhanced bodies."

Peters begins her critique with an analysis of the image of an exuberant wheelchair-bound John Hockenberry from the cover of *Wired* magazine's cover, and its hyperbolic rhetoric: "Your body. Get over it. (Think mind over matter.)" She extends the discussion to the British popular science journal *New Science* and its utopic coverage of actual "brain-machine interfaces" explained to lay audiences in terms of science films like *Johnny Mnemonic*. Peters then contrasts these views with cyberpunk fiction's less optimistic perspectives about the "high price" of technological bodily enhancements, especially as represented in William Gibson's vision of "enhanced bodies" as dystopian "meat puppets" (although Peters correctly points out Gibson's failure to problematize the gendered nature of this technological nightmare). Peters goes on to remind us that bioengineering also has its costs, such as "what happens when there is a new hardware upgrade, or a new software release. . . . Would we still be able to make a distinction between a software bug and psychological illness?" Peters's useful four-part rubric, then, is designed not only to assist us in recognizing some of the terms of the raging posthuman debate but also facilitates the guiding question of her essay: Have we, in fact, become posthuman, and, most important, do we *want* to?

part 2: digitextual aesthetics

The second section of this book asks how scholars, critics, and practitioners can usefully speak of a digital "aesthetics." A number of academic disciplines banished the (ostensibly outdated) concept of "art" long before the world of the Net was either wired or online. After the late 1960s, many arts critics and film theorists celebrated a world of "postformalism." In the 1970s academic cinema studies cast off the straitjackets of style and form almost entirely in quests for subtextual master codes they termed "apparatus" and "ideology." Poststructuralism and postmodernism became ruling orthodoxies in the 1980s, premised as they were on categorical denials of the very stuff around which aesthetics and modernism claimed legitimacy. Yet while these broad strains of theoretical orthodoxy in contemporary theory rightly skewered the universalizing pretensions of traditional "philosophies of the arts" (as if the arts were bounded and timeless phenomena susceptible to generalizations), the contemporary "post-" theories were all premised, problematically, on positions of negation (of form, structure, and maternal specificity).

What the various "post-" theories ignored was that while the objects of aesthetics may have paled and withered in academic and high-culture institutions, commercial mass culture had simply appropriated, exploited, and distributed those aesthetic frameworks on a broad and profitable scale. Style became lifestyle, and lifestyle became—for the most favored demographics in the 1990s, anyway—a social space defined by high-tech consumer technologies and digital media. No longer a philosophical, analytical perspective aimed from the academy, that is, the aesthetic became a clearly valued form of industrial performance and consumer confidence. The very self-consciousness through which commercial culture deploys aesthetic schemas provides the basis for more fully considering what the "art" of digital media has become within contemporary culture.

In the digital age, style has become a form of cultural capital that can be leveraged by digital boutiques and multinational media conglomerates alike. Headhunters now engage art and design school graduates not for the institutional ghettos of high culture but for the proliferating worlds of computer-generated images, animation, and motion graphics. Whether traditional philosophies of art are bankrupt or not, aesthetics, style, and lifestyle have become linguas francas of global culture, as well as a critical vocational competence highly valued by startups, dot-coms, advertisers, and entertainment corporations. Aesthetics, if taken to refer to popular and industrial theorizations about artistic value and digital form, presents a specific challenge to theorists of new media. Whether critical and politically engaged, or descriptive and analytical, the aesthetic stands as a central sociological and cultural discourse, one that we as theorists would do well not to ignore.

Modernity's complicity in the unfortunate split between the arts and sciences remains a subject of contemporary debate in the academy. But the bracketing of these former unities of human endeavor often hides our ability to recognize the literal beauty of science and the science of artistic practices that were commonplace during the Renaissance—a linkage most evident in Leonardo da Vinci, who was, after all, a scientist, artist, *and* technologist. In this section of the book, issues of digital media technology aesthetics and technology users' enjoyment and mastery thereof will be explored. These essays should remind us that the original Greek meaning of *technologia* was the systematic treatment of an art. This section will provide useful conceptual and discursive approaches to articulating the affective dimensions, formal properties, and cultural dimensions governing a range of new digital media and their users. Aesthetic analysis of digital media might mean asking a series of related questions. What, for example, are the visual pleasure principles of web-surfing and immersion technologies, or the cognitive implications of software "authoring" and interface designs? What are the formal properties of interactive music and software, virtual character designs, streaming I-films, computer-animated art, digital space, time renderings, and so on? The articles in this section outline a range of perspectives, and respond to questions about the forms, frameworks, and expectations that govern and value digital works and practices.

Peter Lunenfeld's essay, "Space Invaders: Thoughts on Technology and the Production of Culture," rethinks what "avant-garde" new-media practices might consist of in the context of post–Cold War theorizing. Lunenfeld refuses to consider digital media in the standard, now tired categories of either futurist "mercantilism" or "pseudoreligious noospheric fantasy," or the subtle ironies and faux radicality of cultural studies. He traces instead a proposal for digital theory that resists linear approaches that chart and periodize radical new media practices according to linear teleologies (whether they follow the lockstep progress and "daring moves" vectors inherent in avant-garde assumptions or the celebratory periodization that apologists deploy to celebrate the present victory of capitalism).

Lunenfeld's account is particularly good, first, at shifting the kinds of questions one might ask of new media (suggesting how the cultural studies of resistant fan practices reinforce multimillion-dollar game industry interests); second, at contextualizing digital media within the contested history of its twentieth-century precursors (competing capitalist and soviet forms of industrialism); and third, at drawing out an alternative to the dominant place the cyborg has assumed in recent media theorizing. In place of the traditional or alien cyborg figure, Lunenfeld proposes a model of "dynamic nonconsciousness" attendant to the "machine part" of the human-computer interface. This approach enables the author to consider whether an open-source operating system like Linux is as influential on practice as many experimental new media artists have been. It is in this tension between paradigms of artistry and technology that Lunenfeld finds possibilities for breaking out of the endless quotation and inertia of postmodernism's premature closures.

Chapter 6, Lev Manovich's "The Poetics of Augmented Space," provides readers with a synthetic account of the relatively short (but already complicated) "history" of new-media aesthetics even as it argues for a new conception of space as a digitalized phenomenon. The author is particularly well-positioned to provide this account, given his earlier studies of new media within the context of the history of the twentieth-century arts and modernism, and his influential book, *The*

Language of Digital Media.[2] In contrast to the seemingly endless talk about the disembodied nature of cyberspace and virtual reality in the 1990s, Manovich makes the novel argument that the material world and physical spaces may in fact emerge as central components of digital culture. The chapter discusses how the widespread proliferation of portable digital technologies (like global positioning satellite devices and personal digital assistants), along with dispersed input/processing devices (like computer projection surveillance in public spaces) portend an even greater movement away from "virtuality" and toward the notion of what the author terms "cellspace."

Manovich defines "cellspace" as a physical space filled with data that can be retrieved by a user using a personal communications device of some sort. Unlike traditional forms of video surveillance (which convert visual/sound information into data taken and used elsewhere), cellspace delivers data to "mobile-space dwellers." The chapter gives readers a useful survey of currently developed and utilized digital devices that function in this way, but it also provides the kind of historical grounding that many new-media theorists leave out. That is, Manovich places these current trends within a trajectory of existing art world practices—including the "audio walks" of artist Janet Cardiff and the architectural design of Daniel Liberskind's Jewish Museum of Berlin. Finally, Manovich draws out the contradictions in another institutional register parallel to digital media: that of motion pictures. The chapter discusses a range of art historical practices—from Russian futurism to 1950s assemblage to 1970s installation art—to show not just how the art gallery and museum have been transformed from "white cubes" to "cellspaces" but how they have ironically reduced themselves (via data projection) to their nemesis, the "black box" of the motion-picture theater. Manovich raises the interesting question about the future of artistic practices. At one time they were premised as the antithesis of mass culture. Now, installation art and projection have made the electronic augmented space of commercial culture the paradigm for the art world as well.

Chapter 7, "Too Many Notes: Computers, Complexity, and Culture in *Voyager*," examines an area far too undertheorized in film and new-media studies—sound and music—even though both are integral parts of most interactive and multimedia forms. As a critically acclaimed performer, George E. Lewis brings to this essay both a theoretical and practical knowledge of computer applications in music, one that goes back several decades before the dot-coms and the Internet came to define something as amorphous as commercial digital culture. This chapter stands as an exemplary model for how other scholars might look beyond current critical approaches to digital media that focus on technologies, networks, interfaces, and the like, in order to more fully consider perspectives frequently left out of contemporary discussions on digital media—issues of culture, ethnicity, and race, in particular. Based on a fundamental critique of trans-European aesthetics, Lewis describes the process by which he moved from the "anti-authoritarian" impulses of jazz improvisation toward his goal of "de-instrumentalizing" the computer for use in music. Most computer music applications before Lewis's work on his composition *Voyager* invoked traditional distinctions between "player" (the musician) and "instrument" (the musical instrument, and then computers and synthesizers "played by" performers). But Lewis's work shatters this distinction by creating a program that functions as a "player" as well. The result makes possible interactive and improvisational music performance that has what the author terms a "bidirectional transfer of intentionality."

Lewis describes how *Voyager* employs a computer-driven, interactive "virtual improvising orchestra" that analyzes an improvisor's performance in real time, generating both complex responses to the musician's playing and independent behavior arising from the program's own internal processes. The author contends that notions about the nature and function of music are embedded in the structure of software-based music systems and that interactions with these systems tend to reveal characteristics of the community of thought and culture that produced them. Thus, *Voyager* is considered as a kind of computer-music-making embodying African-American aesthetics and musical practices. By defining *Voyager* as involving generative (or intentional) as well as responsive forms of interactivity, Lewis's work challenges the implicit racial politics that have influenced many aesthetic theorizations about new music. Through this process, Lewis shows how personal and cultural identities become articulated through digital musical forms and technologies. By creating a digital musical program that combines "indeterminacy and empathy" and in which "all communication takes place sonically," Lewis shows how new music composition (here defined as "a bringer of structure") no longer has to invoke regressive views of improvisation as unstructured and therefore critically and culturally suspect practice.

Issues of authorship have long been at the center of key debates in the field of aesthetic theory. Tarleton Gillespie's essay "The Stories Digital Tools Tell" provides new ways of thinking about the role and nature of authorship in the world of digital media. Various scholars have premised their digital apologetics around notions that new media will alter traditional notions of the solitary authorship (of bounded artistic or cultural texts) in favor of "collaborative" authorship possibilities (somehow inherent in "interactivity" and the "open" texts that result from networked forms). Gillespie examines the ways that culture (which includes issues of power and politics) is embedded in the software design of programs like Macromedia Director and Dreamweaver. What he finds at work in these commercial software programs is a complex interplay of heterogeneous metaphors, all of which are drawn from very different traditions of art and media (theater, painting, animation, video, and film). Among the contradictions considered here is the fact that while the culture of software design at companies like Macromedia is organized as a collaborative enterprise around open texts, the actual organization of the software available to users tends to employ very traditional metaphors. In this way, web-authoring programs use familiar symbols that encourage users to think of their tasks as forms of individualized authorship, even though the digital technologies involved actually create the potential for more innovative or radical forms of authorship.

Gillespie's essay brings to the study of new media a set of disciplinary approaches not typically deployed in the tradition of film studies. Gillespie draws on the important work of Bruno Latour (on the "actor-network" theory), Edwin Hutchins's critique of cognitive psychology (which theorizes that technologies structure human thought), Michael Cole's "cultural psychology" research (with its view of the tool as a "cultural artifact"), and Phil Agre's view of critical technical practices (which includes the argument that metaphors operate as a "medium" of cognitive and cultural exchange). The goal in this synthesis is to move beyond the standard positions of new media theorists (i.e., that technologies cause change, or that cultures implement new technologies as part of existing commitments). Gillespie reconsiders more moderate questions, such as how new technologies *mean*, how they favor certain uses and not others, how they stand as artifacts that "encrust" the discourses of all previous users and designers in their interfaces, and how the "politics of design" might work to regulate social practices and animate social relations. Interface design, and the visualized metaphors and icons deployed in software, are celebrated industrially if they are seen to be "intuitive." Yet Gillespie shows how this commonsense attribution (used to judge the quality of a new technology) is also an indicator of whether the interface metaphor comfortably fits the status quo world that the metaphor has already structured. It is in this sort of analysis—of interface metaphors as cultural discourses and new technologies as cultural artifacts—that Gillespie demonstrates the provisional ways that new media technologies can also be political.

part 3: prefiguring digitextuality

New media, by its very name, perpetuates one long-standing myth about technology: that the advent of any new technology inevitably brings with it marked change. Decoupling the two terms (*new* and *media*), however, allows scholars to sift through the various and at times competing claims of those that broker and promote the "new." Commercial interests typically build their marketing cases and promotional campaigns on promises of radical change and therefore discontinuity with the past. In a highly competitive market economy, corporations must likely do this for survival. A niche in any market is only possible if buyers and users perceive that some unique break or benefit is offered by a new technology.

While many academics have moved beyond old dystopian critiques in favor of critical forms of futurism that speculate on the kinds of breaks and leaps that each new digital media technology will somehow bring, another tradition in media studies has sought to ground any such account of new technologies with questions about how the past informs the present. Some scholars, like Raymond Williams and Brian Winston, systematically challenge histories and theories premised on radical discontinuities with the past.[3] Others—even those highly critical of capitalist media culture, like Bertolt Brecht and Hans Magnus Enzensberger— have embraced the chance to exploit the very forms of technological novelty that capitalist corporations are selling.[4] If new technologies do in fact cause social change, such critics assert, then artists and activists would do well to exploit those causal possibilities for progressive causes.

The third section of this book takes as its subject the notion that digital and new media are in fact historical and social formations, composed of and influenced by a number of intertwined and competing interests. Far from the clean, value-free logic of the open-market ideal, the scholars here attempt what might be termed "archaeologies of the digital," seeking to understand specific historical circumstances, trends, practices, and interests that "prefigure" or inform the advent and accommodation of any new technology. We take as our working assumption here that technologies are far more than mere machines. They are the total constellation of conceptual and ideological investments that animate and perpetuate those machines. These antecedent investments—as the four chapters here by John Caldwell, Stephen Mamber, Mark Williams, and Jeffrey Sconce demonstrate—include the prefiguring forces of broadcasting (and television programming), visual modeling and topographic analysis (here applied in a film studies context), commercial motion pictures (and the anxieties about digital technology that they perpetuate), and finally the traditions of culture and media theorizing itself (academic practices that establish certain predispositions to any new media technology).

Can film studies, for example, continue to theorize productively about new media by invoking its old stand-by perspectives—aesthetics, textuality, ideology, and identity—without also talking about the industrial landscape that animates and fuels new-media development on a wide scale? Answering such a question, argues John T. Caldwell in the first chapter of this section, unsettles a number of recurrent assumptions and critical tendencies. Caldwell's "Second-Shift Media Aesthetics: Programming, Interactivity, and User Flows" seeks to consider the ways that long-standing strategies in television and broadcasting—programming, syndication, licensing, branding, and flows—have emerged as textual engines in the design of new media forms. This chapter examines a range of textual forms used in TV/dot-com sites, and looks closely at several the author considers to be both influential and symptomatic of new forms of user flows: homicide.com, freakylinks.com, dawsonscreek.com, futurama.com, thexfiles.com, and several websites tied to new reality shows, game shows, and fan sites.

The chapter first builds on theoretical models of the flow and supertext to describe how what the author terms "first-shift" aesthetics has functioned in mainstream network television programming. Programmers have used various strategies (counterprogramming, tent-poling, hammocking, stunting, seamlessness, etc.) to attract viewers organized around the concept of "day parts" (daytime, prime time, off-prime time, late night, etc.). To this Caldwell contrasts the "second-shift" aesthetics of digital media, which he considers a logical outgrowth of several congruent historical shifts: from broadcasting to multichannel narrowcasting; from mass economies of scale to niche economies of scope; and from serial flows to tangential and cyclical flows. Instead of the linear textual compositing inherent in flow theory, TV/dot-com synergies learn to master "textual dispersal" and user navigations that involve the "migration" of users across brand and conglomerate boundaries. In essence, programming strategies have shifted from notions of program "flows" to tactics of audience/user "flows." Caldwell shows how programming tactics have helped facilitate, prefigure, and implement new-media development, but also how new media technologies have in turn altered those same tactics. The net result, the author argues, should compel scholars to shift from their favored emphasis on notions of boundaryless space and collapsed geographies (that Marshall McLuhan and others have favored), to notions of marketed and programmed temporality. New-media economies and texts, in this account, are based not on the now familiar schemes of networking and simultaneity, but on tested, institutional practices rationalized around forms of dispersal and temporal seriality.

The practices of visual modeling and cartography preceded digital media by centuries, and new-media technologies have provided sophisticated tools that have transformed both the possibilities of and applications in these fields. Stephen Mamber provides an innovative proposal for the use of digital media in the topographic analysis of aesthetic and cultural forms. While his essay "Narrative Mapping" might as easily fit with the other essays that comprise the preceding section of the book on digital media "aesthetics," Mamber is not concerned with an aesthetic analysis of digital media narratives (such as how digital media narratives function) per se. Rather, he demonstrates how digital media tools can provide—in the areas of media and film studies—a range of new methods for the analysis of preexisting narrative forms (in cinema, literature, and reportage). Narrative mapping, as Mamber sees it, attempts to articulate what he terms a "visual information space." This process is especially important when a viewer, user, critic, or analyst attempts to understand works that are particularly complex, like a novel (which might include thousands of pages of text) or a feature film (which involves tens of thousands of specific image-sound events that the average viewer is seldom conscious of while watching). The overall goal here, as in traditional cartography, is to provide a user-accessible reconstruction that enables the viewer-user to have an "all-at-a-glance" understanding of the work or narrative being analyzed.

This chapter proposes, after establishing an informational "database" from discrete parts of the work under analysis (which might include shot descriptions, camera angles, scenes, plot points, image vectors, camera and actor blocking diagrams, script pages, storyboards, or location geographies), developing interactive "maps" that digitally visualize—and thus greatly aid in giving coherence to—the complex object of analysis. This general approach, of course, is analogous to the methods of textualism that have been so fundamental in the development of cotemporary film studies and critical theory. At times, Mamber's narrative mapping methodologies evoke the techniques of formal and narratological analysis and the textual deconstruction so familiar to cinema and literary theorists. At other times, however, Mamber shows how digital maps can actually be thought of in cybernetic terms as "user interfaces," and as electronic simulations that provide experiential possibilities every bit as primary as the initial object of critical analysis. The ability to "temporalize" maps over time, for example, produces experiences potentially as engaging as those of the original motion picture being mapped. Narrative mapping, as proposed here, proves to be a useful tool for analyzing critical objects of complexity, ambiguity, density, and information overload. In a way, the new and complicated digital environments that increasingly define culture increase the need for narrative mapping even as digital media enhances the possibilities for its deployment.

In light of the rise of what has come to be known as digital culture, Mark Williams's "Real-Time Fairy Tales: Cinema Prefiguring Digital Anxiety" discusses the potential significance of a return to what was termed in the 1970s *apparatus theory*. The return proposed here, however, would work specifically to raise questions of difference among aspects of the apparatus rather than collapse them. Williams suggests two important changes in how we might consider the rise of the digital in media history; both are related in a way to what has been termed the concept of "disavowal." One form of disavowal is the commonplace erasure or casual denigration of television prevalent in many digital discourses. Williams builds on Anne Friedberg's influential work to show how important television is to thinking about the historical issues of the interface with digital apparati. This discussion sets up a second point, an argument Williams makes about "liveness" versus "real time."

Both phenomena, that is, refer to an act of mediation but also to the desire to experience liveness and reality as unmediated. This attention to disavowal suggests a useful distinction between "TV liveness" (which is constructed around notions of history, as Mimi White has argued) and "cyberculture real time" (which is premised on the promise of a state Williams terms the "near future").

Having established these key temporal and ontological distinctions, the chapter turns to the analysis of two feature films. Each analysis demonstrates a related but distinct "figuring" of anxiety about digital culture. One film (*Fairy Tale: A True Story*) reconsiders a significant incident in the history of mediated representation. The other film (*A.I.*) ultimately imagines a literally posthuman future, in which humans are "history" amid a world of advanced informational dynamics. Both films are invested in the concept and representation of children, and both blur the distinction between "fairy tale" and "true" story. Significantly, then, both films also construct or figure digital anxiety via an unpacking of apparatus issues (in relation to the process of subjectivity). In doing so, it becomes clear that the rise of what has come to be known as the digital, and its "pressure" toward the near future (real time), might be seen to have produced, in popular culture, evidence of an analogous pressure. That is, it has produced a pressure for a different equilibrium of "belief" as regards our relationship to media—an address to what we typically disavow about our relationship to the media. The shift in the economy of avowal (i.e., the typical way to think about digital anxiety, such as, How can one trust what one sees?) therefore also entails a changing economy of disavowal. This economy of disavowal may be a space in which different sorts of intervention can reside and occur. Media history, Williams argues, has a responsibility to negotiate such spaces.

Proving that new-media theory need not act as a shill for either the high-technology or higher-education sectors, Jeffrey Sconce, in "Tulip Theory," critiques a range of flaws in the ways that film and media studies have construed and engaged new media.[5] Whereas the other contributors in this section examine digital media within the existing and established contexts of television programming (industrial branding and repurposing); visual modeling (the topographic analysis of films, narratives, and complex events); and the film industry (recurrent cultural anxieties about digital technology), Sconce considers how the development of digital media has created great (and unfortunate) instabilities in the ways that film and media are theorized and studied in the academy. The essay traces the rapid emergence of new-media studies in film and media studies departments, and links them to parallel developments in the now-vilified dot-com, high-tech run-up of the 1990s. The account lays bare comparable areas that have been "oversold" by intellectuals and university administrators, all for apparent institutional and financial (rather than scholarly) gains. Sconce takes aim at the fetishization of technologies by new-media wanna-bes in academia, along with a range of positions that have become part of the orthodox canon of new-media studies (including the influential work on identity by Sherry Turkle and others, and the almost religious overdependence of early new-media theorists on the "biblical" works and fantasy speculations of cyberfiction writers like William Gibson).

The recurrent critical trope in Sconce's account comes in the form of glaring contrasts he makes between elite (and irrelevant) cyberpractices and the far more ubiquitous practices that recur in television and mass consumer cultures. Why is it, Sconce askes, that scholars desperately grab at the exceptional if mostly unremarkable and irrelevant cyberpractices of a few as a basis to build their theories on, even as they ignore the many everyday accounts (of identity, pleasure, and consumption) that define users of older forms of electronic media like cable and television? In taking this position, Sconce discusses recent new-media writing within the notion of the "velocification" of scholarship that Andrew Ross has proposed, by connecting it to its corallary: a "deceleration of critical reflection." In making these arguments, the chapter stands as a valuable elaboration of the current state of critical theory as well: its excesses and "promiscuities"; its institutionalized inertias; and its tendencies to bifurcate the field of media studies into crude conceptual binaries. The author's account of the caste system operative in what he terms the "culture of theory" is an innovative take on the current state of affairs. Yet far from neo-Luddite, the chapter stands as a useful read for any scholar wishing to move beyond the speculative, celebratory phase that defined the early years of academic new-media theory. Such a shift promises to develop more informed ways to answer important questions about digital media today.

part 4: digitextual practices

Media studies, and the academic institutions that house them, have traditionally made a needlessly clean split between *theory* and *practice*. Media studies undertaken in the context of the humanities, for example, have regularly broached practice as the province of writers, artists, and alternative-media producers—all essentially outsiders to the commercial imperative of the culture industries. Media studies from an activist orientation, on the other hand, have engaged practice to mean forms of mobilization, critique, and resistance—again promulgating practice as an outsider's pose, albeit a largely political one. Such approaches needlessly constrict the domain of analysis open to digital media scholars and students, especially given the immense amount of activity now available and proliferating on the World Wide Web.

This section provides readers with a range of case studies that demonstrate the complex ways that individuals, groups, and institutions utilize digital media. Understanding digital practice in the present age requires elaborating the forms of critical competence that fuel the work of artists, academics, and other intellectuals, the digital spaces of domestic users, producers and fans, and the products of digital industry conglomerates. Indeed, panics about new media, often promulgated by those with vested interests in old media, are lore and encompass the first arrival of cinema, radio, comic books, TV, video games, the Internet, and, most recently, wireless telephony (we are thinking here of all the alarmist reports of how cell-phone usage poses health threats). This section will reconsider the rhetorics of dystopia by focusing on the actual ways that different people, constituent groups, and organizations use digital technologies. Although cultural studies' emphasis on the use value versus the exchange value of media commodities will underpin these discussions, these will not merely be celebratory essentialist treatises. The multivalent nature and practices of these media as good, bad, neutral, or innocuous is what these discussions should convincingly demonstrate.

What Karen S. F. Buzzard's essay, "Net Ratings: Defining a New Medium by the Old, Measuring Internet Audiences" points out about the current development of Internet ratings' emerging standardization is the familiar story of the best system not necessarily winning out in the end. We are most familiar with the bitter rivalry between the Japanese Betamax and the American VHS technical formats for determining the videocassette recorder (VCR) industry standard. And as we all are aware, the VHS format won the all-important, lucrative winner-take-all consumer market standard. Although both systems initially sold in the tens of thousands worldwide, consumers did not arguably win in this competition, given the success of the technically inferior VHS standard. Buzzard alerts us to a similar dynamic being played out in the quest for market dominance in the business of quantifying the increasingly valuable traffic on the Internet; she investigates the convergence-media phenomenon by painstakingly chronicling the economic imperatives and established marketing practices of older business models as they are imposed on the Internet during its formative stages. She discovers that despite the essential and vast differences between television and the Internet's information flows and user practices, "the economic model employed so successfully by the television networks was transferred increasingly to the Internet industry." This model, she finds, advances through the development of monopoly-like portal structures dubbed "portalopolies."

Buzzard also reveals how the Nielsen television ratings company emerged as the dominant force for measuring the increasingly valuable measurements of the Internet. Not surprisingly, she finds that the Nielsen company used its dominant position from an older medium to take over its new media rival, the Internet start-up Jupiter Media Metrix. As she points out, "market-dominating firms tend to be slow in developing new

products, but 'roar back like lions' when smaller rivals challenge them."
Among her more telling findings that bear on contemporary concerns
about new technologies' threats to individual privacy rights is the extent
to which Internet metrics become far more invasive in their data collection than their older media counterparts. For example, Buzzard finds that
not only could individuals' visits to particular websites be tracked, but
their ages, gender, household size and composition, income and education levels, and geographic location could also be monitored for the purpose of linking this data to specific product purchases. Finally, Buzzard's
tracking of the mergers between Internet search engines and directories is
comprehensive; moreover, she enables us to understand how these economic decisions and machinations are accelerating media convergence,
which ultimately updates the familiar adage "television is the business of
delivering audiences to advertisers." Now, the Internet ratings industry is
in the business of delivering our online searches to advertisers. In the
words of musician Sylvester (Sly) Stone, "Somebody's Watching You,"
and as Buzzard points out, someone is getting paid handsomely to do so.

In her capacity as production supervisor at Pixar Animation Studios,
Katherine Sarafian presents an insider's view of the digital revolution's
centrality to the successes and growing popularity of film's animation
industry. In her essay "Flashing Digital Animations: Pixar's Digital Aesthetic" Sarafian lets us in on a secret of her studio's amazing successes.
Sarafian stresses that Pixar adheres to "a production design that prioritizes story and art over digital bells and whistles." She makes it clear
that the studio's masterful use of digital technologies' high-tech bells
and whistles is always subservient to its ultimate goal of achieving compelling and even traditional storytelling forms. In this way, Sarafian
suggests that the technological and narrative accomplishments of
Pixar's films manage a fealty to some important tenets of classical film
history and theory while simultaneously embodying certain aspects of
new-media discourse. For example, when Sarafian talks about the pull
of new media's potential to tempt digital animators to create either
purely dreamlike imaginative or "realist-looking or realist-seeming
worlds" she evokes the influences of such classical filmmaker-theorists
as Dziga Vertov, the contemporary theoretical speculations of Donna
Haraway, and the neoformalism of Lev Manovich to make her points.

As she indicates, the reality of digital animation's functioning in the
era of convergence between so-called old- and new-media representational regimes dissolves this either/or dichotomy, for in fact, both traditions and sensibilities are at the heart of "the Pixar aesthetic."
However, through her detailed discussions of Pixar's engagements with
storytelling, the computer animation process, the digital artists and
their digital tool kits, and the digital image for the video/DVD audience,
Sarafian illustrates how this complex old-media/new-media mesh gets

realized in such films as Pixar's *Toy Story*, *A Bug's Life*, *For the Birds*, and *Monsters, Inc.*, among others. Here Sarafian makes us privy to the specific technological and narrative challenges, limitations, and innovative stragegies that digital artists and producers at Pixar routinely address to render the believable characters and engrossing story worlds that have come to define Pixar's digital animations and its recognizable product. Today, we have become accustomed to Hollywood's ubiquitous "the making of" subgenre of films that essentially remystify the multimillion-dollar, blockbuster filmmaking process, but in Sarafian's disclosures some honest demystifying is going on.

In "Log On: The Oxygen Media Research Project," Constance Penley, Lisa Parks, and Anna Everett examine and participate in digital media's role in facilitating new modes of feminist praxis, from both academic and corporate imperatives. "Log On" examines the Oxygen Media Research [Project], a three-year interdisciplinary and collaborative study of Oxygen Media, an Internet start-up and cable TV company founded by Marcy Carsey, Geraldine Laybourne, and Oprah Winfrey that works to develop women's programming across different media platforms. Oxygen Media, noted for its aim to "superserve" women, is taken as a test case to determine the possibilities of new media for creating feminist friendly democratic public spheres within commercial multimedia networks. The research includes: (1) historical precedents for Oxygen Media (i.e., the Lifetime cable TV channel, women's reading groups, women's magazines, etc.); (2) participant observation of development meetings and program production; (3) textual and ideological discourse analysis of trade and popular press coverage of Oxygen Media; and (4) formal and aesthetic analyses of Oxygen's television programming and its interactive website agenda. Also important to the project is the team's international research collaboration with European feminist scholars, and the research project's website, "Hydrogenmedia," which serves as a forum for research and commentary on the strategies of Oxygen Media as well as other projects that are attempting to democratize global media for women and other digitally disadvantaged groups.

Chapter 15 is Henry Jenkins's essay "From Barbie to Mortal Kombat: Further Reflections." The importance of Jenkins's contribution is its engagement with an important element of digital media's ascendancy—the phenomenal popularity of computer/video games as both a successful industry unto itself, and as a formidable mass-media rival to both the film and television industries. After his "chance encounters" with the elite Electronic Entertainment Expo (E3) convention of 2001 (where the computer games industry congregates to devise its annual business strategies), and the goings-on of a Melbourne, Australia, games arcade, Jenkins found it necessary to reflect upon some of his ideas concerning gender and gaming culture. What Jenkins points out is the prematurely optimistic view of women's participation in the gaming industry as it is represented in the 1999 book *From Barbie to Mortal Kombat: Gender and Computer Games*, which he coedited with Justine Cassell. From the vantage point of hindsight, and the troubling realities manifest in his "chance encounters," Jenkins rethinks some of that text's key assumptions. Although he found more women participating in the production and consumption of computer games at both the E3 convention and the Melbourne games arcade, Jenkins observed a disquieting reality. The increased proportion of women as gaming entrepreneurs and master players "at a rate significantly higher than men" did little to revise the attitude that female gamers "remain a remarkable spectacle within a commercial and cultural space still dominated by male designers and male consumers."

The painful reality that Jenkins discovers is that far from the utopic vision of a gender-neutral gaming culture thought to be looming on the horizon five years ago (replete with "a growing pink aisle at the software stores"), the fact now is that major games companies have co-opted the spirit of the girls game movement to shore up their "existing franchises that have already proven successful with their predominately male consumers." Jenkins goes on to define gaming culture's renewed sense of bifurcated game play according to a problematic logic of proscribed, socially constructed gender-specific role-play.

The final essay is Joe Amato's "Endnotes for a Theory of Convergence." It is one of the more challenging chapters in this volume due to its web-inspired discursive style. In many ways Amato's unique narrative approach is a literal manifestation of new-media theorizing about the rhyzomatic structure of digital textualities' self-reflexivities and self-referentialities. At first view, Amato's article seems strange and perhaps it seems to create a Brechtian form of distanciation; but on closer inspection and reflection, his writing structures our reading along more familiar lines. In fact, "Endnotes" reads like the very familiar cataloging of Internet search engines and directories responding to computer users' "keyword" entries, data "searches," and "site" matches. But, unlike Hotbot, Ask Jeeves, Alta Vista, Google, Yahoo! and the rest, Amato does not order his endnotes data according to some privileged and opaque heirarchy that resembles retail markets' and superstores' eye-line placement on shelves for maximum profitability.

Amato's writing does, however, challenge the reader to strain at reaching some of the intellectualism that informs his references to a host of writers, poets, and artists who engage with new media and digital technologies in familiar and unfamiliar texts—and just in time. For at the moment that digital media technologies are being colonized by the traditional media establishment with their "least-common denominator" anti-intellectualism, for the purpose of effecting a collective digital labotomization on us so that we don't know or care if we have exited the meat (as Peters suggests in this volume), Amato jolts us back to idea that complex ideas can be informative, rigorous, and playful. Does anyone remember Max Headroom? The important contribution that Amato's essay makes is that it is chock full of useful data. Moreover, it reappropriates the commercial Internet search engines' appropriation of the annotated bibliography for new media literacy "stickiness," as opposed to what Buzzard argues in this volume as web surfer and eyeball stickiness for marketing profitability. For example, in his sampling of useful data from journalists of popular newspapers to Trotskyite socialist thinkers and many in between, Amato informs us that "Genealogy evidently ranks second only to pornography in generating web traffic." Amato also gives a comparative analyses of these disparate literary nodal points on new media discourses, and he surveys how writers interested in new media discuss science fiction films such as Spielberg's *Close Encounters of the Third Kind*, and *A.I.* A poet himself, Amato concludes with an endnote that teases us to speculate a bit about his, and our, own cyborg experiences.

notes

1. For a lively discussion of the posthuman thesis and new media culture, see Chris Hables Gray, *Cyborg Citizen: Politics in the Posthuman Age* (New York: Routledge, 2001).
2. Lev Manovich, *The Language of Digital Media* (Cambridge, Mass.: MIT Press, 2001).
3. See Raymond Williams, "The Technology and the Society," 35–50, and Brian Winston, "Breakages Limited," 77–89, in *Electronic Media and Technoculture*, ed. John T. Caldwell (New Brunswick, N.J.: Rutgers University Press, 2000).
4. See Hans Magnus Enzensberger, "Constituents of a Theory of Media," in Caldwell, ed., *Electronic Media and Technoculture*, 51–76.
5. Sconce develops and builds on the concept of vaporware in a way that complements the work of two other authors in this collection: Peter Lunenfeld has noted that "vaporware, the most ineffable of products . . . is to be sold only to the exceedingly gullible venture capitalists." He raises the questions, "Are critics to follow suit, offering a brand of theoretical immaterialism—a vapor theory of ruminations unsupported by material underpinnings?" Peter Lunenfeld, *Snap to Grid: A User's Guide to Digital Arts, Media, and Cultures* (Cambridge, Mass.: MIT Press, 2000), 34. In an account published the same year, John Caldwell describes vaporware as an aggressive, preemptive strike against competitors used in the marketing of digital media products; see Caldwell, "Theorizing the Digital Landrush," Caldwell, ed., *Electronic Media and Technoculture*, 6–7. He then contextualizes the strategy (à la Thomas Kuhn) as an example of industrial "troping," "niche-ing," and a form of "corporate paradigming . . . (one that provide[s] the kinds of explanatory aspirations that academics presuppose in general theory")—a process, in essence, that is reminiscent of the speculative tendencies favored by critical theorists in the arts and humanities.

digitextual

part one   deconstructions

digitextuality

and

click

theory

theses on convergence

media in the digital age

a n n a   e v e r e t t

The advent of the digital revolution in late-twentieth and early-twenty-first-century media culture apparently confirms both Jean-Luc Godard's belief in the "end of cinema" and other media critics' claims that we have even entered a posttelevision age.[1] Driving this ontological shift in the infrastructures of many Western media forms and practices is the near ubiquity of difficult-to-regulate satellites, cable TV, analog, and digital video recorders, computer camcorders, and other mass-market technologies outside the proprietary panopticon of big media corporations. Moreover, the rapid fin-de-siècle diffusion of such consumer-grade digital technologies as the CD-ROM, the DVD, the Internet, virtual reality, and wireless communications systems portends even more radical challenges to traditional media industries and their increasingly vulnerable representational hegemonies, as the symptomatic and infamous case of the Napster music-file-sharing system and other open-source code technologies have denoted. In response, big media corporations have begun a frenzied bout of high-profile megamergers, and concomitant new-media colonization—or is it cannibalization? (We'll return to this later.)

Still, the spectacular proliferation of these new technologies has multiplied exponentially that which W. Russell Neuman and other observers describe as "the fragmentation of the mass audience."[2] After abiding the economic, production, exhibition, storytelling, taste, distribution, and scheduling dictates of traditional media powers, this fragmented mass audience has seized upon and been liberated, after a fashion, by a plethora of on-demand media services for consumers, (including what Hakim Bey and others call "data piracy"). These audience dispersal services and outlets include Replay; MSN TV Service (formerly WebTV); TiVo; both so-called mom-and-pop (independent) video rental stores and their super retail agent counterparts (Blockbuster Video, for example); private and professionally produced home-video archives, computer game arcades, the Internet, MP3 and Freenet peer-to-peer audio and video file swapping (downloading) systems; and direct broadcast satellites.

At the same time, film and television studies' theoretical and pedagogical foundations are similarly being shaken. At stake for our expanding discipline is nothing less than a necessary rethinking of the field in the face of these seismic shifts and ruptures.[3] A continued failure by cin-

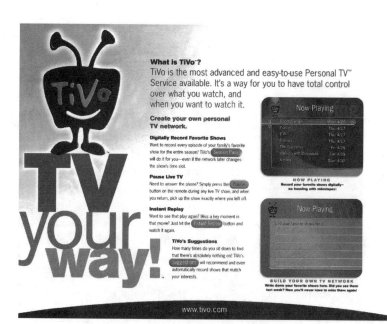

Figure 1.1. TiVo: One of several time-shifting digital videorecorder systems that upset traditional television industry practices and reconfigure television flow for consumer use. ©TiVo.

ema and television scholars to keep current with and, preferably, take the lead in redefining the discipline's continuing relevance as these new media paradigms take shape and power will result in cinema studies' repositioning from avant-garde to rear-guard formation in the unrelenting battle of late capitalism's culture wars. Ours must be an aggressive and accessible participatory agenda in this emergent new-media landscape. Otherwise, the field's relegation to the margins of the ascendant information economy is all but assured. Yet cinema and TV studies are still painfully negotiating mutually acceptable disciplinary boundary crossings, which the evolving digital media have already, to some extent, necessarily hastened despite our willingness and preparedness to engage with this inevitable brave new world. After all, we have only recently reached an attenuated consensus on the differing natures of cinematic and televisual texts as unique objects of study. With this battle barely in a state of field-expanding détente, the digital revolution has introduced new visual and aural media codes that draw extensively from the medium specificities of film, video, and radio while introducing new characteristics and imperatives that are properties of digital technologies alone. These are some of the primary issues that have inspired my thinking about digital matters and that lead to my formulation of the neologism *digitextuality*. Among other concerns, this concept focuses on the intersection of established media modes, codes, and payloads, and those emerging within the frameworks of new media. It also strives to examine and proffer useful ideas about the unique features and characteristics of the evolving new-media technologies that separate them from the old without forcing an untenable equivalence in either instance.

Although my formulation of digitextuality chronologically follows such important recent publications on new media dealing specifically with their indebtedness to film and TV studies and practices as John Caldwell's *Televisuality: Style, Crisis, and Authority in American Television* (1995), Margaret Morse's *Virtualities: Television, Media Art, and Cyberculture* (1998), Peter Lunenfeld's *Snap to Grid: A User's Guide to Digital Arts, Media, and Cultures* (2000) and Lev Manovich's *The Language of New Media* (2001), digitextuality has been conceptually central to my work for some time now.[4]

digital matters: what is digitextuality?

Digitextuality, then, is a neologism that at its most basic combines two familiar word images: the overdetermined signifier *digital*, which denotes most of computer-driven media's technological processes products, and Julia Kristeva's term *intertextuality*. (It also is indebte John Caldwell's far-reaching work on televisuality.) With the terms conjoined in this way, digitextuality suggests a more preci

ilitarian trope capable at once of describing and constructing a sense-
aking function for digital technology's newer interactive protocols,
sthetic features, transmedia interfaces and end-user subject posi-
ns, in the context of traditional media antecedents. Moreover, digitextuality is intended to address, with some degree of specificity, those
marked continuities and ruptures existing between traditional ("old")
media and their digital ("new") media progeny and, especially, how
new media use gets constructed. Given this explanatory agenda, it is
useful at this point to invoke Kristeva's ideas about intertextuality to
better clarify the term's influence on my thinking and theoretical formulation of digitextuality.

When Kristeva first deployed the term *intertextuality* in her 1974 doc-
toral thesis *Revolution in Poetic Language,* it was at the height of psychoanalysis, structural linguistics, semiotics, and other high theories' phenomenal
influence in the humanities fields, in literary and creative circles, and
especially in film studies. In her discussion of certain processes of linguistic structures and practices, Kristeva uses *intertextuality* effectively as a
heuristic trope. She writes, "In this connection we examined the formation of a specific signifying system—the novel—as the result of a redistribution of different sign-systems: carnival, courtly poetry, scholastic
discourse. The term intertextuality denotes this transposition of one (or
several) sign-system(s) into another . . . [and] demands a new articulation. . . . If one grants that every signifying practice is a field of transpositions of various signifying systems (an intertextuality), one then
understands that its 'place' of enunciation and its denoted 'object' are
never single, complete and identical to themselves, but always plural,
shattered, capable of being tabulated."[5] More concisely, Kristeva has
remarked, that " 'Every text builds itself as a mosaic of quotations, every
text is absorption and transformation of another text.' "[6] For me, Kristeva's point that the novel's literary comprehensibility obtains in its
intertextual redistribution of several preexisting cultural sign systems
into a "field of transpositions" demanding a new articulation is
extremely salient when we think about digital media's imbrication in
and rearticulation of analog and other traditional media significations.

For example, we comprehend the information-richness and graphic
density of websites and other Internet data because we are habituated to
the dense image, text, and graphic design schemes previously developed
by newspapers and magazines during the late nineteenth and early
twentieth centuries. Similarly, we can recognize digital media's increasing sophistication in flash animation and streaming media technologies
as a field of transpositions because their sources of sound and animation
are recodings or rearticulations of cinema, television, and radio's
unique signifying systems. As Kristeva notes, "The new signifying system may be produced with the same signifying material; in language,

for example, the passage may be made from narrative to text. Or it may be borrowed from different signifying materials: the transposition from a carnival scene to the written text, for instance" (111).

Where digitextuality departs from Kristeva's notion of intertextuality is that the former moves us beyond a "new signifying system" of quotations and transpositions, to a metasignifying system of discursive absorption whereby different signifying systems and materials are translated and often transformed into zeroes and ones for infinite recombinant signifiers. In other words, new digital media technologies make meaning not only by building a new text though absorption and transformation of other texts, but also by embedding the entirety of other texts (analog and digital) seamlessly within the new. What this means is that earlier practices of bricolage, collage, and other modernist and postmodernist hybrid representational strategies and literary gestures of intertextual referentiality have been expanded for the new demands and technological wizardry of the digital age.[7] Nonetheless, our abilities to understand the new modes and codes of digital media texts today are still often predicated upon successfully decoding their semiotic densities and "semiotic polyvalence" in terms of earlier media structures, what Kristeva calls "an adherence to different sign-systems" (111).

Digitextuality, then, is not only concerned with digital media's *remediation* (to borrow Jay David Bolter and Richard Grusin's term) of our practices of intertextual reading and writing given our need to negotiate between radically different sign systems (historical and contemporary), but also explores digital media's own emerging aesthetics, ethics, and rhetorics in light of the media convergence phenomenon in this time of ascendant globalization and corporate media monopolization. An important part of digital media culture is bound up with the idea of interactivity and expectations for its functionality. As media convergence strategies evolve, a contest is now afoot to determine and delimit how this crucial feature will look and perform. The question is, Will interactivity achieve a political economy in terms of a proconsumerist idea of use value, or a procorporate, profit-motive imperative of exchange value? I return to this issue through a discussion of the significance of bits, sound bites, and digital media's computer determinism later on in the chapter.

I begin with a schematic outline of digitextuality as process, product, and discourse; I continue with what will be a polite rant of sorts against new media's reified rhetoric of the posthuman in which I discuss digitextuality as a representational process and end-user practice—that is, what I am calling "click theory" and the lure of sensory plenitude. Subtending all this is my contention that we are witnessing the rise of a new cultural dominant, one marked by the digital convergence of film, television, music, sound, and print media. To start, let us consider, briefly, some familiar exemplars of digitextuality's signifying systems, practices, and processes.

ontologies of digitextuality

In *Televisuality*, John Caldwell rightly rejects a distillation of film and television spectatorship into opposing ontological camps. Here, film studies' gaze theory proposes a spectatorship consisting of sustained, dream-state hallucinations "focused on the *pleasures of the image*" (original emphasis) in contrast to television viewership imagined as a distracted or " 'more casual' form of looking," termed "glance theory," due to television's interruptible cluttered image and sound flows.[8] For Caldwell, such "regime of vision" approaches miss important commonalities of reception existing between the two media systems.

I suggest that digitextuality is a concept capable of bridging this epistemological chasm because it strives to understand digital media's technological proficiency at cannibalizing both media's modes of production and consumption techniques, particularly those of television. Whereas glance theory denigrates "television based on the viewer's 'fundamental inattentiveness' " (26), user practices of digitextuality, especially as practiced by that generation who have grown up with computer games, MTV-style television aesthetics,[9] and the Internet, suggest an alternative. Increasingly, today's sophisticated media consumers use television, the computer (the Internet, computer games), print material, and the telephone all at once. Such a radically transformed media environment suggests that perhaps we are witnessing media users' development of what might easily be described as a *fundamental hyperattentiveness.* Have apparatuses of convergence and new multimedia texts necessitated an activation of more than the proverbial 10 percent of new media consumers' brainpower when interacting with new technologies? It seems that consumer mastery of digital media's requisite multitasking behaviors and composite texts challenges accepted theories of cognition and spectatorship. Apparently we are becoming more adept at processing and appreciating the gestalt of digital technologies' multimedia barrage.

With this in mind, I propose we think about something approaching a *pixilated gaze* or *hyperattentive theory* of spectatorship, reception, and new-media interaction more compatible with how people today actually engage with the emergent contours of digital encodings, semiotics, and aesthetics. Let us also consider, for example, the frequently changing and interchangeable semiotic systems and aesthetic codes that unquestionably redefine the look of television programs, commercial advertisements, Internet content, and special-effects-driven films that dominate our media topography these days. Talking about the reciprocal nature of film audiences' and especially reflexive films' "look back" at each other, Wheeler Winston Dixon offers an interesting perspective on reception and the apparatus. In *It Looks at You: The Returned Gaze of Cinema*, Dixon argues, "This is the gaze of the object returned—of the frame that possesses the object—of the projected image that possesses the viewer."[10] This certainly seems pertinent for the immersion thesis of new-media engagement.

digitextual semiotics and aesthetics: where is digitextuality?

Film

Since popular culture audiences today understand and expect that most contemporary media texts, including films, are produced with some degree of digital manipulation, processing, and computer generated images (CGI), expressions of cinematic realism, escapism, and formalism as representational incommensurabilities arguably become less significant, especially for digitextuality's *über*-real image constructs. For convergence media, fealty to "a unified set of related, interdependent elements," principles, and laws such as genres, narrative and nonnarrative categories matters less than a film's digitextual processing.[11] More important is its ability to technologize the sublime and convincingly render what was once considered unrepresentable.

Lev Manovich enables us to view such a situation as inhering in the fact that "[t]he iconic code of cinema is discarded in favor of the more efficient binary one. Cinema becomes a slave to the computer."[12] This remark may be hyperbolic, but the point remains. And from this perspective, the success of films like *Forrest Gump* (1994), *The Truman Show* (1998), *The Matrix* (1999), *Run Lola Run* (1999), *Crouching Tiger, Hidden Dragon* (2001), *Final Fantasy* (2000), and *Monsters, Inc.* (2001), among many others, does not hinge on the recognizable separations between representational strategies of realism or verisimilitude, artifice or animation, experimentation or virtuoso formalism to elicit spectators' willing suspension of disbelief. Rather, it is these films' ability to challenge the digital literacy and scopic competencies of contemporary media audiences more concerned with questions of technological magic ("How'd they do that?") than with believable representations of reality as markers of success.

Moreover, media-savvy audiences today apparently understand that the rhetoric of the real has, since modernity, been menaced and exterminated by new-media signifying systems.[13] Deftly simulating the real—an always already compromised state—therefore, is not the issue in digital media culture; overcoming reality's limitations and representing the sublime by any technique necessary apparently is. This is what I mean by *digitextuality's über-real*—an *overreal* or *grand real* construction with signifying powers beyond the simulacrum. Through digital-image manipulation we come to expect and enjoy talking pigs, as in *Babe* (1995), or cats and dogs, as in *The Truth about Cats and Dogs* (2001), in our popular family films. Digitextuality achieves its affective dimensions when it can seamlessly construct enthralling diegetic images of Tom Hanks as Forrest Gump greeting the late president John F. Kennedy in an unprecedented stroke of visual precision and acuity, or assist Natalie Cole in fabulations of "Unforgetable" music in a popular video with her deceased dad, Nat King Cole. Thus, digitextuality is the technological process whereby digital fabrications function as real-time experience of a sort to overcome not only time and space, but life and death.

Television

"I have seen the future of television, and it looks like Fred Astaire dancing with a vacuum cleaner—forever." When Zack Stentz made this memorable statement about digital technologies' obvious semiotic encroachments on analog television's representational regime, he was attending a conference of "movers and shakers in the computer, entertainment and legal industries" at Universal Studios.[14] The meeting concerned these industries' intentions to harness digital technologies' capacities to " 'create' virtual humans' " as "a legion of immortal pitchmen" and women. Consider this telling comment from Jeffrey Lotman, CEO of Global Icons: " 'So, if you had the rights to a Michael Jordan . . . you might not need him to appear personally at every promotional event or in each commercial. You can use his digital clone instead.' "[15] While there is neither need nor time to retread through scholarly and popular writing about virtual reality, or what Margaret Morse terms "virtualities as fictions of presence,"[16] it is interesting to get a glimpse of future plans for digital media's wide-ranging capacities from within the restricted spaces of the industry's managerial class.

What I would like to address, briefly, about digitextuality on television is its function that simultaneously enables aesthetic enhancement and diminution of the televisual image. At one extreme is television's much-improved image resolution and overall production values as the industry makes its grudging shift to overdue court-mandated standards and time schedules for achieving high-definition television (HDTV) in accordance with the proindustry 1996 Telecommunications Act. At the other is television's brand of data compression, used to create its own information-rich look or environment to compete with its growing rival, the Internet, which from an intertextual reference point appropriates its own polysemy from print media. In between these poles is television's more widespread use of cinema's letter-box feature to better present high-income advertising (shot on film instead of videotape), and TV's self-repositioning as the nation's trustworthy, reliable, and preeminent medium of transmedia convergence in the information economy—particularly after the catastrophic events of September 11, 2001.

Digitextuality's visual aesthetics and technological virtuosity are most recognizable on television in special-effects-driven texts such as: (1) commercials, many shot on film (e.g., the striking *Blade Runner–*inspired First Union Bank ad campaign or the Cingular Wireless' *2001: A Space Odyssey–*inspired depiction of unbound connectivity); (2) music videos (e.g., Jennifer Lopez's "Waiting for Tonight" and Korn's "Freak on a Leash"); and (3) science fiction shows like *The X-Files* and *Outer Limits*. What they all share is computerized textual production and image manipulation using high-end digital editing, two- and three-dimensional painting and compositing software compatible with both film and video.[17]

Another important marker of digitextuality in the televisual flow of naturalistic, fantastic, and realistic images is the presence, especially, of commercial images that stand out due to their *sumptuous color saturation*, or that move from Technicolor to what I am calling *"technocolor."* Where the exuberant coloring schemes in postwar 1940s Technicolor musicals countered the expressive but gloomly black-and-white chiaroscuro tones of mid-1940s film noir, contemporary film and video production make use of digital paint tools to effectively and seamlessly merge these seemingly incommensurate modalities. For example, in commercials for luxury automobiles, makeup and hair products, and telecommunications and tourism businesses the color-saturation levels separating these income-generating texts from television's high-cost regular programming is stark. To capture the eyeballs of mass numbers of viewers, television ads use digital software tools like Amazon 2D and 3D (a digital paint system for film and high-definition TV) to intensify their products' look,[18] either as muted color intensities diffused with black or white tonalities, or fully enriched RGB (red, green, and blue) color filters that often seem to trump Technicolor's excesses in Hollywood musicals and melodramas from the 1940s to 1960s. Successful global soap operas like CBS's *The Bold and the Beautiful* and *The Young and the Restless* now simulcast in HDTV, and effects-driven prime-time shows such as CBS's hit drama *CSI* (*Crime Scene Investigation*) often hold their own against the digitally enhanced high production values of high-income-generating commercials. With the incredible allure of such lush, sumptuous, and compelling imagery, an assertion of one CBS promo for *CSI* makes us aware of the stakes involved here. Promoting the show's remarkable popularity and buzz, the promo states, "A lot's been said about *CSI*. One thing is certain: you can't look away."

To ensure that we don't avert our gaze, television producers are experimenting with several strategies to keep us looking, including the pervasive use of data-compression techniques, and program tie-ins with the Internet. Most characteristic in this regard is the obvious embrace of what I am calling the *congested* or *overwhelmed image* by cable networks such as CNN, MSNBC, Fox, and Court-TV. The fact that cable television's news and information programs increasingly construct new epistemologies of the screen where images are frequently overrun by word texts indicates that some media critics' lamentations about "the rise of the image, the fall of the word" in modern culture apparently were premature.[19] Instead, the apparent parity between video image and text combinations on television is symptomatic of that industry's desperate mimicry of the so-called information-rich look of commercial websites. Where CNN's *Headline News* was at the forefront, and continues to lead among all the others who followed in this practice, the events of September 11, 2001, upped the ante. Now virtually all networks and programs have transformed and redeployed the long-standing public service function of the emergency news crawl into a round-the-clock (24/7) attention-grabbing "ticker" device or contrivance. Shows like ABC's *The View* and others attempt to accommodate the industry's discomfiture with the early stages of television and Internet convergence, imploring audiences to "go to our website *after four o'clock*" for additional information covered on the program. To have it both ways, the shows promote their Internet content in the last minutes of the program to avoid competing with themselves and others for the dwindling television audience.[20]

A less successful approach to countering the Internet's poaching on its highly valued youth audience and its ideological "gatekeeping function" was the production of Generation X television shows like UPN's now defunct *Level 9* and *Freakylinks*—with messages implying that kids avoid the dangers of the Net by simply watching it on TV—sutured to the programs' young, hip, and attractive hackers working as government agents. More explicit, however, were television's shrill demonizing and scapegoating of the Internet and video games in the 1999 Columbine High School shooting tragedy, which essentially indicted them "as virtual accomplices to mass murder."[21] Traditional media messages of new-media culpability continue today with the profiling of Arab-Americans (since September 11, 2001), and the persistent yoking of the Internet with child endangerment, pornography, and video games with excessive violence.

how we experience digitextuality

An important part of our ability to experience digitextuality as a visual pleasure or as a potent force for either good or ill seems intertwined with our expectations for digital media's interactive capacities. No sooner had virtual communities' popularization of the Internet relay chat (IRC), bulletin boards, usenets, listservs, MUDs (multiuser domains), MOOs (multiuser object-oriented environments), and multiplayer, text-based computer games oriented people toward a view of interactivity that advances interpersonal communication and "rules of social interactions

[that] are built, not received" than the corporate interests taking over the Web necessarily curtailed this vision.[22] In *Life on the Screen*, Sherry Turkle describes how these and other experiences of the web's interactivity continue to make it a formidable rival for traditional media concerns. Interactivity constructed by "old" media restricts its functioning through predetermined, binary logics (i.e. the ubiquitous "yes" or "no" survey / poll questions), or narrowly focused and limited e-mail commentary tied to TV and print texts. In contrast, Turkle observes, "it is on the Internet that our confrontations with technology as it collides with our sense of human identity are fresh, even raw" (10). A quote by an avid computer-games player articulates well the exchange-value problematic of tradiational media where digital media's version of interactivity is concerned: "This is more real than my real life" (10). Unfortunately, the current media-merger mania that holds the maturing information age in its grips signals nothing less than postmodern society's predictable return to the vertical integration schemes of the early film industry. This means that the corporation's vision of interactivity will eviscerate the more expansive vision of the Internet's early days. Convergence media determined by the economic realignment of big media conglomerates, the Federal Communications Commission's (FCC) 1996 Telecommunications Act, the 1998 Digital Millennium Copyright Act (DMCA), and deregulation policies are the true millennial (or Y2K-year 2000) threat that we should fear and fight.[23] In fact, as globalization gets further advanced by the tidal wave of actual and proposed corporate media mergers (creating such giants as AOL Time-Warner and Disney-ABC; the News Corporation and Twentieth Century Fox; Bertelsmann, Doubleday-Random House, and RCA Victor; Seagrams and Universal; General Electric and NBC, Viacom and CBS, and MCI and Sprint), these mega-corporations threaten to usurp the societal reproduction function of the Althusserian ideological state apparatus (ISA) with an even more potent ideological corporate apparatus (ICA).

In support of my own transposition, I proffer Bill Gates's Microsoft empire as emblematic of the new media convergence industries' powerful role in ensuring the "ruling ideas" thesis through the political economy of the post–Marxist era ICA. When thinking about this idea of the ICA it is not difficult to view the congested and overwhelmed televisual images on CNN, MSNBC and Fox as visual renderings of Louis Althusser's elaboration on the Marxist base and superstructure metaphor for capitalism. At the level of form and composition, for example, both the static and streaming text positioned at the bottom of the televisual frame that conveys stock market information and news headlines evokes the base. The top portion, containing live, in-studio images of reporters and videotaped images of current events, becomes an articulation of the superstructure. Such an image-text condensation of important news and information functions efficiently to reify or naturalize our economic mode of production and societal propagation. Finally, it is likely not an overstatement to say that the once attempted merger of MCI and Sprint (at $108 billion, the *New York Times* estimates it would have been "the largest acquisition in corporate history"[24]) heralds even more empire building, and power consolidation, by the ICA.

In shifting my discussion of digitextuality now to its most pervasive experiential phenomena in our contemporary society, I also argue for a reembodiment thesis in digital culture in terms of an intervention into the hype of new-media formalism. I would like to demonstrate how the hyperbolic discourse of the posthuman in the digital age might be rethought to recuperate a politics of the body in the wake of digital formalism's decade-long preoccupation with an art-for-art's-sake depoliticization imperative.

click theory and the lure of sensory plenitude

An important part of understanding digitextuality centers on what I see as an emerging "click fetish" in the production and consumption of new-media discourses and practices. I propose that a fetishizing of the term *click,* and its attendant iconography (the ever-present computer mouse, its onscreen arrow or white finger icon), operate through new media's lure of a sensory plenitude presumably available simply, instantaneously, and pleasurably with any one of several clicking apparatuses. These newer apparatuses of click pleasure include video game joysticks, wireless cell phones with Internet connectivity, PDAs (personal digital assistants), and handheld computers, what David Pogue and others term "Internet appliances."[25] Also included here are the more familiar apparatuses of click, the TV remote control device and cable TV boxes, both newly adapted for MSN TV services, Replay, and the TiVo systems of convergence media applications, what "old" media executives call PVRs (personal video recorders).[26] As these new proliferating hardware devices saturate our physical spaces and consume our mental energies, they turn us, some argue, into either empowered posthuman cyborgs or disempowered lobotomized borgs in "the cult of information"[27]—that is, New Age couch potatoes. The question is, How can we better understand the emerging codes of digitextuality in our information society and our putative pleasurable situatedness therein? There must be some pleasure to be had—otherwise, why buy? Why buy the rhetoric of plenitude or the expensive machines and services of click culture?

privileging the body in the nature-versus-science split in click culture

Relying on several observations found in Jean-François Lyotard's book *The Inhuman*, especially the chapters "Can Thought Go On without a

Body?" and "Rewriting Modernity," I imagine click theory as a useful heuristic engagement with what Lyotard terms a "meta-function." For Lyotard, a meta-function is a "faculty of being able to change levels of referentiality" almost instantaneously.[28] Clearly, this idea of changing levels of referentiality corresponds to the operations of the Internet and web-based environments with their celebrated hypertext structures and linking functions, and even the channel surfing between television programs. However, its implications for our concerns will be manifest as we progress. As fruitful as the concept of bodily transcendence via the Gibsonian "consensual hallucination" of cyberspace has been for cyberculture and technoculture discourses—especially for imagining a breakout of postmodern society's prison house of socially constructed identities (race, gender, and class constraints)—not all new media theorists are satisfied with this utopian spin, this writer included. Following Lyotard, I too want to understand more precisely and problematize this seemingly reified sublation of body to mind, especially in digital culture and in practices of digitextuality. As Lyotard puts it in considering philosophical thought "the quintessential meta-function":

> The body might be considered the hardware of the complex technical device that is human thought. If this body is not properly functioning, the ever so complex operations, the meta-regulations to the third or fourth power, the controlled deregulations of which you philosophers are so fond, are impossible. . . . In other words, your philosophy is possible only because the material ensemble called "man" is endowed with very sophisticated software. But also, this software, human language, is dependent on the condition of the hardware. (13)

By refusing the elevation of philosophical thought over the materiality of the body, by analogizing the indissociable human body and language to computer hardware and software operations, Lyotard suggests an effective way to consider click theory and the lure of sensory plenitude. The click fetish, then, signifies the persistence of the body despite the powerful rhetoric of the posthuman in new media figurations.[29] Click theory can be viewed as positing a counterpoint to a narratological privileging of disembodied subjectivity in cyberculture.[30] For click pleasure is predicated on an urge to retain the primacy of the body (or the meat), and to rescue it from the phenomenological scrap heap in much of the nature-versus-science debate of our technological era. The fetishizing of the click action, and click pleasure's lure of sensory plenitude, inhere in the bodily tactility of the touch—touching the mouse, the keyboard, the touchpad and screens, and wireless keys. It is not so much that the desire to transcend the body is contested but that the sense of touch, on which this supposed transcendence is predicated, always returns the repressed body in a fort/da move of repression and recall. And, as voice, fingerprint, eyeball recognition and other biomechanical technologies develop, it seems to me that activating the click commands will only intensify a click pleasure—one rooted in the body, as the sensory aspect of speech and other kinesics call forth new modalities of corporeal interactive plenitude.[31] The bottom line for Lyotard, and I concur, is that "thought is inseparable from the phenomenological body" (23).

double-click: on hyperlinks and rhizoplane structures

Again, the new visual and aural representations that define digital texts, such as websites, CD-ROMs, DVDs, and computer games (arcade, console, handheld, and online varieties), construct new epistemologies of the screen that instantiate their own reading strategies, encodings, deciphering practices, and reception contexts. Click theory can allow us to think about the ontologies of new digital images and sound in terms of Immanuel Kant's exhortation to "let things come as they present themselves" (quoted in Lyotard, 32). And, in digital media, things present themselves most often as hypertexts, often designed according to a rhizoplane-like structure of links (the term *rhizoplane* means "the external surface of roots together with closely adhering soil particles and debris").[32] I find this particular terminology and definition metaphorically apt for characterizing the densely packed image, text, and soundscape combinations of websites, video-game menus, and contemporary television programming content increasingly married to the Internet and other digital forms—in a word, *digitextuality*, as I have previously mentioned.

When we understand computerized linking as a system of "nested narratives—a narrative within a narrative,"[33] following the rhizoplane structure, it becomes analogous to Freudian free association, which Lyotard interprets as "a way of linking one sentence with another without regard for the logical, ethical, or aesthetic value of the link" (30–31). It is this promise of infinite narrative possibilies suggested by linkages in hypertexts and digitextuality that corresponds to my idea of sensory plenitude. Digital media texts are capable of simultaneously engaging our senses of sight, sound, touch, and now thought in a heightened manner that is different in degree, if not in kind, from more traditional media texts. Thus, not only do digital media hypertexts promise an immersive bodily experience, but they also present a point-and-click fetish object of unlimited choice and sensory experience. This raises the much-debated issue of a presumed *new* media interactivity supposedly far superior to a putative *old* media passivity. But, if "Click Here" is the command gateway to the plenitude of the World Wide Web and global and local experiences, where do we position traditional and new televisual communication on this problematic active/passive media consumption continuum?

the interactive/passive media problematic and the limits of click

Because the rhetorics of *old* and *new* new-media specifications have unsuitably constructed a binary system of media transmission and reception, I am compelled to question this situational logic by problematizing the construction of, say, TV viewership and traditional print readership as passive consumption in opposition to the view of computer usage as interactive. Again, it is Lyotard who offers me cover. I borrow from his concern about the "already thought" or the inscribed (20). Since the hypertexts' linking functions are delimited by an author's circumscriptions or choices, we can view computer *linking* as a form of interacting with the already thought—the author-programmers' preestablished inscriptions. (That said, it is the case that authors often abdicate their authorial function to those linked texts that escape their discursive control.) Be that as it may, the already thought is compelling, Lyotard argues, because "[t]he unthought hurts" and "we are comfortable with the already thought" (20).

I also find Lyotard's comments about our "faith in the inexhaustibility of the perceivable" (17) useful as I think through the sensory plenitude idea and the "mouse-over," or rollover applets of hypertexts and

Figure 1.2. The Couch Potato as Passive Body.

Figure 1.3. The Mouse Potato as Active Body. Photo by A. Everett

linking. As we become increasingly habituated to hypertexts' encodings of plenitude or "value added" content by "clicking here," for "more" data, I want to suggest that a Pavlovian effect charges the dynamics of mouse-overs and rollovers. Here, our gateway to unlimited sensory pleasures (or displeasures) seems assured as the ubiquitous arrow pointer icon gets immediately transformed into the white finger icon when rolled or "moused" over digital texts that activate supplements to the main texts that "radiate from it in the manner of branches from a tree."[34] In this way, I argue click theory's lure of sensory plenitude functions to affirm Lyotard's idea of our "faith in the inexhaustibility of the perceivable." In other words, by clicking on websites' embedded hotlinks we are instantly transported to other data fields within the site or to separate websites linked to the primary one.

Recently, one cable company advertisement promoted the telecommunications industry's new direct subscriber lines (DSL) service that sums up this idea perfectly. A man is surfing the Internet when he gets a voiced computer message warning him that he has reached "the end of the Internet." He is told, "Please go back." We all recognize within this fictional scenario the essential utility of the "back" button when web surfing to reorient ourselves after going astray amid the inexhaustible information overload of the Internet's ever-increasing but always perceivable content. While we also recognize the fallacy of actually "reaching the end of the Internet," its symbolic or metaphoric relevance to our limited tolerance for experiencing the Web's "inexhaustibility of the perceivable" rings true. In fact, the success of Internet search engines like HotBot, Google, Yahoo, and others, despite the infamous dot-com bust, has been sustained precisely because of their reliable management of the web's daunting, inexhaustible data stream. Now they are what I term *information retailers*.

Unfortunately, today, with the corporate takeover of the web, the apparent unlimited choice of data distributed by these search engines is increasingly ordered and prioritized in ways analogous to the lucrative shelf ordering of retail commodities in supermarkets and superstores like WalMart and others. Google, at this writing, is in a legal dispute with Overture Services over a patent "that lets businesses, for a fee, have Web sites listed in the results of Internet queries."[35] While the outcome of this court battle is uncertain, it is certain that businesses are not lined up to pay for a space on the *bottom* shelf of a search engine's popular "keyword" listings. The gravity of this situation becomes quite apparent when we consider the following context. The web's content may be inexhaustible, but our very human or bodily attention spans and leisure time are not. Thus it is here that the commercial discussed above captures and conveys the conflict between the Nietzscheian will to post-human power and the bodily limitations of physical possibility.

Another area of concern in my click theory argument focuses on some aesthetics of digital texts. When we stop to consider what makes websites alluring despite their semiotic densities and navigational mysteries, or "soil particles and debris," then Lyotard is again instructive, with his discussion of "the concept of the bit," the tyrannical unit of information restriction that characterizes the smallest, yet essential, component of computerized data and information systems. I want to contrast this computerized bit to the televisual "bite," and consider how these shorthand communicative cues engage with Lyotard's discussion of "pleasures in the beautiful" or "a promise of happiness" (33–34). I begin with Lyotard's statement that "Every discourse, including that of science or philosophy is only a perspective, a *Weltanschauung*" (29). For Lyotard, this perspectivization is most acute and discernible through historical knowledge and writing that consists in a double-move of signification most familiar in the English form of " 'putting down'—to write down and to repress," which also "suggests both inscription or recording and discredit" (29–30). For Lyotard, then, this is a form of rewriting, "a double gesture, forwards and backwards" (30). What this means is that to construct a discourse, some information is foregrounded and some erased, some privileged and some discredited. But, most important for Lyotard, all this requires an anamnesis—a reminiscence and a working through, "a business of free imagination" and "the deployment of time between 'not yet,' 'no longer' and 'now' " (35). It is precisely these free-floating imaginative operations that the new technologies inhibit, in Lyotard's view. And that inhibition is most inherent in the basic unit of new technology information transfer, "the concept of the bit, the [basic] unit of information" (34); for as Lyotard puts it, "When we're dealing with bits, there's no longer any question of free forms given here and now to sensibility and the imagination. On the contrary, they are units of information conceived by computer engineering and definable at all linguistic levels—lexical, symbolic, syntactic, rhetorical and the rest. They are assembled into systems following a set of possibilities (a 'menu') under the control of the programmer" (34–35). Although Lyotard's deterministic logic miscalculates the breakout possibilities of hacking through the tyranny of the bit, his sober reflections on the limitations of new media's click culture and its attendant lure of sensory plenitude deserve contemplation. Beyond traditional media's ideologically inflected inscriptions, new-media encryptions get advanced along more restrictive lines of information codification, as anyone (other than hackers) attempting to manipulate or circumvent computerized information protocols quickly discovers via pop-up dialogue boxes alerting one to the errors of one's intent.

Whereas computer bits controlled by engineering fiat crash or fail to respond to users' contrary impulses, the televisual bite (the predetermined basic unit of information/message construct) inadvertently permits contrary message distortion and manipulation at the level of reception and data transfer. Thus, a fifteen- or thirty-second televisual sound bite can be accepted or resisted based on a viewer's or reader's predisposition to the transmitted message at hand. In contrast, a computer user desiring manipulative powers over and beyond the engineer's bit specifications is stopped dead in her tracks. For example, if one tunes in to a TV sound bite a message relay is allowed whether or not one misreads its contents. If, however, one mistakenly keys in an inappropriate alphanumeric code or symbol on a computer, one won't even get connected to a website or be allowed to perform a desired computer function—thus access to the relayed message will be denied altogether. It is this level of medium specificity that supports Lyotard's reservations about the new technologies' limited rewriting or "click" potential.

remediating classical media aesthetics through new-media apparatuses of click culture

Finally, I would like to consider how the click fetish and sensory plenitude of new media production and consumption can be theorized as digitextual "remediations" of classical and traditional media aesthetics and forms.[36] The usefulness of articulating new-media practices' imbrication in old-media precedents is not to proffer a reduction of the former to mere rearticulations of the latter but rather to better outline new media's seductive allures. Moreover, this looking back enables us to grasp how contemporary media users and audiences decode and understand digital technologies' signifying practices and potent representational economies. In fact, Vivian Sobchack, following Martin Heidegger, makes the important observation that "technology is never merely 'used,' never merely instrumental. It is always also 'incorporated' and 'lived' by the human beings who engage it within a structure of meanings and metaphors in which subject-object relations are cooperative, co-constitutive, dynamic, and reversible."[37]

Indeed, many new-media theorists have begun archeologies and hermeneutics of new digital media by way of their situatedness in past cinematic forms and critical theories.[38] And while the focus of many analyses of digital media technologies' indebtedness to classical cinema realist and formalist narrative approaches, as well as avant-garde practices, concentrates on the works of early cinema luminaries such as Dziga Vertov and Sergei Eisenstein, and later theorist-practitioners like Jean-Luc Godard, for example, I would like to take a very brief analytical detour through the works and influence of André Bazin, Germain Dulac, Rudolf Arnheim, and Jean Epstein as well. What I find in returning to Bazin's notion of "the myth of total cinema," Arnheim's discourses on "the complete film," and Dulac and Epstein's medium-specific articulations of cinematic *photogenie* during the avant-garde of the 1920's formalist cinema project, are heuristic predecessors to clarify my conceptions of click theory and its sensory plenitude functions.

In constructing my click theory idea, I share Peter Lunenfeld's view that there are "new artistic communities, emergent technocultures, being built around computer-driven media," and "cybernetic tools" such as "word processors, nonlinear digital video editing systems, database managers, Web server softwares, interactive multimedia programs," and "virtual reality 'world-building' kits."[39] My concern, however, is with how these cybernetic tools recycle, recode, and redeploy classical-media modes and codes to heighten contemporary media users' and consumers' affective responses to new-media functions— especially the computer's immersive click functions. In his influential essay "The Myth of Total Cinema," André Bazin provides the most nuanced way of thinking about how old and new media practices intersect without simplistically conflating the two and thereby losing the specificities of either. He writes, "The cinema is an idealistic phenomenon. The concept men had of it existed so to speak fully armed in their minds, as if in some platonic heaven, and what strikes us most of all is the obstinate resistance of matter to ideas."[40] Here we easily recognize that the advent of what Lunenfeld calls digital media's "cybernetic tools" is the near fulfillment of the idealistic phenomenon that early cinema merely promised. Bazin writes that "it is clear that all the definitive stages of the invention of the cinema had been reached before the requisite conditions had been fulfilled"; what he is arguing here is that it had long been our desire to achieve "a total and complete representation of reality . . . the reconstruction of a perfect illusion of the outside world in sound, color, and relief" (20). In mounting his refutation of the "absurd" belief that silent cinema somehow represented "a state of primal perfection" jeopardized or contaminated by the additions of sound, color, and three-dimensional technology, Bazin hyperbolically states, "In short, cinema has not yet been invented!" (21).

I propose that digital media's new technological advances bring us closer to a realization of Bazin's ideas in the myth of total cinema—in short, finally, cinema *has* been invented! Its invention is achieved through magical digital tools and our unending quest for "a recreation of the world in its own image, unburdened by the freedom of interpretation of the artist or the irreversibility of time" (21). Indeed, click culture now brings us the entire world through the Internet and the web, DVD and CD-ROM, QuickTime and RealPlayer technologies, and satellites where images do not suffer the ravages and degradations of time associated with analog image production. Additionally, MP3 and other digital sound technologies bring us pristine sounds, and cybernetic toolboxes give us sumptuous color, three dimensionaltiy, and virtual reality systems that Bazin could not fathom outside a mythological future vision.

In "What is Digital Cinema," Lev Manovich's observations that "digital filmmakers work with 'elastic reality'" due to digital technologies' "compositing, animating and morphing" features is nothing if not a confirmation of Rudolf Arnheim's 1933 prediction.[41] In "The Complete Film," Arnheim predicts that "The technical development of the motion picture will soon carry the mechanical imitation of nature to an extreme."[42] Although Arnheim is often judged as a silent cinema purist obsessed with denigrating the advances of sound and color (which is true to a certain extent), the reality is that he feared a one-dimensional cinematic hegemony. He writes, "In itself, the perfection of the 'complete' film need not be a catastrophe—if silent film, sound film, and colored sound film were allowed to exist along side it" (159). Despite his miscalculations, Arnheim was inadvertently prescient when he noted that with the arrival of the complete film, "Film will no longer be able in any sense to be considered as a separate art" (49). And with the digital technologies' engendering of convergence media, some of Arhneim's fears of the cinema's eclipse are being realized, if differently than he could have imagined in 1933.

For me, digital media technologies' abilities simultaneously to reproduce and manipulate reality with an unprecedented representational economy and efficacy turn traditional notions of mimesis and diegesis on their heads. And due to their abilities to construct new and synthetic representational strategies and possibilities seamlessly, they not only advance previously unimagined representations of ideas and desires, but are also able to portray the sublime, and that once believed-in idea of the unrepresentable. For click theory, this means that digital media's computerized hypertext structures and linking functions promise and convince us that clicking on hot links, RealPlayer and QuickTime movies embedded within digital texts virtually ensure that the complete film and total cinema have arrived, and that they are available on our desktops, our televisions, and in the numerous handheld computer devices that characterize our new cultural dominant—the age of ubiquitous computing via digitextuality.

As we all set out to articulate key aspects of digital technologies' medium specifities, the relevance of Jean Epstein and Germaine Dulac's elaborations on Jean Delluc's notion of *photogenie*—a conceptualization of the cinema's unique properties or "purest expression"—becomes increasingly apparent. In terms of click theory, I see its lure of sensory plenitude as a sort of recoding of the idea of the cinema of attractions. Again, the impulse here is not to posit an old-media restriction on new-media image processing, but rather to recognize the usefulness of previous critical and theoretical insights for thinking through what is truly new about new-media discourses and practices. At the same time, it is difficult not to see how the much hyped "bullet-time" and "hypertime" slow-motion, "Techno-slammin' visual" special effects of the films *The Matrix* (1999),[43] *Crouching Tiger, Hidden Dragon* (2001), and *Clock Stoppers* (2002) become new media iterations of Jean Epstein's photogenie ideal. In describing "The Spirit of Slow Motion" that suffused his film *La Chute de la Maison Usher* (*The Fall of the House of Usher*, 1926), Epstein writes in 1928:

> In making *La Chute de la Maison Usher*, I deliberately avoided all the visual effects which might have resulted in super-cinema. All I tried to achieve—if I dare express myself so pretentiously—was super drama. At no point in the film will the spectator be able to say to himself: this is slow motion. . . . We are now on the verge of rediscovering lost time as subtly as in literature. . . . This capacity for discrimination in the mechanical and optical super-eye clearly demonstrates the relativity of time. So it is true that seconds last for hours. The drama is placed outside ordinary time. A new, purely psychological perspective obtains.[44] (34–35)

The resonance with late-twentieth-century new-media rearticulations in *The Matrix* and *Crouching Tiger*, for example, and Epstein's own 1920s experimentation with slow-motion cinematic effects seems clear; for here within Epstein's useful explanatory logic are clear premonitory utterances for concretizing my own ideas about the affective dimensions of digital media's technological sway on our cognitive processes of consuming and being consumed by digital texts' visual allures. At the same time, it is hoped that references to this relevant past also help us to be in a better position to thus identify "digital cinema's" own specificities and not negate its indebtedness to literary and classical cinema forebears.

For her part, Germaine Dulac enables us to grasp the need to appreciate and approach a new medium on its own terms and in its own time. What Dulac advocates is the necessity of recognizing what she calls "the moral essence of the cinematic, an art born of our time, and for which we must make an effort, in order to avoid the misunderstanding which so often meets unexpected revelations."[45] (36) Like her contemporary Dziga Vertov, Dulac sees in cinema a second, more powerful eye available for mankind's benefit, "an eye more powerful than our own and which sees things we cannot see" (30). As she puts it in 1925:

> Should not the cinema, which is an art of vision, as music is an art of hearing, on the contrary lead us toward the visual idea composed of movement and life, toward the conception of an art of the eye made of a perceptual inspiration evolving [of] our thoughts and feelings? Only music can inspire this feeling which cinema also aspires to, and in the light of the sensations that it offers we can get a sense of those that the cinema of the future will give us. . . . Among the viewers a few love the cinema for its future possibilities. They will understand. (41–42)

In her desire to see the cinema "freed from its chains and be given its true personality" (37), Dulac points out a way for us to attend to what it is that digital media technologies bring to the changed moment and demands of our own twentieth- and twenty-first-century times. Unfortunately, the data merchants of digital cinema understand all too well the potentialities of a future cinema to tap human beings' thoughts and feelings, as Dulac desired. If you accept the premise that in many ways digital cinema's technological advancements fulfill Dulac's prediction of "pure cinema," Bazin's "total cinema," and Arnheim's "complete film" then you might more easily apprehend my click theory of new media's potent lure of sensory plenitude.

For now, not only are our thoughts, feelings and desires easily rendered and expressed through new media imaging, but our abilities to create and consume those once elusive imaginary ideals as Dulac sets forth are taken for granted and commodified through the various apparatuses of click technology. "Click Here" now means a new porousness of sorts, of such once rigidly constructed geopolitical, national, cultural, techno-logical, economical, gendered, racial, class, and even temporal bound-aries. Again, what motivates this brief detour through some key classical film theory ideas is the urge to temper the hype of the "new" in digital media aesthetics and formalist structures with a sober reflection on its similarities to discourses of the past. But the caveat, which Epstein, Dulac, Arnheim, and Bazin surely would have lamented, is that permeation of all these boundaries and the ability for media con-sumers to alter their spectatorial statuses (either as superconsumers or consumer-producers) is now available *only* if one possesses today's sophisticated (read: *expensive*) apparatuses of click.

I began this latter discussion by interrogating digital technologies' formi-dable impact on our increasingly mediated lives and technology-driven culture. I particularly wanted to point out some conceptual limitations within some of the much-touted posthuman logics and rhetorics, and I attempted to demonstrate how the very notion that the physical and material apparatuses that presumably make transcending the body pos-sible ultimately fails. An important reality of digitextuality is that the apparatuses of click—the primal interfaces granting access to cyberspace, computer-enhanced television, pocket computers, wireless and handheld devices—*always return us to the body activating and making sense of the interface.*

notes

1. Wheeler Winston Dixon discusses Godard's views on the changing nature of the cinema in *The Films of Jean-Luc Godard* (Albany: State University of New York Press, 1997). Michael Nash elaborates on the notion of a posttelevision age in his article, "Vision after Television: Tech-nocultural Convergence, Hypermedia, and the New Media Arts Field," in *Resolutions: Contemporary Video Practices*, ed. Michael Renov and Erika Suder-burg (Minneapolis: University of Minessota Press, 1996), 382–99.
2. See W. Russell Neuman, *The Future of the Mass Audience* (New York: Cam-bridge University Press, 1991).
3. There have been ongoing discussions of new media among interested scholars and members of the Society for Cinema Studies (SCS) for nearly a decade. However, it has not been widely addressed by the or-ganization until recently—notably at the SCS 2002 plenary, in Denver, Colorado, which featured a panel entitled "Cinema" Studies in a New Media Age.
4. I have been working on this idea for some time now, and I have shared these ideas at several conferences and symposia. For instance, in June 1999,

I presented a paper titled "Toward a Theory of Digitextuality: The Internet in the Classroom," at the Interactive Frictions Conference in Los Angeles. See also my article, "The Black Press in the Age of Digital Reproduction: Two Exemplars," in *The Black Press: New Literary and Historical Essays,* ed. Todd Vogel (New Brunswick, N.J.: Rutgers University Press, 2001), 246.

5. Julia Kristeva, "Revolution in Poetic Language," in *The Kristeva Reader,* ed. Toril Moi (New York: Columbia University Press, 1986), 111; hereafter, page numbers will be cited parenthetically in the text.

6. Julia Kristeva, quoted in C. Hugh Holman and William Harmon, *A Handbook to Literature,* 6th ed. (New York: Macmillan, 1992), 251.

7. In their books, both Lev Manovich and Peter Lunenfeld provide excellent and detailed treatises on some specifics of new media's debt to earlier visual media apparatuses, conventions, and philosophies. See Lev Manovich, *The Language of Digital Media* (Cambridge, Mass.: MIT Press, 2001) and Peter Lunenfeld, *Snap to Grid: A User's Guide to Digital Arts, Media, and Cultures* (Cambridge, Mass.: MIT Press, 2000).

8. John Thornton Caldwell, *Televisuality: Style, Crisis, and Authority in American Television* (New Brunswick, N.J.: Rutgers University Press, 1995), 26, emphasis in the original; hereafter, page numbers will be cited parenthetically in the text.

9. In *Growing Up Digital: The Rise of the Net Generation,* Don Tapscott provides an interesting look at how newer generations negotiate their changed status in the information age. As he puts it, "kids use computers for activities that seem to go hand-in-hand with our understanding of what constitutes traditional childhood. They use the technology to play, learn, communicate, and form relationships as children have always done. On the other hand, the digital media is creating an environment where such activities of childhood are changing dramatically and may, for better or worse, accelerate child development"; Tapscott, *Growing Up Digital: The Rise of the Net Generation* (New York: McGraw-Hill, 1998), 7.

10. Wheeler Winston Dixon, *It Looks at You: The Returned Gaze of Cinema* (Albany: State University of New York Press, 1995), 37.

11. David Bordwell and Kristin Thompson, *Film Art: An Introduction* (New York: Knopf, 1997), 78.

12. Lev Manovich, *The Language of New Media* (Cambridge, Mass.: MIT Press, 2001), 25.

13. Jean Baudrillard, *Simulations,* trans. Paul Foss, Paul Patton, and Philip Beitchman (New York: Semiotext(e), 1983), 142.

14. Stentz's full essay, "So Real They're Virtual," can be accessed online at the Metro paper's online archive <http://www.metroactive.com. . ./metro/09.03.98/virtual celeb-9835.htm>.

15. Jeffrey Lotman, quoted in Stentz, "So Real They're Virtual."

16. Margaret Morse, *Virtualities: Television, Media Art, and Cyberculture* (Bloomington: Indiana University Press, 1998), 1.

17. For specific technical information about the software systems used on these and many television and film texts, see the interactivefx company's website at <http://www.ifx.com>.

18. See interactivefx, at <http://www.ifx.com>.

19. Mitchell Stephens, *The Rise of the Image the Fall of the Word* (New York: Oxford University Press, 1998).

20. Television has been competing with the Internet and other new media for nearly a decade, and the situation has destabilized the networks' traditional business model. In his article "Canceled, 'Adventures in Television': Was the Hook Too Quick?" (Los Angeles Times, June 22, 2002, F17) Allan Johnson reports that, " 'They're desperate at this point'. . . . And desperation leads to shows being on for two weeks. . . . With cable, the Internet, DVDs and more competing for viewers' attention, all networks usually can't wait for a show to find an audience, even if it might eventually be there."

21. Anna Everett, "P.C. Youth Violence: What's the Internet or Video Gaming Got to Do with It?" *Denver Law Review* 77, no. 4 (2000): 690.

22. Sherry Turkle, *Life on the Screen: Identity in the Age of the Internet* (New York: Touchstone, 1995), 10; hereafter, page numbers will be cited parenthetically in the text.

23. Wayne Overbeck, a professor of communication, provides an important historical overview of the significance of the DMCA in his article "Let's Give a Toast to Prohibition, Circa 2000," *Los Angeles Times,* July 30, 2000, M5.

24. For details of this history-making deal and more, see Laura M. Holson and Seth Schiesel's article, "MCI to Buy Sprint in Swap of Stock for $108 Billion," *New York Times,* October 5, 1999, C13.

25. David Pogue, "Year of Living Geekely: Even the Dogs Evolved," *New York Times,* 27 December 2001, D1.

26. For a complete discussion of the PVR revolution, see Staci D. Kramer's essay "Content's King" at *Cableworld* <www.inside.com/product/product_p. . .0B8A11C30373&CONTENT=ARTICLE&PRINT=true>.

27. I am posing Donna Haraway's utopic cyborg vision against Theodore Roszak's more pessimistic view for argument's sake.

28. Jean-François Lyotard, "Can Thought Go On Without a Body?" in *The Inhuman,* trans. Geoffrey Bennington and Rachel Bowlby (Stanford, Calif.: Stanford University Press, 1991), 13; hereafter, page numbers will be cited parenthetically in the text.

29. See, for example, various positions espoused on the concept of the posthuman in Judith Halberstam and Ira Livingston's anthology *Posthuman Bodies* (Bloomington: Indiana University Press, 1995), especially the introductory essay "Posthuman Bodies."

30. *Wired* magazine's August 2001 edition has two articles promoting the posthuman ideal; see "The Next Brainiacs," by John Hockenberry (94–105), and "Let's Make Your Head Interactive," by Jennifer Kahn (106–15).

31. *Kinesics* is defined as "the study of body movements, gestures, facial expressions, etc., as a means of communication"; "Kinesics," in *Random House Webster's College Dictionary* (New York; Random House, 2000), 731.

32. This term, *rhizoplane,* which is defined in the 1994 *Merriam-Webster's New Collegiate Dictionary*, does not appear in the later *Random House Webster's College Dictionary*, published in 2000. The 1994 *Merriam-Webster's New Collegiate Dictionary*—which is the later (and still most recent) edition of the 1977 dictionary—does indeed bear a definition (and still the **exact same** definition) for *rhizoplane* on p. 1005. The fact that the 2000 edition *Random House Webster's* does not include the term reflects only the fact that this book comes from a different publisher, and that this publisher chose not to

include the term. Comparing dictionaries that bear the name *Webster* means little these days, as the name itself is no longer copyrighted and virtually **every** dictionary uses it to add an air of authority. What does this say about our ability to know word meanings and etymologies with any sense of certitude beyond a particular corporate reorganization of knowledge regimes? *Merriam-Webster's New Collegiate Dictionary*, 10th ed. (Springfield, Mass.: Merriam-Webster, 1994), 1005.

33. Roland Barthes, *S/Z: An Essay,* trans. Richard Miller (New York: Hill and Wang, 1974), 90.

34. George Landow, *Hyper/Text/Theory* (Baltimore: Johns Hopkins University Press, 1994), 23.

35. "Google Seeks to Void Overture's Patents," *Los Angeles Times,* June 20, 2002, C2.

36. I borrow this terminology from Jay David Bolter and Richard Grusin, *Remediation: Understanding New Media* (Cambridge, Mass.: MIT Press, 1999).

37. Vivian Sobchack, "The Scene of the Screen: Envisioning Cinematic and Electronic Presence," in *Electronic Media and Technoculture,* ed. John Thornton Caldwell (New Brunswick, N.J.: Rutgers University Press), 138.

38. Most notable in this regard are Lev Manovich, Peter Lunenfeld, Vivian Sobchack, Wheeler Winston Dixon, and John Caldwell, among many others.

39. Lunenfeld, *Snap to Grid,* 3, 5.

40. André Bazin, "The Myth of Total Cinema," (Berkeley and Los Angeles: University of California Press, 1967), 17; hereafter, page numbers will be cited parenthetically in the text.

41. Lev Manovich, "What Is Digital Cinema?" <http://www-apparitions. ucsd.edu/~manovich/text/digital-cinema.html>, 5.

42. Rudolph Arnheim, "The Complete Film," *Film As Art* (Berkeley and Los Angeles: University of California Press, 1957), 154; hereafter, page numbers will be cited parenthetically in the text.

43. These are some of the descriptive terms used on the packaging literature that comes with the DVD version of *The Matrix* now available at video retail stores.

44. Jean Epstein, "Bonjour Cinema and Other Writings" (1928), reprinted in *Afterimage 10* (1981): 34–35.

45. Germaine Dulac, "The Essence of the Cinema: The Visual Idea" (1925), reprinted in *The Avant-Garde Film: A Reader of Theory and Criticism,* ed. P. Adams Sitney (New York: New York University Press, 1978), 36; hereafter, page numbers will be cited parenthetically in the text.

the radio as an

apparatus of

communication

b e r t o l t   b r e c h t

In our society one can invent and perfect discoveries that still have to
conquer their market and justify their existence, in other words discoveries that have not been called for. Thus there was a moment when
technology was advanced enough to produce the radio and society was
not yet advanced enough to accept it. The radio was then in its first
phase of being a substitute: a substitute for theater, opera, concerts, lectures, café music, local newspapers, and so forth. This was the patient's
period of halcyon youth. I am not sure if it is finished yet, but if so then
this stripling who needed no certificate of competence to be born will
have to start looking retrospectively for an object in life. Just as a man
will begin asking at a certain age, when his first innocence has been lost,
what he is supposed to be doing in the world.

As for the radio's object, I don't think it can consist merely in prettifying public life. Nor is radio in my view an adequate means of bringing
back coziness to the home and making family life bearable again. But
quite apart from the dubiousness of its functions, radio is one-sided

when it should be two. It is purely an apparatus for distribution, for mere sharing out. So here is a positive suggestion: change this apparatus over from distribution to communication. The radio would be the finest possible communication apparatus in public life, a vast network of pipes. That is to say, it would be if it knew how to receive as well as to transmit, how to let the listener speak as well as hear, how to bring him into a relationship instead of isolating him. On this principle the radio should step out of the supply business and organize its listeners as suppliers. Any attempt by the radio to give a truly public character to public occasions is a step in the right direction.

Whatever the radio sets out to do it must strive to combat that lack of consequences which makes such asses of almost all our public institutions. We have a literature without consequences, which not only itself sets out to lead nowhere, but does all it can to neutralize its readers by depicting each object and situation stripped of the consequences to which they lead. We have educational establishments without consequences, working frantically to hand on an education that leads nowhere and has come from nothing.

The slightest advance in this direction is bound to succeed far more spectacularly than any performance of a culinary kind. As for the technique that needs to be developed for all such operations, it must follow the prime objective of turning the audience not only into pupils but into teachers. It is the radio's formal task to give these educational operations an interesting turn, i.e., to ensure that these interests interest people. Such an attempt by the radio to put its instruction into an artistic form would link up with the efforts of modern artists to give art an instructive character. As an example or model of the exercises possible along these lines let me repeat the explanation of *Der Flug der Lindberghs* that I gave at the Baden-Baden music festival of 1929.

> In obedience to the principle that the State shall be rich and man shall be poor, that the State shall be obliged to have many possibilities and man shall be allowed to have few possibilities, where music is concerned the State shall furnish whatever needs special apparatus and special abilities; the individual, however, shall furnish an exercise. Free-roaming feelings aroused by music, special thoughts such as may be entertained when listening to music, physical exhaustion such as easily arises from listening to music, are all distractions from music. To avoid these distractions the individual shares in the music, thus obeying the principle that doing is better than feeling, by following the music with his eyes as printed, and contributing the parts and places reserved

for him by singing them for himself or in conjunction
with others (school class).

Der Flug der Lindberghs is not intended to be of use to the present-day radio
but to alter it. The increasing concentration of mechanical means and
the increasingly specialized training—tendencies that should be accelerated—call for a kind of resistance by the listener, and for his mobilization and redrafting as a producer.

This exercise is an aid to discipline, which is the basis of freedom. The
individual will reach spontaneously for a means to pleasure, but not for
an object of instruction that offers him neither profit nor social advantages. Such exercises only serve the individual in so far as they serve the
State, and they only serve a State that wishes to serve all men equally.
Thus *Der Flug der Lindberghs* has no aesthetic and no revolutionary value
independently of its application, and only the State can organize this.
Its proper application, however, makes it so "revolutionary" that the
present-day State has no interest in sponsoring such exercises.

This is an innovation, a suggestion that seems utopian and that I
myself admit to be utopian. When I say that the radio or the theater
"could" do so-and-so, I am aware that these vast institutions cannot do
all they "could," and not even all they want.

But it is not at all our job to renovate ideological institutions on the
basis of the existing social order by means of innovations. Instead our
innovations must force them to surrender that basis. So: For innovations, against renovation!

invisible media

l a u r a   u .   m a r k s

With the revolution of mass photographic and electronic media production, the twentieth century was celebrated as the century of visual
media. Twentieth-century visual artists and humanities scholars
devoted themselves to a critical analysis of mass-media images, in laud-
able undertakings such as subversion, reflexivity, and deconstruction.
Prudent academia inaugurated programs in visual studies in the last
decade of the century. But the visible, as Marshall McLuhan predicted,
is no longer the lively and productive arena of struggle it has been. In
terms I will explain below, the image is merely the selectively unfolded
surface of enfolded information.

I propose that the most interesting and urgent areas of communication to study now are *invisible* media; invisible, but not immaterial. The
media of the military, science, financial institutions, and mass communications are increasingly invisible, as advances in chemical and biological
warfare, nanotechnology, the corporate-driven decoding of the human
genome, quantum and other nondigital computing, data encryption, and

other "small-scale" research areas attest. To engage these invisible media on their own territory, more rebellious media adopt similar strategies of invisibility. More precisely, they adopt strategies of enfoldment. These are waiting, hiding, latent media, coiled up like vipers or jacks-in-the-box. Invisible media constitute what Hakim Bey calls the temporary autonomous zone (TAZ): "a guerilla operation which liberates an area (of land, of time, of imagination) and then dissolves itself to re-form elsewhere/ elsewhen, *before* the State can crush it."[1] The TAZ does not achieve permanent revolution but a mercurial liberation; it is defined by stealth and liquidity. After laying out the hiding places in between material experience, information/capital, and image, I will suggest that "temporarily autonomous media" can follow certain strategies of invisibility: these include making visible; sabotage; latency; and hiding in plain sight. My examples will mainly include computer-based media, though cinema, the refuge of the visible, will appear as well.

enfolding/unfolding

A good way to understand the materiality of invisible media is to think of them as enfolded or implicate.[2] Communication entails a material connection between the utterer and the listener.[3] We may think of those communications that haven't happened yet as enfolded, or (in the latinate word for the same phenomenon) *implicate*, while those communications that take place are unfolded, or *explicate*. Physicist David Bohm used the term *explicate*, or unfolded, for that which is apparent in a given system, and *implicate*, or enfolded, for that which is latent in the same system. His elegant illustration is a model of two airtight glass cylinders, one inside the other, with a layer of viscous fluid, like glycerin, between them. When a drop of ink is put in the liquid and the inside cylinder revolves, the ink drop is drawn out into a thread; when it is revolved in the other direction, the thread of ink is enfolded back to a dot. The line is implicate in the dot.

war and invisibility

Two recent wars offer an index of the shift of power from visibility to invisibility. The Persian Gulf War, Paul Virilio argues, was the first real-time war, in which military intelligence could be transmitted and acted upon in an immediate feedback loop.[4] Military information bypassed the mediation by an image, or at least bypassed the delay that translation and transmission previously required. We could say information was potent to the degree that it remained invisible. If the Vietnam War was the media war, the war of extreme visibility, the Gulf War was the first in a new era of invisible warfare. Images from the Gulf War indexed information, not concrete events; the concrete events—the actual deaths—remained enfolded.

John Greyson's film *Law of Enclosures* (2001; based on the novel by Dale Peck), set in Sarnia, Ontario, during the Gulf War, graphically demonstrates how the military-media complex selectively enfolds and unfolds information. For the characters attempting to watch the war on television, poor rural reception further clouds the sketchy images relayed by "smart bombs" of their Iraqi targets. Myra struggles with her satellite dish and shoots her remote in frustration at her TV: "Show us the fucking war! We want to see the fucking *war!*" One character is an American soldier, Stanley, serving in the ground troops. When he returns he refuses to tell his friends what he did in Iraq. Later we learn that Stanley took part in the attack upon fleeing Iraqi soldiers after the cease-fire, part of which came to be called the "Highway of Death."[5] Barely reported during the war, the concealment of this massacre behind the rhetoric of a "clean war" set a precedent for the separation of image and information. Greyson unfolds this doubly concealed information in a stunning montage sequence. An image of the heads of hundreds of Iraqis at a rally dissolves into an overhead shot of contestants at the annual Sarnia kiss-a-thon; the latter release thousands of colored balloons, which dissolve into the black-and-white snow of a television receiving no signal (or too many signals). The true image of the Gulf War, the film suggests, is the image of the disturbed signal: Myra need not adjust her television, because war now is invisible. The war images indexed nothing because the reality of the war remained enfolded.

If the Gulf War was a war whose invisibility benefited the Western allies, then the recent and supposedly ongoing "war on terrorism" was a struggle to define the terms of invisibility. For a while in November 2001 the war seemed to be going horribly wrong. It looked like Osama bin Laden and his cohorts had a kind of invisibility on their side that the Americans and their allies did not. As Britain's Admiral Sir Michael Boyce told the *New York Times*, "This is not like Kosovo. . . . It's not like Desert Storm," he noted, "where you had very clearly defined phases and relatively straightforward objectives. This is a much more murky area in which to work, obviously because the prime element is not actually visible—Osama bin Laden and the Al Qaeda—in the same way that Milosevic and the Serbs were or the Iraqis were. This is something much more intangible."[6] For a while the Taliban seemed to defeat the technically superior Americans because it had the invisibility not of smart weapons (information) but of clandestine networks and caves (caves!)—materiality. Material reality was imperceptible to a military that refused to put soldiers on the ground. Of course, the "war on terrorism," manifest in the bombing of Afghanistan, turned out in the end to be just as ugly in its materiality as the Gulf War: at least as many Afghans were killed as were the innocent workers at the World Trade Center.[7] Meanwhile, as of this writing, the man supposed to be the center of Taliban terror evanesced like a particle of antimatter. As I write, "terror" still retains its power of enfoldment. The global powers of visibility remain daunted by the power of the invisible.

Everybody was trying to unfold the paths traveled by Taliban funds. U.S.-based global capitalism celebrates "transparency" as the basis of fair financial exchange and the smooth transfer of capital. Opacity, in the form of unsanctioned cash flows through fake charities, drug money, trade in diamonds, counterfeiting, tax havens, and the "primitive" Hawala money transfer system, is a slap in the face of global capital.[8] These alternative financial routes were successful because they occurred *far below* the speed of light. In a sort of purloined-letter strategy, the Taliban cash flow remained material, unencoded, and thus resisted detection. It was an affront, a scandal that this money did not flow along the recognized pathways of global capital: How could they do this to us?

experience : information/capital : image

One more concept and we're ready to go. The world of computer-mediated capitalism is well summed up by a triadic relationship of enfolding—experience : information/capital : image.[9] By *experience* I mean the full complexity of material life. Experience enfolds, or holds in latent form, *information* and *capital.* Thus, information and capital selectively unfold experience. In turn, information and capital enfold images. Thus, in the digital world, images (or other palpable expressions, such as sound; computer music is the unfolding of digital information) selectively unfold information and capital. *Image*, being the third term, can also immediately enfold experience. Some photographs, whose images are too specific or banal to be useful as information or for capital, remain the direct index of experience.

Like all Peircean triads, the relationship among these three terms is very fluid. Images, information, and capital become part of *experience*, the first term in the triad. So we can understand the material world of experience to encompass images (not just visual), as well as the abstractions *information* and *capital.* In the rest of this essay, I will look at ways TAZ media can work with properties of invisibility of latency at the three levels I've described.

level 3: image

As I am not very optimistic about the ability of visible images to produce TAZs, I will begin with this third term. As the triadic relationship implies, there are two kinds of image: images of material experience, and images as manifestations of information/capital. Unfortunately for the first kind, as soon as an image is born from the world of experience it gets taken up in the service of something else. Recall a few years back when the clothing designer Benetton piqued consumer interest by appending its logo to the photograph of a boatload of Albanian refugees.

The second kind of image is the skin or visible manifestation of information and capital. It is only a skin. George W. Bush's multicultural cabinet may be understood as the canny deployment of an image that indexes nothing: the image of U.S. state power is different; its function is exactly the same. The relationship of interface : database is a subset of the image : information/capital relationship, and recently the colon between them has become perceptibly loose. Interfaces can unfold information in many ways: they need not be visual.[10] The arbitrary nature of the visual interface is especially apparent in recent digital blockbusters like *Star Wars: Phantom Menace* and *The Lord of the Rings*, where the impossibly spectacular image denotes nothing but information. With digital media, Jean-Luc Godard's dictum, "Money is the film within the film," is truer than ever: the vast onscreen canyons populated by extrahuman hordes quickly become a mental image for costly proprietary software and powerful hardware; these in turn denote megabucks and invisible armies of laboring humans. Aware of the new possibilities of building new interfaces to existing databases, global corporate media have been researching the art of creative unfolding, as in the fountain at the Xerox Palo Alto Research Center, where the strength of the water stream reflects the behavior of the stock market.[11] Unfolding reveals only another surface.

TAZ media can unfold information and capital as well, though we must understand the effects of such manifestation to be temporary. Plenty of activist websites investigate the poor information disclosure (inadequate unfolding) of corporate and state media and create possibilities for radical coalition building. Here are a couple of films that visualize the hidden operations of global capital: *BIT Plane* (1999) by the Bureau of Inverse Technology is an aerial observation of Silicon Valley by a tiny (50-centimeter) remote-controlled plane equipped with mini-camera and transmitter. It sees housing, think-tank buildings, the antlike bodies of engineers and cheap/illegal laborers. It sees only the surface, but this is the unfolded surface of the labor and material infrastructure of military-industrial software and hardware development. *The Subconscious Art of Graffiti Removal* (2000) by Matt McCormick is a faux art-history documentary from Portland, Oregon, home of an anti-graffiti ordinance. The film's thesis is that the inherent impulse to make art is suppressed in our society to such a degree that it is manifested unconsciously in the various creative expressions of graffiti *removal* (blocky, free-form, expressionist). *The Subconscious Art of Graffiti Removal* unfolds the anarchic power of creativity—not only in graffiti, but also among the minimum-wagers hired to paint over it.

level 1: material experience

I've written that experience is encoded only insofar as it is deemed useful, as information or as money. Thus, the first strategy is to be invisible by staying out in plain view, too material to be encoded. Bey is optimistic that the material world is studded with potential infinities, "hidden enfolded immensities," multiplying fractally such that they can never be accounted for, much less put to use, by corresponding "information." I experience such immensities along slush-gray Bronson Avenue in Ottawa, where the squeegee operators work their aggressive dance among the cars waiting at the red light, a jerry-rigged tangle of red and yellow cables decorates the side of the Olympia Meat Market, and a gamely hand-drawn "Smile for the Camera" indicates that we're under surveillance outside Leslie's Garage. I also experience such immensities in conversations that happen for their own sake, such as one in a class on October 5, 2000 where spontaneously the group imaginatively designed a device that would harness live cockroaches to move in a glass box through which we would slide film, emulsion side up, to make a cocko-rayographic movie. Experience is infinite! Its apparent uselessness (comparable to "junk DNA") is what makes it immune to the encoding will of information capital. But as Bey points out, this apparent uselessness is also the seed of creative insurrection:

> If we were to imagine an *information map*—a cartographic projection of the Net in its entirety—we would have to include in it the features of chaos, which have already begun to appear, for example, in the operations of complex parallel processing, telecommunications, transfers of electronic "money," viruses, guerrilla hacking, and so on.
>
> Each of these "areas" of chaos could be represented by topographs similar to the Mandelbrot Set . . . [which] might prove to be useful in "plotting" (in all senses of the word) the emergence of the counter-Net as a chaotic process, a "creative evolution" in Prigogine's term. If nothing else the M Set serves as a *metaphor* for a "mapping" of the TAZ's interface with the Net as a *disappearance of information*. Every "catastrophe" in the Net is a node of power for the Web, the counter-Net.[12]

The Mandelbrot set to which Bey refers is a fractal number set. Fractals are suggestive models of insurrectionary activity because they are complex at both large and small scales, suggesting the interdependency of local and global activity.

Writing in 1990, Bey did not mean by *the Net* only that skein of pallid digital information that so entangles and wastes the time of first-world people now. And by *counter-Net* he did not mean only the aggressive and creative use of the Internet to germinate counterinformation, viruses, and the like, although he anticipated them. Analog hindsight usefully reminds us of the many kinds of invisible media that predate digital applications: happenings, ephemeral performances, pranks, mail art,[13] loitering, and the many "useless" and ephemeral activities—often the work of women—that make life better.

At the level of experience, invisibility sometimes manifests as inactivity, undetectible on the radar. Loitering indexes disenfranchisement from the flows of power. In two movies from poor countries, loitering indicates a kind of enfolded or potential energy. Abderrahmane Sissako's *La vie sur terre* (1999), commissioned by European television for the millennium series "2000 vue par . . . ," is set in Sokolo, Sissako's father's village in Mali. The major activity in this film consists of waiting for information. Nana, a young woman from the next village, waits in vain for a call from her lover on the town's one, malfunctioning, telephone. As the golden daylight moves over the village, time is marked by the row of old men who occasionally shift their chairs to stay within the shadow of a house. They listen on a transistor radio to Radio France Internationale, where live commentators breathlessly describe the millennial festivities at the Eiffel Tower. In a nub of space-time forgotten by the former colonizer, Sokolo marks the difference between visibility and invisibility, mattering to the flow of global capital and not mattering. *La vie sur terre* unfolds the enfolded infinity of the village, heartbreaking in its "useless" beauty.

Loitering also marks the time in Elia Suleiman's film *Chronicle of a Disappearance* (1996) made shortly after the disastrous Oslo Accord but before the second intifada: in other words, during a time in which Palestinian political will was enfolded. The protagonist, like Suleiman a Palestinian living in Nazareth, is invisible to the Israeli police who search his apartment. His friend's tourist shop is invisible to the few camera-toting tourists that still come through. The protagonist and his friend loiter outside the latter's "Holy Land" shop, which remains unvisited all day, the only disturbance being the minute squeaking of the postcard rack. In the stillest, most tentative of movements, the film asks whether there might still be hope for images to unfold—temporarily autonomous images that won't immediately be pulled into the deathly service of signification and surveillance.

level 2: information/capital

One level down in the triad are powers that are invisible except in their effects. Information and capital are infinitely recodable because they have no true nature except for mercurial liquidity. Power now is the ability to toggle information into either a latent or a manifest state.[14]

Thus, another goal of TAZ media in the age of invisibility is the time-honored Marxist strategy of concretizing false abstractions. There are many ways for activists to do this in the digital world, including determining the sources of servers, storage, backbones, and other material sites upon which information media rely. The collective Consume.net invites others to collaborate in building a broadband telecommunications infrastructure that provides a cheap alternative to commercial internet service providers.[15] Other concretizers include programmers who offer their software for free, such as those writing the Unix-compatible GNU (a self-referential acronym for Gnu's Not Unix) software system.[16] These programmers sabotage a system that relies not on quality programming but on copyright, licensing, and expiry dates.

For military, marketing, and surveillance purposes, information is compiled into databases, which lie dormant until they are accessed through interfaces. The kind of interface you use determines what sort of information the database will yield; it unfolds a given database in a specific way. Commercial interfaces pretend to fully unfold the data at their disposal. Search engines, for example, pretend to give access to all the information on the World Wide Web, but (with the apparent exception of Google[17]) they are really just giant Yellow Pages with paid advertisers. Similarly, graphical interfaces to the web, such as Netscape or Microsoft's Internet Explorer, obscure information sources and machine processes. Webstalker, an experimental browser released by the artist/programmers I/O/D in 1997, bypasses the obfuscatory interface. Webstalker graphs the file contents and links of a given webpage, unfolding for users the underlying code of the web.[18]

In the new genres of database art, the work's audiovisual manifestation is secondary to its status as an enfolder of information. Database artists, working with information architectures rather than images, mimic the strategies of the information economy.[19] Many forgo the Flash-y visibility available to web design and work at the level of machine code, making visible (in some cases, imitating the look of) the guts of information. They build interfaces to databases that unfold the choices implicit in the design of information platforms. These include Emmanuel Lamotte (e_rational), "Netochka Nezvanova" (m9ndfukc.com), Marek Walczak and Martin Wattenberg's project *Apartment*, which translates sentences into objects, organized according to linguistic filters; and the famous jodi.org. Often opaque and frustrating, these artists' web works make explicit that an interface is a selective unfolding of data.

A more radical, indeed terroristic, strategy is to bury TAZs within the world of sanctioned corporate and state information. The shadowy collective RTMark deploys the mimic interface for direct purposes of sabotage. Its subsidiary Etoys.com mimics the official site of the company eToys.com. Etoys.com, which appears to sell evil and nasty plastic figures that make explicit the aggression and gender stratification implicit in real children's toys, successfully brought down the stock of the real eToys over Christmas 1999. RTMark's gatt.org mimics the official site of the General Agreement on Tariffs and Trade but unfolds material relations that the real GATT prefers to leave implicit. Gatt.org mimics the drab professionalism of the actual organization's site, but its articles celebrating the advance of global capital link to activist sites that reveal its dark side: for example, "The Bright Side of Efficiency," lauding automated food production, links to Food First's "Twelve Myths about Hunger." These sites are *temporary* autonomous zones because pretty soon users cotton on to the fact that these are fake sites and RTMark is instructed to cease and desist. But they are just those nodes of chaos in the Net that Bey envisioned, causing actual economic damage and giving visitors a taste of anarchy.

Above I suggested that loitering is a form of strategic invisibility. Software can loiter, too. Viruses and worms exist typically in a dormant state but spring into action, making manifest the material connectedness of computers and users. Viruses are not so different from the "cookies" that commercial websites deposit on our hard drives in order to survey our patterns of information usage. Most browsers are initialized with the command "Enable all cookies," presuming computer users' consent. As artist Ardele Lister says, the name connotes the benign invitation that opens an abusive relationship—"Here little girl, have a cookie."[20] Viruses, on the other hand, do not presume the consent of their victim. Virus "art," in making visible the processes of infiltration and co-optation, questions who is allowed such access and what kinds of surveillance are considered acceptable.

The Biennale virus, biennale.py, appears to be the first virus produced as a work of art. Produced for the Slovenian pavilion at the 2001 Venice Biennale by a group of artists and hackers, 0100101110101101.org and EpidemiC,[21] the virus is quite benign. Written in the Python language, it can only attach itself to other files in this currently rare language; in addition, the artists provided antivirus companies with the epidemic.py. Biennale is more interesting in that it draws attention to the mutual implication of all computer users. This sense of interrelationship is the focus of another of 0100101110101101.org's projects, life_sharing. The anagram of "file sharing" describes accurately the project of making the artists' entire hard drive open to any online visitor.

Arguably more creative—or at least more TAZ-like—than Biennale are viruses designed without such careful restraints. Recently a virus called "Creative" infected computers with an activist message for non-proprietary software. The virus does not damage files but moves files with .zip or .jpg extensions to the root directory of the drive, adding to the file's name the admonishment "change at least now to LINUX."[22] Of the thousands of viruses out there, I am especially fond of Joshi. Reported to have originated in India and first identified in 1990, Joshi takes a common Indian surname, perhaps that of its programmer. Every January 5, the virus freezes the systems of infected computers and instructs users to type "Happy birthday Joshi!" in order to liberate them.[23] Joshi indicates its potential power with an annual flex of the claws, commands the ritual obeisance, then returns to dormancy.

A brilliant example of an invisible medium that explicates power relations was the Love Bug virus of 2000. Its perpetrator, Onel de Guzman, failed to graduate from AMA Computer College of the Philippines after the school rejected his thesis proposal involving a software program that steals the Windows passwords of Internet users. The Love Bug was released on May 4, 2000, the date Guzman's class graduated without him. It caused worldwide damages estimated to be $10 million (although the value attributed to hours of work lost is itself a symptom of encoding experience in capital, and probably overestimated).[24]

Guzman's quite reasonable rationale for this illegal program was "to spend more time on Internet without paying." Internet access is prohibitively expensive in the Philippines, where it is common to visit Internet cafés. One of the main purposes of Internet commerce in the Philippines is the mail-order-bride market or, euphemistically, the dating service. North American and European men, drawn by fantasies of demure, submissive Asian brides, advertise for what they want and are answered by women seeking to emigrate. The potential suitors send money with which the women log on at Internet cafés.[25] Perhaps Guzman was protesting the phenomenon of women selling themselves on the international market, a not-ridiculous prospect in a country where teachers' wages are below poverty level. Maybe "I Love You" was an ironic comment on the international, Internet love market: an unfolding of the neocolonial trafficking in women.

I've given several examples of ways that temporarily autonomous media can mimic the invisible processes of information capitalism in order to render its strategies material, and to make manifest things that information capital would like to keep buried. But given the brief life of TAZ media before they are incorporated into the chain of instrumentalization, I celebrate those media that remain latent, viruslike. Invisible media remain enfolded within information, refusing to become an image. Or they remain enfolded within experience, refusing to become information. Bey's examples of poetic terrorism include all-night dancing in the vestibules of ATMs[26]: an activity that is invisible because it is useless, and for the same reason, a source of life against the deathful encoding machine. Just a shade further into visibility are those acts of temporary autonomy that remind people that material life is infinitely richer and more chaotic than the poor bonds of information and capital. I suggest, then, that temporarily autonomous media might work at levels just under the radar of information capitalism: media that are less appropriable, less encodable, less "meaningful," and more potentially disruptive. I suggest we think of invisibility as a kind of degree zero: images and information that are always ready to spring forth but refuse to; refuse to be born.[27]

notes

My hearty thanks go to the participants in the wartime conference for which I initially assembled these thoughts: Blowing the Trumpet to the Tulips: an Exchange on Experimental Media, organized by Gary Kibbins and Susan Lord and held at Queen's University, Kingston, Ontario, October 18–21, 2001. I also thank my smart artist friends Ardele Lister, Eric Rosenzweig, and Benton Bainbridge for their input; Jim Dean for research assistance; Mike Bellemare for information on Mao's Long March, a strategy of disappearance that resides invisibly in the essay; Jukka Sihvonen for a reminder of the "dark matter" of which the universe is primarily and invisibly composed; and Grahame Weinbren, as always a most perceptive and demanding reader, for helping me argue that materiality comprises everything.

1. Hakim Bey, "The Temporary Autonomous Zone," in *T.A.Z.: The Temporary Autonomous Zone, Ontological Anarchy, Poetic Terrorism* (Brooklyn, N.Y.: Autonomedia, 1991), 101. Bey's playful model of the TAZ echoes Guy DeBord's view of revolution as festival, though his focus on the *temporary* nature of autonomous zones precludes revolution in toto.

2. I discuss the strategy of enfoldment in computer-based media in great detail in "How Electrons Remember," *Millennium Film Journal* 34 (1999): 66–80; updated in *Touch: Sensuous Theory and Multisensory Media* (Minneapolis: University of Minnesota Press, 2002). Bohm's illustration is borrowed from that essay.

3. Charles Sanders Peirce, quoted in Vincent M. Colapietro, *Peirce's Approach to the Self: A Semiotic Perspective on Human Subjectivity* (Albany: State University of New York Press, 1989), 18.

4. Paul Virilio, "My Kingdom for a Horse: The Revolutions of Speed," *Queen's Quarterly* 108, no. 3 (2002): 337.

5. See Joyce Chediac, "The Massacre of Withdrawing Soldiers on 'The Highway of Death,'" in Ramsey Clark et al., *War Crimes: A Report on United States War Crimes against Iraq* (Washington, D.C.: Maisonneuve Press, 1992); http://www.deoxy.org/wc/wc-index.htm.

6. Michael R. Gordon, "Allies Preparing for Long Fight as Taliban Dig In," *New York Times*, October 29, 2001, <http://www.nytimes.com/2001/10/28international/asia/28STRA.html>.

7. Seumas Milne, "The Innocent Dead in a Coward's War; Estimates Suggest US Bombs Have Killed At Least 3,767 Civilians," *The Guardian*, December 20, 2001, <http:/www.guardian.co.uk/print/0,3858,4323335,00.html>.

8. "Customs Service goes after terrorist funding," CNN, October 25, 2001. At <http://www.cnn.com/2001/US/10/25/inv.terrorist.funding/>. Rachel

Ehrenfeld, "Funding Terrorism," talk at Aviation Week Homeland Security and Defense Conference, Washington, D.C., November 27, 2001. At <http://public_integrity.org/publications11.htm>.

9. The model of the iterative triadic relationship, so wonderfully useful, is borrowed from Charles Sanders Peirce.

10. Lisa Cartwright demonstrates that in many visual interfaces to nonvisual data, such as ultrasound and other kinds of medical imaging, the visual image is simply a by-product of the data and represents a virtual, rather than physical, object; Cartwright, "Film and the Digital in Visual Studies: Film Studies in the Era of Convergence," *Journal of Visual Culture* 1, no. 1 (2002): 18–20.

11. Lev Manovich, *The Language of New Media* (Cambridge, Mass.: MIT Press, 2001), 330.

12. Bey, "The Temporary Autonomous Zone," 112–13. Note the similarity between Bey's comparison of the dominating Net and the liberating web and Donna Haraway's comparison of the power-serving "informatics of domination" with the liberating, cyborg web in "A Cyborg Manifesto: Science, Technology, and Socialist-Feminism in the Late Twentieth Century," in *Simians, Cyborgs and Women: The Reinvention of Nature* (New York: Routledge, 1991), 149–81.

13. Tilman Baumgärtel traces the prehistory of web art in mail art, teleconferences, and other analog communications works; Baumgärtel, "On the History of Artistic Work in Telecommunications Media," in *Net_condition: Art and Global Media*, ed. Peter Weibel and Timothy Druckrey (Cambridge, Mass.: MIT Press, 2001), 152–61. For the precomputer history of communications and software art, see also Peter Lunenfeld, "In Search of the Telephone Opera," *Afterimage* 25, no. 1 (1997): 8–10; and Florian Cramer and Ulrike Gabriel, "On Software Art," Rhizome.org, September 20, 2001, at <http://rhizome.org/object.rhiz?2848>.

14. As I write, it's being discovered that executives of the failed Enron energy corporation "toggled" their soon-to-be-worthless stocks into personal millions of cool cash before the company declared bankruptcy. Global capital, state interests, and elite shareholders already have the power of selective disclosure.

15. See <www.consume.net>.

16. See <www.gnu.org>.

17. At this writing the stocks of major search engines Ask Jeeves, Lycos, LookSmart, and Yahoo! were exhibiting a sharp decline in 2001 over the previous year, possibly as a result of Google's success. Google does not release financial information.

18. See <http://www.backspace.org/iod/>.

19. Lev Manovich, "The Database," in *The Language of New Media*, 218–43.

20. Ardele Lister, personal communication, January 12, 2002.

21. Web artists are hard to identify and their names do not always index real people: 0100101110101101.org includes Moscow artist Olia Lialina; EpidemiC, based in Italy, includes Gaetano La Rosa.

22. Michelle Delio, "Wild Worm With Pro-Linux Message," Wired.com, December 1, 2000. <http://www.wired.com/news/technology/0,1282,40457,00.html>.

23. Julian Dibbell, "Viruses Are Good for You," *Wired* 3.02 (1995): <http://www/wired.com/wired/archive/3.02/viruses.html>.

24. Associated Press, "Love Bug Indictment Coming This Week," *USA Today*, June 13, 2000, at <http://www.usatoday.com/life/cyber/tech/cti087.htm>.

25. L. Clare Bratten, "Cyber Cherry Blossoms: Online Mail Order Brides," talk at the conference Console-ing Passions: Television, Video, Feminism; Notre Dame University, May 13, 2000.

26. Hakim Bey, "Poetic Terrorism," in *T.A.Z.*, 4.

27. Independent media remains practically invisible due to an old-fashioned lack of access to the means of production. Here are distributors for films and videos described herein:

   > *BIT Plane:* Video Data Bank, <www.vdb.org>.
   >
   > *Chronicle of a Disappearance:* Independent Television Service, <www.itvs.org>; Aska Films, <askafilm@login.net>.
   >
   > *The Law of Enclosures:* Alliance Atlantis Pictures International, (416) 967-1141, Fax: (416) 967-1226.
   >
   > *The Subconscious Art of Graffiti Removal:* Matt McCormick, <matt@rodeofilmco.com>.
   >
   > *a vie sur terre:* California Newsreel, <www.newsreel.org>.

four   **exit meat**

digital bodies in a

virtual world

mischa peters

introduction

The August 2001 edition of *Wired* magazine has a striking cover. It shows a picture of the author of the feature article, John Hockenberry,[1] in his wheelchair. His bodily posture is aggressive, triumphant; his arms are spread wide, his face contorted in a big scream, as if he is jumping up from his chair to support his favorite football team. Although it might be unusual for a disabled person to appear on the cover of a major American magazine, this is not what struck me, and made me turn the pages in a hurry to reach the article. What I considered striking was not even that Hockenberry's wheelchair was depicted as being carried by a drawing of a giant artificial hand, with chips and computer cables connected to it, but that the accompanying text read: "Your body. Get over it. (Think mind over matter.)"

The article discusses alternative interfaces between the human body and its surroundings, such as technological solutions for the sensory-

and voice-impaired (e.g., cochlear-implants for deaf people), or revolutionary technologies, such as a brain implant that allowed a patient who had lost all ability to use his muscles to move a cursor on a computer screen. The article displays an ambivalent attitude toward the body. On the one hand the body is an integrated part of the self; its biological markers like race, gender, physical disabilities, and its attachments to the surroundings, its "being-in-the-world," are seen as contributions to subjectivity. On the other hand the body is also discarded, its material influence played down, since "we don't seem to need it."

In this chapter I will investigate these contradictory attitudes toward issues of embodiment and subjectivity in four texts on alternative brain-computer interfaces. I will connect this to a broader philosophical discussion of the influence of these technologies on humanity at large: Are we becoming posthuman, as, for example, Katherine Hayles argues in her book *How We Became Posthuman*? And, if we answer "yes," then, what defines the posthuman? As we shall see, there are different and conflicting definitions of the posthuman.

Representatives of both perspectives can be found in the four texts under consideration here. My quartet is composed of two different genres: popular science and science fiction. In this endeavor, I follow the works of Anne Balsamo, José van Dijck, and Donna Haraway, who read fictional, literary texts alongside those from the natural sciences.[2] These authors break with tradition and no longer treat fiction and science as two separate discursive realms. Instead they show how the two genres might cross-refer to one another in a very complex sort of way. According to Hayles, "culture circles through science no less than science circulates through culture. The heart that keeps this circulatory system flowing is narrative—narratives about culture, narratives within culture, narratives about science, narratives within science."[3]

alternative brain-computer interfaces

For the general public, the idea of an alternative brain-machine interface is probably best known from the realm of science fiction. In popular movies like *Johnny Mnemonic* (1995), *The Matrix* (1999), or *eXistenZ* (1999) audiences have been confronted with representations of various artificial "sockets" either in the brain or the spine to upload memory (*Johnny Mnemonic*) or connect the human mind to a virtual reality (game) world (*The Matrix*, *eXistenZ*). In many science fiction novels, brain sockets are used to connect the human mind to a computer-generated environment. However, the brain implants described in the *Wired* article are not nearly as sophisticated as the imaginary ones in the science fiction genre, and they cannot cope with the amount of information required for interacting in a virtual reality environment. At best, they enable the patient to move a cursor on a computer screen, making very crude and laborious writing possible. But despite their crudeness, Hockenberry describes them as "a real-world version of the nifty plug Neo/Keanu sported in *The Matrix*" (96).

In *New Scientist*, a British popular science journal, an article on brain-machine interfaces is also introduced by reference to a science fiction movie: the digital memory built into Johnny Mnemonic's head.[4] When the article goes on to discuss actual developments in science, again the crudeness of these devices becomes clear. Moreover, these technologies are not (yet) available to everyone. Because of the risks involved in the surgery they are only available to those who are severely handicapped and who have no other traditional medical options. Still, the results are promising and the article is heavily larded with speculations on what could become possible in the future if only the technology were more developed.

One of the requirements for a more advanced use of a brain-machine interface—for instance, a direct link to a virtual reality world—is the improvement of the connection between the neurons of the brain and the machine electrodes or computer chips. The most promising results to date are, for instance, the experiments with snails at the Max Plank Institute of Biochemistry, in which scientists successfully attached neurons from snail brains to semiconductor chips. This gives an idea of how far removed this future vision remains.

Figure 4.1. Network of snail neurons on a silicon chip. Courtesy of (Fromherz/MPI Biochemistry).

posthuman

The above-mentioned experiments all have in common a view that the boundaries between the human and the technological, or the brain and the digital machine, seem to disappear. For some theorists and scientists the ongoing technologization of the human body is linked to an evolutionary discussion: we are no longer human but have become cyborgs (Haraway) or posthuman (Hayles; Judith Halberstam and Ira Livingston).[5] But does this posthumanist thinking restrict itself primarily to boundaries of the body and issues of machine technology? What about identity and subjectivity—do those change as well? And if yes, how? Does the humanist subject (the rational, reasoning, autonomous "natural" subject, prevalent in Western thinking after the Enlightenment) change into a posthuman subject? And what does this posthuman subject look like?

For Katherine Hayles the posthumanist subject is "a collection of heterogeneous components, a material-informational entity whose boundaries undergo continuous construction and reconstruction" (4). It has no autonomy, nor agency or desire. Hayles stresses that it is not necessary for the posthuman subject to have any technological alterations or adaptations of the body; most important is the adapted, collective heterogeneous subjectivity [MP1]. For Halberstam and Livingston, the posthuman is even more radical. In their book *Posthuman Bodies* (1995) they see the posthuman as "queer, cyborg, metametazoan, hybrid, bodies-without-organs, bodies-in-process, virtual bodies" (19). Both Hayles, and Halberstam and Livingston are adamant about the fact that the posthuman condition is already here and that, to quote Halberstam and Livingston, "lingering nostalgia for a modernist or humanist philosophy of self and other, human and alien, normal and queer is merely the echo of a discursive battle that has already taken place—and the tinny futurism that often answers such nostalgia is the echo of an echo" (19).

Of course, as Hayles, and Halberstam and Livingston, are quick to point out, the posthuman does not mean a total break away from the human. But they hope that the posthuman will eradicate some of the lesser traits of the human subject, such as dichotomizations, whether according to gender, race or class, or the famous mind/body split.

However, the posthuman is still a contested area. Whereas Hayles and other cultural critics link the posthuman to a change in subjectivity and issues of embodiment, for others the posthuman is only about changes of the body, removing any limits to its functioning or improving its durability. For this latter group technology can liberate the human mind from the constraints of the body. This form of

50

transcendence is in line with the liberal humanist worldview that has been prevalent in Western societies since the Enlightenment and that has been severely criticized by feminist and postmodern theorists for its dichotomizing and disembodying effects.[6]

cyberpunk

A genre that is most hailed for its posthuman descriptions is cyberpunk, a science fiction genre popularized by such writers as William Gibson, Bruce Sterling, Lewis Shiner, Pat Cadigan, Neal Stephenson, and Greg Bear. Katherine Hayles, for instance, uses cyberpunk books as examples for her own descriptions of the posthuman in fiction. Cyberpunk novels are influenced, not surprisingly, by actual contemporary developments in science, and often display visions of the new technologies of today. Of course, it is a general topic within science fiction to deal with strange and unknown technologies; however, the attitude toward technology in cyberpunk could be said to differ greatly from more traditional genres of science fiction literature. Where traditional science fiction is concerned with restructuring the boundaries between the human and unexpected others (whether they be animals, aliens, or machines), the attitude toward technology in cyberpunk literature is more in favor of a breaking down of these same boundaries. In cyberpunk literature, technology is not something to be feared or fought against as in classical science fiction, but is used as a means of subversion.[7] Most cyberpunk texts display an overwhelming fascination with as well as anxiety about technology and its immediate effects upon the human. For Veronica Hollinger, this emphasis on "the potential interconnections between the human and the technological, many of which are already gleaming in the eyes of research scientists, is perhaps the central 'generic' feature of cyberpunk."[8] Moreover, she claims that "cyberpunk can be situated among a growing . . . number of science fiction projects which can be identified as 'anti-humanist'" (204–5). Significantly, Hollinger notes, "Bruce Sterling . . . has described cyberpunk as a reaction to 'standard humanist liberalism' because of its interest in exploring the various scenarios of humanity's potential interfaces with the products of its own technology" (205).

mapping the technological body

Both popular science discussions of brain-computer interfaces and cyberpunk novels display a complex and often contradictory attitude toward these new technologies and issues of embodiment and subjectivity. To do justice to this complexity I map out different attitudes in four body concepts. These four concepts can be described according to the following matrix[9]:

	External Technology[10]	Internal Technology[11]
Human[12]	Natural Body	Cyberbody
Posthuman[13]	Modified Body	Enhanced Body

I will investigate the appearance of these four conceptual bodies in two classic cyberpunk novels: William Gibson's *Neuromancer* and Pat Cadigan's *Synners*;[14] both are quintessential cyberpunk novels that describe an elaborate virtual reality or digital world, using advanced brain-computer interfaces. Next to these two works of fiction I will analyze two popular science articles: John Hockenberry's "The Next Brainiacs" in *Wired*, and Peter Thomas's "Thought Control" in *New Scientist*; both describe experimental technology on the subject of brain-machine interfaces.[15]

the natural body

The first conceptual body is the natural body. This is the body without technological modifications or enhancements. This does not mean that the natural body is less marked by technology than the cyberbody, modified body, or enhanced body. Culture and technology also mark the body without direct technological interventions. Technologies, whether they are scientific, medical, industrial, or discursive, determine what counts as a body (Pepper 163). As Balsamo has shown in *Technologies of the Gendered Body*, it is the interplay between the particular materiality of the body (its flesh, bone, skin, gender, race, etc.) and the symbolic construction within a certain culture (or how the body is perceived) that determines and defines the natural body.[16]

It is remarkable that in both Gibson's *Neuromancer* and Cadigan's *Synners* the main characters are relatively virginal when it comes to technological modifications of their bodies, although the novels depict fictional worlds in which technological alterations to the body seem to be an everyday part of society. There is even certain contempt for people who let technology enter their bodies without respecting certain boundaries. For example, when Sam in *Synners* shows her friends that she is using her body as an energy source for her computer—"Sam lifted her shirt just high enough to show where the two needles went into the fleshiest part of her abdomen"—she gets the following response: " 'Oh, God!' Rosa made a gagging noise. 'That's an atrocity! You're sick!' 'I'm a potato clock,' Sam corrected her. 'You're a potato head,' Fez said grimly. 'What's wrong with batteries?'" (54). The novel thus questions the human-machine interface as an unwelcome transgression of boundaries. In this case the boundaries of the body are clearly defined: it should not be used to provide energy for a computer.

Paradoxically, as we shall see even more clearly in the description of what I have called the cyberbody, in these same cyberpunk novels there is also a certain contempt for the natural body, which is described here and elsewhere as "meat."

In the two popular science articles, the natural body is most apparent as the disabled body. Because interface technology is too experimental to try on "healthy, novelty-seekers" (Thomas 42) the appropriate natural bodies described are the "sufferers of degenerative nervous diseases" (40); "people who have lost their sight" (41); or "Johnny Ray", who "suffered a brain-stem stroke . . . which produced what doctors call 'locked-in syndrome'" (Hockenberry 96); and "a quadriplegic" (98). This produces the impression of the natural body as being fallible, with technology as the only solution. Technology seems to serve fundamentally as prosthesis to improve and perfect the frail and failing human body and enable it to multiply its strength and increase its capacities to extend itself in space and over time.[17]

the modified body

The second body in my matrix is the modified body. This is a body that uses technology either as a necessity or as a commodity. Although technology is willingly used, its use is not internalized or seen as an integral part of the self. Technology offers something to the user (e.g. life, health), but at a certain price. This price can be either financial or physical when, for instance, the technology is not advanced enough or still has setbacks—for instance, the electrode skullcap developed to record the user's brain activity which, in turn, triggers software to move a computer cursor, is described as "cumbersome and the whole system a bit rickety. 'Cell phones down the hall at the hospital would cause the thing to go blank . . .' " (Hockenberry 99). But the price to pay for the technology can also be ideological. For example, in *Neuromancer*, Molly works as a bodyguard. She therefore needs all kinds of add-ons to her body, such as optical devices that can see beyond the human scope and enable her to display all kinds of extra information in their field of view, or retractable knives implanted in her hands. But there is a high price she has to pay for them: " 'This cost a lot,' she said, extending her right hand as though it held an invisible fruit. The five blades slid out, then retracted smoothly. 'Costs to go to Chiba, costs to get the surgery, costs to have them jack your nervous system up so you'll have the reflexes to go with the gear. . . . You know how I got the money, when I was starting out? Here. Not here, but a place like it, in the Sprawl. Joke, to start with, 'cause once they plant the cut-out chip, it seems like free money. Wake up sore, sometimes, but that's it. Renting the goods, is all.

53

You aren't in, when it's all happening. House has software for whatever the customer wants to pay for . . .'" (Gibson 177). To pay for the body-guard technology, Molly worked as a prostitute. She literally had to rent out her body because when she had to work an implanted chip in her brain would take over her body movement, reaction, and speech. In the book these women are also referred to as "meat puppets." And although this scenario might suggest for some an easy way to make money, there are side effects: not only would she wake up sore some-times, but she would also have occasional flashbacks or would wake up during the action. Thus, although there is a certain merger between technology and body there are also still clear boundaries, and the subject not fully nor happily embraces the technique.

In the *Wired* article the opposite is happening. Hockenberry uses his own experiences with his wheelchair to explain, "In a straightforward way that needs no psychological jargon to explain, my former [before the accident] body simply does not exist anymore. Like Isaac Stern and his violin, I am now part chair, with some capabilities that exceed my original specifications" (105). Thus, even when there is still an obvious physical boundary between Hockenberry and his wheelchair there is an acceptance of the technology on the level of identity or his *body image*. This is no revolutionary notion, for psychologists and neurologists have long described human beings' abilities to incorporate and accom-modate any beneficial object the body comes in close contact with. This could be clothing, tools, or even bigger objects like cars and boats: Elisabeth Grosz explains it: "The limits or borders of the body image are not fixed by nature or confined to the anatomical 'container,' the skin. The body image is extremely fluid and dynamic; its borders, edges, and contours are 'osmotic'—they have the remarkable power of incorpo-rating and expelling outside and inside in an ongoing interchange."[18]

Hockenberry goes even a step further when he writes, "When you think John Hockenberry, think wheelchair. Think alternative plat-form" (96). The body and its marker—in this case, disability—are inte-grated parts of his identity. This goes further than the liberal humanist view of the body as a mere vessel for the mind and goes more in the direction of what Hayles hopes the posthuman will achieve when "embodiment replaces a body seen as a support system for the mind" (288). That Hockenberry is still ambivalent about this can be seen from his description of the body as "specifications" (Hockenberry 105). I will come back to this in the description of the fourth body, the cyberbody.

the enhanced body

Before we can focus on cyberbodies I will discuss the enhanced body. This is the body whose boundaries are stretched to their utmost and often even transgressed. It is also the place where fears and anxieties about mortality and fallibility of the flesh coalesce with fears and anxieties about technologies. In cyberpunk novels this conceptual body is found in the urge to extend life through the use of various technologies: excessive organ transplantation of aged organs, bioengineering to stop cell deterioration. All kinds of technological interventions are breaking down other limits of the body. Muscles are technologically strengthened and made more powerful to show more endurance, or are replaced by artificial limbs. Optical devices that can see beyond the human scope and enable the user to display all kinds of extra information in their field of view replace the human eyes.

These implants give the human body new kinds of possibilities and continually cross once stable borders and blur familiar boundaries. For instance, when Johnny Ray, one of the examples Hockenberry uses in his article, was able to move the cursor on a computer screen via the electrodes implanted in his brain without consciously thinking about each step of the way, very much in the same way as he once would have used his now paralyzed hand. Hockenberry notes, "The fact that Ray's cursor is indistinguishable from almost any other prosthesis raises an important philosophical question: Because of the implant, is a Dell Pentium cursor now more a part of Johnny Ray than one of his own paralyzed arms?" (98). Indications were there had been a merger on a fundamental level between the technology and the body, maybe even reaching to the level of Ray's identity.

This total blurring of technology and human also surrounds an experimental technology described in *New Scientist*. At the University of Tottori in Japan scientists are working on a device that will enable paralyzed patients to communicate by thought alone. To this end they analyze the electrical brain patterns of subjects concentrating on a specific word. The system then compares this to a database of electroencephalograph patterns for known words, in this way allowing the paralyzed subject to communicate. This is still a laborious activity, and "the computer has a vocabulary of five words" (Thomas 40). In Thomas's description, the boundaries between the database and the subject disappear almost completely when he uses the terms *computer* and *patient* almost without distinction. He even speculates about what would happen if the database contained more words. Who then does the thinking? The computer or the subject? He continues, asking, "[I]f we have software embedded in our brains, . . . what happens when there is a new hardware upgrade or a new software release? What if somebody discovers a software bug or a design error?" These could be interpreted as practical questions. But what about the philosophical implications of a bug in the software ingrained in the human brain? Would we still be able to make a distinction between a software bug and psychological illnesses? It is apparent that when he is describing these philosophical and ethical questions he points to popular culture because "even a Hollywood script writer would be hard-pressed to picture the consequences" (42). Even if hard-pressed, Thomas seems to indicate that there is a role for popular culture in envisioning the ethical and philosophical consequences of these new techniques.

the cyber body

The last of the four conceptual bodies is the cyberbody. Especially in the cyberpunk novels, these are bodies that no longer make the distinction between beings of flesh and blood versus beings made of or mediated by technology. Whether it is a mind uploaded and stored in a computer memory or a temporary virtual body created in cyberspace, the technology has become invisible, internalized, or repressed. For instance, in the case of virtual reality, the interface has to work in such a way that the user represses the material body and only "lives" his computer-simulated life. In cyberpunk, moreover, the general presumption is that the mind can live on in a computer simulation (although the body inevitably dies if it is deserted by the mind for too long). It is remarkable how often the virtual state is preferred over the material state: "Case nodded, absorbed in the patterns of the Sense/Net ice. This was it. This was what he was, who he was, his being. He forgot to eat. Molly left cartons of rice and foam trays of sushi on the corner of the long table. Sometimes he resented having to leave the deck to use the chemical toilet they'd set up in a corner of the loft . . ." (Gibson 76). In Cadigan's *Synners* one of the characters, Visual Mark, has chosen to remain in the virtual world all the time, and not disconnect anymore because "the prospect of returning to the meat of being weighted down, was less appealing all the time" (298). This negative attitude toward the natural body is problematized, say, in contrast to *Neuromancer*, where it is often accepted simply as a by-product of "an increasing infiltration of the body by technologies that seem to take its materiality away."[19]

The *Wired* article by Hockenberry also displays a negative attitude toward the natural body. The way the brain responds to technological solutions for physical disabilities is of concern because "[t]his raises a fairly revolutionary point about brains and the physical world. Bodies are perhaps a somewhat arbitrary evolutionary solution to issues of mobility and communication. By this argument, the brain has no particular preference for any physical configuration as long as functionality can be preserved. . . . The brain-body-machine interface doesn't seem to need the body as much as we believe it does" (105). The body, in this example, is not only regarded negatively, it is even discarded; the brain doesn't seem to need it. This is a typical example of what Hayles calls "a hierarchy in which information is given the dominant position and materiality runs a distant second" (12). As she has shown this attitude has been prevalent in cybernetics and related disciplines, but not exclusively, for within contemporary science this attitude can also be witnessed. Vivian Sobchack (1995) describes this as the "disappearance (or increased 'transparency') of the material, lived-body, its apparent displacement by technological prostheses that can enable and extend our perceptual and expressive powers, provokes in some the 'heady' sensations of having 'beat the meat.' " Or as *Wired* formulated on its cover, "Your body. Get over it. (Think mind over matter.)"

conclusion

The ongoing experiments into alternative brain-computer interfaces have the ability to confront us with some major philosophical and cultural questions. There are no easy answers to the questions raised earlier regarding whether we are becoming posthuman and in what ways. None of the texts discussed here offer clear or unambiguous possibilities. On the one hand there seems to be a familiar and traditional notion of a Cartesian flight away from the body, which is regarded as "meat" or physical "specifications which could be redrawn at will." The body in this view is only regarded as a vessel for the mind; the subject in this view is coherent, in control, unitary, the traditional liberal humanist subject. On the other hand, as we have seen in the modified and enhanced bodies idea, there is also a more embodied view of subjectivity to be found. As Hayles describes so beautifully, the body can be integrated with technology or without it, "being seduced by fantasies of unlimited power and disembodied immortality, that recognizes and celebrates finitude as a condition of human being, and that understands human life is embedded in a material world of great complexity, one on which we depend for our continued survival" (5). These different attitudes are linked to different visions of the posthuman. It is not clear yet which direction will be taken, or whether or not both directions will be chosen. The disappearance of our bodies will not just result in the exit of "the meat," but also likely to go will be parts of our identity, our pleasures and desires. It is unclear as yet whether technology will be able to provide us with suitable substitutes. Therefore, a critical eye needs to be kept on the new technologies, because the fantasies and dreams of transcendence might be too strong to resist, and this could leave us with digital bodies suited only to a virtual world.

notes

Earlier versions of this article were presented at the Science and Literature Conference, Buffalo, N.Y., October 11–14, 2001 and the symposium Culture Studies, Gender and ICT, Utrecht, November 22–24, 2001. I want to thank Rosi Braidotti and Anneke Smelik for their comments and advice.

1. John Hockenberry, "The Next Brainiacs," *Wired*, August 2001, 94–105; hereafter, page numbers will be cited parenthetically in the text.

2. Anne Balsamo, *Technologies of the Gendered Body: Reading Cyborg Women* (Durham, N.C.: Duke University Press, 1996); José van Dijck, *Imagenation: Popular Images of Genetics* (New York: New York University Press, 1998); and Donna Haraway, *Primate Visions: Gender, Race and Nature in the World of Modern Science* (New York: Routledge, 1990).

3. N. Katherine Hayles, *How We Become Posthuman: Virtual Bodies in Cybernetics, Literature, and Informatics* (Chicago: University of Chicago Press, 1999), 21–22; hereafter, page numbers will be cited parenthetically in the text.

4. Peter Thomas, "Thought Control," *New Scientist*, March 9, 1996, 38–42; hereafter, page numbers will be cited parenthetically in the text.

5. Donna Haraway, "A Manifesto for Cyborgs: Science, Technology, and Socialist Feminism in the 1980s," *Socialist Review* 5, no. 2 (1985): 65–107; Hayles, *How We Become Posthuman;* and Judith Halberstam and Ira Livingston, "Introduction: Posthuman Bodies," in *Posthuman Bodies*, ed. Judith Halberstam and Ira Livingston (Bloomington: Indiana University Press, 1995) 1–19; hereafter, page numbers will be cited parenthetically in the text.

6. For a discussion of this critique see Chris Weedon, "Postmodernism," in *A Companion to Feminist Philosophy*, ed. Alison M. Jagger and Iris Marion Jones (Oxford: Blackwell, 1998), 75–78.

7. See Cathy Pepper, " 'I've Got You under My Skin': Cyber(sexed) Bodies in Cyberpunk Fictions," in *Bodily Discursions: Gender, Representations, Technologies*, ed. Deborah Wilson and Christine Laennec (Albany: State University of New York Press, 1997), 163–185.

8. Veronica Hollinger, "Cybernetic Deconstructions: Cyberpunk and Postmodernism," in *Storming the Reality Studio: A Casebook of Cyberpunk and Postmodern Fiction*, ed. Larry McCaffrey (Durham, N.C.: Duke University Press, 1991), 205.

9. This matrix was inspired by the use of similar schedules in Balsamo, *Technologies*, and Hayles, *How We Become Posthuman.*

10. This means that the boundaries between technology and the body are clear. This does not prevent the technology from becoming naturalized or part of the body image.

11. *Internal* and *external* are not just distinctions between inside the body and outside the body. Technology can be inside the body and not be internalized or perceived as part of the body.

12. *Human* in this case stands for liberal, humanist subjectivity.

13. *Posthuman* is in this case defined by, e.g., Katherine Hayles, *How We Became Posthuman.*

14. William Gibson, *Neuromancer* (London: Harper Collins, 1995); and Pat Cadigan, *Synners* (New York: Bantam Spectra, 1991); hereafter, page numbers for these works will be cited parenthetically in the text.

15. These two articles are representative for a larger sample of articles I discuss in my Ph.D. dissertation. Provisional title *Marketing the Posthuman: The Technological Body in Theory, Cyberpunk, and Popular Science.*

16. Balsamo uses the work of cultural anthropologist Mary Douglas to exemplify this: "In her book *Natural Symbols* [New York: Pantheon Books, 1970], Douglas asserts that social perceptions of the human body are never free from determining cultural influences; the body is always compre-

hended as an interaction between the materiality of what is given in a particular body and the symbolic constructions of the 'body' embedded within a given culture;" Balsamo, *Technologies*, 24.

17. Kathleen Woodward, "From Virtual Cyborgs to Biological Time Bombs: Technocriticism and the Material Body," in *Culture on the Brink: Ideologies of Technology*, ed. Gretchen Bender and Timothy Druckery (Seattle: Bay Press, 1994), 50.

18. Elizabeth Grosz, *Volatile Bodies: Towards a Corporeal Feminism* (Bloomington: Indiana University Press, 1994), 79.

19. Dani Cavallaro, *Cyberpunk and Cyberculture* (New Brunswick, N.J.: Athlone Press, 2000), 75.

20. Vivian Sobchack, "Beating the Meat/Surviving the Text, or How to Get Out of this Century Alive," in *Cyberspace, Cyberbodies, Cyberpunk: Cultures of Technological Embodiment*, ed. Mike Featherstone and Roger Burrows (London: Sage, 1995), 211.

exit meat

59

digitextual

aesthetics

space invaders

thoughts on technology

and the production

of culture

p e t e r   l u n e n f e l d

aesthetics for aliens

In the course of my work as an art critic, I was once asked to contemplate the notion of art for aliens. I wondered how to propose, much less define, an alien aesthetic, and then thought about what this might mean for artists, designers, and filmmakers in the first decade of the twenty-first century. I had to first dispense with the notion that my task was to build a full-fledged program for aliens over night, when the idea of an alien had not even been fully defined. Do we restrict ourselves to the kitsch cult of extraterrestrial contact and abduction fantasies, complete with flying saucers, and antinomies between the malevolence of gray aliens and extraterrestrials' treacly sentimentality? Or, are we instead positing a mechanical *other*, one that manifests itself as artificial life and intelligent computation—an alien that we have ourselves created and that may lift us to a new realm as gods, or abandon us as meaty lumps along the road to greater evolutions in consciousness? The cyborg is yet another alien, intimately linked to both the meat and the mechanical, an other best known for its dynamic hybridity, which by constantly reshaping its own boundaries reshapes our own. Finally there are the aliens whose definitions are all too familiar to us, who may even be us—individuals who find themselves on the wrong side of national boundaries in this era of global migrations, instantaneous virtual communication, and well nigh instantaneous jet transport. If aliens do exist—and certainly one or more of the preceding types must—then one task we can set ourselves is to outline the contexts for an alien aesthetic. In so doing, we will be able to get a fix on what aliens will have to learn from our cultural moment and what they could contribute. The goals of this attempt are both modest and absurd: pointing out political markers along the way to an alien aesthetic; proposing a critical model to deal with the productions of this aesthetic; and putting forward what I refer to as "the dynamic nonconscious" as a specific issue with which an alien aesthetic should deal. Finally, I offer a coda that moves past nostalgia for the avant-garde and into an era of aesthetic triangulation.

political economy after 1989

It was 1999 when I tried to develop an aesthetic for aliens; it was also the tenth anniversary of the fall of the Berlin Wall. By coincidence, 1999 also saw the forced retirement of Michel Camdessus from the International Monetary Fund (a post from which he dispensed billions of dollars in aid and loans to the former Soviet Union). In other words, the events of 1999 forced me to consider politics and money regardless of the fact that aliens constituted my erstwhile subject. In Hollywood, politics and money usually manifest themselves in the form of spectacular capital (as opposed to the speculative capital of New York's stock markets and the venture capital of the Silicon Valley). I live in Los Angeles, and in honor of my hometown's devotion to visual storytelling, I will weave a tale across continents, complete with detail and emotion stretching from 1939 to 1989, and conclude with that moment, now our past: the year 1999.

In 1939, in a six-hundred-acre park in the north of Moscow, the Exhibition of the Achievement of the Soviet People's Economy opened. Known as VDNX, this propaganda park was a Potemkin Village, a trade and technology fair, and a model farm, all wrapped up into one. VDNX was a phantasmagoric space in which the Soviet iconography of happy, healthy workers, powerful tractors, and glistening satellites was mirrored by the bounty of prize pigs and luscious produce. VDNX was a central showplace of the Stalinist spectacle, and truly fit Maxim Gorky's definition of socialist realism as "revolutionary romanticism." VDNX showed life not as it was lived, but as it ought to be lived.

That same year, thousands of miles from Moscow, a Sears store opened in Los Angeles at the intersection of Pico and San Vicente Boulevards. This was one of the retail giant's crown jewels, a department store whose building was constructed from the ground up to showcase the merchandise. This syncretic construction was a fairly novel concept in which the tables, fixtures, space requirements for the different merchandise lines, customer flow and width of aisles, as well as the building's shell itself, were all built around the selling-floor plan. At the time, a rival merchandising executive offered tribute: "In my long experience in the retail field," he said, "I have yet to witness a . . . unit which equals Sears' Pico Store in practical efficiency, merchandise engineering, operation, layout and presentation of merchandise."[1]

Setting the story up this way appears to augur a classic dialectic, one pitting communist showplace against capitalist showcase. After the events of 1989, the conclusion would appear obvious: the victory of the market against the failures of the control economy. This would mirror the self-congratulatory prose emanating from the pages of the American media. The tolerant, antistatist, neoliberal tone of established media like the *New York Times* cried out for lampoons, though none were forthcoming in 1999, a year in which triumphalism dominated (in large measure because of the ongoing dot-comedy of the so called "new" economy so dependent on the fantasies of digital omnipotence). The histories we inherit tend to be the stories of conflicts as written by the victors, even when they purport, as with neo-conservative intellectual manqué Francis Fukuyama, to be chronicling the history of the end of history itself.[2]

Discursive excesses aside, 1989 was of central importance in the way we make and think about culture a decade later (even, and perhaps especially, alien aesthetics). That year saw the Czech Velvet Revolution, the fall of the Berlin Wall, the reunification of Germany, the eventual fissioning of the Soviet Union, the emergence of the Baltic States, and the continued extension of market reforms in China (which coincided with the political repression of Tiananmen Square). The Polish trade unionist, journalist, and now capitalist newspaper owner Adam Michnik puts it well when he notes that "The revolution of 1989 was a great change without a great utopia."[3]

So, let's return to VDNX and Sears today, after this "great change." By the mid-1990s the Union of Soviet Socialist Republics was no more, and north of Moscow, a city once again in a country called Russia, VDNX was transformed through that peculiarly post-Soviet mix of Perestroika, privatism, and gangster capitalism. As Jamey Gambrell noted in 1994, the "Exhibition's pavilions, built as palaces for the people, have been transformed into communal apartments of commerce: VDNX is now a bizarre shopping mall. Many of the most opulent pavilions have become congested labyrinths of tiny stalls that sell a jumble of consumer goods."[4] By 1999, the Space Exploration Pavilion was full of used cars, although there were a few satellite and rocket models still hanging from the roof above them. The less grandiose pavilions had been rented out to new Russian companies, many of them protected against Russia's rampant gangsterism by private guard services.

Yet if this is to be the story of triumph, we must follow VDNX's rival in Los Angeles. The only problem was, by the mid-1990s, the building had been sold and was no longer a Sears. Now it stands where the Central-American, Korean-American, and African-American communities meld downtown, the Crenshaw district, and the southeastern-most edges of the rich west side. The first floor was taken over by a massive but always understocked discount hardware store. The second floor became the Pico Swap Mart. Most of the carefully designed walls were knocked down and the whole space was cut up into a series of cubicles separated from each other by metal fencing. Small shopkeepers, primarily Koreans and Guatemalans, filled each little space with a profusion of the sort of off-brand, odd-style goods that you expect to see in Lima, Manila, or Marrakech, but not expected in the very heart of the standardized, homogenized United States of America. In fact, there were probably similar off-brand items available at both VDNX and the Pico Swap Mart. As for the third floor of the former Sears, it has simply been shut off by more of the chain-link fencing.

cultural theories post-1989/post-1968

What looked like it would be a facile history—the victory of one sort of built system over another, the triumph of Sears's capital over VDNX's ideology—turns out to be more complex and problematic. By 1999, the question became how to manage such evidence, to build systematic ways to give context to the culture produced in such political and economic circumstances. This is where the alien returns. The clear antinomies between capitalist and communist, between human and machine, and even between analog and digital are blurred, and if we configure each as an alien to the other, points of commonality and perhaps even communion can enter into the equation.

This essay promised symmetrical narrative, moving from 1939 to '89 to '99, but I'm afraid I'll break the pattern here for a flashback to 1968, for it strikes me that most intellectuals are still using the things they picked up from the generation of 1968 to deal with the culture—especially the electronic culture developed in the computer's wake—that has emerged from the events of 1989. As already noted, this has been an era of capitalism triumphant at least in one of its stages of ascendancy, but we have yet to deal forthrightly with these new circumstances, preferring instead to retreat inside the hermeneutics of suspicion developed more than three decades ago.

It is probably worthwhile going over the events of 1968 once more, just to remind ourselves of how momentous a twelve-month period it was. In the United States, there were the assassinations of Martin Luther King Jr. and Robert F. Kennedy, student revolts at Columbia and dozens of other universities, the days of rage during the Chicago Democratic Convention, and the expansion of the war in Vietnam running headlong into the explosion of antiwar activism back home. The rest of the world was in even greater turmoil: there was the Prague Spring in which Czechs tried to break free from Soviet domination, only to find Warsaw Pact tanks rolling across their borders under orders from Moscow. In China, Mao Zedong's youthful Red Brigades had their so-called Cultural Revolution well under way. Baton charges against Catholic marchers ignited the Troubles in Northern Ireland. Police fired on demonstrators in Mexico City, and the extent of the real death toll has yet to be acknowledged to this day. But of all the events of that year, nothing so crystallized the promise of revolt, the efficacy of reaction, and the change that intellectuals went through in this period more than the events of May 1968 in Paris.

Supported by the student and instructor's unions, five thousand Sorbonne students marched through Paris's Latin Quarter, a demonstration that turned into a riot at the barricades when the police attacked. With echoes of earlier revolts from 1789 to 1848, the fighting in the streets was intense, and garnered sympathy throughout France, with millions of workers going on strike; the country itself seemed to be teetering on the brink. But within weeks, a massive show of force and savvy negotiating with different power blocks by the government of President Charles de Gaulle quelled the revolutionary furor in the streets, and eventually the state reaffirmed its power over the citizens of France.

For a generation, historians and critics have been talking about art and theory in relation to the pivotal year 1968, the assumption being that somehow the failed revolutions of that heady year so demoralized the avant-garde that all cultural production since then has been irrevocably altered. This kind of periodization is what cultural historians *do*, of course, and it has the same relationship to actual developments as the map does to the road—it is a useful guide, but only an approximation of the terrain. Yet other markers have sprung up since then, and in terms of technocultural production especially, it strikes me that 1989 is the new dividing line.

Before the events of September 11, 2001, I wrote that "with tribalism and fundamentalism appearing to be the only other options on the political scene attracting adherents, postindustrial capitalism would seem at this point as inevitable and all powerful to the artists of the West as the Christian Church must have been to artisans of eleventh-century France." I feel that the attack on New York and Washington, and the reverberations thereafter in Afghanistan and around the world, only prove this point. For those coming of age in a post-1989 world who choose not to embrace the rigid certainties of tribe or faith, a viable alternative to capitalism is simply not in the offing, no matter how fervent the desires of antiglobalists manifest themselves on the street. Post-1989 theories of aesthetic production thus begin with the centrality of the market and its forces. This is as opposed to both pre- and post-1968 theories, which were originally predicated on a direct opposition to the culture of the market (classic Marxist/Leninist doctrine).

For artists and critics on the left before the events of 1968, that is, the emphasis was on making art and theory with a specific use value: inciting rebellion. With the repression and/or exhaustion of revolution in the streets, however, the focus shifted inward, from fomenting social action to analyzing social imaginaries. Critics who had been pulling up paving stones moved from the barricades to the text. They, and even more generally their students and interpreters, spent the thirty years after 1968 mining all forms of cultural production for "sites of resistance" to capitalist alienation. By the time that the discipline of cultural studies was firmly established in the 1990s, Anglo-American scholars were lauding so-called subversive consumers who watched *Dynasty*, listened to Madonna, or read *Hustler*. These critics took any smidgen of cultural bricolage as a revolutionary act, and every fan club was seen as a conspirators' cell. Quintessential post-1989 theorist/activist Geert Lovink notes that the cultural studies strategy, which he describes as the embrace of "ambivalent feelings towards pop culture," fulfilled its self-assigned role, liberating "many from rigid and dogmatic antipositions." But Lovink notes that this "creative impulse was still operating from within new social movements which have long gone. It crossed borders, to return safely."[5]

After 1968, what intellectuals had formerly regarded as capitulating to the spectacle was coming to be seen as sly resistance. This leads to bizarre deformations, as when certain academics warn that virtually any attack on pop culture can be read as an attack on democracy itself. There are exhortations to rally to the defense of the multibillion-dollar grossing computer games industry (as if such an economic juggernaut needs, or even would be interested in, the labors of media intellectuals on their behalf). These odd calls for action bear a tenuous relationship to the formal analysis conducted under the rubric of 1968, which was generally predetermined in its purpose—that being to locate "cracks and fissures," those moments in which the ideological mask slips and the repressiveness of the dominant discourse is revealed. Post-1989 theory is more elastic. It is rigorously historicized: it lives in its moment, eschews nostalgia, and acknowledges that often consumption is acknowledgment of, rather than subterranean resistance to, the global market.

At the same time, it is vitally concerned with determining the formal characteristics of contemporary art and culture—especially in their digital and electronic flavors—as opposed to moving directly into a discussion of their "revolutionary" use value. This is not to say that a post-1989 theory worthy of its ambitions functions in tandem with the marketers of the digital "revolution," degrading the latter word more fully than even the most mediocre cultural studies analyses. Post-1989 theory completely rejects the mercantilism of futurism (*Wired*, the Global Business Network, the loathsome George Gilder), and the pseudoreligiosity of noospheric fantasy (the Chardin-inspired discourse of theorists like Pierre Levy).

But, as has been noted, post-1989 theory eschews the spirit of complete renunciation; it lives in, with, and through these technologies in complex and entirely self-conscious ways, wherever that may lead. It is enough to say right now that post-1989 theory is wary of using nineteenth-century analyses of industrial capitalism to engage with the postindustrial, interconnected world. It also takes some of the ideas of 1968 more seriously than those who claimed that mantle. Too often those who identified the death of the author did so only to proclaim the birth of the omnipotent master theorist. For post-1989 theory, not every reflective surface is an invitation to rattle on about Jacques Lacan and the mirror stage. Sometimes a rhizome is just a peanut, after all. It's my hope that post-1989 theory will be able to take itself with a grain of salt, and truly accept that the master discourse is no more, allowing for a more heterogeneous approach to culture rather than simply pulling a coup and swapping its rote assumptions for those of the generation of 1968.

dynamic nonconsciousness versus the alien

I have elsewhere referred to the computer as a dynamic nonconsciousness. Those who throw themselves into binding relationships with the digital then add a third, triangulating element to the psychoanalytic dyad of the conscious and unconscious mind. The dynamic nonconscious, then, is the machine part of the human-computer interface that most interests me, especially in relation to an alien aesthetic. This contrasts with an approach that too often overliteralizes its interests in the alien. In artificial-life art, what we too often encounter is not a replication of life by the machine but a replication of the model of life that has been programmed into it. Likewise, when we take the extraterrestrial too seriously we perform the same alienating rituals that we perfected as a species with religion: taking the best and the worst of ourselves and ascribing these characteristics to an imaginary, anthropomorphized externality. As Chris Kraus notes in her savage memoir *Aliens and Anorexia*, our cultural fantasies about otherworldly encounters tend towards the sanitized or the puritanical, just like established religions: "No one ever says, *I was kidnapped by aliens, and it's the best sex I ever had*."[6] It is too early to describe the boundaries of an alien aesthetic, but we would do far better looking into the dynamic nonconscious that we would to fantasize about artificial life or, worse yet, recycle the spiritual inheritances that all but played themselves out in the first millennium, much less the second, as we enter the third thousand-year epoch of the common era.

the poetics of triangulation

I'd like to close off this discussion of the alien aesthetic and its political economies by mentioning the ways in which a post-1989 theory can bear upon digital media production. I'm very careful about using the term *avant-garde*, even as I spend a great deal of time looking at what other generations did indeed term avant-garde art and media. The very term needs to be given a rest, like a good horse that has been ridden too hard for too long. When stylistic and technical "advances" come from all spectra of digital media production—commercial, artistic, scientific, academic, and the like—the notion we have inherited of a singular, oppositional avant-garde serves little purpose anymore. If our softwares, music videos, computer games, and WAPS (wireless application protocols, for cell phones and other mobile devices) are all to be termed "avant-garde," then that phrase has indeed been reduced to a marketing term like "revolution." I do not see the digital artist as being an avant-gardist in any classical sense of solidarity or shared artistic destiny; in fact, too many mediocre talents have hung on to just such exhausted tropes to support their own, weak brands of practice.

One of these tropes to have emerged over the past decade is the neo-Renaissance figure: the artist as research scientist so prevalent in new-media circles. At conferences, trade shows, and exhibition openings, one hears artists going on about how they are now validated in their choice of art as a profession because scientists and engineers respect their "research," and the fact that they had grants from Intel and Microsoft. This attitude is incredibly odd. Collegiality is a wonderful thing, but in the final analysis, why should artists give a damn about what engineers think about them? This "scientific method" is growing rapidly with the megaversity structure, in which artists who can create a practice that apes the forms of scientific research get hired and funded. They hire and fund others like themselves, and thereby build a peer network to evaluate the "results" of their work. Most artists have some sort of "research" component to their own practice, but this research is generally only important as it relates to the work to which it contributes. There are some, select artists for whom the research is the work, but quite often they are working within a specifically conceptual framework and what they tend to explore ends up being the idea of research itself, rather than a specific topic (a metacritical project that is more ontological than empirical).

Another problem with the artist as researcher is the sense in which the very concept implies that art should be useful to society. Art can be useful, but the glory of it as a sphere of cultural production is that it does not have to be. Researchers and scientists are trained differently and have a different set of expectations for their work—there is an expectation of utility, and often of clarity (avoiding the detours of postmodern science wars for a moment). This whole artist-cum-scientist confusion reminds me of the 1980s when what we saw, especially in the United States, were artists–cum–social workers. For every innovative effort those of Tim Rollins and KAOS there were a thousand dreary "community-based collaborative projects" that existed for one reason and one reason only: to get money from the National Endowment for the Arts (NEA) or local funding agencies. Originally, by putting in some vague prosocial rhetoric, artists could get some support for the work they really wanted to do, but then they came to see the funding scam as their whole reason for being. What began as something of a scam turned into an entire aesthetic. Then, during the "culture wars" of the late 1980s and early '90s, conservatives in the U.S. Congress neutered the NEA and this entire brand of practice died out—though I see some of the same people who went after the social-work funding now going after money and technology from hardware and software companies.

Another post-1989 figure to emerge is the artist as entertainer, a notion that has been much bandied about by the "beauty school" associated with Las Vegas-based art critic Dave Hickey. One of the key debates in the visual arts in the last decade has been over the relationship between art and entertainment. These issues are hardly new to the digital era, going back at least to the postwar critic Clement Greenberg's condemnation of kitsch, and pop art's subsequent embrace of it. Even the vocabulary we might think of as being vital to the most recent debates predates them; think of so e-commercy a word as *infotainment*, which interestingly enough was the title of a show and catalog organized by Peter Nagy in 1985 at Nature Morte, a gallery in New York. I have to admit that when it comes to the intersection of media and technology, my interests and affections are pretty promiscuous. Yet no matter how many times I succumb to the seductions of pop, I know my limits. Mass media and entertainment culture are lovers so self-involved (and so ardently pursued by so many others) that they are deaf to anything more nuanced than the great blaring horns of fandom. So, whenever I slink away from the multiplex, the tube, or the great unwashed bordello that is the Internet, I resolve to return to the more mutual give-and-take of pillow talk with and about art. But I feel guilty upon my return. What are artists to do in times such as these, when the rest of the culture seems ever more obsessed with the minutiae of entertainment and celebrity?

One strategy is to maximize the minimal—to make work that slips into the interstices, that waits with baited breath for the attention the general public may no longer be capable of bringing to bear. This is an honorable choice, with links to the tradition of the artist as obsessive individualist or as avant-gardist working outside, or against, the mainstream. Recently, however, some have chosen not so much to duke it out with the spectacle as to tag along, like lonely little siblings. Usually egged on by critics who are themselves frustrated entertainers, they end up playing a game they can't win, offering amateur theatrics masquerading as installations, performances that play like bad stand-up comedy, and representational imagery that can only be termed orphaned illustration, without benefit of a paying client.

It is my sense, however, that another alternative has emerged for artists who wish to relate to the dominant technologized entertainment culture. I refer to this strategy as *triangulation*, a term derived from a method used by navigators and surveyors to determine the distance between points on the earth's surface by dividing up larger areas into a series of connected triangles. In a like manner, artists can span the territorial divides between art and entertainment by negotiating a series of strategic and interconnected forays from both sides toward new ground. So what work effects this triangulation? It's not painting. This isn't to say that painting is dead—it never was, though it came close with a fifteen-minute coma in the early 1970s—and the only people who still claim that critics think so are dealers trying to sell canvases to collectors, as though buying a painting was a revolutionary gesture rather than the single most conservative transaction in the whole art world. It's not sculpture or photography, either, though both are also selling quite well, thank you.

Right now, works that engage with media technologies but employ them to their own ends, playing with and against the powers of the dynamic nonconscious, are the ones to watch. Artists who master the means of media production—computer graphics, animation, film and video editing, projection equipment, sound technologies, interaction design, and so on—without falling into the wormhole of contemporary celebrity culture's banal self-referentiality have been able to capture the excitement of the electronic, weaving their work all the while into larger cultural and aesthetic contexts. Triangulating toward meaningful work requires a sure hand to escape art-world insularity on the one side, without sacrificing seriousness of purpose in the Narcissus pool of mass media culture on the other.

notes

Meaghan Morris, "Banality in Cultural Studies," *Discourse* 10, no. 2 (1988): 3–29, has had an obvious impact on my thinking. Lawrence Grossberg, Cary Nelson, and Paula A. Treichler, eds., *Cultural Studies* (New York: Routledge, 1992) remains a central document to explore the impact of post-1968 thinking on the then emerging discipline of cultural studies. The literature on 1968 is vast; three places to start are Todd Gitlin, *The Sixties: Years of Hope, Days of Rage* (New York: Bantam Books, 1987), George Katsiaficas, *The Imagination of the New Left: A Global Analysis of 1968* (Boston: South End Press, 1987), and Andrew Feenberg and Jim Freedman, *When Poetry Ruled the Street: The French May Events of 1968* (Albany: State University of New York Press, 2001).

This essay remixes elements of other publications I have written, including *Snap to Grid: A User's Guide to Digital Arts, Media, and Culture* (Cambridge, Mass.: MIT Press, 2000); "Enemy of Nostalgia: Victim of the Present, Critic of the Future: Peter Lunenfeld Interviewed by Geert Lovink," in *PAJ: A Journal of Performance and Art* 70 (2002): 5–15; "Alien Aesthetics: Politics, Theory & Technology," in *Alien Intelligence,* ed. Erkki Huhtamo (Helsinki: Kiasma Museum of Contemporary Art, 2000), n.p.; and "High-Q Art: The Seductions of Broadcast Romanticism," *X-Tra* 2, no. 3 (1999): <http://strikingdistance.com/xtra/XTra100/v2n3/lunenfeld.html>.

1. For information on Sears, see <www.sears.com/company/pubaff/1940.htm>. For VDNX, see Jamey Gambrell, "The Wonder of the Soviet World," *New York Review of Books* 41, no. 21 (1994), 30–35.

2. Francis Fukuyama, *The End of History and the Last Man* (New York: Avon Books, 1993).

3. Adam Michnik, "Ten Years after 1989: Postcommunist Reflections," *Dissent* (1999), Vol. 46, no. 4, 16.

4. Gambrell, "Soviet World," 30.

5. Geert Lovink, "Fragments of Network Criticism," in *Dark Fiber: Tracking Critical Internet Culture* (Cambridge, Mass.: MIT Press, 2002), 165.

6. Chris Kraus, *Aliens and Anorexia* (New York and Santa Monica: Semiotext(e) and Smart Art Press, 2000), 17.

the poetics of

augmented space

six

lev manovich

augmented space

The 1990s were about the virtual. We were fascinated by new "virtual spaces" made possible by computer technologies. The images of an escape into a virtual space that leaves the physical space useless and of cyberspace—a virtual world that exists parallel to our world—dominated the decade. It started with the media obsession with virtual reality (VR). In the middle of the decade graphic browsers for the World Wide Web made cyberspace a reality for millions of users. During the second part of the 1990s yet another virtual phenomenon—dotcoms—rose to prominence, only to be crashed by the real world laws of economics. By the end of the decade, the daily dose of cyberspace—using the Internet to make plane reservations, to check email using a Hotmail account, or to download MP3 files—became such a normal aspect of daily existence that the original wonder of cyberspace so present in the early cyberpunk fiction of the 1980s and still evident in the original manifestos of virtual reality modeling language (VRML) evangelists of the early 1990s was almost completely lost.[1] The virtual became domesticated, filled with advertisements, controlled by big brands, and rendered harmless. In short, to use the expression of Norman Klein, it became an "electronic suburb."

It is quite possible that the emphasis of the first decade of the 2000s will turn out to be about the physical—that is, physical space filled with electronic and visual information. While enabling further development of virtual spaces—from more realistic computer games to new 3-D technologies and standards for the World Wide Web such as Director 3D to wider employment of compositing in cinema—computer and network technologies more actively enter our real physical spaces. The previous image of a computer era—that of the VR user traveling in a virtual space—has become replaced by a new image: a person checking her e-mail or making a phone call using her personal digital assistant / cell phone combo while at the airport, on the street, in a car, or in any other actually existing space. But this is just one example of what I see as a larger trend. Here are a few more examples of the technologies that deliver data to, or extract data from, physical space—and that already are widely employed at the time of this writing (early 2002):

1. *Video surveillance* is becoming ubiquitous, employed in mass no longer by governments, the military, and businesses, but also by individuals; cheap, tiny, wireless and Internet-enabled, video cameras can now be put almost anywhere (for instance, many taxicabs have video cameras continuously recording the goings-on in the cars' interiors).

2. If video and other types of surveillance technologies translate the physical space and its dwellers into data, *cellspace technologies* work in the opposite direction: delivering data to mobile-space dwellers. Cellspace is physical space filled with data that can be retrieved by a user using a personal communication device.[2] Some data may come from global networks such as the Internet; some may be imbedded in objects located in the space around the user. Moreover, while some data may be available regardless of where the user is in the space, it can be also location specific. The examples of cell space applications include using global positioning systems (GPSs) to determine one's coordinates; or using a cell phone to check in at the airport, to pay for the road tool, or to retrieve information about a product in a store.[3]

3. While we can think of cellspace as the invisible layer of information that is laid over the physical space and is customized by an individual user, publicly located *computer/video displays* present the same visible information to passers-by. These displays are gradually

becoming larger and flatter; they no longer require darkness to be visible. In the short term, we may expect large and thin video displays to become more pervasive in both private and public spaces (perhaps using technology such as e-ink); in the longer term, every object may become a screen connected to the Net, with the whole of built space becoming a set of display surfaces.[4] Of course, physical space was always augmented by images, graphics and type; but substituting all these by electronic displays makes it possible to present dynamic images; to mix images, graphics, and type; and to change the content at any time.

Popular media normally does not discuss these three technologies together because they belong to different industries (electronics versus computers) and different markets (consumer versus professional). But from the point of view of their effect on our concept of space and, consequently, our lives as far as they are lived in various spaces, I feel that they very much belong together. They make the physical space into a dataspace: extracting data from it (surveillance) or augmenting it with data (cellspace, computer displays).

It also makes sense to bring together the surveillance/monitoring of space and its dwellers, and the augmentation of space with additional data, because these two functions often go hand in hand. For instance, by knowing the location of a person equipped with a cell phone, particular information relevant to this location can be sent to this cell phone. A similar relationship exists in the case of software agents, affective computing, and similar interfaces that take a more active role in assisting the user than the standard graphical user interface. By tracking the user—her mood, her pattern of work, her focus of attention, her interests, and so on—these interfaces acquire information that they use to help the user with her tasks and automate them. This close connection between surveillance and assistance is one of the key characteristics of high-tech society. This is how these technologies are made to work, and this is why I am discussing data flows *from* the space (surveillance, monitoring, tracking) and *into* the space (cellspace applications, computer screens, and other examples, below) together.

Let's now add to these three examples of the technologies already at work a number of research paradigms actively conducted in universities and industrial labs. (Note that many of them overlap, mining the same territory but with a somewhat different emphasis.) We can expect that at least some of them will become a reality during this decade:

4. *Ubiquitous computing*: the original move (1990–) at the Xerox Palo Alto Research Center (PARC) away from computing centered on desktop machines toward small multiple devices distributed throughout the space.[5]

5. *Augmented reality*: another paradigm that originated around the same time, laying dynamic and context-specific information over the visual field of a user (see below for further details).[6]

6. *Tangible interfaces*: treating the whole of physical space around the user as part of human-computer interface (HCI) by employing physical objects as carriers of information.[7]

7. *Wearable computers*: imbedding computing and telecommunication devices into clothing.

8. *Intelligent buildings* (or *intelligent architecture*): buildings wired to provide cell-space applications.

9. *Intelligent spaces*: spaces that monitor the users that interact with them via multiple channels, and that provide assistance for information retrieval, collaboration, and other tasks (think of the computer HAL in the movie *2001: A Space Odyssey*).[8]

10. *Context-aware computing*: an umbrella term used to refer to all or some of the developments above, signaling a new paradigm in computer science and HCI fields.[9]

11. *Smart objects*: objects connected to the net; objects that can sense their users and display "smart" behavior.

12. *Wireless location services*: delivery of location-specific data and services to portable wireless devices such as cell phones (similar to cell space).

13. *Sensor networks*: networks of small sensors that can be used for surveillance, intelligent spaces, and similar applications.

14. *E-paper* (or *e-ink*): a very thin display on a sheet of plastic that can be flexed in different shapes and displays information received wirelessly.[10]

While the technologies imagined by these research paradigms accomplish this in a number of different ways, the end result is the same: they all place layers of data over the physical space. I will use the term *augmented space* to refer to this new kind of space, which is slowly becoming a reality. As I have already mentioned, this overlaying is often made possible by tracking and monitoring the users—that is, the delivery of information to users in space and the extracting of information about these users are closely connected. Thus, augmented space is also monitored space.

I derive the term *augmented space* from an older and already established term, *augmented reality* (AR).[11] Coined around 1990, the concept of augmented reality is opposed to virtual reality (VR). With a typical VR system, all the work is done in a virtual space; physical space becomes unnecessary and its vision is completely blocked. In contrast, an AR system helps the user to do the work in a physical space by augmenting this space with additional information. This is achieved by laying information over the user's visual field. An early scenario of a possible AR application developed at Xerox PARC involved a copier repairman wearing a special display that overlaid a wire-frame image of copier insides over the actual copier the repairman was working on. Today scenarios for everyday use are imagined as well: for instance, a tourist with AR glasses that overlay dynamically changing information about the sites in the city onto her visual field. In this new iteration, AR becomes conceptually similar to wireless location services. The idea shared by both is that when the user is in the vicinity of objects, buildings, or people, the information about them is delivered to the user—but if in cellspace it is displayed on a cell phone or personal digital assistant (PDA), in AR it is laid over the user's visual field.

The demise of popularity of VR in mass media and the slow but steady rise in AR-related research in the last five years is one example of how the augmented space paradigm is taking over the virtual space paradigm.[12] As we saw, if we use these system for work, VR and AR— the virtual and the augmented—are the opposites of each other: in the first case the user works on a virtual simulation, in the second she works on actual things in actual space. Because of this, a typical VR system presents a user with a virtual space that has nothing to do with the immediate physical space of the user; in contrast, a typical AR system adds the information directly related to this immediate physical space. But we don't necessarily have to think of immersion into the virtual and augmentation of the physical as the opposites. On one level, the difference between whether we can think of a particular situation as an immersion or as augmentation is simply a matter of scale—the relative size of a display. When you are watching a movie in a movie theater or on a large-screen TV set, or playing a computer game on a game console connected to this TV, you are hardly aware of your physical surroundings; practically speaking, you are immersed in virtual reality. But when you are watching the same movie or playing the same game on the small display of a cell phone / PDA that fits in your hand, the experience is different: your are still largely present in physical space; the display adds to your overall phenomenological experience but it does not take over. Thus, it all depends on how we understand the idea of addition: we may add additional information to our experience—or we may add an altogether different experience.

"Augmented space" may bring associations with one of the founding ideas of computer culture: Douglas Engelbardt, and his concept of a computer augmenting human intellect, articulated forty years ago.[13] This association is appropriate, but we need to be aware of the differences as well. The vision of Engelbardt, and the related visions of Vannevar Bush and J. C. R. Licklider, assumed a stationary user—a scientist or engineer working in his office. Revolutionary for their time, these ideas anticipated the paradigm of desktop computing. Today, however, we are gradually moving into the next paradigm, in which computing and telecommunications are delivered to a mobile user. And while it is still more efficient to run computer-assisted design, 3-D modeling, or web-design software while sitting in a comfortable chair in front of a twenty-two-inch liquid crystal display (LCD), many other types of computing and telecommunications activities do not require being stationary. Thus, augmenting the human also comes to mean augmenting the whole space in which she lives or through which she passes.

augmented architecture

In the 1990s, computer hardware manufacturers and the computer game industry drove the development of applications that use 3-D interactive virtual spaces such as computer games. While today's personal computers (PCs) are already too fast for practically all the applications needed for a typical home or business user, real-time rendering of the detailed simulated worlds can use still faster machines; it also requires special graphics cards. The industry therefore has a direct interest in continuously fueling the interest of the consumers in more and more "realistic" virtual spaces—because this is what justifies the sales of new computer hardware.

Augmented space research has the potential for many commercial, consumer, and military applications, and thus it receives funding from diverse groups. Ultimately, it is probably of most concern to the huge telecommunications industry. So if the computer industry thrives on sales of new PCs and graphics boards needed to run the latest computer games, the telecom industry is interested in selling new generations of cell phones and PDAs that will provide multimedia, e-commerce, and wireless location services—and of course, getting huge gains from charging the users for these services.

So much for economics. What about the phenomenological experience of being in a newly augmented space? What about its cultural applications, its poetics and aesthetics? One way to begin thinking about these questions is to approach the design of augmented space as an architectural problem. Augmented space provides a challenge and opportunity for many architects to rethink their practice, since architecture will have to take into account that layers of contextual information will overlay the built space.

But is this a completely new challenge for architecture? If we assume that the overlaying of different spaces is a conceptual problem not connected to any particular technology, we may start thinking about which architects and artists have already been working on this problem. To put this in a different way, overlaying dynamic and contextual data in physical space is a particular case of a general aesthetic paradigm:

how to combine different spaces together. Of course, electronically augmented space is unique, since information is personalized for every user; since it can change dynamically over time; since it is delivered through an interactive multimedia interface, and so on. Yet it is crucial to see it as a conceptual rather than simply a technological issue, as something that already was often a part of other architectural and artistic paradigms.

Augmented-space research gives us new terms to think about previous spatial practices. If before we would think of an architect, a fresco painter, or a display designer working to combine architecture and images, or architecture and text, or incorporating different symbolic systems in one spatial construction, we can now say that all of them were working on the problem of augmented space: how to overlay layers of data on physical space. Therefore, in order to imagine what can be done culturally with augmented spaces, we may begin by combing previous cultural history for useful precedents.

To make my argument more accessible, I have chosen as my examples two well-known contemporary figures. Janet Cardiff is a Canadian artist who has become famous for her "audio walks." She creates her pieces by following a trajectory through some space and narrating an audio track that combines instructions to the user ("go down the stairs"; "look into the window"; "go through the door on the right") with narrative fragments, sound effects, and other aural "data." To experience the piece, the user puts on earphones connected to a CD player, and follows Cardiff's instructions.[14] In my view her "walks" represent the best realization of augmented space paradigm thus far—even though Cardiff does not use any sophisticated computer, networking, or projection technologies. Cardiff's "walks" show the aesthetic potential of overlaying a new information space on physical space. The power of these "walks" lies in the interactions between the two spaces—between vision and hearing (what the user is seeing and what she is hearing), and between present and past (the time of the user's walk versus the audio narration, which like any media recording belongs to some undefined time in the past).

The Jewish Museum of Berlin, designed by Daniel Liberskind, can be thought of as another example of augmented-space research. If Cardiff overlays a new data space on existing architecture and/or landscape, Liberskind uses the existent data space to drive the new architecture he constructs. The architect put together a map that showed the addresses of Jews who were living in the neighborhood of the museum site before World War II. He then connected different points on the map together and projected the resulting net onto the surfaces of the building. The intersections of the net projection and the walls gave rise to multiple, irregular windows. Cutting through the walls and the ceilings at different angles, the windows evoke many visual references: the narrow eye-piece of a tank; the windows of a medieval cathedral; the exploded forms of the cubist/abstract/suprematist paintings from the first two decades of the twentieth century. Just as in the case of Cardiff's audio walks, here the virtual becomes a powerful force that reshapes the physical. In the Jewish Museum the past literally cuts into the present. Rather than something ephemeral, an immaterial layer over the real space, here data space is materialized, becoming a sort of monumental sculpture.

white cube as cellspace

While we may interpret the practices of selected architects and artists as having particular relevance to thinking about how augmented space can be used culturally and artistically, there is another way to link the augmented space paradigm with modern culture. Here is how it works: One trajectory that can be traced in twentieth-century art is from a two-dimensional object placed on a wall toward the use of the whole 3-D space of a gallery. (Like all other cultural trajectories in the twentieth century, this one is not a linear development; rather, it consists of steps forward and steps back, the rhythm of which follow the general cultural and political outline of the twentieth century: its highest peak of creativity in the early 1900s, followed by a second, smaller peak in the 1960s.) As early as the second decade of the twentieth century, Vladimir Tatlin's reliefs broke the two-dimensional picture plane, exploding a painting into 3-D. In the 1920s, El Lissitzky, Alexander Rodchenko, and others moved away from an individual painting/sculpture toward thinking of a whole white cube as one singular surface—yet their exhibitions activated only the walls rather than the whole space.

In the mid-1950s, assemblage legitimized the idea of an art object as a three-dimensional construction. In the 1960s, minimalist sculptors (Carl Andre, Donald Judd, and Robert Morris) and other artists (Eva Hesse, the Arte Povera movement) finally start dealing with the whole of 3-D space of a white cube. Beginning in the 1970s, installation art (Dan Graham, Bruce Nauman) grew in importance to become in the 1980s the most common form of artistic practice of our times—and the only thing that all installations share is that they engage with 3-D space. Finally, the white cube becomes a *cube* rather than just a collection of surfaces.

What is the next logical step? For modern art, augmented space can be thought of as the next step in the trajectory from a flat wall to a 3-D space. For a few decades now artists have already dealt with the entire space of a gallery; rather than creating an object that a viewer would *look at*, they placed the viewer inside this object. Now, along with the museums, artists have a new challenge: placing a user inside a space filled with dynamic, contextual data with which the user can interact.

moving image in space: video installations as laboratory for the future

Before we rush to conclude that the new technologies do not add anything substantially new to the old aesthetic paradigm of overlaying different spaces together, let me note that the new technologically implemented augmented spaces have one important difference from Cardiff's walks, Liberskind's Jewish Museum, and similar works—in addition to their ability to deliver dynamic and interactive information. Rather than overlaying a new 3-D virtual dataspace on the physical space, Cardiff and Liberskind overlay only a two-dimensional plane, or a 3-D path at best. Indeed, Cardiff's walks are new 3-D paths placed over an existing space rather than complete spaces. Similarly, in the Jewish Museum of Berlin, Liberskind projects a 2-D map onto the 3-D shapes of his architecture.[15]

In contrast, GPS technology, wireless location services, surveillance technologies, and other augmented-space technologies all define data space—if not in practice than at least in their imagination—as a *continuous* field completely extending over and filling in *all of* physical space. Every point in space has a GPS coordinate that can be obtained using a GPS receiver. Similarly, in the cellspace paradigm every point in physical space can be said to contain some information that can be retrieved using a PDA or similar device. Surveillance—which in practice includes video cameras, satellites, Echelon (the set of monitoring stations that are operated by the United States and used to monitor all kinds of electronic communications globally), and other technologies—so far can only reach some regions and layers of data but not others; the ultimate goal of the modern surveillance paradigm is to be able to observe every point at every time. To use the terms of Jorge Luis Borges's famous story, all these technologies want to make the map equal to the territory. And— if, according to Michel Foucault's famous argument in *Discipline and Punish*, the modern subject internalizes surveillance, thus removing the need for anybody to be actually present in the center of the panopticon to watch him—modern institutions of surveillance insist that he should be watched and tracked everywhere, all the time. (It is important, however, that in practice, data spaces are almost never continuous: the reach of surveillance cameras means that they can look at some spaces but not at others, the wireless signal is stronger in some areas and nonexistent in others, and so on. This contrast between continuity of cellspace in theory and its discontinuity in practice should not be dismissed; rather, it can itself be the source of interesting aesthetics strategies.)

My third example of already existing augmented space—electronic displays mounted in shops, streets, building lobbies, train stations, and apartments—follows a different logic. Rather than overlaying all of the physical space, here data space occupies a well-defined part of the physical space. This is the tradition of Leon Battista Alberti's window, and, consequently, post-Renaissance painting, the cinema screen, and the TV monitor. However, if until recently the screen usually acted as a window into a virtual 3-D space, in the last two decades of the twentieth century it turned into a shallow surface on which 3-D images coexisted with 2-D design and typography. Live-action footage shares space with motion graphics (titles), streaming data (for instance, stock prices or weather), and 2-D design elements. In short, a Renaissance painting became an animated medieval illustrated book.

My starting point for the discussion of the poetics of this type of augmented space will be the current practice of video installations that came to dominate the art world in the 1990s. Typically, these installations use video or data projectors; they turn a whole wall or even a whole room into a display or a set of displays, thus rehearsing and investigating (willingly or not) the soon-to-come future of our apartments and cities when large and thin displays will become the norm. At the same time, these laboratories of the future are rooted in the past: the different traditions of "image within a space" of twentieth-century culture.

white cube versus black box

Among the different oppositions that have structured the culture of the twentieth century that we have inherited has been the opposition between an art gallery and a movie theater. One represented high culture, the other low. One involved a white cube; the other involved a black box.

Given the economy of art production—one-of-a-kind objects created by individual artists—twentieth-century artists spent lots of energy experimenting with what could be placed inside the neutral setting of a white cube: breaking away from a flat and rectangular frame by going into the third dimension; covering a whole floor; suspending objects from the ceiling; and so on. In other words, if we are to make an analogy between an art object and a digital computer, we can say that in modern art both the "physical interface" and the "software interface" of an art object were not fixed but open to experimentation. In other words, both the physical appearance of an object and the proposed mode of interaction with an object were ripe for experimentation. Artists have also experimented with the identity of a gallery, from a traditional space of aesthetic contemplation to a place for play, performance, public discussion, lecture, and so on.

In contrast, since cinema was an industrial system of mass production and mass distribution, the physical interface of a movie theater and the software interface of a film themselves were pretty much fixed. A 35-millimeter image of fixed dimensions was projected on a screen with the same frame ratio; in dark space where the viewers were positioned in a set of rows; within the fixed time of a movie itself. Not accidentally, when in the 1960s experimental filmmakers started to systematically attack the conventions of traditional cinema, these attacks were aimed at both its physical interface and software interface (along, of course, with its content). Robert Breer projected his movies on a board that he would hold above his head as he moved through a movie theater toward the projector; Stan VanderBeck constructed semicircular tents for projection of his films; and so on.

The gallery emerged as the space of refined high taste while the cinema served to provide entertainment for the masses, and this difference was also signified by what was acceptable in two kinds of spaces. Despite all the experimentation with its "interface," the gallery space was primarily reserved for static images; to see the moving images the public had to go a movie theater. Thus until recently, the moving image in a gallery was indeed an exception (Marcel Duchamp's rotoscopes, Vito Acconci's masturbating performance).

Given this history, the 1990s phenomenon of omnipresent video installation taking over gallery spaces goes against the whole paradigm of modern art—and not only because installations bring moving images into the gallery. Most video installations adopt the same physical interface: a dark enclosed or semienclosed rectangular space with video projector on one end and the projected image on the opposite wall. From a space of constant innovation in relation to physical and software interface of an art object, a gallery space has turned into what for almost a century was its ideological enemy—a movie theater, characterized by the rigidity of its interface.

Many software designers and software artists—from Ted Nelson and Alan Kay to Perry Hoberman and I/O/D—revolt against the hegemony of mainstream computer interfaces such as the keyboard and mouse, GUI, or commercial web browsers. Similarly, the best of video, or more generally, moving-image installation artists, goes beyond the standard video installation interface—a dark room with an image on one wall. Examples include Diana Thater, Gary Hill, Doug Aitken, as well as the very first "video artist," Nam June Paik. The founding moment of what came later to be called "video art" was Paik's attack on physical interface of a commercial moving image—his first show consisted of television with magnets attached to them, and TV monitors ripped open of their enclosures.

the electronic vernacular

When we look at what visual artists are doing with a moving image in a gallery setting in comparison with these other contemporary fields, we can see that the white gallery box still functions as a space of contemplation, quite different from the aggressive, surprising, overwhelming spaces of a boutique, trade-show floor, airport, or the retail/entertainment area of a major metropolis.[16] While a number of video artists continue the explorations of the 1960s "expanded cinema" movement by pushing moving-image interfaces in many interesting directions, outside of a gallery space we can find at least as rich a field of experimentation. I will single out three areas: First, in contemporary urban architecture in particular, many proposals of the last decade incorporated large projection screens into architecture that would project the activity inside, such as: Rem Koolhaas's 1992 unrealized project for the new ZKM building in Karlsruhe; a number of projects, also mostly unrealized so far, by Robert Venturi to create what he calls "architecture as communication" (buildings covered with electronic displays); realized architectural/media installations by Diller + Scofilio such as *Jump Cuts* and *Facsimile*[17]; the highly concentrated use of video screens and information displays in certain cities such as Seoul, Tokyo, or in Times Square in New York City. A second example is the use of video displays in trade show design such as in annual Siggraph conventions. The third is the best of retail environments (I will discuss this in more detail shortly).

The projects and theories of Robert Venturi deserve special consideration since for him an electronic display is not an optional addition but the very center of architecture in the information age. Since the 1960s Venturi has continuously argued that architecture should learn from vernacular and commercial culture (billboards, Las Vegas, strip malls, architecture of the past). Appropriately, his books *Complexity and Contradiction in Architecture* and *Learning from Las Vegas* are often referred to as the founding documents of postmodern aesthetics. Venturi argues that we should refuse the modernist desire to impose minimalist ornament-free spaces, and instead embrace complexity, contradiction, heterogeneity, and iconography in our built environments.[18] In the 1990s he articulated the new vision of architecture "as communication for the information age (rather than as space for the Industrial Age)."[19] Venturi wants us to think of "architecture as iconographic representation emitting electronic imagery from its surfaces day and night." Pointing out some of the already mentioned examples of the aggressive incorporation of electronic displays in contemporary environments such as Times Square, and also arguing that traditional architecture has *always* included ornament, iconography, and visual narratives (for instance, a medieval cathedral, with its narrative window mosaics, narrative sculpture covering the facade, and narrative paintings), Venturi proposed that architecture should return to its traditional definition as *information surface*.[20] Of course, if the messages communicated by traditional architecture were static and reflected the dominant ideology, today's electronic dynamic interactive displays make it possible for these messages to change continuously and to be the space of contestation and dialog, thus functioning as the material manifestation of the often invisible public sphere.

Although this has not been a part of Venturi's core vision, it is relevant to mention here a growing number of projects where the large, publicly mounted screen is open for programming by the public, who can send images via the Internet or choose information being displayed via their cell phones. Even more radical is *Vectorial Elevation, Relational Architecture #4* by artist Raffael Lozano-Hemmer.[21] This project has made it possible for people from all over the world to control a mutant electronic architecture (made from searchlights) in a Mexico City square. To quote from the statement of the jury of Prix Ars Electronica 2002, which awarded this project the Golden Nica in the interactive category,

> *Vectorial Elevation* was a large scale interactive installation that transformed Mexico City's historic centre using robotic searchlights controlled over the Internet. Visitors to the project web site at <http://www.alzado.net> could design ephemeral light sculptures over the National Palace, City Hall, the Cathedral and the Templo Mayor Aztec ruins. The sculptures, made by 18 xenon searchlights located around the Zócalo Square, could be seen from a 10-mile radius and were sequentially rendered as they arrived over the Net.
>
> The website featured a 3D-java interface that allowed participants to make a vectorial design over the city and see it virtually from any point of view. When the project server in Mexico received a submission, it was numbered and entered into a queue. Every six seconds the searchlights would orient themselves automatically and three webcams would take pictures to document a participant's design.[22]

Venturi's vision of "architecture as iconographic representation" is not without its problems. If we focus completely on the idea of architecture as information surface, we may forget that traditional architecture communicated messages and narratives not only through flat narrative surfaces but also through the particular articulation of space. To use the same example of a medieval cathedral, it communicated Christian narratives not only through the images covering its surfaces but also through its whole spatial structure. In the case of modernist architecture, it similarly communicated its own narratives (the themes of progress, technology, efficiency, and rationality) through its new spaces constructed from simple geometric forms—and also through its bare, industrial-looking surfaces. (Thus the absence of information from the surface—articulated in the famous "ornament is crime" slogan by Adolf Loos—itself became a powerful communication technique of modern architecture).

An important design problem today is how to combine the new functioning of a surface as an electronic display with new kind of spaces that will symbolize the specificity of our own time.[23] While Venturi fits electronic displays on his buildings that closely follow traditional vernacular architecture, this is obviously not the only possible strategy. The well-known 1996 Freshwater Pavilion by NOX/Lars Spuybroek follows a much more radical approach. To emphasize that the interior of the space constantly mutates, Spuybroek eliminates all straight surfaces and straight angles; he makes the shapes defining the space actually move; and he introduces computer-controlled lights that change the illumination of an interior.[24] As described by Ineke Schwartz, "There is no distinction between horizontal and vertical, between [sic] floors, walls and ceilings. Building and exhibition have fused: mist blows around your ears, a geyser erupts, water gleams and splatters all around you, projections fall directly onto the building and its visitors, the air is filled with waves of electronic sound."[25]

I think that Spuybroek's building is a successful symbol for the information age. Its continuously changing surfaces illustrate the key effect of a computer revolution: substitution of every constant by a variable. In other words, the space that symbolizes the information age is not a symmetrical and ornamental space of traditional architecture, rectangular volumes of modernism, or broken and blown-up volumes of deconstruction; rather, it is space whose shapes are inherently mutable, and whose soft contours act as a metaphor for the key quality of computer-driven representations and systems: variability.

learning from prada

Venturi wants to put electronic ornament and electronic iconography on traditional buildings, while Lars Spuybroek, in his Freshwater Pavilion, does create a new kind of space but reduces the changing information to abstract color fields and sound. In Freshwater Pavilion information surface functions in a very particular way, displaying color fields rather than text, images, or numbers. Where today can we find interesting architectural spaces combined with electronic displays that show the whole range of information, from ambient color fields to figurative images and numerical data?

Beginning in the mid-1990s, the avant-garde wing of retail industry began to produce rich and intriguing spaces, many of which incorporate moving images. Leading architects and designers such as Droog/NL, Marc Newson, Jacques Herzog & Pierre de Meuron, Renzo Priano and Rem Koolhaas have created stores for Prada, Mandarina Duck, Hermès, Commes des Garçons, and other high-end brands; architect Richard Glucksman colloborated with artist Jenny Holzer to create a stunning Helmut Lang perfume shop in New York that incorporates Holzer's signature use of LCD. Stores featuring dramatic architecture and design, and mixing a restaurant, fashion, design, and an art gallery have become a new paradigm for high-end brands. Otto Riewoldt labeled this paradigm "brandscaping"—promoting the brand by creating unique spaces: "Brandscaping is the hot issue. The site at which goods are promoted and sold has to reinvent itself by developing unique and unmistakable qualities."[26]

Rem Koolhaas's Prada store in New York (2002) pushes brandscaping to a new level. Koolhaas seems to achieve the impossible by creating a flagship store for the Prada brand—and at the same time an ironic statement about the functioning of brands as new religions.[27] The imaginative use of electronic displays is an important part of this statement. On entering the store you discover glass cages hanging from the ceiling throughout the space. Just as a church would present the relics of saints in special displays, here the glass cages contain the new objects of worship—Prada clothes. The special status of Prada clothes is further enhanced by placing small, flat, electronic screens throughout the store on horizontal shelves, among the merchandise. The clothes are equated to the ephemeral images playing on the screens, and vice versa—the images acquire a certain materiality, as though they are objects. By positioning screens showing moving images right next to clothes Koolhaas ironically refers to what everybody today knows: we buy objects not for themselves but in order to emulate the certain images and narratives presented by the advertisements of these objects. Finally, on the basement level of the store you discover a screen showing an interactive multimedia presentation of Koolhaas's team research for his Prada commissions. One can list all Prada stores throughout the world by square footage, look at the team's analysis of the optimal locations for store placement, and study other data sets that underlie Prada's brandscaping. Koolhaas masterfully engages the "I know it is an illusion but nevertheless" effect: we know that Prada is a business governed by economic rationality, and yet we still feel that we are not simply in a store but in a modern church.

It is symbolic that Prada has opened in the same space that was previously occupied by a branch of the Guggenheim Museum. The strategies of brandscaping are directly relevant to museums and galleries, which, like all other physical spaces, now have to compete against the new information, entertainment, and retail space: a computer or PDA screen connected to the Net. Although museums since the 1990s have similarly expanded their functionality, often combining galleries, a store, film series, lectures, and concerts, design-wise they can learn from retail design, which, as Riewoldt points out, "has learnt two lessons from the entertainment industry. First: forget the goods, sell thrilling experience to the people. And secondly: beat the computer screen at its own game by staging real objects of desire—and by adding some spice to the space with maybe some audio-visual interactive gadgetry."[28]

In a high-tech society cultural institutions usually follow the industry. A new technology is being developed for military, business, or consumer use; after a while cultural institutions notice that some artists are experimenting with it as well, and start incorporating it in their programming. Because they have the function of collecting and preserving the artworks, art museums today often look like historical collections of media technologies of the previous decades. Thus one may mistake a contemporary art museum for a museum of obsolete technology. Today, while outside one finds LCD and PDA, data projectors and digital video cameras, inside a museum we may expect to find slide projectors, 16-millimeter film equipment, and 3/4-inch video decks.

Can this situation be reversed? Can cultural institutions play an active, even leading, role as laboratories where alternative futures are tested? Augmented space—which is slowly becoming a reality—is one opportunity for these institutions to take a more active role. While many video installations already function as laboratories for the development of new configurations of image within space, museums and galleries as a whole could use their own unique asset—a physical space—to encourage the development of distinct new spatial forms of art and new spatial forms of a moving image. In this way they can take a lead in testing out one part of augmented space's future.

At the same time, they can play an active role in developing the poetics of augmented space as a whole. For in addition to having the resources of a physical space they have special access to another unique resource: the history of modern art that (as I suggested already) conceptually prepared the augmented space paradigm. Having stepped outside the picture frame into the white cube walls, floor, and the whole space, artists and curators should feel at home taking yet another step: treating this space as layers of data. This does not mean that the physical space becomes irrelevant; on the contrary, as the practice of Cardiff and Liberskind shows, it is at the interaction of the physical space and the data that some of the most amazing art of our time is being created.

notes

1. In the early 1990s the inventors of virtual reality modeling language designed it in order to model and access 3-D interactive virtual worlds over the Internet, and promoted it as the material realization of the idea of cyberspace. (See, for instance, Mark Pesce, "Ontos, Eros, Noos, Logos," keynote address for the International Symposium on Electronic Arts 1995, at <http://www.xs4all.nl/~mpesce/iseakey.html>. As of this writing (May 2002), Internet-based 3-D virtual worlds have still failed to become popular.

2. Coined in 1998 by David S. Bennahum, the term *cellspace* originally referred to the then new ability to access e-mail or Internet wirelessly. Here I am using the term in a broader sense.

3. It is interesting to think of GPS as a particular case of cellspace. Rather than being tied up to an object or a building, here the information is a property of the earth as a whole. A user equipped with a GPS receiver can retrieve a particular type of information relative to the coordinates of his location. GPS is gradually being integrated into various telecommunication and transportation technologies, from cell phones to PDAs to cars.

4. Recall the opening scene of *Blade Runner* (1982), where the whole side of a high-rise building acts as a screen.

5. Mark Weiser, "The computer for the twenty-first century," *Scientific American* 265, no. 3 (1991): 94–104.

6. Wendy MacKay, Giles Velay, Kathy Carter, Chayoying Ma, and Daniele Pagani, "Augmenting Reality: Adding Computational Dimensions to Paper," *Communications of the ACM*, 36, no. 7 (1993): 96–97; Kevin Bonsor, "How Augmented Reality Will Work" <http://www.howstuffworks.com/augmented-reality.htm>, accessed March 16, 2002.

7. See the Tangible Bits project at MIT Media Lab, <http://tangible.media.mit.edu/projects/Tangible_Bits/projects.htm>, accessed March 16, 2002.

8. Guido Appenzeller, Intelligent Space Project <http://gunpowder.Stanford.EDU/~appenz/ISpace/>, accessed March 16, 2002. Intelligent Room Projects, AI Lab, MIT, <http://www.ai.mit.edu/projects/iroom/projects.shtml>, accessed March 16, 2002.

9. Tom Moran and Paul Dourish, Introduction to special issue on context-aware computing, *Human Computer Interaction*, 16 (2001): 108.

10. Ivan Noble, "E-paper moves a step nearer," *BBC News Online*, April 23, 2001, <http://news.bbc.co.uk/hi/english/sci/tech/newsid_1292000/1292852.stm>.

11. For AR research sites and conferences, see <http://www.augmented-reality.org>.

12. Interestingly, this reversal can be said to be prefigured in the very origins of VR. In the late 1960s Ivan Sutherland developed what came down in history as the first VR system. The user of the system saw a simple wireframe cube whose perspectival view would change as the user moved his head. The wire-frame cube appeared overlaid over whatever the user was seeing. Because the idea of a 3-D computer graphics display whose perspective changes in real time according to the position of the user became associated with subsequent virtual reality systems, Sutherland is credited with inventing the first VR system. It can be argued that his was not a VR system but an AR system, however, because the virtual display was overlaid on the user's field of vision without blocking it. In other words, in

Sutherland's system new information was added to the physical environment: a virtual cube.

13. Vannevar Bush, "As We May Think" (1945); Douglas Engelbart, "Augmenting Human Intellect: A Conceptual Framework" (1962); both in *The New Media Reader*, ed. Noah Wardrip-Fruin and Nick Montfort (MIT Press, forthcoming 2002.)

14. I experienced the "walk" that Cardiff created for P.S.1 in New York in 2001.

15. For those readers familiar with these concepts, the artistic augmented spaces I evoke can be thought of as 2-D texture maps while technological augmented spaces can be compared to a solid texture.

16. This passive and melancholic quality of video art was brilliantly staged in a recent exhibition design by LO/TEK for the exhibition *Making Time: Considering Time As a Material in Contemporary Video and Film* at the Hammer Museum in Los Angeles (February 4–April 29, 2001). As Norman Klein pointed out to me, LO/TEK designed a kind of collective tomb–a cemetery for video art.

17. An overview of Diller + Scofilio projects can be found at <http://www.labiennaledivenezia.net/it/archi/7mostra/architetti/diller/open.htm>.

18. Robert Venturi, *Complexity and Contradiction in Architecture* (New York: Museum of Modern Art, 1966); Robert Venturi, Denise Scott Brown, and Steven Izenour, *Learning from Las Vegas* (Cambridge, Mass.: MIT Press, 1972.)

19. Robert Venturi, *Iconography and Electronics upon a Generic Architecture: A View from the Drafting Room* (Cambridge, Mass.: MIT Press, 1996).

20. Robert Venturi, in a dialog with George Legrady, Entertainment and Value Conference, University of California, Santa Barbara, May 4, 2002. The term *information surface* is mine.

21. See <http://prixars.aec.at/history/interactive/2000/E00int_01.htm>.

22. Ibid.

23. See <http://www.manovich.net/IA>.

24. See Ineke Schwartz, "Testing Ground for Interactivity: The Water Pavilions by Lars Spuybroek and Kas Oosterhuis" <http://synworld.t0.or.at/level3/text_archive/testing_ground.htm>.

25. Ibid.

26. Otto Riewoldt, qtd. in Mark Hooper, "Sex and Shopping," *ID*, May 2001, 94.

27. For an insightful analysis of the branding phenomenon, see Naomi Klein, *No Logo* (New York: Picador, 2000).

28. Riewoldt, quoted in Hooper, "Sex and Shopping," 94.

seven

too many notes

computers, complexity,

and culture in *voyager*

g e o r g e   e .   l e w i s

Voyager is a nonhierarchical, interactive musical environment that privileges improvisation.[1] In *Voyager*, improvisors engage in dialogue with a computer-driven, interactive "virtual improvising orchestra." A computer program analyzes aspects of a human improvisor's performance in real time, using that analysis to guide an automatic composition (or, if you will, improvisation) program that generates both complex responses to the musician's playing and independent behavior that arises from its own internal processes.

This work, which is one of my most widely performed compositions, deals with the nature of music and, in particular, the processes by which improvising musicians produce it. These questions can encompass not only technological or music-theoretical interests but philosophical, political, cultural, and social concerns as well. This is consistent with the instrumental dimension or tendency in African musical organization, or what Robert Farris Thompson identifies as "songs and dances of social allusion," one of several "ancient African organizing principles of song and dance that crossed the seas from the Old World to the New."[2]

Voyager's unusual amalgamation of improvisation, indeterminacy, empathy, and the logical, utterly systematic structure of the computer program is described throughout this article not only as an *environment,* but as a *program*, a *system*, and a *composition*, in the musical sense of the term. In fact, the work can take on aspects of all of these terms simultaneously—considering the conceptual level, the process of creating the software and the real-time, real-world encounter with the work as performer or listener. Flowing across these seemingly rigid conceptual boundaries encourages both improvisors and listeners to recognize the inherent instability of such taxonomies.

Musical computer programs, like any texts, are not "objective" or "universal," but instead represent the particular ideas of their creators. As notions about the nature and function of music become embedded into the structure of software-based musical systems and compositions, interactions with these systems tend to reveal characteristics of the community of thought and culture that produced them. Thus, it would be useful here to examine the implications of the experience of programming and performing with *Voyager* as a kind of computer music making embodying African-American cultural practice.

Among the fair number of studies by artists/theorists who have written cogently on issues of race, gender, and class in new technological media (such as Loretta Todd and Cameron Bailey[3]), the ethnographic study of Institut Recherche et Coordination Acoustique/Musique (IRCAM) by the anthropologist and improvisor Georgina Born appears to stand practically alone in the trenchancy and thoroughness of its analysis of these issues with respect to computer music.[4] This viewpoint contrasts markedly with Catherine M. Cameron's rather celebratory ethnography-at-a-distance of what she terms "American experimentalism," in which the word *race* never appears, and in which her notion of a "musical class structure" is framed largely in terms of a now moribund debate about relative privilege between Europe and America.[5]

In contrast, Born's explicit identification of the nearly all-male, all-white musical and cultural canon articulated not only by the French institute but by its American equivalents traces the outlines of the development of a post-1950s aesthetic of trans-European experimentalism. Given her as yet unrefuted thesis that the overwhelming majority of computer music research and compositional activity locates itself (however unsteadily at times) within the belief systems and cultural practices of European concert music, one can easily imagine a work that, like *Voyager*, exemplifies an area of musical discourse using computers that is not viewed culturally and historically as a branch of trans-

European contemporary concert music and, moreover, is not necessarily modeled as a narrative about "composition."

the aesthetics of multidominance

In an influential 1990s essay, the artist and critic Robert L. Douglas sought to formalize an African-American aesthetic,[6] synthesizing visual and musical elements of what the painter Jeff Donaldson, founder of the Africobra art movement,[7] has called "trans-African" culture. The aspect of Douglas's theory that I wish to highlight here is the notion of "multidominant elements," which I will henceforth call "multidominance." According to Douglas, the aesthetics of multidominance, involving "the multiple use of colors in intense degrees, or the multiple use of textures, design patterns, or shapes,"[8] are found quite routinely in musical and visual works of Africa and its diaspora.

By way of introduction to his theory, Douglas recalls from his art-school days that interviews with "most African-American artists with Eurocentric art training will reveal that they received similar instructions, such as 'tone down your colors, too many colors.'"[9] Apparently, these "helpful" pedagogical interventions were presented as somehow universal and transcendent rather than as emanating from a particular culturally or historically situated worldview, or as based in networks of political or social power. Douglas, in observing that "such culturally narrow aesthetic views would have separated us altogether from our rich African heritage if we had accepted them without question," goes on to compare this aspect of Eurocentric art training to Eurocentric music training, which in his view does not equip its students to hear music with multidominant rhythmic and melodic elements as anything but "noise," "frenzy," or, perhaps, "chaos."[10]

In fact, virtually every extant form of black music has been characterized as "noise." As historian Jon Cruz notes, the history of this trope in the United States dates back at least as far as the slavery period: "Prior to the mid-19th Century black music appears to have been heard by captors and overseers primarily as noise—that is, as strange, unfathomable, and incomprehensible."[11] However, as Cruz points out, for slave owners to hear only noise is "tantamount to being oblivious to the structures of meaning that anchored sounding to the hermeneutic world of the slaves." To hear only noise is to "remain removed from how slave soundings probed their circumstances and cultivated histories and memories."[12]

The notion identified by Cruz that "the production of music and other cultural forms enabled slaves to collectively exercise symbolic control" addresses directly the issue of how a formal aesthetic can articulate political and social meaning.[13] Such modern-day (soon to be old-school) hip-hop groups as Public Enemy, in full recognition of the dis-approbation of their music by powerful sectors of the dominant culture of their own day, even appropriated and ironicized this trope, challeng-ing themselves, their listeners, and their detractors with their explicit intention and exhortation to "bring the noise."[14]

Douglas's call for a formalist analysis does not exclude the realiza-tion that the border between form and content is difficult to police. Moreover, these formal abstractions are not universals; multidomi-nance is not present in all trans-African music and art and certainly must not be applied as a sonic litmus test. In the particular case of *Voyager*, however, the composition's African-American cultural prove-nance lends particular credence to an identification of multidominance at the levels of both the logical structure of the software and its per-formative articulation. Moreover, whether or not these multidominant forms have been consciously conceptualized, exploited, and extended by artists with full awareness of their implications, they must be viewed as culturally contingent, historically emergent, and linked to situated structures of power and dialogue.

The African-American composer Olly Wilson has identified a set of tendencies and principles characteristic of African and Afro-American music making,[15] while quite similar principles are identified by Thomp-son in examining African visual forms.[16] In particular, Douglas, Wilson, and Thompson all identify rhythm as a critically important structural element in African-derived music. Wilson notices in African-derived music a "principle of rhythmic and implied metrical contrast."[17] Thompson sees the black Atlantic visual tradition as dis-playing "a propensity for multiple meter,"[18] and his references to Mande cloth work as incorporating a conception of "rhythmized textiles" makes a direct connection with both African and African-American music.[19] Similarly, Douglas connects the visual with the sonic: "the predisposition to use multiple types of rhythm in musical construction speaks equally to a distinct aesthetic as does the multiple use of visual elements."[20]

computer music and trans-african formalism

I conceived and programmed the first version of *Voyager* between 1986 and 1988. The work was created in Amsterdam at the Studio voor Elektro-Instrumentale Muziek (STEIM); I added later ameliorations wherever I happened to be in the ensuing years. Since then, *Voyager* has been per-formed around the world, with improvisors such as myself (trombone); saxophonists Roscoe Mitchell, J. D. Parran, Douglas Ewart, and Evan Parker; pianist Haruna Miyake; and extended cellist Jon Rose. The work has been performed in venues as diverse as the IRCAM Summer Acad-emy, the Groningen Jazz Marathon, International Computer Music

Conferences in 1988 and 1994, Xebec Hall (Kobe, Japan) and the Velvet Lounge in Chicago.[21]

The various versions of *Voyager* have all been written in dialects of Forth, the curiously hybrid compiled/interpreted environment created by Charles Moore around 1970.[22] Seemingly anti-authoritarian in nature, during the early 1980s Forth appealed to a community of composers who wanted an environment in which a momentary inspiration could quickly lead to its sonic realization—a dialogic creative process, emblematic of an improvisor's way of working. As the Forth culture developed, languages such as Hierarchical Music Specification Language (HMSL) and, later, FORMULA (FORth MUsic LAnguage),[23] created by artists working in the field, made Forth and its dialects perhaps the most widely used language group for interactive music before the advent of Max, a language that similarly centers the dialogic as part of the software construction process.

My analysis of *Voyager* as an interactive computer music system uses Robert Rowe's taxonomy of "player" and "instrument" paradigms,[24] although these two models of role construction in interactive systems should be viewed as on a continuum along which a particular system's model of computer-human interaction can be located. In Rowe's terms, *Voyager* functions as an extreme example of a "player" program, where the computer system does not function as an instrument to be controlled by a performer.

I conceive a performance of *Voyager* as multiple parallel streams of music generation, emanating from both the computers and the humans—a nonhierarchical, improvisational, subject-subject model of discourse, rather than a stimulus/response setup.

Both the sonic behavior and the program structure of *Voyager* exhibit multidominance in a number of respects. First, the *Voyager* program is conceived as a set of sixty-four asynchronously operating single-voice MIDI-controlled "players," all generating music in real time. Several different (and to some, clashing) sonic behavior groupings, or ensembles, may be active simultaneously, moving in and out of metric synchronicity, with no necessary arithmetic correlation between the strongly discursive layers of multirhythm. While this is happening, a lower-level routine parses incoming MIDI data into separate streams for up to two human improvisors, who are either performing on MIDI-equipped keyboards or playing acoustic instruments through "pitch followers," devices that try to parse the sounds of acoustic instruments into MIDI data streams.

The aperiodic, asynchronously recurring global "behavior specification" subroutine *setphrasebehavior*, which runs at intervals of between five and seven seconds, continually recombines the MIDI "players" into new ensemble combinations with defined behaviors. This subroutine (or "word," in Forth parlance) first makes determinations as to how many players will be part of the next ensemble. Additional options include turning off all players in all ensembles and starting afresh with this new group, turning off just the most recently instantiated ensemble, or allowing the new ensemble to enter the fray with the groups that are already playing.

The *setphrasebehavior* word also includes constituent subroutines that specify for the new ensemble choices of timbre, the choice of one of fifteen melody algorithms, the choice of approximately 150 micro-tonally specified pitchsets, and choices of volume range, microtonal transposition, tactus (or "beat"), tempo, probability of playing a note, spacing between notes, interval-width range and MIDI-related orna-mentation such as chorusing, reverberation, and portamento, and how such parameters as tessitura and tempo can change over time. More-over, each new ensemble chooses not only a distinct group sonority, but a unique response to input, deciding which improvisors—one, both, or none—will influence its output behavior. Further options include imi-tating, directly opposing, or ignoring the information coming from the improvisors.

The response task word *setresponse*, which runs asynchronously to the phrase behavior task, processes data from both the low-level MIDI parser that collects and manages the raw data and a midlevel smoothing rou-tine that uses this raw data to construct averages of pitch, velocity, prob-ability of note activity, and spacing between notes. This information is used by *setresponse* to decide in greater detail how each ensemble will respond to elements of the input, such as tempo (speed), the probability of playing a note, spacing between notes, melodic interval width, choice of primary pitch material (including a pitchset based on the last several notes received), octave range, microtonal transposition, and volume.

Of particular note here is the fact that in the absence of outside input, the complete specification of the system's musical behavior is internally generated by *setphrasebehavior*. In practical terms, this means that *Voyager* does not need to have real-time human input to generate music. In turn, since the program exhibits generative behavior independently of the improvisor, decisions taken by the computer have consequences for the music that must be taken into account by the improvisor. With no built-in hierarchy of human leader/computer follower—no "veto" buttons, foot pedals, or physical cues—all communication between the system and the improvisor takes place sonically.

The simultaneous multiplicities of available timbres, microtonal pitchsets, rhythms, transposition levels, and other elements in *Voyager*—all emblematic of an aesthetic of multidominance—reflect my inheri-tance from the Association for the Advancement of Creative Musicians' notion of "multi-instrumentalism," where a number of AACM improvisors, including Wadada Leo Smith, Henry Threadgill, Douglas Ewart, Joseph Jarman, Roscoe Mitchell, Anthony Braxton, and others moved to develop multiple voices on a wide variety of instruments.[25] In AACM performances, the extreme multiplicity of voices, embedded within an already highly collective ensemble orientation, permitted the timbral diversity of a given situation to exceed the sum of its instrumental parts, affording a wider palette of potential orchestrations to explore.

The attempt to thoroughly map, parse, and develop the input data is based on the notion that, through the accumulation and articulation of many small details an interactive, adaptive input structure that generates a sufficiently detailed representation of its input can then produce a musical output perceptible by an improvisor as analogous to various states that were experienced during improvisation. This notion of bidirectional transfer of intentionality through sound—or, "emotional transduction"—constructs performance as an intentional act embodying meaning and announcing emotional and mental intention. In this way, I believe, the emotional state of the improvisor may be mirrored in the computer partner, even if the actual material played by the computer does not necessarily preserve the pitch, duration, or morphological structures found in the input.

In improvised music, improvisors often assert both personal narrative and difference as critical aspects of their work. For me, what Jerry Garcia called the "anti-authoritarian" impulse in improvisation led me to pursue the project of deinstrumentalizing the computer. If the computer is not treated as a musical instrument, but as an independent improvisor, difference is partly grounded in the form of program responses that are not necessarily predictable on the basis of outside input. As we have noted earlier, *Voyager*'s response to input has several modes, from complete communion to utter indifference. This seeming lack of uniformity is not necessarily correlated with "lack of structure," as is so often expressed in the vernacular discourse of "randomness." Rather, while tendencies over a long period of time exhibit consistency, moment-to-moment choices can shift unpredictably.

It is a fact, however, that the system is designed to avoid the kind of uniformity where the same kind of input routinely leads to the same result. *Voyager*'s aesthetic of variation and difference is at variance with the information retrieval and control paradigm that late capitalism has found useful in framing its preferred approach to the encounter with computer technology. As I have observed elsewhere, interactivity has gradually become a metonym for information retrieval rather than dialogue, posing the danger of commodifying and ultimately reifying the encounter with technology. As I have noted, "the rapid development of standardized modes for the relationships between humans and computers is unfortunate for such a young and presumably quickly changing technology. The evolution of the language used to reflect the multimedia revolution is a compelling testament to the power of corporate media. Corporate power assumes an important, even dominating role in conditioning our thinking about computers, art, image, and sound. Much of the descriptive language surrounding multimedia (and related areas, such as 'cyberspace') serves to hide the power exercised by corporations."[26]

Finally, Wilson notices in African-derived music a tendency toward a high density of events in a relatively short time frame.[27] It is to be noted that the work of many important African-American improvisors—in particular Cecil Taylor, John Coltrane, and Albert Ayler—exhibits a notion of extended form that involves the sustained use, often for very long periods, of extremely rapid, many-noted intensity structures. Donaldson's 1988 visual work, *Jam Packed and Jelly Tight*,[28] exemplifies the approach of the Africobra artists who, according to Douglas, "used the jampack and jelly-tight concept as a means of filling up the void, to add as much as possible to the act of creation. Africobra members accept these concepts as an African axiom: that to add to life is to ensure that there is more to share."[29]

The *Voyager* program often combines dense, rapid accretions of sonic information with sudden changes of mood, tempo, and orchestration, eschewing the slowly moving timbral narratives characteristic of much institutionally based computer music. Thus, *Voyager* is in clear violation of the dictum that Douglas identifies here as Eurocentric: "Don't overcrowd your composition with too many elements."[30] These real distinctions from much institutionally produced trans-European computer music led one puzzled Italian listener to ask me "why so many things are happening at the same time." Or, to quote the king from the movie *Amadeus*, speaking of Mozart's work, "There are too many notes."[31]

emotional transduction: sound, personality, difference

In the context of improvised musics that exhibit strong influences from African-American ways of music making, musical sound—or rather, "one's own sound"—becomes a carrier for history and cultural identity. As Yusef Lateef maintains, "The sound of the improvisation seems to tell us what kind of person is improvising. We feel that we can hear character or personality in the way the musician improvises."[32] Essentially the same notion was advanced in the 1940s by Charlie Parker, who declared that "Music is your own experience, your thoughts, your wisdom. If you don't live it, it won't come out of your horn."[33]

The incorporation and welcoming of agency, social necessity, personality, and difference as aspects of "sound" distinguish such music from work that "incorporates" or "uses" improvisation, or that features "indeterminacy" or aleatoric practices. "Sound" becomes identifiable not with timbre alone, but with the expression of personality, the assertion of agency, the assumption of responsibility, and an encounter with history, memory, and identity.

Part of the task of constructing *Voyager* consisted of providing the program with its "own sound." In *Voyager,* this notion of sound appears in tandem with a kind of technology-mediated animism, expressed as an interactive aesthetic of negotiation and independent computer agency. This recalls the frequent references by Malachi Favors Maghostut, contrabassist and cofounder of the Art Ensemble of Chicago, to someone he met on his travels as "this African brother who had instruments that played themselves." Further, the trope of musical performance on an instrument as communication between two subject intelligences is exemplified by Francis Bebey's description of an incident wherein an accomplished African musician, after trying an instrument briefly, handed it back to its owner with the remark that he had no way of communicating with "someone who did not speak the same language" as he did. Bebey, in general discussion of African music, further maintains that in a number of African musical traditions a musical instrument "is often regarded as a human being." As evidence he offers the story of another African musician, who described his refusal to sell his drum (despite his near-destitution) by saying that he did not want to "deliver a slave into bondage."[34]

The other important notion that animates *Voyager* is that of the improvising orchestra. While *Voyager* can be seen as appropriating or even playing the dozens[35] with the notion of the nineteenth-century European orchestra, my model in this regard is the Javanese gamelan ensemble, where a large number of players playing a relatively fixed composition nonetheless have considerable latitude in interpretation, even at such primary levels as pitch, duration, and rhythm. Control of musical process is shared among players; interplayer communication takes place without necessarily involving a central authority. Local decisions taken by individual players percolate up to the global level, at which the overall form is maintained.

The Javanese musician Hardja Susilo characterizes "improvisation" in court tradition according to its interactive, social, or intentional role, acknowledging how intentionality of process affects the musical result. For example, the Javanese term *kembangan* (literally, "flowering") refers to an improvisation that adds beauty. *Isen-isen* ("filling") is an improvisation that "pleasantly fills a vacuum." On the other hand, *ngambang* ("floating") refers to musicians who are improvising without clear knowledge of where the music is going, and *ngawur* ("blunder") denotes an out-of-style or irrelevant improvisation.[36] Thus, the success of this heterarchically oriented approach to large-group musical interaction can be seen to depend not only on the performative skills of the players but upon their real-time analytic capabilities.

Finally, it is striking to note how an African-American perspective on improvisation reflects a similarity with recent thinking in the game of basketball, an area in which African-American players have continually presented revolutionary possibilities. The situation with improvisation, conventional classical music wisdom notwithstanding, is remarkably similar to basketball coach Phil Jackson's description of the triangle offense, in which "there are no set plays, and the defense can't predict what's going to happen next." As with improvisation, the ideal of the triangle system is for each player to be "acutely aware, at any given moment, of what's happening on the floor."[37] While in both areas triangle-offense author Tex Winter's dictum that "the offense must utilize the players' individual skills" has major relevance, it is absolutely crucial that both basketballers and experienced improvisors "develop an intuitive feel for how their movements and those of everyone else on the floor are interconnected."[38]

Thus, continuous awareness is the means through which these possibilities are articulated in performance. Part of the analytic task facing any improvisor (whether or not that improvisor is a computer) involves discovering or even positing ways in which seemingly unrelated material can become part of either an existing or a new structure within the emergent music. Depending on context, the responses of the computer to the improvisor's input can potentially be seen as either related or unrelated, either during the improvisation itself or upon further reflection. Moreover, the explicit possibility of encountering completely unrelated material encourages the possibility of changes in the music initiated by the computer as well as the humans players.

Thus, with both computers and humans, the data gathered must be viewed in a variety of contexts and from diverse perspectives in order to decide how the material to be presented next might function in terms of what has already been presented. The relatedness of particular materials need not be, and quite often cannot be, "objectively" demonstrable. Rather, the framing—by all parties to the music making—of the relationship that the new material has to the overall piece at that moment is a crucial factor in structure formation. This process may be subsumed under the general heading of "creativity."

afterword: structure and freedom

Structure, as we understand it in music pedagogy, is highly desirable. On the other hand, at the same time that most students learn fairly early on that "jazz" (whatever that might be) is improvised. The dominant culture informs them, in myriad ways that are continually reinscribed across the breadth of daily experience, that *improvised* is a synonym for *unstructured.* In apparently welcome contrast, we are provided with the role of the "composer," which can be usefully summarized as "bringer of structure." The structure inevitably arrives in the form of a written text, a coded set of symbols, intended for realization in performance by a "performer."

This metonymic dialectic between "composed" and "improvised" ways of producing musical texts serves to obscure a more fundamental constructed binary comprising the two most influential musical cultures of the twentieth century, the trans-European and trans-African. Proponents of each form-complex tend to construct an "other" from proponents of the complementary form—particularly in creating competing notions of "art music"—but the asymmetrical distribution of cultural power clearly rests, for the moment, with the "bringers of structure." In Euro-American art-music culture this binary is routinely and simplistically framed as involving the "effortless spontaneity" of improvisation versus the careful deliberation of composition—the composer as ant, the improvisor as grasshopper.

To move beyond this tendentiously posed opposition, a meaningful distinction between these different ways of knowing—the improvisational and the compositional—must inevitably turn upon the axis of interaction. Improvisation must be open—that is, open to input, open to contingency—and a real-time and (often enough) a real-world mode of production. In machine terms, what we may have in *Voyager* is a composing machine that allows outside intervention. If we do not need to define improvised ways of producing knowledge as a subset of composition, then we can simply speak of an improvising machine as one that incorporates a dialogic imagination.

Thus, if there is to be serious talk about "our" identity as humans, those identities are continually conditioned and reinscribed through processes of interactivity, where negotiation, difference, partial perspective—and in the case of music, sonic signaling—enter the picture. *Voyager* asks questions concerning ways in which historically contingent meanings are exchanged through sound. Even given my emphasis on the personal conception of "sound," *Voyager* is not asking whether machines exhibit personality or identity, but how personalities and identities become articulated through sonic behavior. Instead of asking about the value placed (by whom?) on artworks made by computers, *Voyager* continually refers to human expression. Rather than asking if computers can be creative and intelligent—those qualities, again, that we seek in our mates, or at least in a good blind date— *Voyager* asks us where our own creativity and intelligence might lie: not "How do we create intelligence?" but "How do we find it?" Ultimately, the subject of *Voyager* is not technology or computers at all, but musicality itself.

1. George E. Lewis, *Voyager*, Disk Union-Avan CD 014 (1992).

2. Robert Farris Thompson, *Flash of the Spirit: African and Afro-American Art and Philosophy* (New York: Vintage, 1983).

3. Loretta Todd, "Aboriginal Narratives in Cyberspace," in *Immersed in Technology: Art and Virtual Environments*, ed. Mary Anne Moser and Douglas MacLeod (Cambridge, Mass.: MIT Press, 1996), 179–94. Cameron Bailey, "Virtual Skin: Articulating Race in Cyberspace," in Moser and MacLeod, eds., *Immersed in Technology*, 29–49.

4. Georgina Born, *Rationalizing Culture: IRCAM, Boulez and the Institutionalization of the Avant-Garde* (Berkeley and Los Angeles: University of California Press, 1995).

5. Catherine M. Cameron, *Dialectics in the Arts: The Rise of Experimentalism in American Music* (Westport, Conn.: Praeger, 1996).

6. Robert L. Douglas, "Formalizing an African-American Aesthetic," *New Art Examiner*, Summer 1991, 18–24.

7. Jeff Donaldson, "Africobra—African Commune of Bad Relevant Artists: 10 in Search of a Nation," *Black World*, October 1970, 81–89; Ann Gibson, "The African American Aesthetic and Postmodernism," in *African American Visual Aesthetics: A Postmodernist View*, ed. David C. Driskell (Washington, D.C.: Smithsonian Institution Press, 1995).

8. See Douglas, "Formalizing an Aesthetic," 18.

9. Ibid.

10. Ibid.

11. Jon Cruz, *Culture on the Margins: The Black Diaspora and the Rise of American Cultural Interpretation* (Princeton, N.J.: Princeton University Press, 1999), 43.

12. Ibid., 47.

13. Ibid.

14. "Bring the Noise" is the second track on Public Enemy's second album *It Takes a Nation of Millions to Hold Us Back* (Def Jam Records, 1988).

15. Olly Wilson, "Black Music As an Art Form," *The Jazz Cadence of American Culture*, ed. Robert G. O'Meally (New York: Columbia University Press, 1998), 82–101.

16. See Thompson, *Flash of the Spirit*, xiii.

17. See Wilson, "Black Music," 84.

18. Paul Gilroy describes the "black Atlantic" as an "intercultural and transnational formation" that encompasses Africa and its diasporas, on both sides of the Atlantic Ocean, including Europe (especially Britain), the United States, the Caribbean, and South America. In particular, he argues that "the literary and philosophical modernisms of the black Atlantic have their origins in a well-developed sense of the complicity of racialized reason and white supremacist terror." See Gilroy, *The Black Atlantic: Modernity and Double Consciousness* (Cambridge, Mass.: Harvard University Press, 1993), ix–x. See also Thompson, *Flash of the Spirit*, xiii.

19. See Thompson, *Flash of the Spirit*, 207.

20. See Douglas, "Formalizing an Aesthetic," 19.

21. Recent citations and reviews of this work are included in the following: Joel Chadabe, *Electric Sound: The Past and Promise of Electronic Music* (Upper Saddle River, N.J.: Prentice Hall, 1997), 299–301; Ben Ratliff, "Improvisers

Meet the Machines," *New York Times*, October 14, 1997, E3; Zane East, "George E. Lewis: *Voyager*," *Computer Music Journal* 19, no. 1 (Spring 1995): 109–110.

22. Leo Brodie, *Starting FORTH* (Englewood Cliffs, N.J.: Prentice Hall, 1981). FORTH was spelled in upper case until the late 1970s because of the prevalence of upper-case-only I/O (in/out) devices. The usage "*Forth*" was generally adopted when lowercase became widely available because the word was not an acronym. E. D. Ratner, D. Colburn and C. H. Moore, "The Evolution of Forth," *ACM SIGPLAN Notices* 28, no. 3 (1993); online at <http://www.forth.com/Content/History/History1.htm>.

23. Phil Burk, Larry Polansky, and David Rosenboom, "HMSL: A Theoretical Overview," *Perspectives of New Music* 28, no. 2 (1990): 136–78. D. P. Anderson and R. Kuivila, "Continuous Abstractions for Discrete Event Languages," *Computer Music Journal* 3, no. 13 (1989): 11–23. D. P. Anderson and R. Kuivila, "Formula: A Programming Language for Expressive Computer Music," *Computer IEEE* 24, no. 7 (1991): 12–21.

24. Robert Rowe, *Interactive Music Systems* (Cambridge, Mass.: MIT Press, 1992), 8.

25. References to the AACM, one of the most creatively diverse organizations of the last thirty years, are present in international abundance, so I present here just three citations that detail the organization's structural and cultural strategies: George E. Lewis, "Singing Omar's Song: A (Re)construction of Great Black Music," *Lenox Avenue* 4 (1998): 69–92; Ronald M. Radano, "Jazzin' the Classics: The AACM's Challenge to Mainstream Aesthetics," *Black Music Research Journal* 12, no. 1 (1992): 79–95; Ekkehard Jost, "The Chicagoans," in *Free Jazz* (New York: Da Capo Press, 1994).

26. George E. Lewis, "Singing the Alternative Interactivity Blues," *Front* 7, no. 2 (1995): 18–22.

27. See Wilson, "Black Music," 84.

28. Jeff Donaldson, *Jam Packed and Jelly Tight*, 1998; mixed media on canvas, 36 × 50 inches. The work is reproduced in Driskell, ed., *African American Visual Aesthetics*, plate 10.

29. See Douglas, "Formalizing an Aesthetic," 21.

30. Ibid., 18.

31. *Amadeus*, dir. Milos Forman, 1984.

32. Yusef A. Lateef, "The Pleasures of Voice in Improvised Music," in *Views on Black American Music: Selected Proceedings from the Fourteenth, Fifteenth, Sixteenth and Seventeenth Annual Black Musicians' Conferences, University of Massachusetts at Amherst*, no. 3, ed. Roberta Thelwell (1985–1988): 43–46.

33. Michael Levin and John S. Wilson, "No Bop Roots in Jazz: Parker," *Down Beat* 61, no. 2 (1994): 24–25.

34. Francis Bebey, *African Music: A People's Art* (Westport, Conn.: Lawrence Hill, 1975), 119–20.

35. "Playing the dozens" is a form of insult-play common in African American communities. The game emerges in social gatherings as a kind of competition in improvised rhetoric in front of an impromptu audience.

36. Hardja Susilo, "Toward an Appreciation of Javanese Gamelan," unpublished paper, 1992.

37. Phil Jackson, who during the 1990s won six National Basketball Association championships as head coach of the Chicago Bulls as well as the 2000 NBA championship with the Los Angeles Lakers, adopted as part of his

winning scheme coach Fred "Tex" Winter's unusual system of basketball offense, variously known as the "triple-post" (Winter's term) or the "triangle" offense. Jackson often describes the offense in terms of its spiritual and cultural implications, as well as its efficacy in basketball. See Phil Jackson and Hugh Delehanty, *Sacred Hoops: Spiritual Lessons of a Hardwood Warrior* (New York: Hyperion, 1995), 87. See also Fred Winter, *The Triple-Post Offense* (Englewood Cliffs, N.J.: Prentice-Hall, 1962) for the original documentation of Winter's conception.

38. Jackson and Delehanty, *Sacred Hoops*, 91. See also Winter, *The Triple-Post Offense*.

selected discography

George E. Lewis, *Endless Shout*, Tzadik TZ CD 7054 (2000).

George E. Lewis, *Homage to Charles Parker*, Black Saint BSR 0029 (1980).

George E. Lewis, *Voyager*, Disk Union-Avan CD 014 (1992).

George E. Lewis and Douglas Ewart, *George Lewis/Douglas Ewart*, Black Saint SR 0026 (1979).

Richard Teitelbaum, *Concerto Grosso*, hat ART CD 6004 (1988).

the stories digital

tools tell

e i g h t

t a r l e t o n   g i l l e s p i e

The modernist belief that technology is neutral has been so discounted that it seems almost unnecessary to reiterate it. We know the design of a technology has consequences that go well beyond the explicit "functions" the tool is expected to perform. It seems like ages, though it's been only a few decades, since anyone could have asked, "in view of the simplicity of technological engineering, and the complexity of social engineering, to what extent can social problems be circumvented by reducing them to technological problems? Can we identify Quick Technological Fixes for profound and almost infinitely complicated social problems, 'fixes' that are within the grasp of modern technology, and which would either eliminate the original social problem without requiring a change in the individual's social attitudes, or would so alter the problem as to make its resolution more feasible?"[1] We're now amused, or a bit shocked, by the naïveté of Alvin Weinberg's tragically optimistic question—not to mention that his answer was a qualified "yes," pointing to, of all things, the hydrogen bomb as a successful technological fix for the problem of war.

We can only hope that we'll never be so oblivious to the consequences of technologies, but it's a surprisingly slippery lesson. We still look for, and long for, "technological fixes." We hope trigger locks will reduce criminal violence, cameras fitted with facial recognition algorithms will ensure public safety, smart ID cards will squelch terrorism, or the V-chip will protect children from sex and violence on TV. These technologies hold out the promise of attaining progressive social goals, and of doing so effectively and without discrimination—a promise built upon the persistent belief that technologies exist outside the frailty and selfishness of human politics.

And, as more of our interactions with the world around us—commercial, political, communicative, and artistic—are in digital form, it's been surprisingly easy for us to once again forget what we've learned. Caught in the blood-in-the-ears rush of hype, smitten by novelty, we regularly overlook the most glaring of continuities. The immateriality of digital tools has often been pointed to as proof that they do not work like more earthly artifacts; our fantasies of frictionless digital transaction and intuitive interfaces preach the same mistaken faith—that our tools are our silent partners, helping us in our goals with no agendas of their own. So, as we work to develop increasingly sophisticated insights into digital culture, it is important to rehearse this critical lesson, to remind ourselves to apply it to new technologies, and to develop a language in which it will be less easily forgotten.

artifacts have politics

Technology is, from the start and at every moment, fully embedded in a social matrix of institutions, activities, and values; at the same time, every human activity is both bounded by and fundamentally in negotiation with a range of technologies. As Wiebe Bijker notes, "All relevant social groups contribute to the social construction of technology; all relevant artifacts contribute to the construction of social relations."[2] An analysis of software, then, must begin with a sense of the way technologies may have powerful consequences for the social activities that happen with them, in the worlds imagined by them; as Langdon Winner put it, these "artifacts have politics."

The tendency to treat technology as neutral is so pervasive that it is literally difficult to question it. Winner notes that "to argue that certain technologies *in themselves* have political properties seems, at first glance, completely mistaken. We all know that people have politics, not things. To discover either virtues or evils in aggregates of steel, plastic, transistors, integrated circuits, and chemicals seems just plain wrong, a way of mystifying human artifice and of avoiding the true sources, the human sources of freedom and oppression, justice and injustice."[3] If we are to take this approach seriously, we must adopt a different perspective on the "things" we surround ourselves with. No longer mere tools subordinated to the human will, things must be studied as artifacts—"an artifact is an aspect of the material world that has been modified over the history of its incorporation into goal-directed human action."[4] Once we can see artifacts as crystallized forms of human labor, communication, and value, the importance of how they shape activity becomes clearer. And it requires a subtle understanding of how a technology can have distinct political valences, picking and choosing among human practices according to a veiled agenda.

Most of the discussions of such political valences focus on technologies that, on the surface, do not claim to regulate behavior. Winner turns, controversially, to the Long Island highway overpasses designed by Robert Moses.[5] In building particularly low bridges, the highway—and the beaches they led to—would be more accessible to wealthier New Yorkers with cars, but less so to the (mostly African-American) working class, who needed public busses to leave the city. The material design of the bridges, their height and inflexibility, combine with the class "dimensions" of public and private transportation to enforce a particular social politics. The technology itself can "engineer relationships among people that, after a time, become just another part of the landscape."[6]

Bruno Latour focuses on an even more mundane object, the hydraulic "door-closer" that shuts the front door of his department. He notes that technologies are nonhuman "lieutenants" designed to replace the work of people—but they always come with consequences: these devices may help shut the door behind us, but they are kinder to me than to the small child, the disabled, or the deliverer of heavy packages. "If, in our societies, there are thousands of such lieutenants to which we have delegated competencies, it means that what defines our social relations is, for the most part, prescribed back to us by nonhumans. Knowledge, morality, craft, force, sociability are not properties of humans but of humans *accompanied* by their retinue of delegated characters."[7]

Winner hopes to show not only that architecture regulates, but that architecture can be made to regulate; he is quick to imply xenophobic intent (which, considering Moses's other contributions to New York's landscape, is not a hard case to make). Latour speaks more of consequences—particularly the unanticipated ones. This raises the question of *intentionality*: must the politics of the artifact be deliberate? Or, to put it another way, if we discover what we think are political valences in a tool, can we safely assume that they represent the politics of its designer?[8]

It's easier to spot the political valence of technologies that are explicitly designed to regulate. A familiar example is the "panopticon," a prison imagined but never built by Jeremy Bentham, and discussed by

Michel Foucault. By designing the prison as a cylinder, with light coming from outside and through each cell, a single jailer at the center could see every prisoner simultaneously. And, the prisoners could not see the jailer, but would know that he could see them; according to Foucault, this would compel prisoners to experience surveillance whether or not anyone was even watching.[9] The particular design of the prison serves political ends because it forces bodies into lines of sight that effectively discourage unwanted behavior.

Lawrence Lessig points to more familiar examples to demonstrate not only that architecture can govern behavior, but that we quite often use it as a basic regulatory intervention, especially when other avenues, such as the law, are ineffective or costly.[10] We may regulate driving by arresting drunk drivers, enforcing speed limits, and posting cops at busy intersections. But we also install speed bumps and guardrails to force drivers into lanes and control their speed; we put disruptive bumpers between highway lanes to keep drivers awake; and we install automated barriers to ensure that no one pulls in front of an oncoming train or leaves a parking lot without paying for the privilege. And, we lay out highways in ways that not only regulate the practices of individual drivers, but are massively consequential for the flow of people into and out of, or right by, certain urban neighborhoods.

This attention to the valences of technologies has been taken even farther, to the very structure of human thought. Some critics of cognitive psychology argue that human thought is not contained inside the head, but is stretched across interactions between people—and between people and things. Latour notes, "Cognition has nothing to do with minds nor with individuals but with the propagation of representations through various media, which are coordinated by a very lightly equipped human subject working in a group, inside a culture, with many artifacts and who might have internalized some parts of the process."[11] Edwin Hutchins points to the nautical chart; more than a computational device, the chart is an artifact encrusted with layer upon layer of the cognition of past participants: "The cartographer has already done part of the computation for every navigator who uses his chart. . . . The navigator doesn't have to know how the chart was made and doesn't need to know about the properties of the Mercator projection that give special computational meaning to straight lines."[12] The navigator is thus engaged in symbolic conversation with everyone who contributed to its construction; cognition literally happens in the space between navigator and chart. And the navigator can only understand the ocean through the features of that tool.

The resolve of this argument must be regularly tested, since it can so easily sound like a sophisticated version of technological determinism. If the description of the technology is not a subtle one, it will seem as if we are ascribing causality, even agency, to the technology. Determinism remains the dark underbelly of discussions about technology; the sense that technology actively intervenes in the world is a more manageable shorthand for the complexity of the social. Our second concern, then, must be the question of the *causality* we attribute to the technology. We need to understand the interaction between people as social actors and artifacts as mediated human activity. "We have to hold the two together," writes Latour. "Commercial interests, capitalist spirit, imperialism, thirst for knowledge, are empty terms as long as one does not take into account Mercator's projection, marine clocks and their markers, copper engravings of maps, rutters, the keeping of 'log books'. . . . But, on the other hand, no innovation in the way longitude and latitudes are calculated, clocks are built, log books are compiled, copper plates are printed, would make any difference whatsoever if they did not help to muster, align, and win over new and unexpected allies."[13] A look to the artifact must quickly look beyond, to see its engagement with communities of people, cultures of practice, institutional and social contexts, and discursive landscapes.

the politics of self-interpretation

Analyzing digital tools to discover their hidden politics is no simple task; not only do we lack the critical language for it, but technologies, like people, obscure their politics—in an attempt to appear universal, or natural, or just true. And technologies submerge their politics in the material itself, making them even more difficult to unearth.

One suggestion has been to borrow the lessons learned in the study of literature and art; to do so, we would need to draw an analogy between tools and texts. Steve Woolgar claims that, like traditional texts, the meaning of a tool is a product of its interpretation in a particular context. At the same time, the tool privileges some interpretations over others, inviting "readers" to occupy carefully delineated positions in relation to it. The artifact configures its user by delineating who the user is and attempts "to define, enable, and constrain" what the use of that artifact will be.[14]

This approach is both productive and treacherous. On the one hand, it helps reveal the meaning-making qualities of the tool—as in the title of this essay, to reveal the "stories" that tools tell. The risk, however, is a methodological one. Treating the material artifact like a discursive one may tend to highlight the discursive elements of the tool, and further obscure those elements that do not present in discursive terms. And these might be the features we should be most interested in.

This is not to say that a look at the discursive elements of a tool is not productive. In the study of material artifacts, we can find plenty of evidence that the tool is intended for particular uses, and that it presumes the world to work in particular ways, by looking at advertising campaigns, packaging, instruction manuals, company documents, press descriptions, trade magazine profiles, and critical reviews. Inside these texts the significance and meaning of the tool is being interpreted, often by its own designers; this "self-interpretation" of what the tool does, and what role it can play inside human activity, frames that activity—such that using the tool in these ways makes "sense," and other uses and purposes seem less familiar, less likely, less viable. In digital tools, these textual supplements are perhaps even more potent because they seem to be part of the tool itself. For the digital tool, promotional splash screens, help menus, and affiliated websites accessible from within the application narrate, with similar connotations in how they envision the world in which the tool is involved. And, packaged with the tool itself, it is more difficult to separate them.

Macromedia Dreamweaver comes with a "guided tour" that introduces its main features.[15] The tutorial is a short interactive design lesson, showing how each feature works on a simulated website under construction. In Dreamweaver 2.0, the mock site is for a fictional gourmet food seller called "Olive Branch"—selling "delicately aged Asiago cheese" and Two Leaves wine, an "oaky, buttery cabernet"; a sweet and tangy "Ocean Cape Cranberry Mustard" is today's mustard special. The company's mission statement is earthy and cultured: "fresh from our organic gardens to your table, delectables to please the palette and the soul." Nonexistent customers are urged to "discover a world of flavors direct from our farms to your table," as well as to utilize the "secure online ordering" system.[16] In version 3.0, the tone of the site hasn't changed, but the scope is dramatically more global: the site is for "Scaal Coffee," a supposed Stockholm-based cafe that has now franchised, Starbucks-style, into "670 cities around the world." "After all," we are told, "coffee is a ritual that transcends all cultural boundaries. It makes us feel alert, energetic and alive." The site sells not only the history and prestige of their "brave new world coffee," with its "fresh taste and rich aroma," but also a CD, a travel mug, and a $3.95 tin of "powerfully refreshing mints." Visitors to this site would be rewarded by a not-so-subtle interpellative sales pitch: "Scaal has been serving fine coffee connoisseurs like you for over 50 years."[17]

Both examples are perfectly legitimate, and could easily be real websites. But the choices are also savvy ones, in that they position the tool very carefully amid an array of possible uses. While the web has been colonized by commercial interests and advertisers, even to this day only a few have discovered reliable ways to "Net" a profit. Even now, the debate continues about what kind of medium the web will be, how it will be funded, what kind of communication will happen there. And even commercial sites exhibit a range of approaches and purposes: book and music superstores, journalistic information providers, boutique specialty shops, pornographers, online investors, do-it-yourself entrepreneurs, and so on.

The examples conjured up by Macromedia make an implicit suggestion to users about what kind of site this program is designed to produce and what the web is for. "Olive Branch" and "Scaal" are commercial sites, vested enough to have secure online ordering. The sites are prestigious and specialized; the products are expensive and posh; the aesthetic is earthy and sumptuous. "Olive Branch" suggests both earthy, Old World natural goodness and regal (and commercial) wisdom, while "Scaal" connotes Scandinavian craftsmanship and caffeinated corporate dominance. These choices are deliberate—a story told by Macromedia about both the use of its application and the Net itself. As their own corporate mission statement proclaims, Macromedia is "helping to define what the web can be."[18]

And not only is this powerful narration embedded in the tool; this self-interpretation appears during the process of learning to use that tool. This means that its audience is likely to be uninitiated users, new to both Dreamweaver and perhaps to the web. This glimpse into what a website "is" and what its most important features "are" sets an early frame for how these users encounter the web, positing a compelling example even before alternatives can appear. Basing the tutorial on this site does not mark it as the ideal website; it marks it as the "everysite," so common that it can stand in for all sites, for the sake of learning the application.

(If only to prove the point, a search on a major web search engine for the word "scaal" turned up hundreds of sites titled "Scaal Home Page." A few were exact copies of the Dreamweaver tutorial site; presumably, someone was practicing and inadvertently posted the pages to their public server. The majority were actual websites, for different products and interests; it was clear that these users had generated their sites by modifying the HTML (hypertext mark-up language) code from the tutorial, but had failed to change the title of the homepage. Many of these sites are strikingly similar to the Dreamweaver site in terms of aesthetics and layout, others less so. Most, though not all, were commercial sites.)

the politics of design

As I suggested earlier, using interpretive strategies drawn from the study of texts can overemphasize the discursive elements of the artifact. The tutorial may frame the debate, may appear to the uninitiated as the typical site, may subtly emphasize the commercial dimensions of the web; but it cannot functionally constrain use. But Woolgar did not intend to limit our inquiry in this way; he proposed that we interpret the tool itself, its material or structural elements, its "affordances," for the assumptions it makes about the user, the activities it encourages, and the uses it literally makes impossible. This is a monumentally more difficult task, of course—we are still relatively untrained at articulating how the material elements of a tool themselves have consequences.

All tools have affordances—hammers are good for forcing nails into wood because of their sturdy and inflexible materials, their flat head, their perpendicular handle, the distribution of weight toward the point of impact. But they are not particularly good for sewing up a wound, for many of the same reasons. The suggestion here is that such affordances shape, urge, and constrain particular uses. Moreover, this regulation of social practice is not random or idiosyncratic; it is systematic, in that the activities encouraged all tend to envision the world in a certain way.

The caricature of this is to say that hammers see the world as a bunch of things to be driven forcefully into other things. But our concern is much less absurd if we talk about the affordances of a prison. The architecture of a prison is not merely a functional means to contain criminals; it suggests and authorizes a mentality in which enclosure, control, and boundaries have a heightened salience, where the walls that demarcate inside and out stand for all sorts of cultural and moral lines—right and wrong, just and depraved, human and other. And the particular design of that prison, as Foucault noted, can have additional significance for the practices and presumptions that go on both inside and out. These affordances are always purposeful, and can typically be validated in terms that justify their presence: safety, security, efficiency. But they have a double life; even as they organize behavior, they also install a worldview by which behaviors they encourage or erase. And while they do not create a mentality in their users—most people inside of a prison, convict and guard alike, have come there knowing what the space is about—they may make it subtly more difficult to envision practices that do not fit these built-in logics once they're inside.

To consider software in this way, we must look at the design of the application itself. When the tool offers a range of choices, we must consider what is left off that list. When the tool works with the hardware in a particular way, we have to uncover the economic arrangements it represents. When the tool anticipates who the user is or what he will likely do, we have to take into account the character of the social world those assumptions represent. And again, these political valences will be hidden, or will appear a natural or obvious element of the technology, or will be praised in the seductive terms of efficiency, simplicity, and empowerment.

There are a number of design features in software applications we might consider. A look at Microsoft's courtroom battles suggest that the interface between applications and operating systems has real implications for their use—so much so that the federal government worried that other uses had been rendered impossible. The struggle between the record industry and file-sharing applications like Napster was not only in the courts but in the technology, where proprietary file formats and software filters aimed to select those activities that honored copyright law and the commercial imperatives the industry championed.[19] Here I will focus on interface metaphors, the names given to the functions and features of a software application.[20]

Software designers rarely invent words for the various functions they offer a user; more often, the menu of choices is composed of words they assume the typical user will recognize, and that suggest what that feature offers. The designers at Apple certainly chose "cut," copy," and "paste" for their linguistic familiarity—and may have designed the features in certain ways to fit the terms. Some applications are designed with a coherent, overarching metaphor, while others are a bricolage of reference points drawn from several domains. Either way, these metaphors evocatively yet implicitly suggest particular uses and purposes for the tool, and the practices of users will, in subtle ways, tap into the assumptions built into these metaphors.

Interface metaphors are considered successful by designers if they seem "intuitive," and if they help the uninitiated to quickly and comfortably adopt the tool in ways that feel productive to them. But we need to be suspicious about something being "intuitive." Metaphors are not culturally neutral; those that achieve circulation do so because they are consistent with the values of the culture. Furthermore, metaphors reinforce themselves; metaphors "may create realities for us, especially social realities. A metaphor may thus be a guide for future action. Such actions will, of course, fit the metaphor. This will, in turn, reinforce the power of the metaphor to make experience coherent. In this sense metaphors can be self-fulfilling prophecies."[21] *Intuitive*, then, is often code for whether the metaphor fits an understanding of the world it already structures.

Phil Agre suggests that "metaphors operate as a 'medium of exchange'" between distinct semantic fields.[22] Their very power comes from the fact that the similarity they claim bridges a significant semantic gap—every metaphor depends on there being a difference between the two domains. "The crucial element in this formula is the difference that exists between 'the thing' and the 'something else,'" notes Steven Johnson. "What makes a metaphor powerful is the gap between the two poles of the equation."[23] In this sense, metaphors are wonderful tools; they take a phenomenon too complex to be understood in its entirety, and name it so that we may evaluate it and put it to use. They are particularly important in the process of learning; "we tend to structure the less concrete and inherently vaguer concepts . . . in terms of more concrete concepts, which are more clearly delineated in our experience."[24]

But if the metaphors we circulate have consequences for how we evaluate the world, then the ones we choose should be judged by the representation of the world they offer. George Lakoff and Mark Johnson suggest that, in every metaphor, some elements are downplayed, hidden, and rejected because they do not fit—"a metaphorical concept can keep us from focusing on other aspects of the concept that are inconsistent with that metaphor."[25] Agre imagines this as a spatial hierarchy of "centers" and "margins": "It is extraordinarily common for a philosophical system to elevate some central category as a 'normal' case, so that the integrity of the system depends on its success in hiding or explaining away the associated marginal category."[26] These hierarchical oppositions can be explicit or tacit, but they structure a semantic landscape into near and far that has implications for how the world is perceived. What is marginalized is what cannot be explained; metaphors suggest which features of the world can be named, are worth explaining, and deserve attention.

In Macromedia Director,[27] the user dictates the placement, movement, interaction, and timing of various multimedia elements—images, sounds, movies, and text. These items, stored as separate files in the computer's memory, are incorporated into the program when the user adds them to the "cast." This database keeps track of every imported item available for use in the current project. The elements are visible in a "cast window" that racks them up like yearbook photos. The user must then put these "cast members" on the "stage"—the window representing the project itself. Cast members can be dragged into place on the stage, or they can be given coordinates and times and will appear on the stage as ordered.

These metaphors from the theater are joined by an array of others in the Director interface, many of which come from other domains of media. The majority of a Director project is designed in three main windows: the "stage" (theater), the "cast" (theater, film), and the "score" (theater, film, music). Cast members are placed onto the score into individual "frames" (film), some of which can be marked as "keyframes" (cel animation) to design character movement. There are "scenes" (theater, film) that can be given "transitions" (film, video). Cast members can be expanded into graduated variations of a single image through an "onion skin" technique (cel animation), combined into a single "sprite" (computer programming) and given movement across frames by "tweening" (cel animation) between keyframes. The project can be viewed in progress using a "control panel" (video); your place within the score is marked with a "playback head" (video). When the project is complete, it is a "movie" (film) and is shown using a "projector" (film).

Lev Manovich argues that metaphors drawn from existing media have something to offer the digital interface because their projects are similar. He argues that "each of these traditions has developed its own unique ways of how information is organized, how it is presented to the user, how space and time are correlated with each other, how human experience is being structured in the process of accessing information."[28] Each cultural tradition becomes a "reservoir of metaphor" from which the interface can borrow pretested dynamics.

Digital media therefore negotiate a precarious relationship of allegiance, rivalry, dependence, and transcendence with the media that surround them. These metaphors establish a structural comparison between the two domains, based on an uneasy tension between similarity and difference, stability and change, novelty and familiarity. This metaphoric comparison highlights some features for comparison while relegating others to the margins. Our perceptions of task and context are structured in part by the metaphors we use and how they narrate the world. Most old media metaphors seem intuitive not because of familiarity of language, but because all these forms share familiar, underlying metaphors and patterns of organization—offering comfortable expectations for audience, representation, performance, and content.

the "author" in the authoring software

The question then is, how might these choices, and the worldviews they imply, shape and constrain activity when the tool is used? J. David Bolter and Richard Grusin argue that, whichever medium we happen to be experiencing, one of the pleasures is seeing ourselves within and through that medium: "When we look at a traditional photograph or a perspective painting, we understand ourselves as the reconstituted station point of the artist or the photographer."[29] This process of identification is nothing new, and has been considered before. But, when a new media "remediates" older media forms, we also must negotiate the different available subject positions inscribed in each. Our sense of ourselves, and our identification with the medium, is partially structured by the old senses of self associated with the forms being invoked.

The same kind of intersection occurs when producing for a medium. When the tools articulate multiple metaphoric relations, as in the Director interface, users find they must coordinate and negotiate multiple roles. "Cast" and "stage" and "script" suggest a theatrical production, with us as "directors"; using "keyframes" and "tweening" suggests that we consider ourselves animators, a very different role in the cultural imagination in terms of both status and relationship to the product. Working the "editor" on "pages" and "layout" suggests that we act as editors; "sprites" and "graphics" may suggest that we are computer programmers; "palettes" and "workspaces" posit us as artists. With this confluence of media metaphors comes a confluence, or perhaps a contradiction, of roles the user is invited to inhabit.

But it's less important to tease out the differences between these implied subject positions, and more important to understand what assumptions they all share; to do this, we can look at how these tools and their metaphors imagine the "author." Multimedia applications such as Director and its competitors have come to be known as "authoring software"; on Macromedia's website, Dreamweaver 2.0 got the same treatment, dubbed a "professional Web authoring environment."[30] Here a claim is made about what is being done when these tools are used, and by whom. This is only one articulation of the user offered here; there are others. But it is one situated at an interesting juncture, or disjuncture, between the assumptions about old and new media.

The character of the "author" has a long-standing but complex cultural history, and has come under fire in recent critical theory, specifically in relation to the prominence of digital media. The most common image of the modern author has been of the solitary writer at his drawing table, his nimble mind feverishly conjuring imaginary worlds of his own creation and putting them down on paper for the benefit of all humanity. Even though the act of authorship takes on many forms, very few resembling this at all, the image still enjoys a cultural resonance available to those who produce and encounter texts. Our Western attachment to a robust notion of individualism, our dependence on identity as a sign of originality and authenticity, and our mentalist theories of cognition converge to reinforce this icon of authorship.

Some new media scholars have argued that digital technologies, especially in their emphasis on collaboration and recombination, expose the fallacy of modern authorship more than previous media. The excitement around the possibility of "interactivity" anticipated a new collaboration between author and reader, where the user has the chance to wander through a landscape of information, rather than being fed a sequence of choices premade by the author—the work itself would be "authored" by both. Digital design seemed to emphasize the mixing and matching of preexisting and readily available elements, something the more traditional notion of the author minimizes in its valorization of originality.

Both Director and Dreamweaver appear to put collaboration and recombination at the forefront of digital design as they envision it. For instance, Dreamweaver allows for the placement and manipulation of digital objects, but offers little help in creating those objects. There is even an odd silence about where these "objects" are supposed to come from. In one moment of the Dreamweaver 2.0 tutorial, it says "the Objects palette contains buttons for creating various types of objects, such as images, tables, and horizontal rules . . . clicking a button creates the specified object at the cursor location." But when you "create" an image in Dreamweaver, you are actually only marking the space for an image to be placed. The tutorial later says "to insert an image, click the image button." The verb has changed to one of "insertion"; the tool presumes that preexisting elements are being recombined, whether they are borrowed from another website, designed with another tool, or scanned from another media source.[31]

We could argue that these tools, because their affordances privilege collaboration and recombination, will shape design practices in this way and will help transform the practices of authorship. Many have argued that digital technology is doing so as we speak. However, the classic notion of the author has a long cultural tradition, and will not expire so easily. And it is the media metaphors built into these tools that may powerfully curtail this transformation. While the software seems to encourage an unexpected range of authorship strategies, it dresses those strategies in a language drawn from media forms that have long supported more traditional principles.

It's not clear which is more compelling—the function, or its metaphoric name. Perhaps I should pose it as a question: Do familiar, old-media metaphors help timid users find their way into a dramatically new set of cognitive and communicative arrangements? Or do they translate everything innovative about these tools back into a conventional and conservative set of cultural relations? To begin to answer this question, we must remember that these tools are part of a moment of transition, as the software industry looks to develop an ever broader consumer base. As computers have become common household objects and the Net has expanded its reach far beyond academics, researchers, and hobbyists, the designers and corporations that create software now aspire to compete with more mainstream media forms. Where tools like these were once designed for users who very much resembled the designers, now they are made for and promoted to a wider consumer audience—and must resonate with users who do not consider themselves part of this technical design community, and who bring to the table a very different set of assumptions.

These tools must now serve as boundary objects between two different communities—those of designers and users—and thus must reconcile two significantly different investments in the notion of authorship. Software designers affiliate themselves with the worlds of science and engineering; as such, they often share their opinions about the nature of authorship, which tend to highlight collaboration as much as originality. But these tools now must appeal to users outside of this relatively limited circle. The users they seek are less familiar with or dependent on these distributed notions of authorship. They are likely to assume that "authoring" carries the connotations they know best—the solitary genius mind that produces original works of art and knowledge.

There is a tension being negotiated here; a design community that embraces a distributed notion of authorship and an open text, using tools that destabilize the more arcane of the cultural assumptions about authorship, finds it must tap those very assumptions in order to distribute that tool and have it resonate with users. This means that tools that might otherwise renovate traditional power relations are marginalized in the very effort to make them available to a wider audience. And—no surprise—this fits the commercial logic of the companies that produce these tools; as they desire both the innovation of the new and the status of the old, they must strike an awkward, compromised, and metaphoric balance between those competing impulses.

conclusion

These tools do not exist in a vacuum. Rudi Volti suggests that we think about technologies not as material artifacts, but as "technological systems" with a material artifact at the center. "When technology is seen as a combination of devices, skills, and organizational structures, it becomes natural to think of it as a *system*. For an individual technology to operate effectively more is required than the invention of a particular piece of hardware; it has to be supported by other elements that are systematically interconnected."[32] Macromedia Dreamweaver is not a program; it is a tool, a community of designers, an array of users, a medium, a corporation, and a series of cultural expectations; its implications can only be made clear once this "system" is brought into focus.

This is a way to remind ourselves that an inquiry into a piece of software may begin with interface metaphors, but cannot end there. And it is also the solution to the problem we began with, of ensuring that we never slip back into treating technologies as neutral objects. It was precisely this erasure of the social and institutional elements that helped us imagine technologies as neutral. Because we drew the boundaries around a technology at its metal or digital edges, we could not see how its affordances were crystallizations of social arrangements, its narrations were the claims and aspirations of its designers and distributors, and its functions were a staging point of a conversation between makers and users about the world they intend to create.

notes

1. Alvin M. Weinberg, "Can Technology Replace Social Engineering?" in *Technology and the Future*, ed. Albert H. Teich. (Boston: Bedford/St. Martin's, 2000), 32.

2. Wiebe E. Bijker, *Of Bicycles, Bakelites, and Bulbs: Toward a Theory of Sociotechnical Change.* (Cambridge, Mass.: MIT Press, 1995), 288.

3. Langdon Winner, "Do Artifacts Have Politics?" *Daedalus* 109, no. 1 (1980): 122.

4. Michael Cole, *Cultural Psychology: A Once and Future Discipline* (Cambridge, Mass.: Belknap Press of Harvard University Press, 1996), 117.

5. Bernward Joerges discusses the way the Moses parable has been mythologized in the literature on technology, noting especially that Moses's bridges may have been that height because of federal statutes, or architectural traditions that nostalgized low bridges as an American tradition. His point is not to discount Winner's theoretical claim, but to note how the intellectual discourse picks and chooses how and why it circulates such "splendid pieces of ready-made discourse" as parables. Steve Woolgar and Geoff Cooper question Winner's story for its apocryphal power in their field as well, noting that anecdotal evidence seems to suggest that buses *did* travel to Jones Beach along the parkways. Their task is more epistemological, taking both Winner and Joerges to task for putting too much faith in technologies as definitive artifacts and dismissing articulation (even their own) as somehow secondary. Instead, they urge a renewed sense of "the essential ambivalence of artefacts." See Bernward Joerges, "Do Politics Have Artefacts?" *Social Studies of Science* 29, no. 3 (1999): 420; Steve Woolgar and Geoff Cooper, "Do Artefacts Have Ambivalences? Moses' Bridges, Winner's Bridges, and Other Urban Legends of STS," *Social Studies of Science* 29, no. 3 (1999): 443.

6. Winner, "Do Artifacts Have Politics?" 124.

7. Bruno Latour, "Mixing Humans and Nonhumans Together: The Sociology of a Door-Closer," *Social Problems* 35 (1988): 276.

8. This is worth leaving as an open question, although we should start by taking particular care about whom we assume to be the "designer" of a particular technology. The question of intentionality presumes that an individual can be reliably labeled as the tool's originator, a presumption that deserves some skepticism. It may also be that focusing too much on intent ends up limiting the means for change; when the disabled community sponsored laws requiring wheelchair access, they did not get far by pointing only at the deliberate, malicious intent of particular architects and designers. It was more compelling to argue that the architecture itself discriminated against them, not the people; making the technology the enemy meant making fewer political enemies in the process.

9. Michel Foucault, *Discipline and Punish: The Birth of the Prison*, 1st American ed., trans. Alan Sheridan (New York: Pantheon Books, 1977), 195–228.

10. Lawrence Lessig, *Code and Other Laws of Cyberspace* (New York: Basic Books, 1999).

11. Bruno Latour, "Review of Edwin Hutchins' *Cognition in the Wild*," *Mind, Culture, and Activity* 3, no. 1 (1996): 56.

12. Edwin Hutchins, *Cognition in the Wild* (Cambridge, Mass.: MIT Press, 1995), 173.

13. Bruno Latour, "Visualization and Cognition: Thinking with Eyes and Hands." *Knowledge and Society: Studies in the Sociology of Culture Past and Present* 6 (1986): 6.

14. Steve Woolgar. "Configuring the User: The Case of Usability Trials," in *A Sociology of Monsters: Essays on Power, Technology, and Domination*, ed. John Law (London: Routledge, 1991), 69.

15. Macromedia is one of the most prominent producers of such tools, focusing primarily on applications that produce for CD-ROM and online environments. Macromedia was incorporated in 1992 when two existing software companies, Macromind and Authorware, merged; now it's traded on NASDAQ. In the nine months ending December 31, 2001, Macromedia earned $249.1 million. (Macromedia website, <http://www.macromedia.com/macromedia/ir/>, accessed January 20, 2002.) That revenue is drawn almost entirely from sales of its design applications: Director and Dreamweaver, as well as Flash, Freehand, Authorware, Fireworks, and ColdFusion.

    Introduced in 1997, Dreamweaver marked Macromedia's entrance into the market of WYSIWYG—"what you see is what you get"—web editors. Like multimedia presentations, web sites were originally all written in the computer code called HTML. But as the web reached a wider audience, a market developed for tools that would bypass the need for HTML expertise, offering users the chance to design websites simply by arranging text and graphics visually. Programs like Dreamweaver provide the design space and the controls, then compose the HTML to match.

16. Macromedia Dreamweaver 2.0, guided tour.

17. Macromedia Dreamweaver 3.0, tutorial.

18. Macromedia website, <http://www.macromedia.com/macromedia/>, accessed January 20, 2002.

19. For more on this subject, see Tarleton Gillespie, "Sleight of Hand: Law, Technology, and the Moral Deployment of Authorship in the Napster and DeCSS Copyright Cases"; Ph.D., diss., University of California, San Diego, January 2002.

20. I have to note at this point that I am, despite my own warnings, choosing a discursive feature of the technology to analyze; it's possible that I'm falling into the same trap as I noted before, where treating technology like a text à la Woolgar leads us to notice the most text-like aspects. However, interface metaphors are, I would argue, fundamentally different than something like a tutorial; the tutorial narrates the tool through example, whereas the interface metaphor literally stands for the function of the tool. Since these metaphors are the only visible element of a feature of the tool, what they fail to represent is, for argument's sake, simply not a part of the tool.

21. George Lakoff and Mark Johnson, *Metaphors We Live By* (Chicago: University of Chicago Press, 1980), 156.

22. Phil Agre, *Computation and Human Experience* (Cambridge: Cambridge University Press, 1997), 37.

23. Steven Johnson, *Interface Culture* (San Francisco: Harper Edge, 1997), 58–59.

24. Lakoff and Johnson, *Metaphors*, 112.

25. Ibid., 10.

26. Agre, *Computation*, 43.

27. Director, introduced by Macromind in 1984, was originally conceived as a two-dimensional computer animation tool. But after weak sales, a version 2.0 upgrade in 1990 significantly reimagined Director as a multimedia

design tool for business and education professionals—particularly by adding Lingo, a scripting language that allowed the possibility of interactivity in the presentations it produced. Director quickly found and dominated its market just as the CD-ROM seemed to have become a viable medium for business and a consumer market. When the CD-ROM format faltered and the web came to prominence, Macromedia again shifted Director's focus by developing Shockwave, a plug-in application for web browsers that can present Director projects delivered via the Internet. Macromedia released Director 8.0 in 2001.

28. Lev Manovich, "Cinema as a Cultural Interface." Available at <http://jupiter.ucsd.edu/~manovich/text/cinema-cultural.html> (1998).

29. J. David Bolter and Richard Grusin, *Remediation: Understanding New Media* (Cambridge, Mass.: MIT Press, 1999), 231.

30. Macromedia website, <http://www.macromedia.com>, accessed February 18, 1999.

31. Ironically, Macromedia's copy editors caught this incongruency; the language was changed in version 3.0, to "the Object palette contains buttons for *inserting* objects such as tables, layers, and images." See Macromedia Dreamweaver 3.0, Help menu, "Dreamweaver basics; Object palette".

32. Rudi Volti, *Society and Technological Change*, 3d ed. (New York: St. Martin's Press, 1995), 5.

prefiguring

digitextuality

second-shift

media aesthetics

programming,

interactivity, and

user flows

j o h n t . c a l d w e l l

The show will flow back and forth between the Web and
TV. We're going to be laying some new ground (with
Homicide.com).
>   —*writer/producer Ayelet Sela on new flows resulting*
>   *from Web-TV tie-in.*

The much-heralded Internet series (Homicide.com) has
amassed numerous awards, including two Inovision
Awards for Story/Script and Web Design, and a prestigious 1998 *ID* Magazine Media Design Review.
>   —*Microsoft press release promoting Windows MediaPlayer as*
>   *the means to witness NBC's convergence of the series*
>   Homicide: Life on the Streets, *the website Homicide:*
>   *The Second Shift, and a special "Homicide.com" episode.*

Both new and old media trade publications continue to invoke modernist notions of "cutting-edge" originality, innovation, and radicality

to promote progress in their respective industries. The "Homicide.com" sweeps-week stunt during February 1999,[1] for example, served as curatorial bait for an eclectic phalanx of trade writers and vested interests intent on promoting the expansion of the digital and dot-com worlds. This event, many surmised, represented the ultimate integration and seamless convergence of old and new media. Since 1997, the website Homicide: The Second Shift had depicted life on the flip side of the show. That is, as the prime-time stars left their one hour broadcast "shift," web surfers could watch the precinct and replacement personnel on the Internet during the other "23 hours" of the day. The acclaimed sweeps stunt began with second-shift detectives investigating webcast crimes committed on Wednesday and Thursday of the week. On Friday night, the "first-shift" detectives on NBC's televised series continued the same investigation and sought to solve the ritualistic murders that had earlier been webcast. This search involved a descent into the frenetic and dark world of Internet culture, with producers and consultants bragging that there would be eighty scenes in this special episode rather than the normal forty to sixty.[2] This dramatized, televisual cyberworld included fake e-mail solicitations, chat rooms, and recurrent hacker interventions.

To solve the murders the onscreen detectives eventually enjoined all members of the composite precinct to help solve the crime online, even as they themselves were shown between acts playing a computer arcade game featuring a female figure blasting away at her animated prey. As the show built up to its cliff-hanger, NBC ended the hour by advertising the website where the narrative would continue after the TV show ended. Homicide.com then showed the second-shift detectives continuing the investigation, sifting through video fragments that had earlier been webcast (before) or broadcast (after) the first crime had been committed. The site also gave web users at home the ability to sift through audio and video clips of the evidence itself, to interview the suspects, and to play an online version of the very arcade computer game that detectives of both shifts had played in the analog and digital worlds. Frenetic web use now pervaded each register of reality available in the integrated convergent stunt: the televised cast, the webcast cast, and actual web users all now logged-on, chatted, threatened, downloaded, and played the same digitized video and audio clips and computer games, and sifted throught the same clues, in an ostensibly synergistic ecstasy of digital euphoria.

My suspicions at the time about the significance of the critically acclaimed, seamless stunt proved warranted, as the award-winning but low-rated series and integrated site came and then went off the air and offline. And while other shows like Fox's *Freakylinks* and Freakylinks.com continued to angle for critical acclaim to get a leg up in the ratings wars in the next season (by hyping radical aesthetic innovation and online integration with content), the vast majority of TV/dot-com sites today are far less ambitious narratively and aesthetically than these showcased exercises in visionary convergence. Sifting through the various technical and economic interests involved in the Homicide.com stunt suggests that institutional relationships and industrial leveraging may have been far more important than the aesthetic forms that comprised the event. "Authorship" for the show was claimed by many involved in the effort: NBC (which aired the show), NBC Digital Productions (which produced the integrated project), NBC.com (which promoted the show's site on the web), the Homicide.com Internet producer Ayelet Sela (who pitched and then cowrote the televised script), and Barry Levinson and Tom Fontana's production company (which produces and owns the show in syndication). Authorship of this screen-Net stunt was also claimed by the coalition of business partners that created the event, including ZDTV (an internet programming and consulting firm);[3] Internet piracy consultants from the Web series "Cyber-CrimeTV" (lawyers Alex Wellen and Luke Reiter);[4] and the Microsoft corporation.[5]

Each partner leveraged the TV/dot-com stunt to increase market share in its own industrial sector. ZDTV (an Internet "technology publisher whose website covers tales of hacking, [and] electronic eavesdropping") hyped its own marginally rated webcast programming.[6] Consultant Wellen used the experience to create a segment for his own Net series.[7] Internet personnel at Homicide.com earned a prime-time television screenwriting credit via the stunt. But Microsoft worked and spun the event with as much intensity as any of the other players. With a summary of the event's aesthetic features as mere icing on its lengthy press release, Microsoft proceeded to promote not just its Windows MediaPlayer as "the" way to access the celebrated synergy,[8] but also devoted considerable promotional copy to describing the wide-ranging extent and nature of its contractual business relationships throughout digital and electronic media: "With Microsoft, NBC owns and operates MSNBC, a 24-hour cable news network, and (the) Internet News Service at www.msnbc.com. Also, together with Microsoft and Dow Jones, NBC operates CNBC/Dow Jones Business Video. . . . Other new media innovations from NBC include interactive television initiatives with Microsoft WebTV for Windows and the WebTV Network Plus service, Wink-enhanced programming with Wink Communications, NBC Intercast with Intel Corp., electronic program guides with Gemstar, and on-demand video services with Intertainer. . . . Microsoft, Windows, WebTV, WebTV Network, Windows NT, and NetShow are registered trademarks in the United States."[9] Executives at NBC hyped Homicide.com as if it were akin to the second coming: "more than a simple tie-in between a

Web-site and a television show: *it is an actual convergence of entertainment media.*"[10] Microsoft, however, more deftly deconstructed the subtext of this convergent art form via the (now essential) financial market lexicon: "Founded in 1975, Microsoft (is listed on) Nasdaq as 'MSFT.'"[11] Like a predatory male marking its turf, Microsoft invoked an endless series of proprietary, brand-related trademarks. Like an all-knowing conglomerate, Microsoft sketched a networked empire so broad that the sun might never stop shining on its endlessly augmenting parts. Like a boardroom sage turned earnest financial advisor, Microsoft discreetly shared an insider's critically valuable stock investment tip: "MSFT."

As this dense example suggests, cutting-edge accomplishment in digital aesthetics frequently provides pressure points and lucrative contact zones where a broad set of new institutional practices and proprietary strategies interact. This sort of phenomenon begs the question of whether film studies can continue to talk productively about texts, aesthetics, ideology, and identity in new media (all standby analytical perspectives in the field of film studies) without also talking about the industrial landscape that animates and fuels new-media development on a wide scale. Answering such a question, I would argue, unsettles a number of recurrent assumptions and critical tendencies, as I hope to show in the pages that follow.

It is no longer entirely credible, for example, to imagine that digital media is somehow marked by a radical break with traditional media practices. The Microsoft-NBC conglomeration scenario above shows how meticulously managed and prefigured "new" breakthroughs have become. Even mainstream, primetime narratives in the domestic sphere, for instance, now provide unremarkable reflections on the now naive and overly optimistic promises of cybertech, the high-techs, and dot-coms. An episode of *The Simpsons* that aired April 28, 2002, for example, showed Bart struggling to develop his own animated series. After zeroing in on the title "Danger Dad," Bart drew crude images of father Homer in various states of tirade, and then pitched his series to legendary DC Comics founder Stan Lee. The animated Lee—whose real-life counterpart was in the process of premiering his own blockbuster film *Spiderman* worldwide five days later—scoffed at the quality of Bart's comic book. This rejection sent Bart to another possible buyer, and a new digital startup—"Better than TV.com"—which launched the rejected project as an animated "online series."

The Simpsons creators and its audience on Fox were critically mocking online culture (which paid Bart and Lisa with "stock options" dispensed from toilet paper rolls), the naïveté of venture capitalists (whose startup on this show went down in the flames of bankruptcy), and the hubris of dot-com CEOs (who somehow imagined they were creating a viable alternative to the Hollywood animation and television industries). Matt

Groening, James L. Brooks, and company were mocking the fact that the newcomers (like the real-world network TV wanna-bes "Mondo Media," "JoeCartoon.com," and "Spunky" on the Net) had only actually delivered crudely drawn, QuickTime and Flash animations (which stuttered at glacially slow frame rates), with content that embodied infantile, male, adolescent sensibilities. Celebrated cult breakthroughs like the animated series *South Park* had broken through to cable in 1997–98 precisely because of such qualities. In hindsight, however, this discovery turned out to be the exception that proved the rule. *The Simpsons*/ Fox/Newscorp/ Hollywood–versus–dot-com/startup episode, and the Homicide.com/NBC/WebTV/ ZDTV/Microsoft tie-in are more than just displays of postmodern cynicism or conglomerate hype. Both examples also stand as forms of institutional and market deployment; both critically exploit digital media aesthetics to leverage cultural capital, visibility, and financial benefit; and both help—through branding strategies and discourses of distinction—to position and value their respective conglomerates in the capital markets.

The emerging and ever-morphing digital mediascape that these examples map challenges the unfortunate gap that exists between political-economy and industry research on the one hand (which tends to ignore texts and forms entirely), and critical studies in the humanities on the other (which tend to avoid issues of economy, commercialization, and industry). Both practitioners and critical theorists invoke aesthetic schemes, albeit in different ways. This chapter examines a range of textual forms used in TV/dot-com sites, and looks closely at several the author considers to be both influential and symptomatic of new forms of user flows: Homicide.com, freakylinks.com, dawsonscreek.com, thexfiles.com; the websites of the TV series *Futurama* and *Sex and the City;* the networks HBO and WB; and fan sites. Furthermore, the chapter seeks to consider the ways that long-standing strategies in television and broadcasting—programming, syndication, licensing, branding, and flows—have emerged as textual engines that prefigure the design of new media forms.

I draw attention to the rather commonplace example from *The Simpsons* cited above not to show that old media has somehow "won" in its struggle over new media. Rather, I suggest that what we might term "convergence media" in the digital era is not defined by any new technically induced or determined quality or capacity, but instead defines itself in the ways that networks and studios use convergence initiatives to implement long-standing industry practices mentioned above. Scholars that ignore such workaday strategies and practices in theorizing new media place their own studies in doubt. Throughout the 1990s, scholars in the fields of visual arts and film studies in particular rushed to embrace digital and new-media forms in conferences and exhibitions as important parts of their changing disciplines. Yet a recurring pattern in such venues was the attempt to connect digital media with early protocinematic forms (in film studies) and early avant-garde and art-world forms (in the visual arts) that prefigured new media by as much as a century.

As I have argued elsewhere, such scholars somehow managed (through ignorance or intention) to ignore the sixty to seventy years of television and broadcasting history that now seem to have assumed a much more central role in inflecting and defining new media than either film or art-world practices.[12] Television, to many academics in the higher disciplinary castes, represents the world of commerce and easy entertainment. Television's preoccupation with programming and syndication, that is, apparently pales in the face of the theoretical opportunities promised when one presupposes radical experiential and cognitive results from any new technology. I hope to suggest how viewing new media through the lens of old media (and television in particular) can provide a range of insights into the increasingly complex strategies used in the deployment of digital media forms.

I have hijacked and adapted the term *second-shift aesthetics* from the celebrated tie-in cited earlier not to describe digital technologies, interactive programs, or software as bounded objects of analysis; rather, I hope to describe a growing and ubiquitous world of digital that employs traditional and modified "programming strategies" in the design of everything from interface and software design to merchandizing and branding campaigns.[13] The very term *aesthetics* employed here had largely disappeared from film theory by the 1980s, since it was deemed an archaic approach bound up with the retrograde ideologies of classicism and romanticism. Yet I think the term helps bridge the unfortunate gap that has widened between academic studies of industry, from a political-economic perspective, and critical studies in the humanities. Producers and critical media theorists deploy aesthetic schemes, but to different ends. A concern with texts stands as the common ground between the two professional communities. Textualism, of course, is a dominant perspective in both critical and cultural studies, even though revisionists now propose ways to eclipse it.[14]

Media professionals, on the other hand—who (with little prompting) might denigrate the pompous pretensions of critical intellectuals who presume to speculate authoritatively on media—themselves go to great ends to explain, rationalize, perpetuate, and critically evaluate film/video/new-media content. Although the resulting critical discourses rarely seem to intermingle (let alone impact each other), both worlds privilege the stuff at the heart of the aesthetic exchange. For media practitioners this is termed "content"; for critics these are termed "texts." As I have argued elsewhere, it is almost impossible to talk usefully today of conglomeration, globalization, and industry without talking about texts; and impossible to talk of texts or identity today without also talking about their corporate logic and institutional significance.[15] In some ways this assertion is a reaction to what might be termed the "gnostic" inclinations of critical theory to date; that is, to the tendency to disembody and deindustrialize meanings, ideology, power, and identity in theory.[16] The examples examined here suggest that new-media authoring and end-user activities are both integral and strategic parts of most business plans in various media convergence schemes.

first-shift aesthetics: content flows, supertext, and programming strategies

Understanding second-shift aesthetics means re-considering the ways that Raymond Williams's model of television's "flow" and Nick Browne's model of television's "supertext" have both developed and adapted in the increasingly digital world of convergence media. Both paradigms were used to describe electronic media in the analog age of network television and cable (in 1975 and 1984, respectively), and both strategies have been challenged by recent digital media developments. Williams argued that the most significant object of critical research in television was not the individual programs that critics tended to isolate, but rather the cumulative succession of programs, promos, previews, ads, and bumpers that could create a single flow on a network across several programming hours. While this seemed like a radical idea to many scholars at the time, flow theory actually existed in network programming departments since the early 1950s. Browne's insight was to link these flow strategies to several practices, including: programming "day-parts" (daytime, prime time, off-prime time, late night, etc.); the political economy of the industry; and the ideologies that managed these temporal, organizing strategies. The composite, televisual viewing forms that resulted he termed the "supertext"—a paradigm that required critical theorists to privilege the contextual "clutter" (ads, promos, and previews interspersed throughout any broadcast) in addition to and together with any specific show being aired.

The supertext proposition allowed critical scholars to begin considering politicoeconomic issues in industry (context) as integral parts of any program (text). Although few critical theorists acknowledged it, the flow/supertext methodologies in effect allowed critics to "discover" some very basic strategies that broadcast and network programming departments had mastered and deployed for decades in industry. Because I am interested in digital form and aesthetics (as well as institutional analysis), I consider these (predigital) programming strategies to comprise what might be termed "first-shift" aesthetics. Programmers have since used various means to attract viewers organized around the concept of day parts, which include the segments: morning, afternoon, early fringe, prime access, prime time, late fringe, late night, and overnight. "Counterprogramming" tactics can be deployed in any given day part, and involve airing programs that attract and award distinctively different demographics from those of a competing network. In the late 1980s, for example, CBS programmed Monday nights as "women's night" (with sitcoms like *Murphy Brown*) as a counter to the male-dominant demographics of ABC's *Monday Night Football*. The new Fox network achieved much of its success around the same time by counterprogramming edgier fare like the *Simpsons* against the much older demographic in CBS's Sunday evening lineup. From 2000 to 2002, struggling weblet UPN counterprogrammed the ratings dominance of the major networks with what it termed "UPN Mondays." This attempt to grab a foothold in the market share actually consisted of an evening of "black-block" programming: four successive sitcoms involving African Americans (*The Hughleys*, *One on One*, *The Parkers*, and *Girlfriends*). Herman Gray has demonstrated how this programming marquee racially produced, popularized, and circulated "blackness" as one industrial key to the survival of struggling UPN in the "neo-network" era.[17]

CBS had demonstrated the effectiveness of another programming strategy, "tent-poling," in the design of its Sunday prime-time lineup since 1980. For many years the network showcased the highly rated and venerable *60 Minutes* to bring viewers "into the tent" (as executives described it); that is, to gather viewers around the less distinguished shows that surrounded it on that evening. A third programming strategy is "hammocking"—a technique by which new and untested shows are launched between two successful and ratings-proven series. NBC repeatedly used this strategy as part of its Thursday night "must-see-TV" campaign in the 1990s, when it premiered a succession of new and untested shows in the much-sought-after half-hour slot between *Seinfeld* and *Fraser*, for example. Such a slot guarantees that any new show in it will have the residual benefit of the ratings leaders that precede and follow it. Programming departments spend considerable efforts deploying other tactics as well, including "stunting" (special episodes that break genre formulas during sweeps weeks), and "seamlessness." NBC championed the latter strategy when it eliminated all breaks between shows on the same network and required each successive sitcom to start midaction rather than with obligatory and standardized (but less attention-grabbing) title sequences. The goal of all of these strategies was to keep viewers engaged with a single network's proprietary, ad-sponsored "flow."

Several fundamental shifts upset the effectiveness of these strategies. Cable, the VCR, the remote-control, multichannel cable and satellite services, video-on-demand, and finally the Internet all promoted a fragmentation of the flow, and thus a precipitous decline of the major networks, all of whom had developed and depended upon classical "first-shift" programming campaigns for decades. I would argue that these new technologies did not only increase "churn" (the rate at which viewers cancelled one service for another) or "grazing" (the rate at which viewers turned to and scanned other channel choices while watching a show) but also attacked the fundamental, institutional logic that had served as the very foundation of network television. Producers, programmers, and content developers in the digital era could no longer strategize and sequence their flows around an economy of discrete day-part demographics. Each specific day part had traditionally been linked confidently to the spending practices of very specific audiences sectors—which advertising agencies then focused on in mass target-marketing campaigns, and which network executives custom developed content for. Digital technologies are now integrated widely across industrial sectors and throughout the major media conglomerations. The difficulty of creating or predicting a serial textual composite—within a single convergent multimedia company—makes it very difficult to predict linear viewing patterns, and to realize a viable flow "inside" of the bounded brand of a network. Although programming departments historically have attempted to lock viewers into a linear, sequential viewing pattern within or inside of a single, bounded brand, the Internet, personal video recorders, and multitasking have made this an unrealistic and improbable goal.

second-shift aesthetics: niche-ing, dispersal, and user flows

Many cybertheologists like Pierre Levy and Paul Virilio (following Marshall McLuhan's lead) have cultivated liberatory and utopian assertions in their characterizations of digital as a cyber-neural-spatial revolution in consciousness.[18] Yet digital media, the Internet, and AOL—all ostensibly responsive "pull media" forms rather than "push media" forms (the latter, an "outdated" type favored by Hollywood studios and network television, according to Nicholas Negroponte[19])—did not end the need for programming strategies. In fact, the dispersed, amorphous world of digital networking and multitasking has made the need for content programming in the digital era even more compelling. After the collapse of the virtual economies of the dot-coms, any good business plan will now at least (attempt to) attest to this fact. Instead of cleanly replacing first-shift aesthetics, that is, the new landscape of convergence has forced content providers to continue to adapt and overhaul the means and goals of programming, in order to succeed in far more volatile media markets. These adapted strategies I term "second-shift aesthetics." Second-shift practices attempt to bring new forms of rationality to unstable media economies. Venture capital requires this sort of rationality—imagining that such things deliver a requisite predictability as well.

In many ways, second-shift practices are logical responses to several interrelated historical and industrial shifts: from broadcasting to multi-channel narrowcasting; from mass economies of scale to niche economies of scope; and from serial flows to tangential and cyclical flows. Instead of the linear textual compositing model inherent in supertext/flow theory, TV/dot-com synergies now must learn to master *textual dispersals* and user navigations that can and will inevitably *migrate* across brand boundaries. In essence, programming strategies have shifted from notions of network *program* "flows" to tactics of *audience/user* "flows." Targeted day parts are a thing of the past now that media users can digitally go to almost any content, via multiple channels, at any time of the day or night. Successful multimedia development, therefore, means being able to track, monitor, and predict—or at least respond quickly to—multidirectional user flows and migrations. As a result, digital programmers must develop new units of temporal-user measurement.

Second-shift aesthetics involves the management of ancillary and digital sites that users migrate to from a primary or initial site. In the crudest formulations, network sports and news shows on ESPN or CBS direct viewers to their respective websites (espn.com and cbs.com) to mine the minutiae of sports statistics or financial and "CBS Market-Watch" data. At other times, television networks like the WB use websites (thewb.com) as program indexes and promotional billboards to send viewers back to televised shows. Both of these unremarkable tactics still fit the traditional, unidirectional model of flow/supertext. Yet many other websites design bidirectional or circular protocols in the "click-throughs" they privilege. In the Freakylinks.com/Fox tie-in (fall 2000), online narrative clues directed users to televised plots and clues in prime time, which in turn sent viewers back to the web for further textual elaboration and interaction during the week. The WB's www.dawsonscreek.com site allowed fans to read the personal diaries of characters in the show, and to "hack" into the private e-mails of those same characters. Such tactics elaborate the kind of "back story" that screenwriters typically include in the production company's "bible" that orients the series over its lifespan. This kind of second-shift tactic provides discursive grist for narratological analysis that is easily as complex as that offered by any novel. Websites for series as different at HBO's *Sex and the City* and WB's *Dawson's Creek* also allow users to "direct" their own virtual tours of the "actual" sets used in the show as QuickTime "movies" on the Net.[20] Again, these secondary textual activities can be viewed, in the traditional critical sense, as stylistic augmentations to some original text. Although complicated, these aggregate texts still fit an easily recognizable aesthetic schema.

The *Dawson's Creek* and *Sex and the City* sites also allow user-viewers to click and purchase fashions and commodities used by stars on the show (backpacks and locker paraphenalia on the one hand; t-shirts and martini glasses on the other). Clearly second-shift augmentations here "flow" the viewer outside of any televisual or digital text into the material world of consumerism proper. But the sites go further, and provide what are essentially "narrations" that user-purchasers can employ to choreograph themselves once they enter the world of merchandising. The *Dawson's Creek* site whispers directorial motivations to the viewer-consumer-actors at home: "Buy like Brad, give like Gwyneth, shop like a celebrity, win a $5,000 shopping spree sponsored by NeimanMarcus.com." These second-shift augmentations, while not aesthetic texts in the traditional sense, are still material forms: text-related merchandising scenarios that are being comprehensively programmed as part of allied vested interests.

But what are we to make of flows that exit proprietary texts and merchandising entirely in order to preoccupy the user-viewer in the world at large? HBO encourages viewers, for example, to go to digital simulations (and then to the actual geographic sites) of "the hottest and hippest nightspots" in New York, to bars and restaurants that have no apparent fiduciary relationship to either HBO or the show's producers. This kind of extratextual dispersal gives at least some second-shift programming the profile of entropy—of a declining, then flat-lined dramatic arc—and is about as far from the hard sell of traditional ad-driven electronic media as one can imagine. Granted, we can always surmise that premium services like HBO are really selling lifestyle and not just bottom-line electronic content. I would argue, however, that more is going on here than general affirmations of cosmopolitanism. Current research shows that children and adolescents in particular are very good at multitasking—at using the web, TV, phone, videogame, and CD player all at the same time. Yet what these HBO viewer-users are *not* doing (in the bars, restaurants, and nightlife of any city) is watching TV. How can this goal be a logical part of any cost-conscious programmer's plans? The answer, I think, comes in the programming logic of "tiering" and "branding."

aggregating, tiering, branding

The economic rewards that used to follow from a program's mass-audience share no longer stand as realistic corporate goals. Media corporations now must try to master the cumulative "aggregation" of audiences from across the fragmented demographic niches that compromise the proliferating, multichannel market. The success of narrowcasting as a programming strategy in the 1980s is said to have ended the "economies of scale" that defined the network era. Narrowcasting succeeded because of its ability to return lucrative, "niche" demographic segments of the audience to program suppliers and networks who could, as a result, charge higher advertising rates. The current media conglomerates, however, can no longer sufficiently capitalize their operations by exploiting this kind of limited economy of "scope." Instead, large media companies seek to incorporate diversity and cultural difference (and their attendant revenues) by combining them within a single, integrated corporate structure. The dispersed flows and migrations that I have characterized above—of both texts and viewers—produces highly fragmented revenue streams. Since this kind of fragmentation is difficult to associate with single brand identity, corporations like AOL/Time-Warner/HBO/Showtime/CNN/Turner now specialize in "tiering" numerous brand-inflected niches within the uber-brand. HBO now charges cable and satellite users a gradation of premiums for no less than sixteen "different" channel "tiers." There is no need to go to Lifetime or Oxygen when women viewers have HBO Signature; no need to go to IFC, Bravo, or the Sundance Channel when cineastes and aesthete-viewers can see "cutting-edge," vanguard film on HBO Zone; no need to go to the Disney Channel or Pax TV when children have HBO Family. No need to switch to BET when African Americans are sold on critically acclaimed depictions of African Americans on HBO and its sister brand Showtime (in series like *Soul Food*). No need to switch to general cable channels like MSNBC, either, when HBO news viewers can switch instead to Turner's CNN, an important affiliate in the HBO conglomerate.

What has essentially happened is that individual media conglomerates have attempted to engineer the mannerisms of the multichannel universe within the branded walls of the conglomerate. Brands in the digital era are expected to function in far more extensive and complex ways than they were in the analog age. In the past, a limited set of basic product and trademark names functioned as brands, whose ad agencies sponsored mass-audience television shows in the network era. Branding has now become an obligatory specialization, one that requires continual reinflection as technological, market, and regulatory changes ripple through the industry. Branding aims to market services that are identified not by specific products but by highly individuated and easily recognized corporate personalities. In this scheme, effective branding is frequently praised for having created psychological and empathic relationships with consumers. HBO and its uber-conglomerate have proliferated variants of the mother brand, which invoke cultural difference without straying from the "emotional core" of the original brand. The AOL/Time-Warner/HBO brand is so complicated that most websites within the conglomerate provide either linkages to other corporate affiliates, or schematic descriptions, maps, and users' guides that help the web user understand his location within the uber-brand.

Architects of conglomeration regularly deem such relationship networks in press releases as "synergies." Such practices also show, however, that conglomerates have imposed and adapted flow strategies that are now intended to work within their proprietary, and newly aggregated, world—even though migrations now flow multidirectionally across potentially endless numbers of channels and niches.

This characterization of intrabrand flows, of course, is the boardroom fantasy of many a corporation. What actually occurs in TV-Net usage is that users migrate in all sorts of directions that can only be loosely encouraged with incentives, rather than controlled in any sense. First-shift flow programming is heavy-handed if compared to the management of dispersed flows that takes place in second-shift arenas. HBO is willing to provide minimal links to its affiliates outside of HBO (with links to "free AOL service," to AOL Box Office, and to Turner's Cartoon Network, for example). Other entities try to partner and cobrand in order to steer users to corporations with shared economic interests—even if they are in different sectors of the economy. NBC could viably partner with Microsoft (MSNBC) but not HBO; it could create a portal with Snap.com and ShopNBC rather than with AOL. But even these alliances "leak" on the Net. This inherent leakiness in flow management means that cable executives now strategize (and program) degrees of "stickiness" in the second-shift world (with stickiness being the extent to which providers can induce users to stay with a package of services). At the NCTA (National Cable Television Association) convention on May 15, 2002, management panelists all concurred that the notion of homogenous content "convergence" is, in many ways, a myth. CEOs from Time-Warner Cable, AT&T Cable, Charter Communications, and others asserted that viewer "churn" only improved when companies provided a package of different services within a single delivery system (video, data, telephony, enhanced TV, etc.).[21]

The CEO of Wink Communications (an "enhanced TV provider") summed up the insight that higher customer satisfaction came from packaging different services and thus "creating value on a single platform."[22] In some ways this notion (of diverse packaging/singular delivery) mirrors the ways that branding (in the age of digital) works by producing diversity and difference within a single uber-brand. But textual dispersal and flow leakiness also mean that content providers must now learn looser forms of management to master programming in the second shift. Other interests and sites can (and regularly do) pull users out of branded confines. Following the pattern established by CBS's *Survivor* phenomenon, reality shows like ABC's *The Bachelor* provided Disney/ABC with intrabrand flow and tie-in possibilities. But as each female contestant was exiled from the show, many other news and entertainment shows aired by local stations (KROQ, KISS) or in first-run syndication (*Access Hollywood, Entertainment Tonight*) also solicited and then showcased the banished contestants as part of their own proprietary special segments.[23]

These forms of regular textual appropriation—across competing proprietary brands and technologies—are now pervasive parts of media-business practice. Media companies intending to master the second shift, that is, must move beyond unilateral programming schemes in order to master more nuanced and dialogic forms appropriations. In place of the "command-and-control" tactics of first-shift programming, emerged second-shift strategies oriented more like the fluid responsiveness preached in Lao Tzu's *Art of War*. Matt Groening's series *Futurama* on Fox, for example, quickly generated a range of "unauthorized" fan sites (like "Can't Get Enough *Futurama* [CGEF]). CGEF immediately pirated and offered downloads of each and every episode of the series that Fox broadcast. To add insult to injury, a banner ad on the CGEF site soon boasted "the REAL Futurama site"—a gesture that essentially taunted the producers, and denigrated the poor content, on Fox's "official" *Futurama* website. Fox and Newscorp initiated legal threats against the CGEF site that were only partially successful; the pirating and downloading went on. But Fox had by now learned the potential of endless reciprocity now possible in the second shift. The *Futurama* producing staff established that they knew well the forms of appropriation that were going on (and that they were hardly threatened), when they added a prominent title to each televised episode: "*Futurama*, coming to an illegal DVD near you soon." CGEF countered that their website downloads were still a much better alternative than watching *Futurama* on a "primitive television screen." And so forth.

Far from being a significant legal case or fiduciary threat in any sense, this back-and-forth textual appropriation was actually just very good business for a marginally rated animated series like *Futurama*. Many other examples of two-way textual appropriations pervade the TV/Net relationship. Second-shift aesthetics, however, are not simply about TV/Net relations. They characterize new initiatives to "brand" or "cross-brand" the world of wireless technologies as well. Walt Disney, Vivendi Universal, and AOL–Time Warner have all recently negotiated deals with wireless phone companies, "with visions of wireless phones becoming hand-held entertainment centers."[24] Universal pictures signed with Nokia to provide "logos and ring-tones" from its recognizable studio properties. Disney is providing "games, graphics and ring-tones" to AT&T so its customers can "individuate" and assign various studio songs and properties to the personality profiles of incoming callers. "Sony Ericsson" is introducing what it terms "multimedia phones" as platforms to promote Sony "franchises" (like *Men in Black* and *Charlie's Angels*), and as portable PlayStation videogame consoles. While many now characterize such initiatives as evidence of a move toward (non-PC) "ubiquitous computing" and "digitally augmented *space*", I would argue that these technologies are also about building a user-relationship in *time*. The multimedia wireless experience is an outgrowth and development of second-shift programming. Defining experience away from primary or first-shift content by the brand stands as an exercise in affect, and as a relationship-building gesture. One consultant argues that consistency of message, copy, content, or information is not the issue. Rather, "brand consistency lies in core values . . . and identifiable style—not copy."[25] This emotional bond—based on "core values" rather than information, and defined by temporal duration in cross-channel, cross-media, and cross-technology configurations—is the key to commercial second-shift programming in the era of digital ubiquity. All of these practices indicate that the real "interactivity" in the digital era is not a user-technical process somehow inherent in the technical interface. It is, rather, a form of responsive, multiparticipant textual interactivity that now programs boundary-crossing content as part of second-shift aesthetics.

grazing, herding, navigation

Convergence television's most effective answer to the instabilities of viewer "grazing" does not always lie in an attempt to "corral" the grazer within a single brand-bounded flow. Rather (to stick with the unfortunate animal husbandry metaphor *grazing*, popularized by media management), many of the most effective countermeasures involve the process of coaxing or loosely "herding" the grazing user across hospitable sites, noncompeting third-party brands, and markets. In many cases what is seen as viewer-user "navigation" is actually strongly affected by built-in limits and channeling dictated by the contractual alliances that a major Internet portal (like AOL, Yahoo, or Earthlink) maintains. As any web user has experienced, the very same search—launched from different portals or search engines—hardly ever produces the same results. The strong-armed tactic of the web provider (corralling) is to delimit and direct "click-throughs." The weak-armed, more subtle—and potentially more lucrative—approach (herding) is to provide inducements for click-through patterns that have the cumulative effect of benefiting the conglomerate and its aggregating parts. Standard branding theory now argues that it is essential to cultivate the inclinations and priorities of third-party sites so that any users you link or send there will be recognized and "harnessed" responsively via online "in-store" promotions. This responsiveness and favor adds value to the sending site or content-channel source as well. As branding consultant Martin Lindstrom argues, if success at this kind of "cross-branding" practice doesn't happen, "failure occurs and synergy is lost."[26]

When Time-Warner merged with AOL in January 2001, many analysts announced that this marriage of two worlds—"old media" and "new media"—would usher in the final arrival of "convergence." "Leveraging" the proprietary content of Time-Warner, its networks, and its studios, that is, the Internet (dominated by AOL) would at last provide the missing link: a ubiquitous, worldwide, digital pipeline into the home. The conglomerate's stockholder meeting sixteen months later, however, looked far more like a lynch mob than a marriage ceremony. The once "visionary" Time-Warner/AOL CEO Gerald Levin left the company in disgrace. Analysts from Merrill Lynch (with a born-again wisdom driven by hindsight), reversed their many earlier blessings of the corporate marriage and now eulogized, "It's a sad ending. This is the worst acquisition in media history given the decline in market value of AOL."[27] NBC's news anchor Tom Brokaw (who also served, intentionally or not, as the de facto spokesperson for a competing conglomerate) offered the last rites to a national audience at the burial. He pronounced the earlier boast (that AOL would prove to be the ultimate delivery route for content) a lie, and characterized the pending divorce between AOL and Time-Warner as the "end of synergy" and the end of the myth of any near-term "convergence."[28] One overlooked lesson in all of this analysis, however, was that viable synergies would, arguably, come less from forced marriages of pipeline and content than from programming; less from hard-sell control at the Net portal or cable "gate" (AOL/Time-Warner's original marriage fantasy), than from less-restrictive "value-added" digital user experiences. For those interested in the bottom line—and in a real industrial economy rather than a virtual one—media web strategies today attempt, out of necessity, to develop more effective and responsive management of multidirectional user flows throughout and across second-shift components of the conglomerate.

time versus space/seriality versus simultaneity

Cybertheorists, *Wired* magazine, and scholars of new media have tended to emphasize the impact of digital technologies on space more so than time. This of course follows McLuhan's notions of how electronic media crosses boundaries and collapses geographic identities in the creation of a networked "global village." In some ways, scholars have made mediated geography and space the key to understanding new media. This privileging of space is informed in part by McLuhan's sense of temporal simultaneity, or what he termed the "all-at-onceness" inherent in electronic communication. Television programmers, on the other hand, have been far more interested in the interrelationships between digital media and sequential time. Time has always been the metric that broadcasters have been forced to master. They strategize time to program content and they research and quantify time (rather than "box office") to rationalize their media economies. Programming tactics—adapted from old media—have helped facilitate, prefigure, and implement new-media development; but new-media technologies have in turn altered those same tactics.

The net result of this process should compel scholars to shift from a recurrent emphasis on notions of boundaryless space and collapsed geographies to notions of meticulously rationalized, marketed, and programmed temporality. As this study has suggested, new media economies—and the dispersed and migrating texts that define them—are not determined wholly by the now familiar schemes of networking, virtuality, and simultaneity. Rather, programming practices in what I have termed the convergent industry's second shift are being rationalized around new forms of textual dispersal, reaggregating flows, and temporal seriality. All of the predictions about digital's utopian promise as a responsive, "lean-in," "pull" technology aside, programmers and the financial interests that deploy them will continue to attempt to "push" content, to brand delivery systems, and to schedule media experience. The austere economies of digital and venture capital after the dot-com crash now favor those making the case that they have mastered such nuances as part of an industrial aesthetics of the second shift.

notes

1. Microsoft, "Detectives to Solve 'Homicide' case Online and On-Air," *Microsoft Press Pass*, February 1, 1999, <www.microsoft.com/presspass/press/1999/Feb99/NBCTVpr.asp>.
2. Matt Beer, "Homicide Cops Get Hands-On Lesson in Internet Crime," *San Francisco Examiner*, February 3, 1999, posted online by *The Kansas City Star*, <www.kcstar.com/item/pages/fyi.pat,fyi/30dab8f8.203.html>.
3. Stephen McLaren, "Sci/Tech: TV and Net Combine to Catch Killer," *BBC Online Network*, February 3, 1999, <http://news.bbc.co.uk/hi/english/sci/tech/newsid_271000/271660.stm>.
4. Maria Seminario, " 'Homicide' Tackes Cybercrime," *ZDNet News*, February 2, 1999, <http://zdnet.com.com/2102-11-51-3592>.
5. Microsoft, *Microsoft Press Pass*.
6. McLaren, "Sci-Tech."
7. Beer, "Homicide Cops."
8. See the second epigraph that opens this chapter, in which Microsoft links MediaPlayer with the awards the web coalition has won.
9. Microsoft, *Microsoft Press Pass*.
10. NBC executive Thomas Hjelm, quoted in Microsoft, *Microsoft Press Pass*; emphasis added.
11. Microsoft, *Microsoft Press Pass*.
12. John T. Caldwell, "Aggregating Form and Re-Purposing Content in the Culture of Conglomeration," in *The Persistence of Television*, ed. Lynn Spigel (New York: Routledge, 2003).
13. I use the term *programming* throughout this essay not in the sense that a computer programmer would, but to describe the ways the networks and stations schedule programs and series, usually as part of a "broadcast programming" department.
14. See Toby Miller, "Revising Screen Studies," *Television and New Media* 2, no. 2 (2001): 92; and "Cultural Citizenship," *Television and New Media* 2, no. 3 (2001): 185.
15. John T. Caldwell, "Critical Industrial Practice: Branding, Re-Purposing, and the Migratory Patterns of Industrial Texts," *Television and New Media*, forthcoming, 2003.

16. John T. Caldwell, *Televisuality: Style, Crisis, and Authority in American Television* (New Brunswick, N.J.: Rutgers University Press, 1995), 338–40.

17. For a particularly good analysis about this programming strategy as a production of "blackness" see Herman Gray, "The Travails of Blackness: Black Visibility in the Age of the Neo-Network," in *Identity Globalization, Convergence: Ethnic Notions and National Identities in the Age of Television and Digital*, ed. John T. Caldwell and Bambi Haggins, forthcoming.

18. See Pierre Levy, *Collective Intelligence: Mankind's Emerging World in Cyberspace* (New York: Plenum, 1997); Paul Virilio, *Open Sky* (New York: Verso, 1995); and Marshall McLuhan, *Understanding Media: The Extensions of Man* (Cambridge, Mass.: MIT Press, 1964, 1994).

19. See Nicholas Negroponte, *Being Digital* (New York: Alfred A. Knopf, 1995).

20. The website for HBO's *Sex and the City* is <www.hbo.com/city/cm/city_style>.

21. The CEO of AT&T Cable, for example, found that their churn when providing video alone was 2 percent, but that when they added telephony, the churn rate dropped almost in half to 1.2 percent. Public comments on The Future of Cable panel at the NCTA (National Cable Television Association) Convention, cablecast on CSPAN, May 16, 2002.

22. Maggie Wilderotter, CEO, Wink Communications, in public comments as a panelist on The Future of Cable panel at the NCTA Convention, cablecast on CSPAN, May 16, 2002.

23. The *Bachelor* ran on the Fox network starting in April 2002. Weekly installments of the series selectively culled the "most promising" of the female contestants and banished those considered less desirable by the bachelor judging the bevy of women in search of a potential bride. The show culminated as a sweeps-week showcase in May.

24. See Richard Verrier, "Wireless Outlets: Enticed by the Profit, Carriers and Media Giants Aim to Offer More Audio and Video Content for Telephones," *Los Angeles Times*, May 13, 2002, C1, C7.

25. Martin Lindstrom, "Cross-Channel Branding," *Click Z: Smarter Marketing/Brandmarketing* newsletter, May 21, 2002, <www.clickz.com/brand/brand.mkt/article.oho/t140681>.

26. Lindstrom, "Cross-Channel Branding."

27. Sallie Hofmeister, "Angry Investors Say Goodbye to AOL Chief," *Los Angeles Times*, May 14, 2002, A1, A28.

28. Tom Brokaw, on-air comments on the *NBC Nightly News*, April 24, 2002.

ten   **narrative mapping**

stephen mamber

I would like in this essay to attempt to link up a variety of areas of creative endeavor which I believe have a common goal. As I don't think
these strands have yet been pulled together and given a name, I want to
try to do so here. This is also valuable because digital media bring out
the possibilities for further work here like never before, especially for
suggesting new interface possibilities.

  I call this activity "narrative mapping," and give it a simple and broad
definition: an attempt to represent visually events that unfold over
time. This would be *mapping* (rather than just presenting a picture),
because space, time, and perhaps other components of the events
would be accounted for. A visual information space is constructed that
provides a formulation of complex activities.

  These mappings may be of real or fictional narratives, but my own
feeling would be that the latter presents the greatest challenges, because
mapping becomes a form of critical visualization. (*Critical visualization*

might be a useful alternative term to narrative mapping.) Take virtually any great work of literature or film and ask yourself, What would a mapping of this work look like? While both the fictional and the real can be mapped, it's useful to distinguish between the two to consider possible differences between mapping strategies. Our conclusion may be that the only difference is of available information (finite, in the case of fiction). I am principally arguing that fictional mapping is both possible and productive, and extends from real-world mapping practices.

The kinds of activity that can be linked to this enterprise have been showing up in a lot of places. What has been happening (or could happen) is a merging of information graphics, journalistic diagramming, visualizations, reconstructions, and some conventional-looking (but ambitious) geographic maps, all in service of this idea of looking for approaches to representing a set of spatially located, temporally situated events.

To lay out this territory, I will do two things. First, I will suggest some reasons this might be a productive area of endeavor, and then I'll briefly survey a number of attempts to do this. Taken together, I hope this will put narrative mapping "on the map."

four purposes of narrative mapping

1. Representation
Maps can become that which they represent. They can stand in for, even replace, that which they seek to model. Particularly with complex instances of narrative structure, they can do what all good maps do—offer a visually readable opportunity to see both grand contours and areas of specific interest. A narrative map, as it seeks to provide a visual theory of the work (or the event), subsequently vies with the original (and other possible mappings). A simple example would be a set of visual thumbnails representing scenes in a film on a DVD. When the thumbnails are laid out so that they can then be clicked on by a user, one need never return to the original form. Instead of watching a film from start to finish, the mapping is now an alternative method with which to both conceptualize and access the work.

While in the midst of a succession of events unfolding over time, we might not have a sense of a "larger picture" (or "bird's-eye view") that a mapping can provide. The ability to unpack—to deconstruct, to resequence—can be inviting functions of narrative mapping.

There are some types of narrative that are especially appealing as representation. As mentioned, complex narratives are one such type, as are those that are ambiguous in some fundamental fashion. Narratives where the events themselves and their potential sequencing (and possible simultaneity) have multiple explanations or versions would be good mapping subjects. Examples of such narratives would include crime

146

scenes and accidents. Also, narratives with elaborate temporal constructions, such as flashback films, suggest a need for sorting out or making linear, which a mapping could provide. A form of ambiguity related to temporal construction can also naturally be spatial—it can be difficult particularly when events closely overlap temporally to establish an order or set of relationships. We will look at one such example shortly—Stanley Kubrick's early crime drama *The Killing*. In general, when events are either condensed or dispersed, spatially or temporally—in other words, too much at once, or just a little over a long period of time, or all in close quarters or all over the globe—these are instances where mapping provides a means to represent these events in a coherent and compelling manner.

It can also be said that narratives may contain *implied* mappings, a sense that underlying their creation was a mapping that's been hidden from us, so we can be representing, in a sense, what's already there but hidden. We may be re-creating what an author has worked out, yet chosen not to reveal so explicitly.

2. Analysis

A mapping can itself be a means of theorizing, a way of isolating and exploring specific activities of narrative—particularly those that are not immediately evident. Or, analysis can "go global" in a sense, providing an overview or synthesis that recasts the narrative in a new light.

Aspects can be teased out, grouped, color coded, abstracted, or otherwise reformulated, for the sake of offering some new perspective or approach. Mapping is clearly an interpretation, so it can be a kind of textual analysis—a reading as much as a mapping.[1] While grounded as much as possible in the details of a text, a mapping will likely require a certain amount of conjecture, and also a willingness to accommodate ambiguities and contradictions regarding temporal and spatial questions. Where is a text grounded in the physical specifics needed for an unarguable mapping, and where must the mapper "fill in" a pattern or an uncharted but indicated aspect? Again, this is not so much a reenactment (a picturing of narrative events) as it is an abstraction—a method to translate significant aspects of a work into a theoretical construct.

3. Information Space

To map narrative is to model an information space, or in part to construct an underlying database that is then visually represented. One kind of mapping is to connect aspects of a narrative to things that led to its creation (for example, linking shots in a film to their preceding storyboards) and then to what has subsequently been said about it (like critical texts), so that the work is positioned within an unfolding process of creation, influence, and response. Even without linking to the before and the after, narrative mapping can develop a structure to position and contextualize bits of information, as much as being a visual representation. The map is of a field of linkages, a model of how ideas and like objects connect.

4. Interface

Narrative can shift into becoming its own interface—in fact, I think a well-designed narrative map cries out to be an interactive mechanism leading one back to the source. When a narrative is broken down or segmented—into scenes, shots, actions, or other units—these elements can become the means to access the work. This is why hypertext is already a form of mapping, but any form of abstraction or visual representation is a possible interface. Good maps should allow themselves easily to be clicked on or to be moved through, zoomed in and out or left and right, or from a location to a piece of information. So the map becomes the interface to the work itself, the text its own invitation to user-initiated access.

In a digital environment, an interface is itself a form of mapping in that it can serve as a navigation guide to a set of underlying materials and experiences. Whether one is playing a video game, exploring a museum collection, or reading a web-based newspaper, a well-designed interface will present an orienting representation of an underlying information model. So narrative mapping can be seen as a method to move critical activity (the conceptualizing of a work into visual form, with temporal and spatial dimensions) into the realm of interface design. The restructured views of the narrative map can become the means of access to the work itself, since the map is already a representation of its structure.

the most popular types of narrative mapping

As a last means to underline the purposes of narrative mapping, I'd like to characterize the most common types, after which we'll consider some specific examples.

1. Geographic

As might be expected, many narrative mappings are geographically based. A most useful form is the mapping of fictional characters onto real and constructed spaces.[2] Narrative maps can look like "regular" geographic maps, but it should be remembered that fictional works can enter this realm as well, and that the geography of a fictional work may or may not be any more "real" than the characters being mapped. Particularly in the case of films, it has been easy to assume that the places being depicted, especially when given the names of actual places, are their real-world counterparts. The Bodega Bay, for example, in Alfred

Hitchcock's *The Birds* is mostly a constructed space (drawn and constructed much more than photographed), so apart from mappings that might place the film's characters on an actual map of the place, the altered geography from the world to the fictional work might itself be a concern. In either event, the temptation to use maps of actual places and then incorporate various fictional aspects is often a rewarding enterprise.

2. Temporal

Whether timelines or grids (we see both), an ordering in time marked in units is the expected counterpart to the Cartesian space of geographical mapping. Events can be placed in sequence, revealing gaps and overlaps which are not as apparent in their original presentation. A mapping over the space of time is roughly possible with nearly all narrative works, and in some cases can be accomplished with considerable precision. Two examples, one old and one recent, will be presented here.

3. Thematic or Structural

While thematic mapping has a specific meaning in the world of cartography,[3] narrative mapping can isolate elements within a work and locate them against a model of the work as a whole. A color coding of a film, for instance, could represent instances of moving camera, close-ups, or any other stylistic aspect. Appearances of a character, of different visual motifs, of virtually any repeated device are also mappable qualities.

4. Conjectural

While aspects of narrative mapping can involve reconstruction, we should remember these are often speculative or hypothetical. Mapping may be an attempt to visualize, and to fill in what's either implied or altogether absent. While a drawn or modeled image tends to have greater persuasiveness than a written description, one appealing aspect to narrative mapping is this crossing of the line into the advancement of proposed alternatives. We can picture the plane crash which left no living witnesses or the story told elusively. Narrative maps can be guesses made visible.

5. Conceptual

This may apply to all good narrative maps, but there is a special "all-at-a-glance" quality that shows the work or events under study in a wholly fresh manner that invitingly contends with whatever it is meant to represent—the mapping being the more thought out and unambiguous alternative. When one comes to understand the eloquence of London or Tokyo subway maps, who would choose to visualize instead the underlying chaos they distill? Narrative maps at their boldest can reconceptualize. So much can be ignored, while other aspects are brought to the fore in a concentrated manner, that we see the events under study as is they never made sense before, never had achieved their proper form. And the subject and the map delightedly intertwine.

Having now suggested these broad categories, let's pull together some examples of work from a number of areas and attempt to place them all under this broad umbrella. If they seem to be strange company to each other, that is what I hope for—to try for a merging of disparate work, all as an instance of narrative mapping.

the examples

1. Franco Moretti

Moretti's recent book *Atlas of the European Novel: 1800–1900* is the single most ambitious attempt at what he calls "a geography of literature." Looking at authors such as Jane Austen, Charles Dickens, and Emile Zola, Moretti is often concerned with ideas of class that come out by charting the geographical spheres of all of a novel's principal characters.

While many of Moretti's examples are simple national or city maps upon which he has applied prodigious effort to indicate where certain narrative actions occur (and which characters are involved), sometimes he is prepared to leave geography behind. In a tour de force section on Dickens, Moretti notes that his diagrams here "constitute largely

61. *Bleak House*

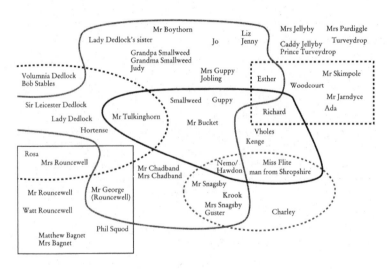

autonomous narrative universes."[4] He ingeniously indicates class and professional spheres of activity so that he can then mark transgressive paths through them.

His map of *Bleak House* will serve as a case in point. Accounting for at least thirty characters, his map can place a single character in a series of realms and also show how one character's plot moves through this series (notice the plot lines—they are literally *lines*). Elsewhere, Moretti convincingly maps major cities through the placement of characters from multiple novels of an author (Arthur Conan Doyle's London, Zola's Paris), but I find him here with Dickens at his most ambitious— leaving the city behind to map structures not entirely dependent upon geography.

2. *The Birds*

This is from work I've been doing on Alfred Hitchcock. It is a few thumbnails short of being every shot in *The Birds*; it is also a visual data-base from which one can get information about each shot, view story-boards and scripts, and drag the mouse to see selected sequences. But I also like it this way, as an opportunity to see a film all at once, a bird's-eye view of *The Birds*, as it were.

While the first shot in the film is at the upper left and nearly the last at the lower right, the full image is a narrative mapping. One can eas-ily see starts and ends of scenes, shifts from day to night, color prefer-ences, and other wonderful things, all in just a single still image

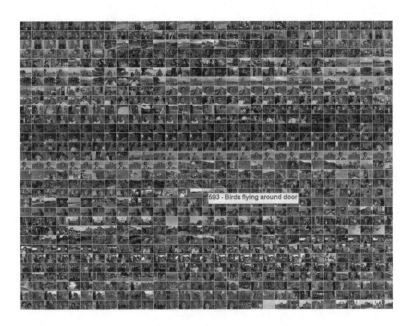

593 - Birds flying around door

composed of many smaller images, each the opening frame of an individual shot.

By altering the frequency (every fifth shot, say) or the size, one can simulate "flying" over the film, just as one can with conventional geographic maps. It is also a good example of the all-at-a-glance mapping again, which shows you a familiar thing (a movie) in an unexpected manner.[5]

3. Etienne-Jules Marey

If narrative mapping has a father, Marey is it. His 1880 masterwork *La Methode Graphique* is replete with examples that are still eminently applicable, as I hope to show. I first saw this chart in one of the three books of the modern master of information graphics, Edward Tufte. Marey is probably still best known as a key precinema figure, for his invention of the chronophotographic gun, but the same Marey is also full of ideas for plotting movements and events over time.[6] While we will only look at one here, even Tufte's first book includes several examples from *La Methode Graphique*.[7]

This twenty-four-hour train schedule of all Paris-Lyon trains is also a beautiful all-at-a-glance image. The steeper the line, the faster the train. Crossings, stops, relative frequency are all easily digested. It is a classic mapping of space over time. While Marey is looking at a train schedule here, he clearly sees the link to other space-time relationships, as mapping motion was one of his principal endeavors. From trains to birds' wings to horses' hooves and on to a wealth of other scientific phenomena, Marey among his many attributes mapped these phenomena in a manner that showed great skill in the "graphic method," and Tufte is quite right to value his work in this area so highly.

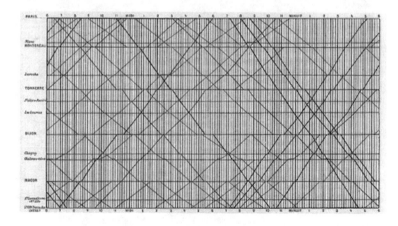

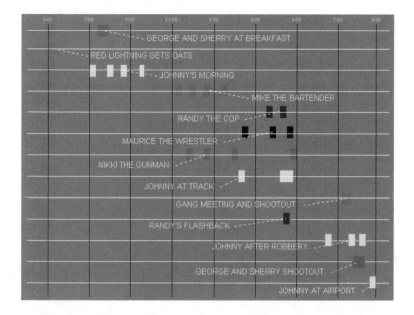

4. *The Killing*

In a direct homage to Marey, I have taken the Stanley Kubrick film *The Killing* and mapped all events on the day that most of the film is interested in—when a racetrack robbery occurs. The film is narrated with to-the-minute precision, so I don't doubt that somewhere a mapping like this exists that was written in Kubrick's own hand.

The order in the film is from top to bottom, and from left to right on each line. I have used this map as an interface to the film, so that one can click on each block (represented as a specific chunk of the movie's space time) and view that sequence from the film—thus allowing for closer viewing of contiguous scenes if one wishes (or in any other chosen order).[8] This is all very useful, but I would acknowledge that it is a mapping pretty close to what Marey was exploring 120 years ago.

5. *News Reconstructions*

Rather than present a single specific example, I want to describe generally a kind of information graphic which has been appearing regularly in newspapers and news magazines. Most particularly, the *New York Times*, *USA Today*, and *Newsweek* have been active in presenting reconstructions of events in the news, including crimes, incidents of violence, and various forms of natural disasters and accidents (especially plane crashes).

The rise of this sort of mapping activity stems from the same kinds of impetus we have been exploring, coupled with a use of computer-based modeling and illustration software to produce the work. Complex (and often controversial) events with multiple components and possibly ambiguous aspects are pulled apart, set in temporal order, and presented often with multiple and magnified angles of perspective. These graphics can contain a wealth of multimedia elements (and a lot of data): pieces of photographs, charts, blow-ups, bits of inset text. They straddle ground interestingly between all these forms of reportage, and have created a fresh and sophisticated form of narrative mapping, suggesting often theoretical arguments difficult to express through other means and certainly lacking in impact if not offered in this new manner.

One such, but quite typical, instance of this work appeared in the *New York Times* as part of its coverage of the shooting of Amidou Diallo by four New York City policemen in 1999.[8] The controversial event in question involved a man who was shot and killed by forty-one shots while removing a wallet from his pocket in a dark hallway. (The officers claimed they believed he was pulling out a gun.) The *Times* graphic, which is worth seeking out, presents a powerful argument for visualizing a sequence of disputed events in this encompassing manner. While appearing to be an illustration, as with many good maps, important components are stripped away to reveal an underlying set of well-selected elements, which are laid out in terms of (spatial) location and (temporal) sequence, emphasizing strongly the firepower involved and the racial components of the incident.

The *Times* Diallo graphic pays particular attention to the bullets fired, including the distinction between shells and bullets, the guns they came from, the officers who fired them, and their ultimate destinations. Some aspects are speculative, such as "likely locations of each officer," and some material would appear to be extraneous, like the photographs of the officers (except of course that they serve as reminder that all four are white). The text information can be laconic in the extreme, such as a line in the lower right corner which says: "Additional bullets were recovered at the morgue." (Presumably they were extracted from the body.) Another common but effective technique is the use of the inset ("Inside the Vestibule," which displays an outline of a body lying on a floor—more drama certainly than information). This further narrativizes the presentation, offering multiple views of the event and also a kind of cinematic close-up—a traditional map technique merged with an equally basic cinematic convention.

There are also extremely effective charts at the bottom of the graphic illustrating individually each of the "rounds available" and the "rounds fired" (in two of the four cases they show the same sixteen bullets). This also clearly sits somewhere between information and editorial, as the enumerating and picturing of each individual round shows the total firepower involved in stunning specificity. (It is surely no accident that one meaning of "graphic" is synonymous with dramatic, plainly visible, and full of impact.) This is among the many non-photographic aspects of the construction, just as is the removal of all automobiles from the representation of the street, though their locations are indicated. This suggests, I think, that the officers were well hidden from on-lookers when this incident occurred and that the *Times* graphic is exposing what couldn't have been seen by an on-looker at the time. And, above all, the reconstruction captures the "all-at-a-glance" quality again of good narrative maps. With the selectivity, re-imagining, and editorializing, we see everything at once in a synthesis of space-time encapsulation.

The numerous examples of such work which appear in *USA Today* function along similar lines. One such case was a graphic reconstruction of a shooting of a possibly deranged homeless man in front of the White House.[10] When presented as a graphic, the result is part information, part editorial, as the illustration appears to express a view that the shooting of the man was not fully necessary. Perhaps to soften or at least contextualize this argument, the graphic places the event in the narrative sequence of other such shootings at the White House. So, one event is broken into component parts, and then other similar events are mapped and accounted for. Also, two views of the same space (the White House and area around it) are offered. The second view does not offer a new perspective on the shooting—it simply locates more clearly where the shooting occurred in relation to the rest of the building.

The shooting is also broken up into five pieces of action, and in common information graphic fashion, a thick directional arrow is offered to indicate somewhat the man's direction of travel. The sequencing of events (here numbered one to five and overlaid upon the space) is a common method for introducing step-by-step order (a method not employed in the *NY Times* graphic discussed above). Some effort is usually made to place the descriptions of these moments close to where they occurred, though when not feasible, the description is still provided. Also, key incidents (such as the actual shooting) are not just described but depicted. Like a kind of comic strip or graphic novel played out over a map, this hybrid form seeks to approach its material through every means it can muster—illustrating what it thinks is essential, geographically mapping all its particulars in two views, and bringing in all relevant events to indicate larger patterns. Ambitious, somewhat overreaching, and almost too-much-at-a-glance, one can see a new form coming into being.

6. A Final Example

I have numerous examples of reconstructions and mappings within my two websites, Instrument of War: The True Story of the Yuba City Draft Board Murders, <www.cinema.ucla.edu\Mamber)>, and the Center for Hidden Camera Research, <www.cinema.ucla.edu\Mamber2>.

The map here (from the Hidden Camera site) is mainly a timeline, but it is also a mapped selection of ten events in a day's videotape of a child and his nanny, taped by a hidden camera. Once again, the map becomes the interface, as the user can click to see the video segments in question.

Hidden-camera footage is often so loose a collection of events (one can wait hours for something to happen) that providing a map can create a narrative. Rather than watch empty space for hours, a map can both situate events and lead the user to them. This is still quite different from narrative constructed through actual editing. It is perhaps closer to a database in this way too, with segments tagged for easy retrieval from the larger collection of video. Also, this kind of footage often requires extensive explanation, which is made available when the video is played.

When visual material is "free form," or ongoing for extensive periods, mapping can provide overlays of narrative structure without forcing the viewer to accept these selections as the only possible method to access the material. Anyone wishing to draw upon larger amounts of the footage may do so. The maps provide what maps often provide—a guide to the terrain, and paths available through it.

some brief conclusions

Narrative mapping is a useful tool for dealing with complexity, ambiguity, density, and information overload. It offers possibilities for approaching and explaining ideas that would otherwise be difficult to express. It is an aid to visualizing—a guide, an interface, an analysis, a critical method.

What has been left unsaid here but is plainly in evidence is that digital environments greatly enhance the potential for narrative mapping, and also increase the need for it. Three-dimensional modeling, information graphics, and what has been called multimedia cartography all play a role in this new form. Many narrative works will contain mappings as a matter of course. (Much hypertext already does.) Almost every DVD, for example, comes with thumbnailed "chapter scenes" now, both to aid access and to provide an overview. When we walk into many planned exhibit spaces, such as malls, museums, and theme parks, the maps we are offered often have narrativized elements to them—bits of schedules, tables of contents, and diagrams to aid in orientation. As space itself is narrativized, so too is the map.

Where narrative mapping can also play a significant role is in theorizing newly emerging narrative forms. While I think digital media provide the most challenging possibilities, existing forms also, of course, are undergoing change. To take one example, there has been a spate of contemporary films that are structured around retelling the same events.[11] Narrative mapping can serve as a tool to chart differences between such versions, and also could be a way to allow a viewer to bring such differences more directly into proximity of each other. Even more important, perhaps, such mapping could be part of an analysis of the temporal notions at work in such films.

A further possibility yet to be explored is the temporalizing of narrative mapping itself: animating such maps so that they themselves unfold over time, perhaps in conjunction with the works they are mapping. The fluidity between the real and the virtual that we are finding in so many spheres is very strongly evident here. We will often have to ask: when is the narrative the map, and vice versa?

notes

1. Norman J. W. Thrower, *Maps and Civilization: Cartography in Culture and Society* (Chicago: University of Chicago Press, 1996), 218.
2. It is the principal subject of Franco Moretti's book, *Atlas of the European Novel: 1800–1900* (New York: Verso Books, 1999), as will be discussed shortly.
3. See, for example, Thrower, *Maps and Civilization,* 95.
4. Franco, *Atlas of the European Novel,* 131.
5. See Mamber, *Media Computing,* for more on visual databases as narrative mappings.

6. See Marta Braun's essential book *Picturing Time* for a full and valuable assessment of Marey's contributions; Braun, *Picturing Time: The Work of Etienne-Jules Marey (1830–1904)* (Chicago: University of Chicago Press, 1994).

7. Tufte, Edward R. *Envisioning Information* (Cheshire, Conn.: Graphics Press, 1990).

8. For more on *The Killing*, see Stephen Mamber, "Simultaneity and Overlap in Stanley Kubrick's *The Killing*," *Postmodern Culture* 8, no. 2 (1998), online at <http://calliope.jhu.edu/journals/pmc/v008/8.2mamber.html>(subscription required).

9. "The Scene: A Carpet of Casings and Bullets," *New York Times*, December 10, 1999, page C21.

10. "Shooting Outside the White House," *USA Today*, December 21, 1994, page 4A.

11. The films *Blind Chance, Run Lola Run, Sliding Doors, The Family Man*, and *Go*, to name but a few.

bibliography

Bounford, Trevor and Alistair Campbell. *Digital Diagrams: How to Design and Present Statistical Information Effectively.* New York: Watson-Guptill, 2000.

Cartwright, William, Peterson, Michael P., and George, Gartner, eds. *Multimedia Cartography.* New York: Springer-Verlag, 1999.

Cubitt, Sean. "Cartographic Instruments, Narcissist Illusions, Regimes of Realism in CGI," *Millenium Film Journal* 34 (1999): 66–81.

Mamber, Stephen, "Space-Time Mappings as Database Browsing Tools," *Media Computing: Computational Media Aesthetics.* Edited by Chitra Dorai and Svetha Venkatesh. New York: Kluwer Academic Publishers, 2002.

Marey, Etienne-Jules. *La Methode graphique dans le dciences experimentales et principalement en physiologie et medécine.* Paris: Librarie de l'Academie de Medécine, 1885.

Monmonier, Mark. *Mapping It Out: Expository Cartography for the Humanities and Social Sciences.* Chicago: University of Chicago Press, 1993.

Moretti, Franco. *Atlas of the European Novel: 1800–1900.* New York: Verso, 1999.

"Shooting Outside the White House," *USA Today*, December 21, 1994, 4A.

Storr, Robert. *Mapping.* New York: The Museum of Modern Art, 1994.

"The Scene: A Carpet of Casings and Bullets," *New York Times*, December 10, 1999, C21.

real-time

fairy tales

cinema prefiguring

digital anxiety

m a r k   w i l l i a m s

This essay will endeavor to ask specific questions about grand transformations—and claims about such transformations—in the contemporary media environment. The contemporary media environment has on occasion been promoted to be unprecedented: in its tendencies toward and dynamics of convergence, in its scale of socioeconomic impact, in its capacity to rerender and reimagine the worlds of representation and mediated expression. Considering such a dramatic purchase on the present, but also on the anxious and awed imagination of its futures, what are the challenges, perhaps even the demands, of work in media history and historiography in this context? Which access to a historicized past affords what range of critical distance or consonance regarding this media environment? What is at stake in positing and investigating these relationships? What role can such work play in better understanding our present, and the variegated tendril holds of new media discourse on the future?

Not surprisingly, this essay will suggest that media history and historiography are crucially important in this context. This is especially due to (and complicated by) the imperative of the new-media environment to inflect and construct both our notion or concept of "history" and the range of particular historical narratives and events necessary to the reality effect underlying normative subjectivity.

More surprising may be the call in this essay for the critical return to a methodology that has been itself regarded as a historicized anomaly: apparatus theory.[1] This approach to media has been variously denounced as elitist, naive, totalizing, and hopelessly partial. What possible advantage or insight could be afforded by the reconsideration of such a methodology? What follows is an initial foray into these questions and issues, inspired in part by two particular digital-era films that render questions about this era in relation to questions about human subjectivity, especially in their depictions of childhood. One film, *Fairy Tale: A True Story* (Sturridge, 1997), reconsiders a significant incident in the history of mediated representation. The other, *A.I.: Artificial Intelligence* (Spielberg, 2001), ultimately imagines a literally posthuman future,[2] in which humans are history amid a world of advanced informational dynamics.

By virtue of their common themes (fairy tales, technology, and the construction of childhood), and their opposite temporal configurations (the past, the future), these films can be seen to configure a range of fundamental questions about the digital age and subjectivity. Or, more accurately, they might be seen to prefigure anxiety about these questions, including the fact that these questions indeed exist. The sweep of real and imagined transformations ascribed to the rise of digital culture, and the nature of certain issues endemic to digital representation, may be understood to have rerendered popular uncertainty regarding core questions about origins and futures, and mediated representations themselves. These films can serve as an index for some of these questions and anxieties.

Part of the significance in returning to methods and questions of apparatus theory regarding such a project is to suggest the importance of considering media specificity in analytical work about media history. This attention is significant to the historical contextualization of these films, and also of course to their consideration *as* films within the convergent technological and industrial practices apparently commensurate to digital culture. An overview of how some of these issues contribute to contemporary issues of media historiography can therefore serve to introduce an analysis of the films themselves.

from "liveness" to "real time": notes toward an electronic culture *dispositif*

One key trope of historical analysis afforded by a return to apparatus theory is an enhanced attention to media specificity, and thus to broad attendant questions of media definition, hybridization, convergence, and dissonance. The most effective deployment of this trope, however, would be in the service of combating the tendency toward overstatement and totalizing pronouncements that characterizes much contemporary discourse about the media.[3] Especially in light of the critique of apparatus theory in its foundational guise, its deployment regarding contemporary media should be precisely to foreground media specificity in the age of presumed convergence, rather than contribute to the erasure of difference in the consideration of quite varied instances of media formats and devices. In other words, the return to apparatus theory may serve to specifically raise questions of *differance* in the consideration of new media rather than elide them.

These are pressing issues endemic to digital culture, especially in light of the vast recent technological changes wrought across media and mediated culture. (These include the rise in home and office computers, communication peripherals such as personal digital assistants and cell phones, digital television in the form of digital satellite and cable delivery, digital receivers and recording devices, computer games, and so on). It is beyond the scope of this essay to provide a cogent history of these developments; in fact, it is one desire of this essay to encourage that work on such a vast historical field be rigorously undertaken. This will entail new understandings of significant emergent intermedial associations and differences, in specific historical instances.

Apparatus theory would therefore place a certain purchase on these issues of media specificity ("the ensemble of the equipment and operations necessary" to the workings of a medium[4]). It would also encourage considered attention to a second major trope within apparatus theory: issues regarding the address to and constructed positionality of subject effects regarding these media. It is significant in this regard to note that as the rise of digital culture has become evident, so has popular interest in media history, including interest in the media as industries. Essays and feature articles about media history/industry now appear regularly in news and cultural magazines (e.g., *Time*, *Newsweek*, *The New Yorker*). The *New York Times* has greatly expanded its coverage of media and technology, and other newspapers have followed suit. Documentaries and talk-show discussions about media technology, media moguls, media conglomerates, and media effects have become standard fare on PBS and several new cable channels. Contemporary media dynamics (textual, industrial, economic, interpersonal, etc.) and an apparently attendant desire to understand how they are and have been determined, now exist at an unprecedented level—as staple topics for news and information media outlets.

This popular attention to media dynamics further suggests the pertinence of apparatus theory, since it seems to involve a desire to understand the media and our mediated experiences with greater detail and complexity. It suggests, in other words, a kind of shift in attention and degree of interest and self-consciousness regarding our knowledge about the media and our mediated selves. I would argue this must entail at some level a recognition or underlying sense that we have tended to ignore or repress, rather than be merely unaware of, some of the media matters we now seek to understand. Such a process suggests a relationship to issues surrounding the *dispositif*, which concerns mediated relationships to attendant dynamics of subjectivity. One key aspect of the trope of *dispositif* analysis is whether and how the process of disavowal may be seen to be constitutive to the power and allure of media. The enhanced public interest in media history today seems to suggest the emergence of new equilibria regarding the particulars and even the valuation of the desire for knowledge about the media, and therefore begs certain questions regarding processes of disavowal within and around these equilibria.

This quality and capacity for disavowal regarding the media is the concern of much of this essay. Disavowal, and the economies of belief related to technology and mediation in digital culture, are topics of study in media history that beckon the methodologies of apparatus theory. They are also topics that can render unstable the unspoken assumptions of normative subjectivity and ideology. The enhanced contemporary degree of interest in questions about media/technology is therefore not unrelated to concomitant questions about our world and ourselves, and therefore the relationships between media/technology, the socioeconomic-political sphere, and subjectivity itself.

I wish to address in some detail one aspect of media disavowal with vast implications and also great utility as a topic within media history and historiography: the electronic mediation of temporality. The potential significance of attending to this aspect of what I am calling an *electronic culture dispositif* includes its contribution to an intermedial understanding of the "new" media environment, and especially a recognition of the often absented consideration of television as constitutive to rather than transcended by this environment.

This involves two moves regarding the consideration of the rise of the digital in media history, both related in a way to the concept of disavowal. One is the ongoing reconsideration of the object and methods of study regarding "cinema" in the contemporary media environment.[5] As assayed by Anne Friedberg, many of the changes in spectatorship vaunted to be distinctive to digital media were inherent to developments in television in the predigital 1970s and '80s.[6] The rise of the remote control, cable television, and the VCR produced an "interactive" mode of viewing that began to dissolve the "historical differences" between film and TV. This shift crucially involved not only changes to corporate hierarchies in these industries (e.g., weakened network hegemony), but also significant manipulations of temporality in relation to these media (e.g., time shifting).

162

Just as key aspects of new media spectatorship can be traced to developments in predigital television, the dynamics of new media temporality must be understood in relationship to the oddly protean temporality of television. Central to this relationship is a contrast between the like concepts of televisual *liveness* and new-media *real time.* Both terms are grounded in the capacity for electronic media to represent something at roughly the same moment it occurs. But each term, in significantly different registers, also designates a key dynamic of disavowal, in that each names an act of mediation but also the desire to experience this act as unmediated.

As I have discussed elsewhere, *liveness* has developed across broadcast history into one of the most semantically saturated terms in the study of media.[7] What began as a description of the technological relation to a referent that a medium was in the process of representing, based on the ontological status of that referent, has become today a description of what an electronic medium is representing at this moment. What is "live" on TV today is what TV is showing/enunciating now, regardless of the status of the referent. Mimi White has suggested a crucial trope in this development, regarding the persistent use of the term *history* in relation to television. As television becomes less ontologically "live," and its temporality grows more complex with the development of surfing, zipping, and time-shifting devices, it relies even more on grounding its discursive address in relation to a range of modalities that approximate claims to the historic and the historical. Televisual liveness, then, can be understood to be a historically mutable, situational *effect* that leans upon or is propped onto history as a key trope of its temporal *dispositif.*

Computer-related electronic media, by contrast, are characterized by the properties and desires attendant to *real time*, which can be understood to be propped onto the near future. The evident demand in contemporary media society for faster processing, fatter data pipelines, and immediate downloads is constitutive of real-time desire.[8] This desire is crucially entwined with the overall purchase on the popular imagination and conceptualization of the near future that relies on the claims and promises made about digital culture.

Like *liveness*, the term *real time* refers to a mediation of the present; like *liveness*, it refers to a situational valuation of this mediation, which appears to proffer a (desired?) virtual transposition of values as its limit point: the act of mediation itself may render something as more live or more real than it would be if encountered unmediated. Taken together, *liveness* and *real time* can be understood to possess the synergistic capacity for a frenzy of the temporal, such that the reference to time as a traditional anchor for certainty is thoroughly postmodernized into a fluidity that questions rather than assumes the relation of the present to what might have or will occur.

163

The resultant potential for what might be called the real-time subjunctive[9] is one way to render the bramble of anxieties and enthusiasms that have captured the public fascination about digital culture. Mark Wolf has suggested that the documentary quality of certain computer simulations has produced an elongation of the indexical link presumed to anchor representations to the real world. Regarding credible images constructed from data, which may represent "speculation as much as or more than existing objects," Wolf posits a semantic slippage from the perceptual to the conceptual. This slippage is grounded less in a critical investigation of what is represented than in a popular and scientific esteem for the status of the mathematical basis for computer simulation, which Wolf suggests is today perhaps even greater than the status typically given to photography.

These concerns and dynamics of the real-time subjunctive characterize the issues and themes explored in the films *Fairy Tale* and *A.I.* Each demonstrates a related but distinct "figuring" of anxiety about digital culture. Analyzed together, they can be seen to demarcate many issues of the electronic *dispositif* introduced in the discussion above. One film engages with issues of "history," and is steeped in an unpacking of issues about disavowal and their relation to the specific technologies and processes of an apparatus of representation. The other is set in the near future, and is engaged in an unpacking of issues regarding disavowal and the process of subjectivity. Each film received a problematic popular response regarding its negotiation of themes related to digital culture. As such, they provide a useful introductory cross-section of the figuring of our cultural response to the complex potentialities of the digital.

prefiguring new economies of belief

Fairy Tale: A True Story (1997), an impeccably appointed film directed by Charles Sturridge, presents by its very title an intentional paradox. How can a fairy tale, part of what is regarded as the most emphatically recreative and fantastic genre, bear an equivalence to actual events? One might recognize the title as a sort of pun, since the film is a rendering of events involving the alleged photos of the Cottingley fairies—perhaps the most widely known and debated instance of reputed contact with the supernatural. But the claim that a standard of absolute veracity (a true story) has been applied to matters typically considered to be incredulous (a fairy tale) seems intractable. What this paradox both implies and announces for the makers of *Fairy Tale* is a license and even an ambition to examine the fluidity between such apparently binary terms (e.g., fairy tales and true stories) so as to recognize and accentuate the blurring of notions of certainty that seem inherent to the characters and events of this historical tale. The film can be seen to attempt, in other words, the kind of truth evoked by many fairy tales: a narrativized reworking of fears, concerns, and problems pertinent to a contemporary audience (that of the digital era), but rendered in a form both familiar and distanced.

The film meticulously constructs the period of the Cottingley incident (circa 1917–1920), establishing a tone that is historically precise but also mythic in quality (see notes for a plot synopsis).[10] The public and collective excitement of audiences in rapt attention is rendered from the start, and is often tied to celebrities that mark the time frame. Clearly meant to reference our own experience of this film (perhaps filmgoing in general), these events are portrayed with an emphasis on the constructedness of theatricalized (staged) intrigue. The famous audience participation segment from *Peter Pan* that is referenced in the opening montage of course foreshadows the encounter with fairies to come in the film. But it also underscores the process of willful desire for belief ("Do you believe in fairies?") that is inherent to the pleasures pursued in such mediated settings. The fuller emotional timbre of the period, however, is rendered by the isolated and comparatively anonymous act of mourning (the mother at the gravesite), a register of emotional duress that is imposed rather than sought out or willfully pursued. The pivotal context of World War I in assigning this emotional timbre as widespread and defining of this era is part of the mythic tone evoked, though not the exclusive determinant of it. (Mrs. Wright, we will learn, mourns her son, who died of pneumonia at age twelve). But mourning is positioned as one key condition of possibility for the complex dynamics of belief which follow. That the celebrities introduced will become involved with and even work to evaluate these dynamics further contributes to the mythic rather than merely prosaic sense of "history" in the film, and contributes as well to the movement toward fluidity across binaries that is evident as part of the film's project (e.g., across public/private, famous/anonymous, fantastic/real).

Much of this fluidity can be seen to be referenced in the semantic nexus of meanings that flow across these images and scenes. Key to this dynamic is a play on the notion of "wings," which tropes and mobilizes the connotations of this term (including the notions of flight, airiness, liberty, perspectives above the ground, etc.). The sense of entrapment and incarceration that introduces a Harry Houdini segment, for example, is ultimately met with his eventual unfurling of the straitjacket, as if molted into a freedom of becoming. (Houdini is later seen to be advertised as "The World Famous Self-Liberator.") More significantly, the depiction of the production of *Peter Pan* extends the "wing" metaphor across not only its most literal depictions (the moths seen to accumulate on the lamps behind the stage), but also what is perhaps its most abstract level of meaning: affording the deconstruction of the site, the production, and the experience of spectacle, "from the wings." (This references the attention to media specificity and disclosure within apparatus theory.) The film is announcing, if you will, at the very out-set, its intention to represent and evoke a range of what I would call *experiences of enthrall*—from popular entertainment, to the experience of the natural world, to that of mourning—that it will place into a kind of critical, historicized consideration.

What consolidates the assignation of *fairy tale* within this historicized and mythic structure, of course, is the attention to and emphasis on children and their perceptions—a set of issues that the film engages with great care. In light of generic tendencies regarding children and their representation, especially as detailed in critical work on the genre by Marina Warner, *Fairy Tale* can be seen to follow the utopian rather than conservative goals of the genre, even in, or perhaps especially in, the often troublesome area of gender roles.[11] Neither as harrowing as many fairy tales nor as mysogynist, the film affords its two central char-acters, Elsie and Frances, a kind of nascent "girl power" as they form bonds with one another and work together to follow the faith of their convictions. These include a keen sense of curiosity and an active sense of the powerful attributes of imagination—at odds with the already-understood character of the adult world around them, but also the larger myths of inquisitive females as the downfall of man. (In this, the film bears a resemblance to early Spiritualist movements, which are of course a topicality within its diegesis.)[12] The girls' sense of imagination, upon which many of the questions about the Cottingley incidents arise, is handled somewhat obliquely, and never in the conventional assump-tion of a child's point of view (i.e., child as "person through whom we see"). Warner complains that the conventional point of view is often an excuse for adult denial in the name of a prelapsarian ideal: the cor-rupted innocence of the child's gaze as inevitable guarantor of the loss of ideals the adult spectator wishes to naturalize. The film rather auda-ciously adopts a more omniscient point of view regarding the appear-ance of the fairies within the diegesis, introducing these "characters" explicitly outside the shot/reverse-shot conventions that would "con-tain" their rendering within the points of view of the children.

The omniscient perspective in the rendering of the fairies has been the locus for criticisms of the film, many of which claim it confuses the issues the film wishes to raise by insisting on the facticity of fairies. (Even Roger Ebert was among the many critics who complained that the film somehow wanted to "have its cake and eat it too.")[13] This seems to indi-cate what in Barthesian terms we can call a *hermeneutic split*, a difficulty in the narrative economy of knowledge and epistemology. I would sug-gest that one result is that the film offers an opportunity to reflect on the uses and implications of what has become a fulcrum of contempo-rary Hollywood cinema: the proliferation of digital special effects. It offers, first of all, a kind of spectacle and attraction that is in some ways unprecedented and at the same time has come to be seen as necessary to the appeal and "promise" of this kind of film. Indeed, I would suggest that by the dictates of contemporary cinema, for a film of this budget you can't *not* show the fairies. (Such a dynamic is part of a larger series of questions to pursue along these lines, regarding the "pressure" to represent according to what digital technology affords us.) As such, *Fairy Tale* takes part in the tradition of enthralling popular entertainment invoked earlier, but also raises questions about implicit and explicit dynamics of the real-time subjunctive.

It does so in what seems to me an enlightening way. As opposed to the plot-and-character-lite, pseudocarnival rides that can dominate the box office (e.g., *Jurassic Park*, *Twister*, and *Star Wars Episode I: The Phantom Menace*), with digital effects that attempt to approximate an immersive ideal or virtual enclosure within the world created, these creatures in *Fairy Tale* seem to me positioned as precisely contingent and conditional, begging the question of the credulity of digital effects and especially placing into a new perspective the legacy of mediated fairy images that the film shares with the Cottingley photos.

Centrally important is the film's unpacking of the process of photography in its deliberation of the issues of belief regarding the Cottingley incident. The truth claims readily ascribed to photography—which are generally tied to a collapsing of its process and a fixation on the moment of shuttered exposure—are parsed out across various permutations in the analysis of the photographic process. In this way, the film participates in the trope of historicizing our consideration of the mediated "moment," such as is pursued in work on the constructedness of liveness and real-time mediation today.

The decision to omnisciently image the fairies outside of this investigation, then, can be recognized to figure the question of the fairies' existence as irrelevant to the determination of whether the fairy photos were falsified. (This is in fact how the events were ultimately described by the real-life Elsie and Frances Cottingley, late in their lives: they admitted they did fake the photos, but also insisted they had actually seen fairies.) The simple binary on/off model of belief typically ascribed to the photos is expanded by virtue of the film's fuller contextualization of the photographic process (from issues of camera operation, to production of the negative, to the development of a positive print, to the range of degrees of reception).[14] The film works through, in other words, the refusal of an expected indexical assurance, toward the insistence on an attention to questions of process—an attention that is now recommended by theorists of digital media to be constitutive of the new condition of reception in our postphotographic era. The call for such methodological complexity further recommends a utility for apparatus theory regarding digital culture.

Steven Spielberg's 2001 film *A.I.: Artificial Intelligence* (famously based on a project gestated by Stanley Kubrick, with Spielberg's participation) registers a different degree of self-consciousness regarding media, media history, and desire.[15] Like *Fairy Tale*, it participates in the still-viable tradition by which motion pictures adopt a special purchase on the realm of public fantasy, especially via narrativized renderings. Also like *Fairy Tale*, it affords a reflexive perspective on the anxieties about digital culture, though with an emphasis on the component process of subjectivity itself.

This emphasis is perhaps ironic in light of the critical response to the film, which has tended to focus on the "paternity" of its final realization (e.g., Kubrick or Spielberg as the auteur/pater; the film as problematic "hybrid," etc.). My discussion will not be especially invested in such auteurist debates (as indicated above, I refer to it as a Spielberg film), and my interest in responses to the film has more to do with its narrative trajectory. Like many Spielberg films, *A.I.* reworks a classic narrative from the Disney studios, in this case *Pinocchio*. But the inflections on this narrative raise intriguing questions and issues regarding the definition of "human" subjectivity less from its distinction to prehuman forms than from its potential relationship to posthuman forms.

Within *A.I.*, the concerns with subjectivity are quite literal, even somewhat clinical, and infused with a variety of figures and scenarios that can be seen to be friendly to post-structuralist theories of the subject. The film concerns the introduction of a domestic robot boy, David, into a nuclear family, and David's exploits in enacting his desire for a level or kind of subjectivity that can fulfill the subjective demands he is wired to respond to. The attendant issues of his subjectivity in relation to parentage are quite precisely focused on the (m)other as the site of an emotional interface that approximates David as human-like, and the subsequent problems that David's artificiality produces in this regard.

The scene of David's transformation into a loving/loved object is especially redolent of poststructuralist theories of subjectivity. His "mother" chooses to trigger the program that will engender David's emotional attachment to her. Looking directly into his eyes, she engages a physical interface (pressure points on the back of David's neck) while speaking an arbitrary series of words. Through this combination of maternal gaze, physical proximity and touch, and especially the introduction of language as an abstract code that accesses and promises to define the "human" interface, the scene approximates a condensed performance of the Lacanian imaginary and mirror stage. David's need for evidence and assurance of his (m)other's love ultimately proves unwieldy for the long-term comfort of the family, especially due to the jealousy he instills in his "brother," and David is discarded/abandoned in the woods.

This scenario already connotes the fantastic and emotionally charged terrain of the fairy tale. As with the title of the film *Fairy Tale: A*

True Story, A.I. also explicitly demarcates a blurring of the expected boundaries of this genre, which is consonant with other issues of blurring in the film, but the film equivocates between blurrings of epistemological categories versus gendered categories.

David eventually comes in contact with a public spectacle known as Flesh Fair that involves the extravagant destruction of artificial life forms. Accompanying its credo that this activity is an avowed celebration of "life" is the condition that such a celebration is predicated upon the demolishing of "artificiality." Such an insistence on a pure binary definition and distinction is therefore equated with the will for violence and a marked brand of (virtual) incivility on the part of the participants.[16] But when David is teamed with another recluse robot, Gigolo Joe, the implicit gendered modalities of subjectivity are somewhat more binarily secured. Joe is like an ideal big brother to David, especially in that his sexual persona as a gigolo robot becomes merely supplementary to his pedagogical and epistemological function: he introduces David to the city (characterized by blatant sexual figurations), and works to find someone who can provide an answer to David's riddle-like inquiries.

The segment with the perhaps ironically titled Dr. Know literalizes the blurring of generic boundaries, as David and Joe realize they must combine Dr. Know's categories ("flat fact" and "fairy tale") in order to render an answer that satisfies David's inquiry. The resultant journey culminates in a two-stage reencounter with David's origins of subjectivity, which mobilize the most troubling and suggestive aspects of the film's treatises on subjectivity.

David's return to the lab at which he was developed conflates a return to the "father" (his inventor) with a stark recognition of the myth of his individuality. His encounter with another David unleashes his own violent response to "artificiality," as he demolishes the doppelganger robot in a manner not dissimilar to that seen at the Flesh Fair. This is followed by what is perhaps his culminating crisis, as David recognizes not only that his subjectivity is mass-produced (scores of Davids boxed for distribution), but that sexual differentiation appears to be far less stark a binary than he might have expected (scores of boxes of a female variant of his model). The effect of this new and disorienting knowledge—which again approximates the understanding of subjectivity according to poststructural theories—drives him to the brink of despair. David sits dejectedly at the edge of the building, and soon simply falls off into the depths below.[17]

This quasi-suicide ultimately leads to David's fantasmatic encounter with the Blue Fairy, the very goal that he has been seeking for much of the film. Her appearance in the flooded and decaying carnival setting (which again literalizes a fairy tale) designates a culmination of sorts to David's narrative. His eventual semipermanent interface with this statue is one of the most compelling figurations in the film, and in my experience is the place where many audience members (actually, everyone I have spoken to about the film) believe the film should have ended.

The apparent displeasure that results from the film moving beyond a (literally) frozen mirror stage with the Blue Fairy is intriguing. The scenario of subjectivity figured here seems to condense (1) the perpetual cycling of desire that is produced by and directed toward the Imaginary dyad, with the Blue Fairy representing both the ur-mother and the supposed font of ur-knowledge, and (2) the machinic subjectivity of David, which can only register the dynamic "lack" at the center of his subjectivity, with no self-awareness of such. The section of the film that follows this sequence therefore seems to suggest that there is more to examine in the issues of David's subjectivity. His discovery by still more futuristic robots, and the subsequent scenario of desire they are capable and willing to construct for him, imply that he has been programmed for "lack," and has yet to experience "loss"—the emotional timbre of which will constitute his move toward the "human."

One irony of this movement is that it occurs in a wholly posthuman context (2000 years later), when apparently only robots now exist on the frozen earth. David is prized as a rare historical find, since he is the last sentient artifact to have experienced an indexical contact with human life forms. This quality and capacity for transience, and more specifically for mortality, is the final aspect of subjectivity that David accesses. Again this is rendered in decidedly gendered and Oedipal terms, as David is afforded one day to spend with his "mother" (based on a regenerated DNA sample), at the end of which she, and apparently he, will drift off to sleep and death. The tone established for this conclusion is quietly powerful, and disturbing in its elegance and beauty. Sleep, with which David had no previous acquaintance, is designated as the place where dreams are born—and by relation, creativity and art. Yet the scene renders this via a decidedly precise form of classical oedipal "perversion," as David lies contentedly in bed with his mother—or, more specifically, her corpse.

some conclusions

Although representing a significantly different historical address than *Fairy Tale*, *A.I.* shares with that film a figuration of digital anxiety via an unpacking of apparatus issues in relation to processes of subjectivity. The rather startling frankness of the concluding scenario, in conjunction with the overall trajectory of references to difficult and uncomfortable issues of mediated psychic demands, drives, and determinations, suggests a relationship of the film to theories of subjectivity and disavowal significant to apparatus theory.[18] The evident trope of blurring in both films—in the most general sense, their crossing of fairy tales with true stories and flat facts—can be seen to trouble standardized modes of knowledge and belief, including those of genre, gender, and even species, and is redolent of the dynamics of the real-time subjunctive: *Fairy Tale*'s unfettered broaching of a hermeneutics of mediated knowledge and epistemology via the figuring of what might be called the "extra-human" (fairies, angels, etc.), and *A.I.*'s foregrounded actualization of fairy tale scenarios and literalization of the post-human (robots only)—what might even be called the ex-human.

This real-time subjunctive, I have suggested, describes in part the creative dynamic of these films (a new representational license, for example, but also a pressure to represent digitally). It also describes in part the anxieties that they mediate. It arose in relation to the juggernaut cyber-economy and culture of the late 1980s and '90s, with its attendant complex of what I have called real-time desires, which are recognizable via a frenzy of temporality understood to be in lineage to the "liveness" of television. The saturation of the term "live" in relation to television can be described in relation to a series of semantic slippages regarding the growth of that medium, especially sliding notions of its enhanced "present" and "presentness" in everyday life—spatially, temporally, and in relation to the determination of just-in-time cultural capital.[19] A similar kind of dynamic might be seen to be true of cyber-culture, with its extraordinary purchase on the near-future. Its accelerated growth was promoted and projected forward, in a seemingly totalizing way (packed with disavowals about the credulity of these projections), toward a transformative, charged tomorrow—as if Moore's Law could guarantee perpetual expansion—what might be posited as the ultimate "real-time" fairy tale. What had become a "future" that you did not want to *not* be part of, became what in another context has been called The Not Yet Meets the Already Gone.[20]

Like the televisual "live," cyber-culture's "real-time" can also be referenced via semantic saturations and slippages—this time in the terms "current" and "currency"—regarding its ties to cultural capital (and eventually literal and virtual economic capital). To have a grasp on, to have access to the near-future defined what it was to be "current," happening, promising—eventually, perhaps worth investing in. To be current (to assume or affect the state of "currency"; perhaps even to attract invested currency/dollars—to be "money") was to be directly linked to the newest electronic media, which was to be "wired," to be jacked into the escalating, accelerating promise of the near-future: perhaps even literalizing and performing that promise via day-trading of dot-com stocks on a PC laptop. The basis for such a spiralling configuration, the actions and effects of which both blurred and mutually reinforced one another, is a large part of what I am referring to in this essay as "real-time" desire.[21]

My claims for these films can therefore be seen in relation to other recent and significant work on new media and theory (although more precisely rendered relations will be deferred to a subsequent version of this essay). Indeed, the notion of "pre-figuring" digital anxiety directly alludes to David Rodowick's work on the "figural," a term which he defines and describes in relation to new media's capacity to invent and critique and even to be produced by dynamics "*ahead* of philosophy." The figural, for Rodowick, is a concept (more than a thing) "meant to describe a distinct mutation in the character of contemporary forms of representation, information, and communication," to "help character-ize the social physiognomics of postindustrial capitalism and the infor-mation society," not by the logic of identity, but by "tracing out what Modern philosophy has systematically excluded or elided."[22]

The rise of digital culture, and its attendant "pressure" to render and actualize the near future (which determines in part the aesthetics of the real time subjunctive), might be seen to have produced, in popular cul-ture but also elsewhere, evidence of a likewise pressure toward different equilibria of "belief" as regards our relationships to media—relation-ships that we typically take for granted, the complexities of which we disavow.[23] This has significant implications regarding the role and responsibility of media studies in this cultural context. Digital anxiety is often rendered in relation to shifts in the economies of avowal: for example, as a result of digital culture's crisis of indexicality, how can one trust what one sees? Apparatus theory can help us to recognize that changes in the economies of avowal also necessarily entail changes in the economies of disavowal (and, more broadly, occlusion, repression, foreclosure, etc.).[24] These may be the spaces where different, even radi-cal sorts of intervention can reside and occur. Media studies and work in media history have a responsibility to facilitate this negotiation.

notes

1. By the phrase apparatus theory, I am referring generally to the develop-ment of a set of critical methodologies in the 1970s (but also since), related to theoretically-informed studies of spectatorship and constructions of mediated subjectivity. This range of studies can be implicitly or explicitly materialist in nature, and is informed by post-structural theory (espe-cially Marxism and psychoanalysis) in the attempt to address specific technologies and modes of address in relation to theories of subjectivity and subject effects. The list of critics and theorists I would consider perti-nent to these critical methodologies may be more expansive than is typi-cal: Baudry, Metz, Comolli, Dayan, Heath, Bellour, Vernet, Kuntzel, Mulvey, etc. The pertinent texts by these authors are not therefore sug-gested to evidence one coherent or boiler-plated set of critical operations, nor a reified and closed historical object termed "apparatus theory." My contention is instead that apparatus theory, especially in light of its grounding in dynamic theories that identify and interrogate contradic-tions, is less necessarily totalizing and tautological than perhaps even some of its founders and practitioners may have decreed or implied. In

our contemporary critical and theoretical context, such a dynamic perspective on both the theoretical foundations of apparatus theory and the historicized responses that worked to contain-disdain it may better afford a re-engagement of its premises regarding contemporary media (if only situational re-engagements). As indicated by the scope of work by the writers noted above, the range of factors and determinants assessed in the materialist terms of apparatus theory are certainly not exclusive of sociohistorical concerns such as industrial history and political and ideological context, including historiographic aspects of fields such as gender, race, ethnicity, and queer studies.

2. The key text in defining and elaborating on the notion of the post-human is N. Katherine Hayles, *How We Became Posthuman: Virtual Bodies in Cybernetics, Literature, and Informatics* (Chicago: The University of Chicago Press, 1999).

3. John Caldwell discusses such totalizing tropes in his essay "Introduction: Theorizing the Digital Landrush" in *Electronic Media and Technoculture*, ed. John Thornton Caldwell (New Brunswick, N.J.: Rutgers University Press, 2000), 1–31.

4. This demarcation of two aspects of apparatus theory is drawn from Jean-Louis Baudry, "The Apparatus: Metapsychological Approaches to the Impression of Reality in the Cinema," in *Narrative, Apparatus, Ideology*, ed. Phil Rosen (New York: Columbia University Press, 1986), 299–318; see especially note 2. For an example of how various theoretical and critical approaches—including those of apparatus theory—can be utilized in assessing issues of media specificity in digital culture, see Lev Manovich's discussion of computer animation in relation to Bazin, Comolli, and Bordwell-Staiger in *The Language of New Media* (Cambridge: MIT Press, 2001), pp. 185–191.

5. My interest in this topic was inspired by the work of artist Zoe Beloff, who visited a course I co-taught with Brian Miller in 1999. Her website entitled Philosophical Toys is premised on her contention that the rise of digital culture allows us to reconsider the age of pre-cinema, with both eras at opposite ends of a more constrictive media continuum. Implicit to the strata of pre-cinematic "toys" is the potential for a great multiplicity of "cinemas," each with a distinct "philosophy." The development of dominant cinema, however, severely constrained and delimited this multiplicity for nearly a century, until the rise of contemporary digital culture, which again promises a new plethora of "cinemas." A similar model of cinema history was enunciated by Tom Gunning in his closing remarks at the 2000 GRAFICS Conference at The University of Montreal on "Stop Motion and Fragmentation of Time: Cinematography, Kinetography, Chronophotography." Gunning's governing metaphor was a rope of cinema history, with strands of pre-cinematic devices that became woven tightly into dominant cinema, coming unwound again in the digital age. Recent publications that evidence some of the historiographic potential for such reckonings of cinema history include Barbara Maria Stafford and Frances Terpak's catalog for the Devices of Wonder exhibit, published by the Getty Research Institute. A related historiographic trope is the reconsideration of cinema history from the "lens" of the digital era's essentially electronic characteristics, a project which seems to me more genealogical than archaeological. Donald Crafton's important volume in the History of Cinema series, *The Talkies: American Cinema's Transition to Sound, 1926–1931*,

173

for example, reconsiders the early sound era of U.S. cinema as a founding transformation of the medium in relation to burgeoning electronic culture. Also pertinent to this line of inquiry is my own research on early television history in Los Angeles, in which I found that one key audience for the first experiments with "electronic" television in the city were electrical engineers and sound technicians newly arrived to assist with the development of "talkies."

6. Anne Friedberg, "The End of Cinema: Multimedia and Technological Change," in *Reinventing Film Studies*, ed. Christine Gledhill and Linda Williams (London: Arnold, 2000), 438–52.

7. Mark Williams, "History in a Flash: Notes on the Myth of TV 'Liveness,'" in *Collecting Visible Evidence*, ed. Jane M. Gaines and Michael Renov (Minneapolis: University of Minnesota Press, 1999), 292–312.

8. See for example Joseph Turow, *Breaking Up America: Advertisers and the New Media World* (Chicago: The University of Chicago Press, 1997), Damien Broderick, *The Spike: How Our Lives Are Being Transformed by Rapidly Advancing Technologies* (New York: Tom Doherty Associates, 2001) and Jeremy Rifkin, *The Age of Access: The New Culture of Hypercapitalism Where All of Life is a Paid-For Experience* (New York: Jeremy P. Tarcher/Putnam, 2000) for three very different explications of the effects of the rise of new media and technologies.

9. My interest in thinking about the subjunctive in relation to contemporary and cyber-culture was initiated by Marjorie Garber's positing of the "prurient wishful subjective," regarding celebrity biographies and the marked role that rumors of homosexuality can play in them. See Marjorie Garber, *Vice Versa: Bisexuality and the Eroticism of Everyday Life* (New York: Touchstone, 1995), p. 137. The term has been directly applied to computer-mediated culture in Mark Wolf's fine essay "Subjunctive Documentary: Computer Imaging and Simulation," in *Collecting Visible Evidence* edited by Jane M. Gaines and Michael Renov (Minneapolis: University of Minnesota Press, 1999): 274–291, which is briefly discussed above.

10. The basic plot of the film (which is not especially steeped in the historical facts of the incident) involves 12-year-old Elsie and her visiting cousin, 8-year-old Frances, who are both committed to fairy lore, and who take photographs of what they claim are actual fairies. As the film opens, it cross-cuts between the lives of two celebrities and that of the girls' family, touched by World War I and the flu epidemic that arose in its wake. Arthur Conan Doyle attends a public performance by Harry Houdini, who escapes from a strait-jacket; the mother of the family, Polly, grieves at the headstone of her son lost to illness; Frances attends a performance of the play *Peter Pan* enthusiastically exclaiming her belief in fairies; Elsie is at play with the fairy cottage and furniture that her late brother designed. The fuller dynamic of their respective emotional states soon becomes more clear. Frances arrives at the family home, awaiting word about her father, who may have been lost while serving in the war. Elsie's father Arthur is concerned that Polly will not accept her son's death; she believes in angels and contact with the afterlife, and attends events such as a meeting of The Theosophical Society. The girls are more empathetic to her, and take an interest in Elsie's father's camera, borrowing it for their excursions into the woods. When the resultant photos of fairies come to the attention of Conan Doyle, a believer in Spiritualism who lost his own son during the war, he elicits opinions

from a skeptical Houdini and also the chemists of Kodak labs before working to publish the pictures in the popular magazine *The Strand*. A more broad public speculation and interrogation of the girls and their claims ensues, before a climactic return of the fairies on the night that Frances' father arrives home.

11. See Marina Warner, "Through a Child's Eyes," in *Cinema and the Realms of Enchantment: Lectures, Seminars, and Essays by Marina Warner and Others*, edited by Duncan Petrie (London: British Film Institute, 1993): 36–50.

12. See Alex Owen, *The Darkened Room: Women, Power and Spiritualism in Late Nineteenth Century England* (London: Virago Press, 1989); Ruth Brandon, *The Spiritualists* (Buffalo: Prometheus Books, 1983); and Tom Gunning, "Phantom Images and Modern Manifestations: Spirit Photography, Magic Theater, Trick Films, and Photography's Uncanny," in *Fugitive Images: From Photography to Video*, edited by Patrice Petro (Bloomington: Indiana University Press, 1995): 42–71.

13. This phrase is not literally taken from Ebert's review, but did appear in more than one review with sentiments similar to this, obtained via a Lexis-Nexis search.

14. For a solid introduction to some of the ideological issues implicit to photography and its processes, see Suren Lalvani, *Photography, Vision, and the Production of Modern Bodies* (Albany: State University of New York Press, 1996).

15. My analysis of the film that follows contains a plot synopsis sufficient to this working paper. It should be mentioned that I intend to expand my discussion of both films at a later date.

16. This scene also establishes a relationship between the experience and fate of the discarded robots and certain thematic connotations regarding the history of slavery, including a parallel between the Flesh Fair and practices of lynching. (The robots, like slaves, are mandated to be non-human property, whose existence nevertheless threatens to blur the boundary with the human. The public spectacle of their subjugation is intended to reify a "human" stature which assumes the "natural" power to perform such a violent scene of demarcation.) The casting of African-American comedian Chris Rock is significant, as the first robot to be decimated.

17. This scene is strikingly similar to the conclusion of Rosselini's *Germany Year Zero* (1947), the culmination of his war trilogy, which follows a young German boy in war-ravaged Berlin. The purpose of such a reference is not entirely clear, although it seems to reference an utter bleakness of spirit in both characters. It also perhaps raises an odd tension within the Spielberg ouvre, crossing David's gendered crisis of subjectivity with that of German post–World War II subjectivity. (Spielberg of course has become a major figurehead in contemporary Holocaust studies.)

18. For more on issues of disavowal and the "utopias" implicit to much of the discourse on digital and cyber-culture, see Philip Rosen, *Change Mummified: Cinema, Historicity, Theory* (Minneapolis: University of Minnesota Press, 2001), especially chapter 8, titled "Old and New: Image, Indexicality, and Historicity in the Digital Utopia." Rosen's book, which in signal ways continues his reflections and analysis of what he terms 1970s film theory, will clearly be an important text to consider regarding any future deployment of apparatus theory. Michael Renov has discussed the significance of disavowal and ambivalence in the digital era in "Documentary Disavowals, or, the Digital, Documentary and Postmodernity" *Polygraph* 13 (2001): 93–111.

19. A significant transition in these representational dynamics that occurred partially in relation to the rise of digital effects is analyzed as "televisuality," in John Thornton Caldwell, *Televisuality: Style, Crisis, and Authority in American Television* (New Brunswick, N.J.: Rutgers University Press, 1994).

20. See Steven Holl, *Parallax* (New York: Princeton Architectural Press, 2000), especially the chapter entitled "Duration."

21. James Gleick suggests that the very phrase "real time" began with the invention of computers, but attained special significance upon the recognition of a demand for computer processing in bank transactions and money exchanges. See James Gleick, *Faster: The Acceleration of Just About Everything* (New York: Pantheon Books, 1999), pp. 66–67.

22. D. N. Rodowick, *Reading the Figural, or, Philosophy After the New Media* (Durham, NC: Duke University Press, 2001), p. 43, 49. Other recent work that seems keenly related to a re-deployment of apparatus theory includes Patricia Ticineto Clough, *Autoaffection: Unconscious Thought in the Age of Teletechnology* (Minneapolis: University of Minneapolis Press, 2000), which directly addresses Richard Dienst's important work on television, and Mark Hansen, *Embodying* Technesis: *Technology Beyond Writing* (Ann Arbor: University of Michigan Press, 2000). Each of these books is explicitly engaged in assessing the value of psychoanalytic discourse to work on new media. Psychoanalysis may itself become recognized as a historicized relic of epistemology, available for its mythic potential to contain the realization and dread of new media and posthuman dynamics.

23. It is worth mentioning that Spielberg's subsequent futurist film, *Minority Report*, can be described in the terms of this essay as invested in PVR temporarily and desire. PVR's, which are a cross between a VCR and a computer hard-drive, produce their own inflections upon the real-time subjunctive. Their capacity, for example, to "freeze" the "live" image, and then provide "real time" options by which to subsequently delay, fast-forward to, or simply jump to re-synchronize with the "live," represents the newest wrinkle of temporal frenzy within mediated culture. The premise of *Minority Report* can be seen to perform the desire implicit to PVR temporality: to (subjunctively) fast-forward and "record" into the future, for later playback. There are a number of aspects of this film to discuss in relation to the other films analyzed here. One interesting point to note is that like *Fairy Tale, A.I.* also concerns a family grieving the apparent loss of a child: Henry (the father), concerned about the emotional state of Monica (the mother) due to the coma suffered by their son Martin, arranges for a new experimental robot child named David to be provisionally adopted. *Minority Report* again situates its dramatic premise about subjectivity and mediated temporality in relation to a protagonist who still grieves the traumatic loss of a child. This trope suggests the likely pertinence of trauma theory as well to the consideration of these films and their attendant themes.

24. One important aspect of foreclosure in the digital discourse, for example, is the privileged absenting and re-positioning of labor issues within the digital economy, issues that began to reappear with the recognition of the dot-com bust. See for example, Jonathan Weber, "A Worker's Paradox," *The Industry Standard* 3:30 (August 14, 2000): 11, and Jill Andresky Fraser, *White Collar Sweatshop: The Deterioration of Work and Its Rewards in Corporate America* (New York: W.W. Norton & Company, 2001).

bibliography

Baudry, Jean-Louis. "The Apparatus: Metapsychological Approaches to the Impression of Reality in the Cinema." In *Narrative, Apparatus, Ideology: A Film Theory Reader*, ed. Philip Rosen. New York: Columbia University Press, 1986.

Beloff, Zoe. *Philosophical Toy World.* <http://www.turbulence.org/Works/illusions/index.html>.

Binkley, Timothy. "Camera Fantasia: Computed Visions of Virtual Realities," *Millenium Film Journal* 20–21 (1988–89): 6–43.

Brandon, Ruth. *The Spiritualists.* Buffalo: Prometheus Books, 1983.

Broderick, Damien. *The Spike: How Our Lives Are Being Transformed by Rapidly Advancing Technologies.* New York: Tom Doherty Associates, 2001.

Bukatman, Scott. "The Artificial Infinite." In *Visual Display: Culture beyond Appearances*, ed. Lynne Cooke and Peter Wollen. Seattle: Bay Press, 1995.

Caldwell, John Thornton. "Introduction: Theorizing the Digital Landrush." In *Electronic Media and Technoculture*, ed. John Thornton Caldwell. New Brunswick, N.J.: Rutgers University Press, 2000.

——. *Televisuality: Style, Crisis, and Authority in American Television.* New Brunswick, N.J.: Rutgers University Press, 1994.

Cha, Theresa Hak Kyung, ed. *Apparatus: Cinematographic Apparatus: Selected Writings.* New York: Tanam Press, 1980.

Clough, Patricia Ticineto. *Autoaffection: Unconscious Thought in the Age of Teletechnology.* Minnneapolis: University of Minnesota Press, 2000.

Crafton, Donald. *The Talkies: American Cinema's Transition to Sound, 1926–1931.* History of the American Cinema, Volume 4. Berkeley: The University of California Press, 1997.

Dienst, Richard. *Still Life in Real Time.* Durham, N.C: Duke University Press, 1994.

Fraser, Jill Andresky. *White Collar Sweatshop: The Deterioration of Work and Its Rewards in Corporate America.* New York: W. W. Norton, 2001.

Friedberg, Anne. "The End of Cinema: Multimedia and Technological Change." In *Reinventing Film Studies*, ed. Christine Gledhill and Linda Williams. London: Arnold, 2000.

Garber, Marjorie. *Vice Versa: Bisexuality and the Eroticism of Everyday Life.* New York: Touchstone, 1995.

Gleick, James. *Faster: The Acceleration of Just about Everything.* New York: Pantheon Books, 1999.

Gunning, Tom. "Phantom Images and Modern Manifestations: Spirit Photography, Magic Theater, Trick Films, and Photography's Uncanny." In *Fugitive Images: From Photography to Video,* edited by Patrice Petro. Bloomington: Indiana University Press, 1995.

Hansen, Mark. *Embodying Technesis: Technology beyond Writing.* Ann Arbor: University of Michigan Press, 2000.

Hayles, N. Katherine. *How We Became Posthuman: Virtual Bodies in Cybernetics, Literature, and Informatics.* Chicago: University of Chicago Press, 1999.

Lalvani, Suren. *Photography, Vision, and the Production of Modern Bodies.* Albany: State University of New York Press, 1996.

Manovich, Lev. *The Language of New Media.* Cambridge, Mass.: MIT Press, 2001.

Mayne, Judith. *Cinema and Spectatorship.* New York: Routledge, 1993.

Metz, Christian. *The Imaginary Signifier.* Bloomington: Indiana University Press, 1977.

Morse, Margaret. *Virtualities: Television, Media Art, and Cyberculture*. Bloomington: Indiana University Press, 1998.

Owen, Alex. *The Darkened Room: Women, Power and Spiritualism in Late Nineteenth Century England*. London: Virago Press, 1989.

Petrie, Duncan. *Cinema and the Realms of Enchantment: Lectures, Seminars, and Essays by Marina Warner and Others*. London: British Film Institute, 1993.

Poster, Mark. *The Second Media Age*. Cambridge: Polity Press, 1995.

Renov, Michael. "Documentary Disavowals," *Polygraph* 13 (2001): 93–111.

Rifkin, Jeremy. *The Age of Access: The New Culture of Hypercapitalism Where All of Life is a Paid-For Experience*. New York: Jeremy P. Tarcher/Putnam, 2000.

Rodowick, D. N. *Reading the Figural, or, Philosophy after the New Media*. Durham, N.C.: Duke University Press, 2001.

Rosen, Phil. *Change Mummified: Cinema, Historicity, Theory*. Minneapolis: University of Minnesota Press, 2001.

———, ed. *Narrative, Apparatus, Ideology: A Film Theory Reader*. New York: Columbia Unviersity Press, 1986.

Sobchak, Vivian. "Nostalgia for a Digital Object: Regrets on the Quickening of Quicktime," *Millenium Film Journal* 34 (1999): 4–23.

Stafford, Barbara Maria and Frances Terpak. *Devices of Wonder: From the World in a Box to Images on a Screen*. Los Angeles: Getty Research Institute, 2001.

Turow, Joseph. *Breaking Up America: Advertisers and the New Media World*. Chicago: University of Chicago Press, 1997.

Warner, Marina. "Through a Child's Eyes." In *Cinema and the Realms of Enchantment: Lectures, Seminars, and Essays by Marina Warner and Others*. Edited by Duncan Petrie. London: British Film Institute, 1993.

Weber, Jonathan. "A Worker's Paradox," *The Industry Standard* 3, no. 30 (2000): 11.

White, Mimi. "Television: A Narrative—A History." *Cultural Studies* 3, no. 3 (1989): 282–300.

Williams, Mark. "History in a Flash: Notes on the Myth of TV 'Liveness.'" In *Collecting Visible Evidence*, ed. Jane M. Gaines and Michael Renov. Minneapolis: University of Minnesota Press, 1999.

Wolf, Mark. "Subjunctive Documentary: Computer Imaging and Simulation." In *Collecting Visible Evidence*, ed. Jane M. Gaines and Michael Renov. Minneapolis: University of Minnesota Press, 1999.

twelve **tulip theory**

jeffrey sconce

After the NASDAQ/dot-com crash of 2000, business reporters searched for a historical parable to put the disaster in proper perspective. Several settled on Charles Mackay's account of "tulipomania" in his canonical chronicle of human folly, *Extraordinary Popular Delusions and the Madness of Crowds* (1841). For those unfamiliar with this work, Mackay recounts the introduction of the tulip to Western Europe in the seventeenth century and how German and Dutch aristocrats became so enamoured of this Turkish import that a "mania" drove the price of the flowers to unbeliev-able heights. Rare, exotic, and in demand (though essentially useless except as ornamentation), tulips became the foundation for a whole new speculative economy. Mackay reports of one man trading twelve acres of land for a single tulip! Comic stories abounded of unwitting bystanders mistaking a precious tulip bulb for a deformed onion and accidentally eating an investment equal to a year's wages. By 1636, as tulipomania spread beyond the moneyed classes, even the "lowest dregs" (Mackay's words) began to speculate in the tulip trade, pooling their money to buy and sell tulip futures on the Dutch stock exchange. Mackay takes this story to its inevitable conclusion: "At last . . . the more prudent began to see that this folly could not last forever. Rich people no longer bought the flowers to keep them in their gardens, but to sell them again at cent per cent profit. It was seen that somebody must lose fearfully in the end. As this conviction spread, prices fell, and never rose again."[1]

As a parable of the stock market, the parallels are obvious. This is what happens when people wake up and realize that there is no "there" there—that the economy is based on tulips (or online services with slick pitchmen, great graphics, and no customers). The following rant considers how this tulipomania has spread beyond the corridors of NASDAQ market power and into the hallways of university programs in film, television, and other mass media. As any fossil still teaching film and television realizes, it's all about "digital culture" now. This is true in terms of funding, hiring priorities, and general institutional enthusiasm. At the same time, however, I think most of us would be hard-pressed to think of a discipline in which more pages have been printed about things that haven't happened yet (and may never) or phenomena that in the long run are simply not very important (Jenni-cam, anyone?). Of course, only an idiot would claim that digital media are not worthy of analysis, an assertion that would sadly replicate the hostility toward film and television studies encountered in the last century. No one doubts the importance of digital media as a new form of distribution for the culture industries or as a new mode of telecommunications for bored office workers. The place of digital media in both the political and cultural economies of the future is certain. But generally, this isn't really what new media scholars are interested in studying. Academic "tulipomania" can be found in the seemingly endless claims that the internet, MUDS (multiuser domains), avatars, virtual reality (VR), TiVO, Palm-pilots and whatnot have led to radical redefinitions of identity, race, gender, narrative, subjectivity, community, democracy, the body, and so on. "The more visionary proponents and analysts of cyberspace come to virtual technologies from a variety of backgrounds and perspectives," notes Robert Markley, "but they share the belief that cyberspace marks a revolutionary expansion—and liberation—of our senses of identity and reality."[2] All too frequently such academic claims depend not on any tangible historical or sociological evidence concerning anyone's actual identity or reality but on theoretical posturing buttressed by little more than science fiction or digital gallery installations said to "explore" issues of identity and reality.

Digital pundits refer to fantastic but as yet unrealized computer applications as "vaporware." Given the continuing emphasis on tulipy speculation that permeates many new technology claims, we might do well to explore the implications of building more and more media departments around "vapor studies." While such scrutiny may seem a rather solipsistic pursuit, changes in the academic zeitgeist do eventually trickle down to our students while also setting the boundaries for future research in the field (indeed, such changes help define the "field"). With the emerging field of new-media studies, we have the chance to see an academic discipline in its embryonic stages. And, at least in the early days of digital studies, there seems to be a disconnect between the increasingly banal applications of digital media in the "real world" and the favored objects of digital study in the academy. Cyberstudies continue to trade in tulips despite the fact that evidence of sweeping transformations in identity, reality, art, and politics remains scant. Yes, a few iBook anarchists used e-mail to rally more people to jump up and down on police cars during the World Trade Organization meetings in Seattle, but many more "Netizens" are interested in organizing to protest how slow AOL is for downloading porn. Despite the incredible freedom and creativity promised by hypertext fiction, few people (beyond its practitioners) seem to be clamoring for it. There may come a day when people throw over Stephen King and John Grisham novels for the pleasures of hotlinking through a tortured bohemian's interactive account of her perceived childhood abuse—but I doubt it. Digitally based visual and performance arts, finally, are even less popular than middle class culture's previous whipping boys—abstract expressionism and atonal music. Though cyberenthusiasts have tempered their claims in the past few years (often through an obligatory and half-hearted reference to the "digital divide"), there persists in new media culture a revolutionary discourse "implying some larger social change, as if the major structural problems confronting our democracy were merely technical shortcomings."[3]

There are of course many scholars doing excellent work in the political, financial, and cultural economies of new media, examining digital culture less as a giddy revolution than as product and extension of more entrenched social forces. But let's face it: thumbing through the course schedules of many media departments and the catalogs of major university presses, this isn't the sexy, grant-grabbing, tenure insurance that makes for a career these days. Reading the more vapory work on new media, one gets the feeling that most of its claims about the recasting of body, identity, and subjectivity are based on either popular representations *of* these technologies, avant-garde art *incorporating* these technologies, or critical theory projected *onto* these technologies. In the pop-cult realm, calling William Gibson's *Neuromancer* the "bible" of cyberstudies is not far off the mark. Like the bible, Gibson's novel has also become a fiction divorced from history, a mystical document of parables that the faithful take as absolute truth.[4] Meanwhile, as the lowly masses clamor for TiVO, WebTV, and other digital technologies that will aid in a more interactive and emancipated consumption of *Everybody Loves Raymond*, gallery installations featuring digital media give the impression that we are all experiencing such a crisis of cybernetic fragmentation that it's a wonder anyone can find their way to work in the morning. New media theory, finally, often places the cyber-applecart before the virtual horse—discussing a world of digital speculation as if it were in fact already digital reality.

As a media historian and intermittent new-media pedagogue, I think the impact of digital culture, digital media, and digital studies on the academy raises fascinating and important questions. What exactly is the mission of new media studies? As more and more academic programs change their names to accommodate digital media, what exactly is being added? How does the addition of digital media to film and television departments impact other research projects and paradigms? How, finally, did we get to a state of affairs where the cybercontortions of Stelarc the Magnificent stand as a more important commentary on technology and the body than the daily travails of an overworked telemarketer? Part of the answer, I believe, is to be found in the fluctuations of two academic economies, the marketplaces of university resources and media theory.

cybercarrots

Media scholars who have read this far (and who else *would* read this far?) are no doubt feeling the pressure around funding for their departments. Many of us, I imagine, began in the humanities as English majors or art history majors, looking forward to the day that we would have tenure, a decent office, and the opportunity to consume the texts of our choice, think about them, and then teach and write about them. Of course, over the past few years, such a model of scholarship has been rearticulated in popular culture and university administration as rather rarefied and parasitic. Now we are all greatly encouraged to find "external funding," make lucrative connections to potential donors, and contribute to pecuniary—that is, pedagogical—advances through "distance learning." All of these activities will help fill the coffers of our various institutions and offset the cost of us hanging out in coffee shops, engaged in the unproductive labor of thinking, writing, and mentoring. Some take to this challenge like a fish to water—so enthusiastically that one wonders what attracted them to academic life in the first place. Others have to be dragged kicking and screaming out of the library to hustle for grants, donations, and the spare cash that might fly out the window of a passing CEO's Mercedes.

This often creates tension in media departments between those who study "new media" and those who remain mired in "old media" (film, television, radio, the telegraph, books, semaphores, cave paintings, and all other extinct technologies). As it so happens, the people interested in "new media" are often much better at networking and raising money—which administrators love. They're also very good at convincing deans and provosts that "old media" like books, film, and television are actually *old* media. The fact that many, many more people still read books, go to movies, and watch television than explore the frontiers of cyberspace matters little. Digital media are the future, we are told, and no one wants to be left behind. In any case, the creation of new-media studies provides a strategic point of entry for renegotiating resources, priorities, and profiles within media studies itself more broadly conceived. Often at stake here is a vision as to what should constitute media studies—future-looking techno-boosters ready to wire and fund the department for the new millennium, or bedraggled historians trapped in their musty cubicles worried about days long gone. "While the two types sometimes meet at conferences, the terms of engagement are typically only superficial," notes Lynn Spigel. "The historians . . . get carted out to present colorful anecdotes about 1950s housewives decorating their TV sets or nineteenth-century kooks using x-rays to mutilate their hands. . . . Meanwhile, the future is narrated by the new-technology crowd, many of whom are so steeped in enlightenment notions of 'progress' and romantic dreams of community and transcendence on the Net that history seems only a dead weight bogging utopia down."[5] The constant repetition of this narrative in individual departments and throughout the larger discipline has solidified the idea that new technologies are a "growth field"—a place where money, opportunity, and prestige await all willing to forge ahead and stake their claim.

Thus, at many institutions of hired learning, digital media have become one of the juiciest carrots ever to hang in front of the sad, downtrodden little donkey that is now the liberal arts. In the new corporate mode of university organization, digital media hold the promise of channeling revenue streams into (gasp!) humanities programs, allowing them to at last fall in line with the vocational model that many students, parents, and regents want to see in a university education. Having your son or daughter become one of the state's leading experts on *Finnegans Wake* is somehow less painful if they also learn how to design a *Finnegans Wake* website—at least that's *practical* experience that might be of interest to prospective employers. That's all well and good to the extent that it helps departments survive, gives graduates another career path, and perhaps even underwrites those cranks still interested in old media and old history. What is troubling, however, is when the integration of such vocational training leads to ramping up programs with resources and personnel that overrepresent a very narrow (and potentially fleeting) intellectual and technological moment. As many would no doubt agree, these are boon years for those who know (or can fake their way through) basic software packages. Since so many of us in media departments are middle-aged farts still dazzled every time we figure out how to access our e-mail from a remote location, freshly minted Ph.D.s who can put up a website without starting a minor housefire become as valued (or more so) than those tying to survive on intellectual or scholarly ability alone. Sadly, given the choice between hiring a brilliant logocentric and someone who can teach Photoshop, many media departments will now choose the latter in fear that someone else on campus will end up teaching all the Photoshop courses. If said Photoshop instructor can teach courses like "Photoshop and the Body," "Globalization and Photoshop," or "the Visual Culture of Photoshop," so much the better. Nevermind that any reasonably motivated thirteen-year old armed only with a six-pack of Pepsi, a Walkman, and an operator's manual can teach herself Photoshop in an afternoon.

This influx of hardware into the humanities has also led to a reconceptualization of what constitutes productive labor in an academic environment, a fantasy that can appeal to both administrators and faculty. Again, administrators do not mind if one uses departmental resources to design a devastatingly subversive Theodor Adorno CD-Rom, as long as in the process the exercise helps students find jobs in corporate graphics departments on down the road. For faculty, meanwhile, new media liberate a lifetime of frustrated creative fantasies. Those who have studied film and television over the years have generally been excluded from meaningful arenas of production. Digital technologies, however, make the production of websites, hypertexts, CD-Roms, digital video, and other creative formats relatively easy. This indulges academics in the vibrant fantasy that they can be both producers and critics of media (or even worse, producers of critical media). For once, academics seem to be building the future rather than simply watching it arrive. This move from reflection to production is not without its hazards. The "gush of workaday, real-time analysis of the future may seem to provide a bandwagon opportunity for media studies scholars, who have waited patiently for their place at the table of commercial, public discourse," notes John Caldwell. "But technospeak also issues an effusive density of conceptual clutter that may actually muddy the waters and meanings of digital technologies."[6]

This shift in academic media culture from "thinking" to "doing" is also a function of our continuing fetishization of the technology itself. We've all seen (and probably participated) in this drama—the glazed look that comes over a colleague's face with the announcement that the new powerbook has hit the stores. "Have you seen the new G4? Heard the iPod?" In the halcyon days of film studies, we all admired the intrepid souls who could take an old Bolex camera and a cranky Nagra out into the world and bring back something that could be edited together into a compelling work of art. Jean-Luc Godard using a shopping cart for a dolly while shooting *Breathless* was a story of heroic improvisation and creativity. Now, however, we have all been so thoroughly interpolated by *Wired* magazine's marketing discourse that the shame of technolag is forever upon us—often activating infantile regression in departments around who has the newest computer. Those of us who simply write for a living could probably still get by on a Commodore 64, but not if the dude in the next office is gettin' a Dell! So strong is this impulse that we occasionally see the sad spectacle of once highly committed Marxists sincerely debating whether or not the new iMac design is a good move for Apple.

Beyond enabling our forays into media production and stirring our love of the hardware, digital media's most profound impact on the marketplace of academe may well be in how we conceptualize our relationship to research and writing. Obviously, computers have vastly accelerated our ability to organize information and generate manuscripts. We are that lucky minority in the digital age who thrive on the acceleration of information. As Andrew Ross observes of information professionals, "Our tools are viewed as artisanal, and they can help us win comparative advantage in the field if they can access and extract the relevant information and results in a timely fashion. In such a reward environment, it makes sense to respond to the heady promise of velocification in all its forms. . . ."[7] Ross's concern is to delineate the cybercaste system that supports the more sublime manifestations of digitopia ("Let's not forget that for every one of us who wants our PCs and software to go faster, there are fifty others who want them to go slower," he notes[8]). We should also consider, however, what this "velocification" has done within our own realm of professional information. As an undergraduate English major, I remember being highly impressed by a professor's assertion that William Faulkner wrote *As I Lay Dying* on a typewriter in six months while he was working forty hours a week in a General Electric plant. While it has been rather unfashionable to talk about creative genius in the past few years, this story (if true) certainly speaks to a drive and focus I'm sure many of us wish we could harness today (my TV-addled brain certainly couldn't when it came time for my term paper on Faulkner). There has been much written about how computers change the act of writing itself, but if we were to boil this trend down for its impact on academic culture, we might consider if the ease of writing afforded by the computer is countered by a lack (or at least an acceleration) of critical reflection. Imagine, for example, the terror sweats we would experience today if we were to embark on the *Arcades* project or *Negative Dialectics* armed only with a notepad or a typewriter! Indeed, the idea of a master-

185

work—the culmination of a life's thought and reflection—seems almost absurd now in the age of ephemeral digitality. No doubt some will regard such concerns as the residual anxiety of a cranky modernist—the paradigms of work and knowledge now have the potential to change in liberatory and progressive ways, we are told. All technologies, of course, open new possibilities while ending others, and I'm certainly not arguing that we should go back to hunting and pecking on our Smith and Coronas. Still, who among us has not wondered if it is a bit *too* easy to write and publish today. On the bright side, this hyperacceleration of our work may lead to more timely interventions in public debate and an eventual facsimile of academic truth. Then again, it may mean, in the spirit of Henry David Thoreau, more and more of us will realize faster and faster that, in the end, we have less and less to say.[9]

theory club

If digital media in the academy have accelerated funding opportunities, the lust for hardware, and overall writing output, they have also presented a fertile terrain for the cultivation of Theory with a capital *T.* Many of us still imagine theory to be simply an intellectual tool: questions exist, and theory helps us explain them. And yet, there is also a "culture of theory" in academia that is equally important. Here theories exist as commodities subject to the vicissitudes of any other market of exchange, competing for fleeting status as the discipline's "cutting edge" in what Pierre Bourdieu might call the "intellectual field."[10] Perhaps because media studies is a young discipline, it has been highly interdisciplinary in nature; indeed, one might argue the explosion of interest in film studies in the 1970s marked the beginning of the increasingly vibrant interdisciplinary nature of all humanities research today. As with any strength, however, there is also a weakness. The theoretical "promiscuity" of media studies—its constant quest to assimilate other paradigms so as to reinvent itself—can also lead to accelerated cycles of theoretical fashion (not to mention rampant dilettantism). Thirty-year veterans of media studies have seen a dizzying parade of paradigms march by: auteurism, genre theory, semiotics, Marxism, psychoanalysis, structural anthropology, performance theory, gender theory, queer theory, formalism, neoformalism, cultural studies, ethnography, postmodernism, and postcolonialism, just to name a very few. Some paradigms find a place and remain a vital part of the institution; others fade away into historical oblivion. And, at any given moment, new approaches vie for ascendancy as a means of reconfiguring a prior set of questions related to the study of media.

Those with an "instrumentalist" interest in theory employ it to "solve" problems and avoid charges of naive positivism. Within the "culture of theory," however, rote "application" becomes less important than creative "performance." As the stakes of theoretical performativity become higher, the culture of theory increasingly engages in dialogue with itself rather than the ostensible "objects" and "problems" it once distantly addressed. Defenders of "grand theory" (as it is sometimes called) might argue that such metaspeculation is essential to intellectual progress, constituting a laboratory where the theory of tomorrow takes shape. I would agree that theoretical research and development is an essential component of the discipline—even if it does occasionally lead to blind alleys or open up academia in general to charges of irrelevance by the various anti-intellectual dullards so popular on the Fox News network and elsewhere. Citizens of a poststructuralist age, most of us probably feel there is no final answer to any critical question, and that the split between theory and object, like that between form and content, is at best a heuristic convenience. Theories and objects constantly redefine one another through the dialogue of history and critical practice; therefore, we should resist the empiricist temptation to dismiss even the most impenetrable metatheory as mere speculative posturing.

Nevertheless, the current intersection of theory culture and digital media has presented a particularly fascinating historical conjuncture, a moment when the acceleration of digital theorization threatens to outrun the development and deployment of any actual digital media. "The future," writes Caldwell, "has never been so systematically envisioned, aggressively analyzed, and grandly theorized as in the present rush to the cyber and digital."[11] Raymond Williams once said of television that it was the first telecommunications technology to be devised without regard to its eventual content. "It is not only that the supply of broadcasting facilities preceded their demand," he writes, "it is that the means of communication preceded their content."[12] A Marxist salvo hurled at the seemingly intuitive logic of technological determinism, his point was that social forces *implement* technologies; they are not radically transformed by them. If broadcasting technology developed in advance of its content, grand theory's discovery of digital media goes one step further, creating an academic discipline in advance of its "object." More accurately, new-media studies may well be the first discipline where "theory" does not derive from a study of the "object"; rather, the object of new-media studies derives (so far) more from theoretical conjecture than demonstrable impact. As society implements media, so too the academy implements theory.

In this respect, the language of theory (dismissed as "jargon" by its foes) is a much a productive force as a descriptive rhetoric. Say, for example, I'm interested in pornography. I want a research grant from my university to study pornography, but I'm undecided between two media-specific projects. I write up two proposals:

> "Midwestern Distribution Strategies in the Video Pornography Business: 1982–1990."

> "The Story of the (Electronic) Eye: Cybersex and the Deterritorialized ~~Perverse.~~"

Now, both proposals are essentially about industries serving people who like to masturbate in front of a video monitor. The first, however, conjures images of pot-bellied workers coming home and popping "Cathy does Cleveland" into the VCR—tasteless, exploitative, and to your average university grant reviewer, a little bit scary. But cybersex—that's the wanking of the *future*—evokes images of rubber-suited Thors fearlessly forging new sexual identities in the bodiless realm of cyberspace. While the first is about depressingly embodied subjects—firmly situated in history and on the couch, the second evokes the future wonders of mystical disembodiment, foretelling of that day when we all will be just miasmas of liquid pleasure surfing from mainframe to mainframe. In short, the second proposal evokes a world that exists more as theoretical improvisation than as actual social practice. The jargon, allusion, and parenthetical play evoke not so much a study of sexual desire but an abstract desire for the abstract play of theory. Of course, I'm not arguing we shouldn't study webcams, MUDs, telematic stimulation, VR vixens, adult websites, and whatever new paths to orgasm humans devise in the coming years. We should recognize, however, that an academic chain of desire binding theory and technology is as important here as the "new" libidinal economies of the imaginary "Netizens" we purport to study.

In *Making Meaning*, David Bordwell discusses the "routines and practices" that have guided interpretative approaches to cinema studies. Every few years or so, a critic will produce an "exemplar," a work that "influentially crystallizes an approach or argumentative strategy." As Bordwell reminds us (sadly), "most critics do not produce exemplars" but instead engage in "ordinary criticism," an "ongoing program . . . using approved problem/solution routines to expand and fill out the realm of the known."[13] If we were to map the "culture of theory" attending digital media, we would no doubt see a volatile terrain open for colonization and contestation. The "Wild West" profile of the discipline is captured in the very ambiguity of the terms used to describe it: *virtuality, digital culture, cyberspace, Internet studies, new media, the information age*—each term is a homesteader's stake in an as-yet-unclaimed field. And as with all homesteading, the field often constructs itself around a feud—

debates that are about the debates as much as the culture of digital media itself. Indeed, new media studies may well be the most self-reflexive discipline yet encountered in academe, a reflexivity befitting its embryonic status and the potential for economic and symbolic prestige that await its "pioneers." For example, discussions of digital culture often begin by defining two "warring" factions. Thus, Erik Davis warns of a "Manichean" conflict in new-media discourse that continually pits "the doomsdays of the neo-Luddites" against "the gleaming Tomorrowlands of the techno-utopians."[14] The ritual evocation of this "Manichean conflict" has become a prerequisite for many exploratory forays into the analysis of "digital culture," suggesting that early theory building in the field has displayed a trend toward irrational bifurcation. In this vein, Allucquere Rosanne Stone discusses the binary of "deification/demonization" in new media.[15] Timothy Druckrey follows in the same volume with the terms *telephobia* and *teletopia*.[16] Others begin with a laundry list of binaries (male/female, human/machine, subject/object) said to be confused by new media. From these all or nothing binaries comes skepticism. "Binary oppositions that characterize power struggles," notes Mary Ann Moser, "are often treated as though they might evaporate in the disembodied flux of electronic communications. But, so far, there are few signs this is the case."[17] Unbridled theoretical play in cyberculture is like "tulipomania," chimes another.[18] From skepticism over the state of the field comes compromise. "All too often," write the editors of *Race in Cyberspace*, "when it comes to virtual culture, the subject of race seems to be one of those binary switches; either it's completely "off" (i.e., race is an invisible concept because it's simultaneously unmarked and undiscussed), or it's completely "on" (i.e., it's a controversial flashpoint for angry debate and overheated rhetoric).[19] Reasonably, the answer must be somewhere in between.

Why is so much of the writing on new media concerned with other writing on new media rather than new media itself (present essay included)? In large part, this is because the study of "digital culture" has yet to generate a true "exemplar," though it is certainly not for a lack of trying. Who exactly is involved in this competition? We might posit a hierarchy within the culture of theory, ranked according to one's relationship to the production of exemplars. At the top is *the visionary*, a theorist who has in fact produced an influential, groundbreaking work of critical theory. Whether explained as an accident of historical circumstance or as biochemically hardwired genius, certain theorists emerge to shift the paradigm, to produce the model that serves as the foundation for subsequent debate in the field. All of us would like to attain the visionary class, of course, for it means we have exited the pursuit of mere ordinary criticism to instead become the model for the ordinary criticism of others. Just behind the visionary is *the synthesizer*, the critic who demonstrates a mastery of almost every relevant theoretical paradigm, generating work in the points of contact and conflict between visionary exemplars. The synthesizer often sets the overall terms of debate for a field and brokers what is or is not "hot" in the world of theory. Below the synthesizer is *the dogmatist*, a critic who masters one theoretical approach, applies it to all cultural phenomena from opera to car repair, and then learns how to reasonably defend himself from the assaults of other paradigms. Behind the dogmatist is *the bricoleur*, the low version of the synthesizer, pillaging the "greatest hits" of various theoretical paradigms with no real sense of their history or interconnection. At the bottom of the heap: insufferable *positivists*.

At present, I would argue the study of "digital culture" involves competition among many "synthesizers" vying to generate the visionary exemplar. This competition has many faces. In his introduction to *Electronic Media and Technoculture*, Caldwell demonstrates, rather unnervingly, the almost mirrored relationship between academic and industrial tropes of new media, suggesting that each domain places its own interpretive spin on shared assumptions about technology and the future.[20] The industry's spin, as we might imagine, derives from the hope of expanding profits and marketplaces. The academic spin on new media, however, seems more a competition among former critical exemplars, bodies of theory conceptualized in a logocentric universe now pressed into setting terms of debate for the digital future. One of the most promising candidates for an exemplar in new media studies (judged in terms of course assignments and number of citations) is Sherry Turkle's *Life on the Screen*. In her introduction, Turkle quite explicitly addresses the current "synthetic" intersection between old theory and new media. She writes, "More than twenty years after meeting the ideas of Lacan, Foucault, Deleuze, and Guattari, I am meeting them again in my new life on the screen. But this time, the Gallic abstractions are more concrete. In my computer-mediated worlds, the self is multiple, fluid, and constituted in interaction with machine connections; it is made and transformed by language; sexual congress is an exchange of signifiers; and understanding follows from navigation and tinkering rather than analysis. And in the machine-generated world of MUDs, I meet characters who put me in a new relationship with my own identity."[21]

Turkle's comments here map quite nicely some of the exemplars that have held sway over media studies (indeed, all of the humanities) for the past twenty years or so. First, there is the post-Foucauldian move toward post-Enlightenment accounts of the body, agency, identity, power, and space. While the ideal of rational agents working toward secular democratic equality seemed like a good idea earlier in the century, we now find it is actually a trap! New media, it would appear, will help us out of this fix through "multiple," "fluid," "cybernetic" identities. Second, we have an ongoing recasting of the Baudrillardian strain of postmodern theory. For those who remember the 1980s theoretically, simulation and hyper-reality used to be rather sinister concepts, seen (perhaps wrongly) as the final electronic victory of advanced capitalist spectacle. Now, of course, simulation and hyperreality are states to be desired—digital media promising us any reality we care to construct, even helping us to better understand our own core identity.[22] Finally, there is the residue of seventies era film theory (via Jacques Lacan and Louis Althusser) that posited media (as a form of language) must have some direct, productive relationship with subjectivity. "Apparatus theory," as it was called, stumbled a bit when applied to television, and yet its fundamental premise that media technologies produce "subjectivity" remains an influential concept.

Turkle's work with MUDs presents an interesting intersection of the abstractions of high theory and the specificity of media ethnography. The more vapory wing of new media studies, however, does not so much map theory onto "real" people as cite digital art as evidence of significant transformations in culture and society. Like the world of high theory, avant-garde art is often more a dialogue among a closed circle of connoisseurs than a dialogue with audiences or their world. As yet, we do not have fully immersive VR, or unnervingly sentient artificial intelligence, or even very impressive cybernetic prosthetics; but we do have plenty of art premised on the idea that the attending changes in vision, identity, reality, subjectivity, the body, the human, and so on have already taken place. In this respect, the field we call "digital culture" is a product of the dialogue between theory and avant-adventurism, a critical discussion that implies, as is fitting of vapor, that somewhere, somehow, a really interesting pot of ideas is on the boil. Many of the titles sound promising: race/gender/identity/subjectivity/the body and cyberspace/virtuality/the Internet/digital media. But, given the current speculative configuration of digital media, surely these are examples of a single, wispy electronic tail wagging several humongus dogs. If one encounters a gallery installation that examines the relationship between race and digital media, for example, it doesn't necessarily follow that there actually is a significant relationship between race and digital media (or more to the point, digital media may not be the most vital arena of cultural power in which to explore the politics of race). By the same token, if I analyze a gallery installation that examines the relationship between race and digital media, then I'm really writing more about the vicissitudes of art and theory than about a world out there that contains race and digital media.

Many vapor studies seem to recognize this is a potential problem. A common rhetorical strategy, therefore, is to showcase an esoteric and isolated example of digital practice, universalize it as if it has some larger importance, and then close with a passing reference to the "digital divide" so as to absolve oneself of the guilt associated with seeming to ignore more concrete issues of race, class, and gender. What makes these invocations of the digital divide particularly annoying is that they still carry the assumption that the digital is more important than the divide, rather than confronting the unpleasant fact that the digital is more a function *of* the divide. Ten years ago academics laughed when Newt Gingrich proposed solving the nation's poverty by giving welfare mothers their own computers, but one wonders what the reaction would be today if the same suggestion were made by a member of the "digerati," appealing to issues of malleable "identity" rather than economic empowerment.

Theory is like a shark; it must keep moving or die. No doubt it will (and should) find new ways for scholars (and their students) to reinvent, resee, and reshape their worlds. In this respect, high theory and high art may have a similar goal. The danger, to the extent that any development in academia can be called dangerous, is the potential for distorting our relationship to media, and in turn, the media's relationship to the "real world" (however it may be conceived). When the allocation of university resources and the culture of theory join forces to trade in tulips, to study vapor, it creates a formidable apparatus of potential misdirection. As Caldwell asks, "What becomes of critical theory when the showcased digital art, hacker, and counter practices that first set theory in motion fade; when boutique cyberaesthetics recede in the gush of the workaday e-commerce and e-business onslaught; when digital activity finally becomes as commonplace, pervasive, and ubiquitous as television?"[23] As the digital mundane continues to outpace the digital sublime, this process is already in motion, challenging us to ask what will be left after the vapor clears. Will we have an institutional and critical apparatus in place to address all media in the twenty-first century, whatever form they might take; or, will we still be gleefully reigning deathblows on the already well-bruised body of René Descartes? A relentless alchemy continues to stalk electronic media and electronic media studies, determined that cyberwizards will one day turn bodies into machines, consciousness into information, reality into simulation. Turkle captures this metaphysic succinctly in a single question: "Are we living life *on* the screen or life *in* the screen?"[24] But there is a third option. Perhaps we should begin exploring the more banal yet productive possibility that we are simply living life *with* the screen.

notes

1. Charles Mackay, *Extraordinary Popular Delusions and the Madness of Crowds* (1841; reprint New York: Farrar, Straus and Giroux, 1992), 95.
2. Robert Markley, "Introduction: History, Theory and Virtual Reality," in *Virtual Realities and Their Discontents*, ed. Robert Markley (Baltimore: Johns Hopkins University Press, 1996), 2.

3. Jesse Drew, "Media Activism and Radical Democracy" in Markley, ed., *Virtual Realities and Their Discontents*, 72. The discussion of vaporware and theory in this chapter builds on two previous accounts both published in the same year. See Peter Lunenfeld's critical elaboration of "vapor-theory" in *Snap to Grid: A User's Guide to Digital Arts, Media and Culture* (Cambridge, Mass.: MIT Press, 2000), 33–36; and John Caldwell's examination of vaporware as a theorizing practice in "Introduction: Theorizing the Digital Landrush." *Electronic Media and Technoculture*, ed. John T. Caldwell (New Brunswick: Rutgers University Press, 2000), 6–8.

4. For a more complete discussion of Gibson's influence on the culture of new media, see Allucquere Rosanne Stone, "Will the Real Body Please Stand Up? Boundary Stories about Virtual Cultures," in *Cyberspace: First Steps*, ed. Michael Benedikt (Cambridge, Mass.: MIT Press, 1991), 81–118.

5. Lynn Spigel, "Yesterday's Future, Tomorrow's Home," in *Welcome to the Dreamhouse* (Durham, N.C.: Duke University Press, 2001), 404.

6. Caldwell, Introduction, in *Electronic Media and Technoculture*, 2.

7. Andrew Ross, "Jobs in Cyberspace," in *Real Love* (New York: New York University Press, 1998), 25.

8. Ibid., 20.

9. Henry David Thoreau, *On Walden Pond.* (New York: Vintage Books, 1991).

10. For a more detailed discussion of the "intellectual field" (as constituted in France in the 1960s), see Pierre Bourdieu, *Homo Academicus* (Stanford, Calif.: Stanford University Press, 1998).

11. Caldwell, "Introduction," 1.

12. Raymond Williams, *Television: Technology as Cultural Form* (Hanover, N.H.: Wesleyan University Press, 1992), 12.

13. David Bordwell, *Making Meaning: Inference and Rhetoric in the Interpretation of Cinema.* (Cambridge, Mass.: Harvard University Press, 1989), 24–25.

14. Erik Davis, *Techgnosis: Myth, Magic Plus Mysticism in the Age of Information* (New York: Three Rivers Press, 1998), 9.

15. Allucquere Rosanne Stone, preface to *Electronic Culture: Technology and Visual Representation*, ed. Timothy Druckery (New York: Aperture, 1996), 9.

16. Timothy Druckrey, introduction to Druckery, ed. *Electronic Culture*, 15.

17. Mary Anne Moser, introduction to *Immersed in Technology: Art and Virtual Environments* (Cambridge, Mass.: MIT Press, 1996), xxii.

18. Jeffrey Sconce, "Tulip Theory," in *Digitextuality*, ed. John T. Caldwell and Anna Everett. (New York: Routledge, 2003).

19. Beth E. Kolko, Lisa Nakamura, and Gilbert B. Rodman, introduction to *Race in Cyberspace* (New York: Routledge, 2000), 1.

20. Caldwell, "Introduction," 7–8.

21. Sherry Turkle, *Life on the Screen: Identity in the Age of the Internet* (New York: Touchstone, 1995), 25.

22. See Jeffrey Sconce, "Simulation and Psychosis." in *Haunted Media: Electronic Presence from Telegraphy to Television.* (Durham, N.C.: Duke University Press, 2000).

23. Caldwell, "Introduction," 28.

24. Turkle, *Life on the Screen*, 21.

digitextual

practices

thirteen   **net ratings**

defining a new medium

by the old, measuring

internet audiences

k a r e n   s.   f.   b u z z a r d

In the 1990s, the economic model employed so successfully by the television networks increasingly was transferred to the Internet industry through the development of sites, known as portals, which, like the TV networks, conglomerated content. A key part of this emerging Internet business model was the rise of a system of audience measurement to identify and track its users. Wall Street investors; banner, pop-up, and pop-under advertisers; domains; and web-property owners desired such information in a variety of breakdowns.

Although traffic measurements offered Internet companies a means of product differentiation in order to enter the market, the second key business objective was the ability to dominate the marketplace, or gain market power. As Barry Litman has suggested, market power has its roots in the framework of the economics of cost efficiencies, product differentiation, and vertical integration. It is derived from creating an inelastic demand (loyal following of customers) for the product. With no close substitutes the product is indispensable to customers and thereby enables firms to charge high prices and earn excessive profit.[1]

By 2002, A. C. Nielsen's business tactics, employed so successfully in the traditional world of TV, led to its dominance of the Internet ratings marketplace. To better understand this process, this article examines the entry, methods, and business tactics of what were four major players in the race to measure the Internet and why Nielsen was able to dominate this new media despite its later entry into the marketplace. It examines the system of metrics developing to measure the Internet audiences and compares them to traditional TV ratings. Finally, it examines the dominant business model developing in light of the current focus on merger mania within the Internet business today, what some call a trend toward "portalopoly."[2] As the market has contracted to one provider of Internet ratings, the methodology has become rooted in a model provided by the traditional media in order to give company and advertisers comparability of data across media. In fact, Doug McFarland, president of Jupiter Media Metrix (JMM), until recently the dominant Internet ratings service, has criticized Nielsen's NetRatings for "shoehorning the Internet into an outdated model." According to McFarland, "We [Jupiter Media Metrix] are in essence, children of the Net. We grew up with the medium. When Nielsen views the world, everything looks like a TV screen."[3]

industry shake down: the battle to be the "nielsen of the net" goes to nielsen

Nielsen, the foremost TV ratings company, was slow to enter into the Internet ratings fray. This delay was because of an intense battle it was waging against four potential entrants into its TV "peoplemeter" market.[4] Because of its later entry, the door to the market was wide open for such pioneer ratings services as Media Metrix, Relevant Knowledge, and NetRatings.

Crucial to traditional analysis of technological innovation and its relationship to market structure has been some kind of first-mover advantage. The first firm to complete its research and development successfully receives a patent that allows it to monopolize the relevant product market more or less permanently. However, in the case of Internet ratings, as we shall see, Nielsen was not a first mover in terms of development of the technology—downloadable software—that monitored surfer activity on the Internet. Patents did not prove to be the key to its success. In fact, JMM had filed a patent infringement suit against Nielsen.

Instead, as the empirical evidence bears out, Nielsen found it more profitable to pursue a fast second policy allowing smaller pioneers modest inroads before responding aggressively. Rather than take a leadership role in innovation, it followed the business policy—in this instance, letting smaller firms initiate new forms of technology and methods, entering when its own research and development produced a virtual knockoff of rival products and methods and when it could use its economic muscle to merge with more experienced rivals—enabling it to gain their advantages. As F. M. Scherer notes, market-dominating firms tend to be slow in developing new products but "roar back like lions" when smaller rivals challenge them.[5] Competition from rivals had been the driving force behind many of the technological and methodological changes made: Neither Nielsen nor its clients·was willing to upset the status quo without an external threat.

Just as in other markets, in the world of Internet measurement, having multiple services makes for lower prices and better products, but it also made for conflicting traffic figures. As Eileen Meehan has suggested concerning TV measurement, having multiple contradictory ratings for any single time slot complicates and disrupts the routine of buying and selling. In fact, this disruption had predisposed networks and advertisers to accept a monopoly.[6] Ralph DeMuccio, research manager at AltaVista, puts it this way: "It's like having 3 watches on that all have a different time. You don't know what the hell time it is."[7] As a result, the driving engine of the TV ratings industry had traditionally been a combination of both monopoly and competition. As economists F. M. Scherer and David Ross note, "Much theory and empirical evidence suggests that the most successful market structure for rapid technical progress is a subtle blend of competition and monopoly, with more emphasis on the former than the latter and with the role of monopolistic elements diminishing when rich technological opportunities exist."[8]

the history of internet services and their methods

Web tracking services allow advertisers to put a face as well as age, gender, and household income on Internet surfers. Unlike the peoplemeter, the device used to measure network TV, the web software provides information as it occurs in real time and does not depend on its recruited sample to remember to perform some task, such as push a peoplemeter button, to indicate viewer demographics.

The oldest pioneer service for Internet ratings was Jupiter Media Metrix. Until its 2001 purchase by Nielsen, some felt it was destined to be the industry leader since it accounted for 85 percent of the advertising dollar before the dot-com crash. JMM was owned and (until recently) managed by Todd Johnson, president of NPD Group, a marketing service. The origin of what was first known as PC Meter came in 1994, when Steve Coffey, heading up the advanced research and development team at NPD Group, had the idea of creating a metering device that could measure actual software usage in computers. Previously, purchase data were among the only figures available to estimate software ownership and usage.

A year later, Coffey and his team began installing meters on panelists' computers to monitor and project usage of those computers. This invention would be critical in building what would be one of the Internet's most influential companies, as well as paving the way for the growth of e-commerce and e-marketing. For not only did the meter indicate what software was used, it also had the capability to specify the webpages users visited. JMM patented its meter device, which measures actual software usage in computers.[9]

With the meter patent in place, the NPD Group launched PC Meter as a separate company in 1995, then renamed it Media Metrix in 1997 in order to reflect its expanded coverage of digital media. The earliest subscribers to Media Metrix's syndicated reports included leading New York advertising agencies and media companies who had learned about its products through promotions at industry conferences and trade shows.

Jupiter Media Metrix pursued a path of technological innovation and aggressive expansion and soon developed new generations of its patented metering methodology. The technology worked with personal-computer operating systems and Internet browsers to passively monitor *all* user activity, including that of the World Wide Web, proprietary online and e-mail services, software applications, and hardware ownership and usage in real time, click by click, page by page, and minute by minute. The company offered monthly, weekly, and daily data collection. Moreover, Media Metrix captured in-depth demographics for each sample member including age, gender, household size and composition, income, education level, geographic location, and more, allowing user behavior to be linked with product demographic characteristics.[10]

In addition to its own innovations and organic growth, a key strategy for Media Metrix's continued leadership was to acquire and partner with other leading companies: In 1998, Media Metrix merged with Relevant Knowledge, a top internet ratings competitor. Founded by two former executives from Turner Broadcasting, Relevant Knowledge added local market ratings and analysis of fast-breaking events in real time, adding speed of delivery to Media Metrix's numbers in providing overnight reports, rather than the previously used monthly mail-in diary. The merger ended a war between the two companies that previously criticized each other in the press for both the size and quality of their samples and the timeliness of their data.

In February 1999, Media Metrix forged a strategic research alliance with McKinsey and Company to develop an understanding of online consumer behavior and its implications for e-businesses. In October 1999, Media Metrix acquired AdRelevance, an innovator and pioneer in

Internet advertising measurement technology. In July 2000, Media Metrix bought Jupiter Communications to become Jupiter Media Metrix (JMM) in order to add more analysis to its reports and to better position itself to compete with Nielsen NetRatings.[11] To protect its position from competitors using the same or similar software, JMM soon filed infringement suits against key competitors. It was successful in forcing a two-year upstart, PC Data, from the field and had filed two additional suits—against Paris-based NetValue, a company owned by Taylor, Nelson, and Sofres, a European research leader, and against Nielsen NetRatings.[12]

Another major competitor in the field, NetRatings, was a spin off of Hitachi, and was the only service to provide lifestyle and consumption information that helped advertisers to target niche groups. However, it was criticized for its method of soliciting panel members from web banner ads. In November 1998, just two weeks after the Media Metrix-Relevant Knowledge merger, it teamed with Nielsen Media Research to form Nielsen NetRatings. The merger helped NetRatings overcome its weakness in panel size and selection (originally 3,500 compared to 40,000 for JMM) by offering the benefits of Nielsen's considerable experience in audience panels to the newly combined service. The partnering also offered NetRatings the ability to launch a global service, eRatings, as Nielsen NetRatings had earlier joined with A. C. Nielsen to invest $500 million over the next two years to get a service running in thirty-three companies by 2001.

With the competition reduced to two main competitors, it was Jupiter Media Metrix who buckled under the financial pressure. In 2000, JMM recorded revenues of $143 million compared to Nielsen NetRatings' $20 million. But by 2001, the situation had reversed with Nielsen NetRatings making $335 million to JMM's $20 million.[13] The dot-com meltdown had resulted in a loss of 22 percent of its subscriber base leading to a net loss of $48.2 million in 2001 compared to $7.6 million in 2000. In response, the company underwent major restructuring changes in top management. In an effort to help bail out the troubled company, Todd Johnson loaned JMM a $25 million letter of credit. By late October, JMM, struggling to remain afloat, had slashed operating expenses by $40 million and had laid off 300 employees.[14]

Later that same month deals were underway for the purchase of JMM by Nielsen NetRatings, who also purchased A. C. Nielsen's eRatings, its international Internet ratings business, in order to streamline Internet ratings into a single brand and create a de facto standard for the Internet. The merger would have effectively made the California-based Nielsen NetRatings the largest player in audience measurement. (The only remaining competitor, at this writing, is the upstart Com-Score Network.) Nielsen NetRatings agreed to loan JMM $25 million to replace its letter of credit between Jupiter and Todd Johnson. The loan was considered crucial for JMM to last long enough to consummate the merger. Interestingly, JMM and Nielsen NetRatings had both been criticized for reporting widely disparate figures for the number of unique visitors to the same sites. With the merger, this problem would disappear. However, NetRatings and Jupiter Media Metrix were forced to call off their $71.2 million merger agreement after federal trade officials raised concerns about the competitive impact of the merger that would consolidate much of the Internet measurement business in the hands of NetRatings.

The economic incentives toward monopoly had been strong, encouraged by the advantages offered in reaching optimal size (through economies of scale, diversification, and vertical integration) and by the Internet ratings industry it served, with its desire for only one set of noncontradictory numbers. This time that incentive was foiled due to antitrust concerns.

developing a system of web metrics

Let us consider now the value of web-tracking services over log files. Web services offer what may be called audience-centric over site-centric measures. Log files measure hits to a site and page requests, as well as how long visitors remain on a site. However, the technology has several faults. First of all, serve logs can be misleading since caches can skew information collected. Second, they are faceless.

By comparison, Internet ratings estimate the number of site visitors by capturing the surfing behavior of a particular audience. Compared to the expensive hardwiring of the set-top box that pollsters use to measure TV viewing, those recruited install (by downloading) monitor software. The number, age, and sex of surfers' eyeballs on a website correlate directly to compensation for any pixelating corner of the real estate of its pages, just as ratings do for television. Unlike their old-media counterpart, web raters offer their clients not only size and demographics breakdowns of their sites, but also specific data on what site visitors bought. This information is used by the Internet industry to set advertising rates.

the sampling process

Just as it does with TV viewers, Nielsen NetRatings recruits samples of surfers who agree to provide data on site visits, including when and how often the visits occur. Their samples are called *panels*. Although NetRatings (prior to its merger with Nielsen) originally recruited surfers from websites, it came under heavy criticism from industry observers because web-recruited surfers tend to be heavier users, disproportionately male and much more experienced than typical web users. After its merger with Nielsen, NetRatings began using enumeration studies to decide how to project data and how to weigh its sample, to make it representative of the overall Internet-using population. The company also switched to a technique known as random digit dialing to gather recruits.[15] Based on the premise that the telephone is the most pervasive technology in the home in the United States, phone numbers are chosen at random and recruits are asked to disclose information about their Internet usage. Recruiters convince them to load monitoring software on their computer. Nielsen samples have grown to 165,000 worldwide (as of January 2002) with 70,000 in its U.S. panel, including 8,000 people at work. But because the universe of websites is greater than the number of TV channels, the industry desires a much larger sample.[16]

who uses web-tracking services?

The first web-ratings clients included stock analysts and certain business or commercial websites. All were hungry for information about the people visiting their sites and eager to set themselves apart from the crowd. Ratings helped analysts value the various web properties in hot stock markets and these figures were used for buying and selling. Websites sought to give advertisers as much information as possible about how many and who were the people viewing or surfing their sites. According to Beth Haggerty, vice president of world ad sales at InfoSeek, "Viewership ratings and measurement will have a major impact on how the Internet is perceived as a mainstream media, to how Wall Street values Internet companies, to how our customers measure value of market investments."[17]

metrics, or what do they measure?

Both Nielsen and JMM have been trying to establish a definitive system of web metrics. So far, this had resulted in four types of measurements: web property rankings; website rankings; domains; and unique visitors to each site, typically reported by week and month, as well as the amount of time each person spent at a website. A *web property* is defined as a collection of websites owned by one company. Some have criticized JMM for using the terms *site* and *web property* synonymously, which masks individual sites and produces obfuscated rating figures. They have been criticized as well as for letting site owners control what information was included in their web measurements rather than JMM providing an independently standardized metric formulation. For instance, Lycos owns, in addition to its flagship portal, the HotBot search engine, and the Tripod home page.[18] The combined traffic of all these sites and all the other Lycos-owned property sites make up the Lycos web property figures (see table 13.1). A website, by comparison, is an individual site, such as the Google search engine. JMM and Nielsen define unique visitors as the actual number of total users who visited the Web site once in a given time period.

All unique visitors are unduplicated (only counted once). Unique visitors are a measure of reach, the percentage of the population that visits a website or web property over a specific time period. If we multiply the percentage of unique visitors by the number of times an average person visits a website during the same period, or frequency, we can get estimates of gross, terms familiar to the traditional world of advertising.

In addition, Nielsen's reports were unique in reporting banner ad click-through and their demographics on a weekly and monthly basis. As such, it established a special category for top web advertiser and banner ads. JMM had been widely criticized for ranking a little-known camera-maker website, the X10, among the Internet's five top destinations. This was because the X10 had used pop-ups (advertising that is automatically launched by webpages) and pop-unders (advertising that opens a news browser window beneath the webpage) to boost its audience counts. Nielsen had weeded out advertisements from the numbers aimed at judging the popularity of websites.

JMM ranked both the top fifty websites and web properties. Nielsen, by comparison, only ranks web properties. Subscribers to Nielsen, as a result, had to make a special request to receive individual site data. Some feel that the absence of standardized individual site data potentially poses a critical problem. Significantly, Internet ratings are similar to the ratings used for television. TV ratings measure how many people tuned into an entire network during a given week or month (the counterpart to the web property) or how many watched a particular program (the counterpart to the website). Web property numbers, like network numbers, indicate how many people a web media owner can reach. For example, in February 2000, the Yahoo! network had forty-five million people, compared to thirty-two million for Lycos and twelve million for AltaVista.[19] Website numbers are comparable to individual TV show ratings. They indicate how popular a website is among surfers, just as you might wish to determine how popular a particular show is. If, for example, I want to know the popularity of a particular

Table 13.1 Rating Traffic Patterns
The Top Five Web Properties for December 2001, U.S. Source: Nielsen NetRatings

Property	Unique Audience	Reach %	Time per person
1. AOL Time Warner	65, 522, 808	62.72	0:44:54
2. Yahoo	58, 030, 507	55.55	1:20:31
3. MSN	49, 551, 935	47.43	1:08:28
4. Microsoft	30, 160, 176	28.27	0:10:22
5. Amazon	23, 733, 016	22.72	0:17:18

search engine, then, the web-property ratings are useless since they mix in people who went to Lycos, HotBot, and Tripod as well.

This explains how in January 1999, Go.com jumped from 21 to 34 percent in surfer numbers in JMM's reports. Go.com had decided to include web-property figures, not just website figures. According to an April 4, 2000, *Search Engine Reports* article, this practice is "comparable to Fox combining ratings for shows like *Ally McBeal* and the *Simpsons* into ratings for *Titus*, to show it was more popular than *Friends*."[20] Just as with TV, it is crucial to know the hit shows since they can make or break a network. The combination of different sites into one number allows web media owners to hide bad shows, and it obfuscates true data about which of the sites' business partners are the actual hits for the property. Some search engines have begun reporting the number of queries per day to give a better measurement of search-specific traffic.

how are web ratings shaping the dominant business model for the Internet today?

The central metaphor that illuminates the dominant business model operating today on the web is the board game *Monopoly*. Similar to *Monopoly*, Internet businesses, both new and established, have rushed to stake claims to Internet properties in order to own and rent valuable Internet real estate, a game, as I've mentioned, that some analysts call "portalopoly." The game is played like this: Internet companies are racing to build sites (known as portals) that serve as hubs or gateways to the larger Internet. Just as local TV stations served the needs of their local audiences until networks came along to aggregate content, traffic, and revenue, so do portal sites serve a similar function. Portals function like the mass circulation magazines or TV networks: they are sites that meta-aggregate content and offer a range of services in order to be the home page for as many users as possible, thereby attracting more advertising revenue. The space they occupy has become the coveted promised land.

These portals have evolved to include a laundry list of free services such as e-mail, news, and weather. Some see these portals as the new shopping malls, town centers, and news hubs all rolled into one.[21] Many of today's portals were once known as innocuous search engines but are now on the verge of maturing into the new media conglomerates of the new millennium. The new media giants include Yahoo, Excite, Lycos, AOL, AltaVista, Snap and InfoSeek, not to mention Microsoft.

the distinction between a search engine and a portal: google is a search engine; yahoo is a portal

The six or seven traditional portals are facing competition from such content sites as the *New York Times on the Web*, Charles Schwab, and Fidelity, which are beginning to lure customers through free e-mail service and other features. Schwab's start page, the Market Buzz, aggregates content from other financial sites such as The Street.com and Thomson's MarketEdge. Sports sites such as CBS's SportLine.com also have the potential to be portals.[22]

In this landscape, the name of the game is market share. Competition for eyeballs has led to a spate of acquisitions, partnerships and distribution deals. Given estimates numbering 580.78 million world wide Internet users as of 2002, companies are spending millions in the hope of eventually cashing in before the window of opportunity closes. Presently, portal stocks are soaring and companies are in turn using this stock to acquire new properties. Since the major portals market has become homogenized with sites that contain similar customization features, it may take longer and exclusive content deals for these sites to develop identities of their own. According to Patrick Keane, an analyst at Jupiter Communications, "At one time differentiation was adding features. Now the true search and directory players all provide the same things. Search has become a commodity."[23]

the portal business or home page as one-stop gateway to the web

In an effort to attract new Internet users, portals are spending millions of dollars. The goal is to get users to designate a specific company's portal site as *the* homepage on their browsers. Once that is done, the page is the first one seen on logging in and launching browsers. To keep the surfers there, portals are loading their sites with customized features and accessories. The longer users stay, the more features they may use, and the more revenue they generate for portals. Apparently, the future will be determined by those who control the first screen to be seen on whatever user device of the future is tuned in (i.e., computer, TV, or some combination thereof), whether it be called the homepage, portal site, electronic programming guide, system interface, or "first boot."

A portal site can earn the coveted spot of homepage in two ways: getting users to manually plug its address into their web browser or by delivering a preprogrammed browser to the users with its sites already designated as the homepage. Most prefer the latter strategy and are making deals with Internet service providers. For example, AT&T has signed deals with three portals sites—Lycos, Excite, and InfoSeek—to form a "web-based online service." MCI and Yahoo have also joined forces to form a "web-based online service," a homepage linked to a portal. (This idea was pioneered by SNAP of CNET, but their version lagged behind others such as Yahoo and Excite.) The traditional TV networks, fearful of being left behind, have major portal investments: ABC in Go.com (owned by Disney), CBS in iWon.com, and NBC in NBCi.

The portal idea is an expensive business model, but becoming the gateway for millions and translates into millions with lucrative advertising deals and multimillion deals in renting out valuable real estate to commerce partners. For example, Excite will pay $70 million for a two-year period to power Netscape's Netcenter Search Engine.

As the industry becomes more concentrated, search engines and others are competing to demonstrate their dominant position to advertisers. Portal site suppliers and community sites are pairing up to create vertically integrated media companies. Yahoo has merged with GeoCities, AOL with ICQ/Netscape, InfoSeek with Disney, and AltaVista with Compaq. (The logic is that community sites, e-mail, and the like attract viewers/visitors who tend to be "sticky," to stay longer in a site, thus creating advertising opportunities.)

Portals offer a business model similar to network television. They are big advertisers, audience-gathering sites that act as hubs, feeding traffic to other sites and gathering content from sites for an integrated community—not unlike the networks' role in television. Although TV has become fragmented, with hundreds of channels available, the big four TV networks still are the focus of a lot of viewing.

Studies indicate that the same gigantism that afflicts the old media now dominates the new. Despite the Internet's myth of indestructible diversity, cyberspace is also vulnerable to monopolistic tendencies. Two years ago 60 percent of all time spent on the Internet was on sites owned by 110 companies. By 2001, fourteen companies captured the largest share of the user's time and 50 percent of all time is spent with four companies.[24] These companies now steer visitors to other sites they own or cross-promote. Mergers and marriages have whittled down the field while the evaporating dot-coms have forced weaker sites to close. Although anyone can still get online, having a powerful voice once you get there is becoming a different matter.

notes

1. Barry Litman, "Network Oligopoly Power: An Economic Analysis," in *Hollywood in the Age of TV*, ed. Tino Balin (Boston: Unwin Hyman, 1992), 115–16.
2. Jim Hu, "Racing to the Start Line," *C/NET News*, May 14, 1998, <http://news.com.com/2009-1023-211162.html>.
3. Doug McFarland, quoted in Justin Oppelaar, "Web Ratings Gladiator," *Variety* 380, no. 9: S34, 2002.
4. Karen S. F. Buzzard, "The Peoplemeter Wars: A Case Study of Technological Innovation and Diffusion in the Ratings Industry," *Journal of Media Economics*, forthcoming (winter 2002).
5. F. M. Scherer, *High Technology Competition* (Cambridge, Mass.: Harvard University Press, 1992), 158.

6. Eileen Mehan, "Why We Don't Count: The Commodity Audience," in *Logics of Television*, ed. Patricia Mellencamp (Bloomington: Indiana University Press, 1990), 126.

7. Ralph DeMuccio, quoted in "Media Matrix: First Ever Multi-County Internet Audience Measurement Results Released by Media Matrix," *CNN Disclosure*, June 19, 2000, 5.

8. F. M. Scherer and David Ross, *Industrial Market Structure and Performance*, 3d ed. (Boston: Houghton Mifflin, 1990), 660.

9. Material provided to the author by Jupiter Media Matrix, 2000.

10. "Company Measures Web User Patterns," *Dot.Com* 5 (1998), 1.

11. Ken Kerschbaumer, "Media Metrix—Jupiter Merge," *Broadcasting and Cable*, July 5, 2002, 35.

12. Maryann Thompson, "Ratings Firms Vie for Global Domination," *Industry Standard*, October 25, 1995, 3.

13. Erin Joyce and Christopher Sanders, "NetRatings to Buy Jupiter Media Matrix, eRatings.com," *Advertising Report*, October 25, 2001, 3–4.

14. "Jupiter Feels the Dot.com Loss," *Advertising Report*, July 30, 2001, 1–2.

15. Oppelaar, "Web Ratings Gladiator," S34.

16. Pete Barlas, "Rivals Vie to Be Nielsen of the Net," *Investors Business Daily*, July 9, 1998, 3.

17. Beth Haggerty, quoted in "InfoSeek Hosts 'Great Ratings Debate,'" *PR Newswire Associate*, July 11, 1998, 12.

18. "The Problem with Ratings Services," *Search Engine Reports*, April 4, 2000, 2.

19. Ibid.

20. Ibid.

21. Dawn Kawamoto, "Cashing In on the Portal Fever," *C/NET News*, May 14, 1998, <http://news.com.com/2102-1023-211086.html>.

22. Beth Lipton Kriegal, "Content Sites As Portal Competition," *C/NET News*, May 14, 1998, <http://news.com.com/2009-1023-211089.html>.

23. Patrick Keane, quoted in Hu, "Racing to the Start Line."

24. Catherine P. Taylor, "Jupiter Offers Vertical Reports for Nine Areas," *Advertising Age*, April 9, 2001, 28.

flashing digital

fourteen   **animations**

pixar's digital aesthetic

k a t h e r i n e   s a r a f i a n

> Art challenges technology and technology inspires art.
> —John Lasseter, Executive Vice President of
> Creative at Pixar Animation Studios

The computer-animated feature film is the all-digital product of a production process that joins traditional filmmaking techniques with
emerging technologies and tools. Production designers might consider
a wide range of possibilities in defining a computer-animated movie's
visual world, which will be manufactured completely, pixel by pixel. A
digitally created world can have a unique, never-before-seen aesthetic
or a kind of hyperrealism that only digital art, in all its precision, mathematical perfection, or programmed randomness can achieve. Will the
computer moviemaker, with a team of traditional and digital artists,
programmers, animators, and cinematographers, use the versatile digital medium to create a world that has lived only in artists' imagina-
tions? Or will the artist attempt to represent the most real-looking or

real-seeming of worlds—manufactured to evoke the very imaginings of the populace, the expected dream lives?

The *Forrest Gump* visual effects tricks and *Titanic* constructions of pasts and presents, commingling both the whimsical and true, are intended to deceive audiences, to have them suspend disbelief for the time it takes to tell stories. A computer moviemaker, video game creator, or digital graphic artist can attempt the opposite: computer moviemakers create fantasy worlds that cannot be seen elsewhere, and will not be seen without their particular kinds of eyes. These are not the kino-eyes of filmmakers past, nor the literal eyes and camera lenses of live-action auteurs. These are the tools of a different trade, and they make possible techniques and looks that expand the imagination and stretch the cinematic aesthetic.

The computer moviemaker's eyes are part of a tool kit of digital and nondigital parts. These artists have a virtual camera, with a field of view set wholly in the computer. They select lenses for the effects they desire; a different lens means a different view on the artist's monitor. The workstation might consist of a hard drive, keyboard, mouse, stylus pen, digital shot recorder, playback monitor, and earphones. Artists have characters, sets and props: digital sculpts, three-dimensional objects existing in virtual space, placed into layouts, arranged in the computer's virtual set and lit with key, fill, and rim lights. Characters' costumes are texture maps, shaders and digital paintings applied with computer paint brushes to the 3-D objects. Digital dailies are run off a shot recorder, which plays back computed, rendered scenes for the director and crew.

storytelling

At Pixar Animation Studios, the computer feature-filmmaking process begins traditionally. Artists sketch, paint, pastel, and doodle by hand, on paper. They sculpt sets and characters in clay or they construct scale models. Pixar art directors design productions as other filmmakers would, but with an almost endless world of possibilities for the completely created, pixel-by-pixel digital aesthetic. Then, technical artists, animators, and digital painters revise productions in the computer, object by object and shot by shot. They plan on paper and in clay and with databases; then they build fantastic worlds in the computer, layer by digital layer. With so many kinds of artists touching each shot, from modeling, shading, and layout to animation, simulation, lighting, and effects, the computer animation process is truly collaborative. All of these artists use different kinds of tools, both new and traditional, enabling them to see with different kinds of eyes. If the late twentieth and early twenty-first centuries have been times of revolution and technological development leading to the formation of a digitally saturated culture for everyday life, work and play, then earlier revolutions and revolution-era filmmaking practices readily come to mind. It is true that we now live in an increasingly digital world, an ever more automated workplace, home, automobile, gym, and movie theater. But, there are precedents.

In 1928, Dziga Vertov's *The Man with a Movie Camera* was created as a mirror reflection of the revolution of its time. The film, made "in the transitional period immediately preceding the introduction of sound . . . joins the human life cycle with the cycles of work and leisure of a city from dawn to dusk within the spectrum of industrial production." The production includes segments about filmmaking itself, which Vertov presents as a "range of productive labor processes," as well as communications, construction, mining, and the textile industry assembled on film "in a seamless, organic continuum, whose integrity is continually asserted by the strategies of a visual analogy and rhyme." Film scholar Annette Michelson's characterization of Vertov's storytelling in the silent cinema is instructive: "The rhythm and rhymes are in fact the formal instantiation of a general community, of the common stake in the project that retains both division of labor as indispensable to industrialization and rationalization as indispensable to the construction of socialism, a project that has radically reorganized the property relations subtending industrial production."[1]

Now, in a twenty-first-century digital culture, the formal moviemaking process uses every available technology, as Vertov surely would have, and it also mirrors the surrounding contemporary culture of labor, production, productivity, and communications—all processes more technologized than ever. If almost no part of day-to-day life has gone untouched by digital technology, then the kino-eye is alive and well in computer moviemaking. But instead of striving after a "truth" attempted by Vertov's kino-eye, the constructs of computer cinema range from the manipulated fantastic (special effects, over-the-top explosions, ghouls, and *Dragonheart*'s digital monster) to the "real" (*Titanic*, with digital effects created to make the re-creation of a past reality as accurate as possible). Clearly, revolutionary media practices drive the industry today, just as in the past. This is nontraditional filmmaking produced with some highly traditional methods. Today, computer animation may be a different kind of moviemaking, but it is rooted in the most traditional of storytelling and motion-picture-production techniques. In some ways, this is standard, familiar movie production: a motion picture aesthetic with a motion picture vocabulary and process that are at once rooted in and different from live action and two-dimensional animation production. Audiences of computer animation may expect to experience a look they have never seen, a completely new, inventive visual world, but no matter what dazzling, groundbreaking looks computer imagery achieves, feature film audiences expect a good story, well told.

Digital moviemakers use new and evolving tools to tell their stories, but however new the tools, the techniques still must be rooted in effective storytelling. Like any other storytellers, computer artists use the tools that best tell their stories. These tools range from paper, pen, and paintbrush to 3-D computer models, pixels, lines of code, and digital paint. Character performances are not computer-animated at all, but are hand-animated by artists whose work is grounded in puppetry, acting, dance, and 2-D animation. It is human work, not computer work. It is art and story translated through an apparatus, like most movies, paintings, books, and plays. The apparatus is not a wood puppet with strings, but a 3-D model with digital textures and lighting.

the computer animation process

The first computer-animated feature film was born not just of *Toy Story* director John Lasseter's love of toys and the idea that toys could come to life; it was born of the rich look Lasseter knew he could achieve with the 3-D qualities, detailed textures, emotive lighting, and depth of computer animation. Making the attempt to achieve the distinct look of plastic toys and the angular surfaces in Andy's bedroom in *Toy Story* also made sense for artists working with Pixar's developing computer tools. Before *Toy Story*, Lasseter's short films *Luxo Jr.* and *KnickKnack* presented the worlds of inanimate objects—lamps and snow globes, respectively—with a 3-D realism mixed with a colorful cartoonishness. The computer was Lasseter's tool for achieving moods, character animation, and acting nuances in a pair of gray lamps that 2-D animation might have expressed quite differently.

Figure 14.1. Luxo, Jr., copyright Pixar Animation Studios.

Developing the story for Pixar's second feature film *A Bug's Life*, director Lasseter was taken with the idea of a cast of insect characters. "In thinking of subject matter that lends itself to this medium, one that came up very quickly was insects—because of their physical attributes: exoskeletons, color, iridescence, translucence. All of these properties translate to our medium beautifully."[2] As technology and storytelling sophistication for the medium have progressed through the years, directors have challenged the computer and the digital artists, asking for what is most difficult for machines to compute: soft lines, organic forms (i.e. human hair), water, fire, and fog. Consequently, directors and artists have pushed the machines beyond existing technology standards, designing movies that use simulated cloth and fur, all the while asking software engineers to develop innovative processes that will allow artists to achieve these more complicated looks.

the artist

Are computer animation artists working with digital limbs and keyboard prosthetics? Are they the cyborgs hybrids of Donna Haraway's human/machine unity? Surprisingly, the qualities of the digital artist are not what one might expect. At first glance, the digital artist is the ultimate wired studio employee. The machines—keyboard, mouse, foot pedal, playback monitor, earphones—are the tools, and a digital artist at work in a computer animation studio wears the machine, at times, as an extension of the hand. Like any users who have become intimately familiar with a piece of software, digital artists anticipate what the software will do next. They are as at one with keyboards and commands as the pastel artist is with the chalk and the carpenter is with the hammer.

So it becomes clear that, per Haraway's vision of a digital culture, "One consequence is that our sense of connection to our tools is heightened."[3] But something else is happening: the digital artist surrounds herself with the nondigital as well. Hand-drawn art, sketches, animation thumbnail studies on paper, pastels for color reference, clay sculpture: these are the tools piled on top of computer artists' monitors and desks. Computer animation, as it is practiced today, is still a manual artistic process. It is not automated. The very term *computer animation* can be deceptive; the computer does not animate. Animators animate; the computer is the tool, like a pencil or paintbrush. Haraway's cyborg suggests a creature so unified that it is "not clear who makes and who is made in the relation between human and machine. It is not clear what is mind and what body in machines that resolve into coding practices."[4] Pixar's digital artist, in contrast, is a separate and distinct partner working in tandem with his tools. Thus, artist and tool are not at union, but at times are in partnership, collaboration, and communion to achieve a set goal.

How does one create for a nascent medium that simultaneously is grounded in and transforms its predecessors—that is, live-action film-making, 2-D animation, sculpture, painting, print, photography, film, computer science, and the Internet? It is the partnership of traditional and nontraditional techniques and practices that forges innovative and new methods. The artist who places the digital lights keeps a hand-drawn pastel, the true color reference for the scene, pinned to her bulletin board. A computer animator doodles thumbnail sketches on paper, or videotapes himself acting out the movement of the scene. The layout artist flies a small camera around a clay model of the set to scout locations, inspiring camera angles well before the virtual set is built. The process is less a transformation from classical art to high-tech art than, again, a partnership—a coproduction of established art practices with emerging technology's tools.

the tools

If the keyboard becomes an extension of the artist's hand, according to the cyborg analogy, then the computer screen is a kind of augmented eye, displaying the artist's defined field of view. With these enhancements, the possibilities may be endless, but the parameters are not; they are set by the computer artist. The virtual camera does not fly anywhere that the layout artist has not predetermined. If a computer layout artist moves the camera outside the boundaries of a designated shot, she might find that the sets have not been built to be seen so wide. If the camera zooms in on an area and the textures on objects in that area were not designed to be seen close-up, the resulting scene may have an undesired plastic, unfinished look. Computer artists have many tools at their disposal, but they do not have the option of visiting a physical studio to find that ideal weathered old chair. Instead, they must build a 3-D chair model and paint the wear and dirt onto it digitally; then they prepare the chair model to be seen either in close-up or in wide shots, depending on what level of digital dirt a scene requires.

animation

The digital artist's tools come complete with possibilities and challenges. Details like very slight facial squashes (contortions), flesh jiggles, or other bodily subtleties are possible to render in the 3-D computer animation medium, but they come from a different way of working. Animation, like other phases in the production process, involves a gradual, step-by-step layering of detail, motion, and acting. With early-stage animation blocking, a computer animator can see a rough version of a shot very quickly. First, a basic character body, broad-strokes motion, and overall physical acting are roughed in. An animator may start a character scene without the character's arms, for

214

example, keeping the animation software working quickly and efficiently. Finally, he might load more elements into the shot: a character's feet, arms, and mouth.

"You can do anything in animation, performance-wise," notes Pixar animator Andrew Gordon. "You can capture something, manufacture a performance sometimes with more control than even an actor would."[5] Many human actors would not consider the minute details of a performance the way computer animators must. Human actors study the motivating details of a character, then they might improvise the acting once they are "in character." Computer animation characters, by contrast, are always in character. They were born in character. Animators need to finesse certain details and make the acting seem improvised, matter-of-fact, *natural*.

The layering of digital detail in computer animation continues beyond the animation department. Shading, set dressing, lighting, rendering, and digital paint add more detail into shots, well after the animator's work is done. The actor/animator herself may not know all the details that will be visible in a shot until the shot is completely computed or digitally rendered. Results are not always immediate, as computers, often heavy with artistic data, render images a frame at a time for playback at film speed. Speed is an issue in computer animation; what might be perceived as the most advanced interactive medium of all is actually slow much of the time. An artist's interaction with computer tools depends on how an individual artist works, how he sets up the scene and layers in the details.

Thus, with the intricate process comes a kind of delayed gratification for the artists. They learn to create for a medium that responds gradually as solitary frames compute, rather than immediately as a paint brush moves across a canvas. The artists' interactions with tools of the new technology are such that they experience the actual manifestation of their creative energy and output incrementally, as lines of code compute or as frames render finally in completed form. The reward for this delayed gratification is the performance created from almost nothing—not motion-captured from live movement, and not the result of an automated, programmed task list in the computer. The reward is a complete performance manufactured through a collaboration of art and technology, a performance not determined wholly by mechanical means of reproduction and data processing. It is, at its best, an exceptionally natural, organic performance, which arguably is achieved in Pixar's recent film *Monsters, Inc.*

computer models

A character's shape (termed "geometry" in computer animation), once approved by directors as a computer model, is like a toy action figure: it is fixed. Animators create performances from the very birth of the computer model when they request particular articulation points from the technical team. An animator may require certain facial articulation controls, limb stretches, and flexibility that would not be built into a rigid action-figure model. So the technical team places articulation points into the models, developing characters that can act with as much subtlety or largeness as an animator can imagine will be necessary. Fortunately for animators who need a range of acting tools for characters, only the character's geometry is fixed early. Animators work with the technical team for many months to define the necessary motion points. If an animator tests a model and cannot get the desired acting from the existing version, additional articulation points can be placed in the model and finer detail can be achieved. Once a character's shape has been fixed and articulated, animators work with the limitations and possibilities of the model, knowing that if they push it too far it might literally break. The computer model is a digital being. It can have glitches, imperfections, system errors, and crashes. If a human actor is pushed to a point of extreme emotion, he might break down and weep, become exhausted, or giggle. Similarly, computer characters react to extreme manipulations like overbends, overextends, smiles too large for faces, and eyes that open too wide. An eyelid might intersect a cheek; teeth might penetrate lips; elbows might buckle and contort if bent along unintended axes. Although it seems counterintuitive, Gordon informs us that "the best thing you can do in animation is push something too far. You're caricaturing life in animation. Better stuff comes through experimentation, once you know the point of the scene." Directors' shot briefings give animators the guidance they need to create shots that will work and thereby avoid a very specific problem. "We have to watch out not to get too live action-y", warns Gordon.[6] Indeed, computer animation artists walk a very fine line. Characters built in the Pixar aesthetic can appear quite lifelike, with real-looking hair or fur, detailed expressions, and emotive eyes. Pixar's digital universe is not a hyperreal world, nor is it a surreal world, nor a real world that mimics life. It is an *other*world, neither more nor less real than the actual, physical world outside. It is wholly different at the same time that it is familiar, familiar enough that audiences have come to expect a certain level of believability from Pixar's brand of productions.

letting computers do what they do best

Creating a believable world means using technology and special effects as storytelling tools, not as attention-grabbing eye candy for the audience. Animators needed special controls and acting skills to make *A Bug's Life*'s individual insect characters expressive, and they needed sophisticated techniques unique to computer technology to give the film's core group of characters—the ants—the attributes most essential to the story. Ants live in colonies, and they needed to be grouped into massive crowds and animated as a multitude rather than as individuals. For director Lasseter, the story *required* computer crowd technology; the story's success would not have been possible without it: "The living organism is the entire ant colony, it's not the individual ant. It's such an important thing, and it became the theme of the story . . . individually, [the ants] could be defeated, but if they stand up together and they work together, there's nothing they can't do."[7] Pixar technical artists developed computer tools to generate ant "crowds" in *A Bug's Life* and, more important, to make those crowds believable so that they would work as the critical storytelling tool the film required.

The idea of ants as a multitude was essential to the audience's understanding of the power of ant colonies, and digital technology made the replication of the ant colonies possible. Computer artists did not build one ant, then "copy and paste" it into batches; instead, they animated scenes of crowds with techniques that traditional 2-D animation could not have achieved. Computer artists created technology that would allow the crowds of ants to display individual characteristics. Dale McBeath, the supervising animator of *A Bug's Life*'s crowd team, notes, "The crowd should be treated as a character in and of itself, with a personality and attitude, made up of individuals who are reacting together but not identically to each other." The goal of animating more than a thousand ants in one shot was most successfully achieved with computer technology, which can assign specific attributes and "instructions" to the crowds of characters: "The [crowd] team built up a very large library of ant 'behaviors' such as curious, angry, incredulous, happy, and nervous. Each of these behaviors was given a number of named characteristics, and each character was fully animated with its own distinct personality," McBeath explains. "We broke up the animation of each crowd ant into smaller animation snippets called 'states'. . . . When provided a set of rules about how these states could be connected, and the probability that a state would happen next, we achieved great flexibility in meeting our needs. What we ended up with were very large crowds made up of unique individuals."[8]

Pixar technical artists even wrote special software to add antenna twitching and general motion to the ant bodies. The *A Bug's Life* crowd technology resulted in over four hundred scenes with anywhere between twenty-five and one thousand ants per scene, and those ants did what they needed to do: they furthered the story as colonies made up of alive, "acting" individuals, without calling specific attention to any particular ants or actions within the crowd. The result was a digital ant colony that acted like an actually existing ant colony. The computer was the tool whose characteristics—logic, response to instruction, linked dependencies—were best suited to the storytellers' needs. As Lasseter notes, "This is where the technology with computer animation . . . really worked for [the] movie. There's no way you could do this by hand."[9]

the aesthetic

Toy Story is particularly notable for the impact it did *not* have. The world's first computer-animated feature film was known for its story and for its endearing characters, Woody and Buzz Lightyear, the cowboy and the space toy, and not primarily for its deft use of high-tech computer imagery. The same is true of Pixar's early short films, from *Red's Dream* to *Luxo Jr.* These films told stories; computer animation was the medium that expressed the message. In 1995, audiences were given a traditional genre picture: *Toy Story* was a buddy film that was created in the emerging medium of computer animation. The computer animation aesthetic, as Pixar defines it, is not "computery" at all. In fact, the computer movie and its techniques are rooted in a traditional aesthetic. Painting, live-action motion picture production, and a more traditional filmmaking vocabulary are all at work in the studio's computer animation production pipeline.

A digital artist in the current feature film climate may fight the computer aesthetic, avoiding a "computery" look. Just as live-action filmmakers work to make their computer effects appear as seamless as possible, computer animation artists create looks that move toward the real. As technology and the digital artists' tools have evolved, artists have come to realize that the robotic, high-tech look most readily achieved with a computer and software are appropriate only for certain kinds of stories and worlds. For Pixar films, the most successful looks are achieved with a production design that prioritizes story and art over digital bells and whistles.

In the computer medium, finding the look—that appealing character quality and design—is among the greatest of challenges. A character design does not only have to be wonderful on paper. It needs to be appealing from all angles, and it needs to support the story and fit into a rich, textured world. For Pixar films, a character design needs to walk a line between "photo-real" and cartoon. A 3-D character is seen fully formed and fully rendered; it has dimension, depth, and cinematic lighting that make the form look so real that audiences can hold the character to a certain standard of believability. For *A Bug's Life*, artists designed a detailed world of leaves, foliage, dirt, and dandelions. Nature's shapes and forms were difficult to create in the computer, which prefers geometric shapes, straight lines, and right angles. Against this tendency, *A Bug's Life* required soft, organic shapes. "Some of the most difficult things to do in computer animation are organic," John Lasseter explains. "A rule of thumb is: the more organic something is, the more difficult it is to do. The more geometric and rigid, the easier."[10] *A Bug's Life*'s characters presented a different kind of challenge. Bugs with exoskeletons might have seemed easy at first, but "they had to be visually interesting enough to hold your attention. The faces still needed to convey all the range of expression any character actor would have, which means the faces actually have as much control and flexibility as any human face."[11]

The Pixar aesthetic represents a convergence of these stylized-yet-believable character designs and environments with a real-looking world of props and sets. *A Bug's Life, Toy Story, Toy Story 2,* and *Monsters, Inc.* are set in realistic fantasy worlds. *Final Fantasy,* also a computer-animated feature film in recent release, has a more photo-real aesthetic, while *Jimmy Neutron: Boy Genius* is more cartooned and whimsical. Pixar films have tended toward a convergence of the real with the stylized.

the digital image for the filmmakers

From the computed digital movie comes the pristine movie output, the digital image. Frames of animation are combined and layered with textures, backgrounds, lighting, and effects, then rendered. Computation is the fixative that adheres the elements together, making them "actual" instead of virtual. It is the archive and the quality control. Rendering is in some respects the ultimate cinema of the computer moviemaking process: it layers the details beyond acting, camera direction, textures and lighting. The rendering stage is about processing the digitally created world, making it appear real. Rendering is what makes computer images accessible to audiences. Before it is rendered, work may appear broken, plastic, and rough. Finessed work is processed to make the images digestible and real. Digital projection, increasingly available in the United States, does not take digital movies to the next level so much as it *keeps digital movies at their pristine, high-resolution level.* It avoids the downgrade step of transferring high-resolution digital images to analog film. Digital presentation is a computed, manufactured world at its most accurate and pure.

The vocabulary of digital projection differs from that of traditional analog presentation terminology. Gone are words like *flicker, jitter, weave, film grain,* and *transfer.* Replacing the analog language are terms like *pure, clean, sharp, perfect,* and, as presentation (not representation), *from the digital source.* It is a vocabulary of purity and mathematical perfection for a world that has been created to appear as real, organic, and non-"computery" as possible. The digitally created, digitally produced, digitally projected motion picture is at once pure and organic, born as much of clay sculpture, paint on paper, and ink drawings as of lines of technical code. Lev Manovich sees digital cinema as a kind of return to cinematic roots. He writes, "The history of the moving image thus makes a full circle. Born from animation, cinema pushed animation to its boundary, only to become one particular case of animation in the end."[12]

One consequence of a new digital cinema production practice is a shift in the way special effects are treated in the computer animation process. When part of a computer-animated movie needs to look particularly "analog"—a shot that shows static on a television monitor, for example—the special effects team is the group that simulates the analog look. Pixar effects artists make selected images impure, while digital painters apply dirt, weathered textures, or visual noise to those images. So, as Manovich points out, "The relationship between 'normal' filmmaking and special effects is . . . reversed. Special effects, which involved human intervention into machine recorded footage and which were therefore delegated to cinema's periphery throughout its history, become the norm of digital filmmaking."[13]

the digital image for the video/DVD audience

An all-digital production process presents computer moviemakers with unique opportunities for home video and DVD audiences. Pixar artists make family films that need to hold up to repeat viewings on video. They considered this critical when preparing A Bug's Life for home video release. One artist states the case thus: "As filmmaking purists we wanted to make a no-compromise wide screen film. As storytellers we also knew that millions of people would be watching the movie over and over again on video. We didn't want to compromise their expectations either."[14]

If artists create a digital movie for theaters at a theatrical 1.85:1 aspect ratio or in Cinemascope, then they can also create alternate versions of the movie and recompute the images for other kinds of exhibition presentations and formats. International theatrical presentation may require 1.66:1, while home video for standard televisions fits a 1.33:1 aspect ratio.

For A Bug's Life's home video release, artists could literally go back into the shot files and rework, recompose, and restage scenes to fit the action into a different kind of frame. As images were revised for the home video aspect ratio, technical artists recomputed the shots—in essence, remaking the movie for a different aspect ratio. Pixar artists were free to make a widescreen theatrical version without compromising for video; later, they were able to create a video version by "reframing" the theatrical images. In this way, "Reframing A Bug's Life breaks new ground in delivering a single motion picture to two vastly different markets: The big screen of the theatre on 35 mm film and the small screen at home on VHS tape. It allowed the film to be made with no compromises imposed by a future film-to-tape transfer."[15]

Even with widescreen television sets becoming more common, most homes still have square TV screens. Computer filmmakers can

katherine sarafian

Figures 14.2–14.4. Progression of frames from Pixar's animated short film *For the Birds* (dir. Ralph Eggleston, 2000) shows rough, unfinished computer images progressing as rendering stages are completed. The final rendered image (bottom) includes light, textures, shadows and detail that early, rough frames do not.

reframe for the television aspect ratio and deliver a more powerful full-frame experience in that medium. For most viewers, a letter-boxed film is less compelling on a square monitor. Bill Kinder, senior manager of editorial and postproduction at Pixar, appreciates the rewards of reframing for audiences and filmmakers: "You're throwing away part of your visual space. We have the freedom in our medium to reinvent, reperform, repackage the work for a different distribution channel." Whether for IMAX, television, or international theatrical, "versions of the film can be specially-created in ways live action pan-and-scan historically has not."[16] A computer animated movie can be deconstructed, recoded, reconstructed, and re-presented for virtually any audience or distribution channel. It can be reconstituted as a series of new realities from the same narrative source material.

conclusion: story rules

Digital artists have moved toward a vocabulary of digital cinema. In creating a completely manufactured world of sets, props, and characters, traditional cinematic terms have been the major point of reference and have been made to apply. Depth of field, motion blur, fog, atmosphere, grain, even video lines or static when downgrading a scene to simulate analog quality—all of these are manufactured in the computer. A traditional cinematic vocabulary has been repurposed and adapted to fit a developing medium and the many traditional cinematic artists who now work in that medium.

If everything is manufactured, then everything must be considered. If artists imagine everything in the computer movie world, then they must construct everything in that world. They build shots, plan locations, even edit digitally before they shoot the images to film. They know film grammar from a structural point of view. Kinder notes, "Maybe you need to know how to deconstruct a film before you can construct one from scratch. . . . You have to know that a camera has depth of field, and you have to make the computer simulate that."[17] For the non-"computery" aesthetic to work and be believable, the convention must exist as seamlessly as possible. Audiences need to forget that the work is computer animated. When this happens in a Pixar film, it is the effective materialization of that convention. The computer-animated movie, a manufactured otherworld of infinite visual possibilities, is not a hybrid art of human unified with machine. It is the ultimate collaborative storytelling work: partnership of human artist with machine; of artist master with her own digital and nondigital tools; of art challenging technology; and of technology inspiring art.

notes

1. Dziga Vertov, *Kino-Eye: The Writings of Dziga Vertov,* ed. with an introduction by Annette Michelson, trans. Kevin O'Brien (Berkeley: University of California Press, 1984), xxxvii.

2. As quoted in Jeff Kurtti, *A Bug's Life: The Art and Making of an Epic of Miniature Proportions* (New York: Hyperion, 1998), 20.

3. Donna J. Haraway, *Simians, Cyborgs, and Women: The Reinvention of Nature* (New York: Routledge, 1991), 178.

4. Ibid., 177–78.

5. Andrew Gordon, interview with author, Emeryville, California, December 27, 2001.

6. Ibid.

7. John Lasseter, interviewed by Terry Gross. *Fresh Air.* National Public Radio broadcast, February 27, 2002.

8. Kurtti, *A Bug's Life,* 100.

9. Lasseter interview (see note 7 above).

10. Kurtti, *A Bug's Life,* 46.

11. Ibid., 48.

12. Lev Manovich, "What Is Digital Cinema?" <http://jupiter.ucsd.edu/~manovich/text/digital-cinema.html>.

13. Ibid.

14. Craig Good, "Reframing *A Bug's Life,*" unpublished paper presented to National Association of Broadcasters, January 20, 1999.

15. Ibid.

16. William Kinder, interview with author, Emeryville, California, January 4, 2002.

17. Ibid.

fifteen   **log on**

the oxygen media

research project

c o n s t a n c e   p e n l e y ,   l i s a   p a r k s ,
a n d   a n n a   e v e r e t t

The Oxygen Media Research Project is an exciting and challenging
research initiative focusing on women, new media, and democratic
access to technology. It is an experiment in devising multidisciplinary
and collaborative approaches to studying the unprecedented formation
of a large, corporate media entity created by and for women. Oxygen
Media, an Internet startup company working to develop women's programming across different media platforms, was founded in 1998 by
some of the most powerful women in television, including Marcy
Carsey and Caryn Mandabach of Carsey-Werner-Mandabach Productions, the largest independent television production company in the
United States (*The Cosby Show, Roseanne, Third Rock from the Sun*); Geraldine
Laybourne, who built Nickelodeon, the first and very successful network for children; and Oprah Winfrey, the talk-show host, film and

television producer, and, until recently, organizer of the largest reading club for women in the world. The Oxygen website launched in 1999 and the cable channel began broadcasting in February 2000.

Oxygen Media is an appealing and intriguing feminist media research object. Never have there been more powerful women in American television and never have they joined together, financially and creatively, to build a specifically feminist media corporation. Although Oxygen's feminism is decidedly liberal and couched in the language of consumerism, it has staked out a different feminist stance than that of rival networks such as Lifetime and Women's Entertainment (WE). Part of our project then will be to try to understand this new phenomenon of "corporate feminism."

Oxygen has widely publicized its "commitment to enriching the everyday lives of women and families" and suggests that this is what gives the new multimedia channel "its unique spirit and depth of purpose." Not only are we interested in Oxygen's self-proclaimed commitment to women's lives, we are also concerned with the way in which Oxygen's executives have taken advantage of this moment of technological convergence to carve out new opportunities and spaces for women. As historians and theorists of media technologies we believe that Oxygen Media represents one of the most promising efforts today to democratize the mass media landscape. More than any other project, Oxygen Media has understood how to use an actually existing and widely available technology—television—as the way into the world of the Internet, not only for women but potentially for people around the world who likely do not have a computer but who probably do have a television set.

Although we appreciate the critiques of global media conglomeration by such scholars as Robert McChesney, Ben Bagdikian, and Noam Chomsky, and we accept that corporate control over media has had the effect of eroding traditional forms of participatory democracy, we believe there is a need to examine how these economic conditions may have also created new opportunities for women. Our project, therefore, is designed to use Oxygen Media as a test case to determine what the possibilities might be for creating democratic public spheres within commercial multimedia networks. This is a particularly urgent issue in the United States, which has far less bandwith devoted to noncommercial public media than any other Western country. Because Oxygen is funded in part by the Markle Foundation, which is committing all of its $100,000,000 endowment over three years to organizations devoted to democratizing the Internet, we will also have an opportunity to study whether alliances between nonprofit agencies and commercial media might result in new forms of democratic media.

We think that the Oxygen Media Research project can make an illustrative comparison between Oxygen's media strategies and those of that much-touted media triumvirate, Dreamworks SKG. We could also learn a great deal from the way these two projects have been covered in the popular and industry press. Oxygen wanted to create something that was fluid and fast, that spoke to the realities of new media. Dreamworks SKG wanted to pour concrete, to build a behemouth 1930s-era studio in the last remaining wetlands in the Los Angeles basin. The formation of Oxygen got headlines like "Ladies Home Internet." Dreamworks SKG was covered as a heroic, if Sisiphyean, and visionary project, even with the controversy about its ecological incorrectness.

The Oxygen Media Research project determined to understand the Oxygen producers' strategies for shaping a feminist public sphere in the world of commercial television, first through tracking the television programming and web creation and then focusing on the ways television and the web interacted. At the outset the Oxygen producers said that they wanted to draw the content of their shows from the richness of the web, present the web content telegenically, but always sending the viewer back to the web for further research. With few exceptions, however, such as a show called *Oprah Goes Online*, where she and her best friend Gayle learned how to use the Internet, most of the programming is standard TV fare: talk shows, game shows, morning exercise shows, celebrity interviews, movies, sex and relationship advice, animation, sports, and personal growth, some of whose topics relate to Oxygen's increasingly pared-down number of websites. It remains to be seen whether Oxygen's success lies in its ability to be a successful web-TV entity (where so many have failed) or in its talent for creating programming that women find useful and entertaining. In a strikingly honest revelation, Geraldine Laybourne said of recent programming changes on Oxygen, "When we started, we thought women really needed our help. Focus groups showed us that women are not that pathetic. They want to be entertained."[1] The head of Oxygen's focus group research put it even more pointedly: "At the beginning Oxygen erred on the side of sensitive. It turned out that smart sensitive women want to watch dumb TV."[2] We will be closely tracking Oxygen as it tries to negotiate how to be smart and dumb at the same time.

Another strong feature of Oxygen that made it an intriguing object of feminist media analysis was the commitment to intergenerational feminism in its mix of programming that appealed to both second and third wave sensibilities. But beyond that Oxygen's efforts to create programming for girls and adolescents set it apart from the demographics of Lifetime, which targets its programming to a large audience of women aged 25 to 54. So, too, Oxygen promised to be *the* place on television for women's documentary, which offered a challenge not only to Lifetime but to PBS, given how cautious and conservative its programming, especially its choices of documentaries, has become in the face of its corporate underwriters and a hostile U.S. Congress.

The Oxygen Media Research Project would not have the descriptive and explanatory power it hopes to have without its resolutely comparative and international approach. Research partners in Europe (with connections to eastern Europe, central Europe, and southern Africa) are examining, among other issues, the history of women's entry into variously conceived public spheres through consumerism[3]; the differences and similarities between European "state feminism" and U.S. "corporate feminism" in reshaping television to better promote the interests of women and minorities[4]; and young women's negotiation of the cyberworld.[5]

As we conduct our research we will present it on the Hydrogen website, which has been designed as the digital public interface of the Oxygen Media Research Project (see fig. 15.1). The design of our website is a playful *détournement* of the design of <www.oxygen.com>. We chose the name Hydrogen because of what happens when hydrogen and oxygen combine—they either generate an explosion or water. We hope that the Hydrogen website will pressure Oxygen to remain explosively energized in its efforts to enhance women's technoliteracy worldwide, while serving as a reminder that women should be as integral to the formation of new media technologies as water is to human life. On the Hydrogen website, users will find information about our methods, our findings, and they will discover links and spaces dedicated to multimedia literacy and criticism. They will also encounter a list of questions and a space to respond to them. As it develops, we hope that the site will attract an international community of scholars and activists, beyond our established research team, concerned about the democratization of digital media. Our international partners in the Netherlands are forging connections with digitally disadvantaged communities in southern and eastern Europe and southern Africa, and <www.hydrogenmedia.ucsb.edu> is the place where all of the data will be published. Our international partners also post their ongoing research questions and discuss this project with other interested media researchers and policy analysts. In the future, television and Internet producers will perhaps interact with our website and respond to our research iniatives. Whatever the fate of Oxygen in the intensely competitive climate for new forms of media convergence, the Hydrogen website will continue to serve as a forum for the discussion of women, new media, and democratic access to technology (see fig. 15.1).

228

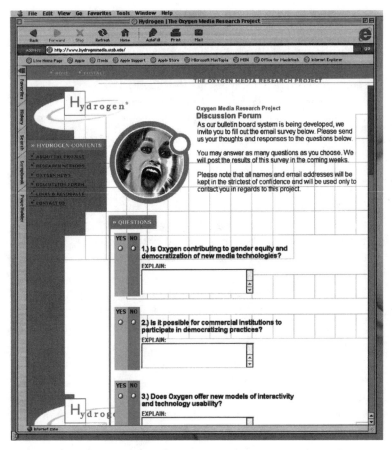

File Edit View Go Favorites Tools Window Help

Figure 15.1. The Hydrogenmedia Website, the public face of the Oxygen Media Research Project. Design by Jon Lapointe.

studying a media institution in the age of convergence

During the past decade, technological changes have happened so quickly that the mere task of describing them has itself become a great challenge. One of the central tasks of our project has been to develop a methodology that will allow us to keep up with the speed of capital. That is, we have tried to develop an analytical model that will enable us not just to study but to *intervene in* new-media technologies and institutions as they take shape. In an effort to address this issue, we have created an interdisciplinary method that combines approaches from media and cultural studies, history, anthropology, sociology, communication, and feminist criticism. Our method is designed to foster multidisciplinary thinking and learning, recognize new possibilities for media analysis and criticism, foreground our dual position as both consumers and scholars of media, and describe the specific material and textual conditions that define technological convergence.

Since Oxygen is a site of media convergence, a site where relations between television, satellite, and computer technologies and industries are being renegotiated, it represents the potential to revise and extend some of the premises of existing critical media approaches. Our project involves five overlapping research clusters. First, we consider the formation of Oxygen's emergence in relation to the broader history of women's media. We discuss the historical precedents for Oxygen including women's reading groups, women's magazines, genres such as the soap opera and the talk show, and the Lifetime network.[6] In other words, our project explores how the cultural and economic viability of Oxygen Media is predicated upon a set of already existing women's cultural forms. Our research examines how Oxygen adapts and transforms "women's media" through both derivative and novel uses of television and computer technologies.

The second cluster of our research involves ethnographic methodologies. More specifically, we plan to conduct on-site participant observation of executive board meetings, workplace conditions and practices, and program production. We believe Oxygen's executives, producers and staff have much to teach us about their organization.[7] We hope that participant observation will not only provide us with insights about women's work within this new media institution but also reveal the specific ways in which women are shaping new forms of programming packaged for television and digital distribution.

Third, our research employs textual and ideological analysis of Oxygen's websites, television programs, network promotions, advertising, and multimedia products. Given recent technological transformations, we have had to rethink how television and computer convergence refigures what we understand to be the "text." And in the context of global media conglomeration, where media synergies have become common practice, we need to also consider how textual formations often function in relation to the branding of products, the marketing of lifestyles, and the formation of cultural tastes.[8] Some companies now use the term "omnimedia" to refer to a set of intersecting media formats all linked to and supported by the same brand name.[9] Since Oxygen fits this omnimedia model, it is an important site for rethinking practices of textual analysis, which in some television studies have historically been tagged to one television series and/or flow segment. We believe that the many texts of Oxygen will likely have to be studied in a way similar to *The Many Lives of Batman* or the phenomena of intertextuality that Tony Bennett and Jane Woollacott explore in *Bond and Beyond*.[10] Oxygen has as many textual incarnations (and fights as many battles) as some popular superheroes.

The fourth cluster of our research examines issues related to audiences and fandom. Our analysis of audience and fandom will consider Oxygen executives' attempts to imagine and construct an audience (in the industrial discourse Ien Ang describes in *Desperately Seeking the Audience*) as well as fans' own reworkings of Oxygen texts (as Constance Penley and Henry Jenkins have described of *Star Trek* fans). Oxygen has struggled to build an audience with multi-platform (online, cable, and satellite) distribution and a website designed to solicit ideas from and interact with viewers and fans. Because of the network's online presence, computer users around the world that are beyond the range of Oxygen's cable and satellite delivery can still access its content. Since one of the network's early promises was to "superserve the interests of women," we explore this issue in a global context: who has actually been watching and surfing Oxygen, and do they feel their interests have been "superserved"? This part of our research, which clearly entails the most practical difficulties, involves interviews with executives about the construction of the Oxygen audience, studies of Oxygen's ratings, exchanges with Oxygen viewers/users/fans, analysis of fan productions, and discussion of Oxygen's place in everyday life.

The fifth area of our research is an analysis of Oxygen's coverage in the trade and popular press. Since Oxygen's emergence (as a convergent women's television network–computer interface) was largely unprecedented, critics in the press responded in different ways. While some noted the ambitious and noble goals of the network, others have been dismissive, skeptical, and even discriminatory in their remarks about Oxygen's viability and future. This part of our research will enable us to better understand the role that press discourse plays in shaping public sentiment about and consumer interest in new media institutions and technologies.

watching oxygen on cable, online, and in print

When Oxygen Media ran its attention-grabbing "I Am Baby" ad during one of television's most coveted viewing slots, Super Bowl 2000, it announced to a global television audience the birth of an audacious women's new media start-up company keeping pace with the revolutionary changes occurring in the media industries as a result of new digital technologies, especially the Internet. The memorable ad was compelling for its rendering of a normal-looking delivery room full of newborn babies, suddenly disrupted when crying baby girls begin throwing off their pink knit caps as the sounds of the popular 1970s song "I am Woman" crescendoed in the background. Providing impact and order to the ad's seeming narrative chaos was the digitally enhanced close-up of one lone, newborn baby girl's defiantly raised fist (see fig. 15.2). Accompanied by intertitles that simply state, "A new voice. For Women, by women. Oxygen, it's in you," the ad also displays Oxygen's now famous ubiquitous black "stripe" at the bottom of the televisual image featuring the ever-present Oxygen logo and its web address, oxygen.com. This powerful image and sound mesh renders perfectly Oxygen's literal and figurative message that indeed a new voice for women's media had been born on February 2, 2000. The ad, as metaphor, articulates unambiguously Oxygen's aim to refashion the Net's so-called "'pink content' market," and cable TV's male-centered programming landscape,[11] for a new breed of women who refuse to accept traditional gender roles and who are impatient with normative media industry practices targeted at women. As Laybourne put it in 1998, "The traditional media have missed the boat with modern women. . . . There is nothing that serves women the way ESPN serves men or Nickelodeon serves kids. We want to create a brand on television and the Internet that brings humor and playfulness and a voice that makes a woman say, 'you really understand me.'"[12]

When we began our study in 1999 we wanted to understand Oxygen's programming philosophy, and explore what distinguished Oxygen from other media entities targeted at women. At the time we, like the mainstream media, were intrigued by the very idea of Oxygen, especially with its unprecedented plan to launch fifty-five hours of *original* cable TV programming weekly, and thirteen online sites.[13] Our approach came from the realization that more than two decades of feminist film scholarship and pedagogy have so far had little impact on

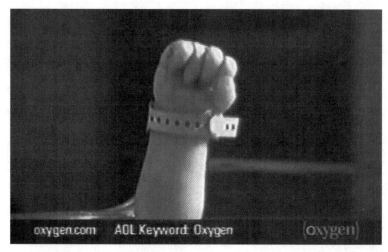

Figure 15.2. Television frame-grab of Oxygen's "I Am Baby" ad. Courtesy of Oxygen Media, LLC.

the films or corporate structure of Hollywood, which is still almost entirely closed off to the issues and constituencies that women care about (despite the "decade of the woman" and "girl power" rhetorics of the 1980s and '90s respectively). We note, however, that women have made a great deal of headway in both the creation of television shows and entry into the corporate structure of the television industry, and we wanted to see if Oxygen was a new beginning. Moreover, we were as struck by Oxygen's willingness to utter the *F* word, *feminism,* as we were by its ambitious programming agenda and the vision of its founders to lead the field in convergence media.

At this writing it is now two years since Oxygen began its bold experiment. For us this presents an opportunity for reflection on and digestion of Oxygen's programming (both actual and reported, online and on TV). Oxygen launched the first phase of its convergence in 1998 with its purchases of Concrete Media's Girls On Net franchise, and Thrive, Moms Online, and Electra, three preexisting websites owned by America Online (AOL), which were then joined by the Oprah.com website that same year. The second phase occurred in 2000 when Oxygen's television content began airing on cable to an estimated ten million households. Despite its often unfair comparison to Lifetime's audience numbers of over seventy-five million households after more than twenty years of operation, media industry insiders found Oxygen's market share promising as an indication of its future success. For example, Jefferson Graham of USA Today.com writes, "Oxygen's launch numbers top most recent cable launches. TV Land, in 45 million homes today, premiered in 1996 with 5.4 million subscribers. E! Entertainment Television's Style, at 6 million today, began in late 1998 in 3 million homes."[14] These figures are important because they temper debates about Oxygen's viability in a crowded cable market.

From the start, we closely followed news of Oxygen, including its late-1999 "Oxygen rocks the tank" publicity campaign and national bus tour. We caught the Los Angeles stop of this tour to promote Oxygen's February 2, 2000 cable TV launch, and immediately became very interested in conducting textual analyses of the content and aesthetics of Oxygen's brand of women's media. We were particularly interested in the intersection of these formal aspects and Oxygen's stated goal of "superserving" women of diverse ages, races, nationalities, and even political persuasions. At the same time, we realized that Oxygen's bold move to integrate its new cable television programming with its women's and girls' online properties was important to study because it was happening at a crucial moment in the development of television and Internet convergence. Thus we recognized the significance in this instance of powerful women in media (Laybourne, Winfrey, Carsey, and Mandabach) using their economic and cultural clout to ensure constance penley, lisa parks, and anna everett

women's participation in these converging and increasingly globalized media technologies. The significance inhered not only in Oxygen's potential to better democratize the Internet, and push for gender equity in the cable industry, but also for what it augured for the emerging aesthetics and stylistic practices of digital media production in general. One media analyst reported that "Oxygen's plan is to beat rivals with content and reach beyond the mainstream. Winfrey has said the company 'will focus on women and treat us like the busy, smart, and complex people we are.' But [Oxygen partner Tom] Werner puts it more bluntly, 'Not everybody has to be 28 years old, white, and pretty,' he said. 'You're going to see all sorts of colors and ages on our shows.'"[15] Finally, we were interested in the question of whether or not Oxygen's programming might be thought to represent what we are calling "corporate feminism," a liberal feminist mode of media production and design capable of disrupting the male-dominated media's representational hegemony and ideological imperatives in ways that twenty years of second wave feminist activism could not.

This latter question became even more intriguing when we noticed a disconcerting component of the popular press's often dismissive speculations about Oxygen's viability as a media player simultaneously competing with and sometimes collaborating with such cable TV giants as Time-Warner's CNN, NBC's cable networks, HBO, Disney's Lifetime, and others. Most of the negative ink devoted to pillorying Oxygen, we discovered, appeared well in advance of the network's availability in most markets or following the first installments of its shows. To counterbalance this myopia, we set out as a research team to watch Oxygen's television programming and visit its websites so that we could devise more informed critiques of the network's actual intermedia content, organizational goals, and initial achievements. Oxygen's founders understood the risky nature of experimentation in the formula-driven environment of television, and apparently early on they trusted the audience. "I think if we're clear about our intentions and make mistakes the first year," Tom Werner said, "the audience will forgive us—as long as we respect them."[16]

watching oxygen for an aesthetics of corporate feminism

Our watching of Oxygen's cable network programming flow yielded some interesting findings when compared to that of its chief competitor, the Lifetime network. Despite its slogan, "Television for Women," Lifetime's prime-time movies and miniseries are remarkable for their narrative recuperations of patriarchal institutions and the status quo. Lifetime's highly successful formula of endangered and dangerous women narratives, often "inspired by actual events," features plucky, determined women surviving a host of societal and personal crises. However, the movies tend to undermine their messages of female agency and autonomy with representations of women's survival invariably requiring rescue by benevolent patriarchal structures—especially the courts—and handsome, goodhearted, strong men. Lifetime's movie offerings for the month of October 2000 are indicative with such titles as: *To Love, Honor, and Obey: The Last Mafia Marriage* (1993), *The Killing Secret* (1996), *No One Could Protect Her* (1995), *One Woman's Courage* (1994), *Nothing Lasts Forever* (1995), and *Trial by Fire* (1995), among others. These movies and others of their ilk (which, we admit, some of us love to watch) accompanied such original Lifetime shows as *Intimate Portrait* (biographies of prominent women), *Strong Medicine* and *Any Day Now* (fictional dramas), and *Beyond Chance* (a reality-based show about the paranormal).

By comparison, Oxygen TV was launched in 2000 with such news and information shows as *Exhale, Pure Oxygen, She Commerce, Trackers, Oprah Goes Online, As She Sees It,* and *Daily Remix.* Other Oxygen shows included an animation show *X-Chromosome*, a sports show *We Sweat*, and a game show *I've Got a Secret.* In contrast to Lifetime's docudrama and fictional narratives about women, Oxygen's original programming emphasized non-fiction and documentary narratives about adventurous and determined women and girls, successful in their own right. Moreover, these Oxygen shows attempted to avoid the trap of exacerbating the supposed conflicts between both its stay-at-home and career-oriented women audiences by refusing to structure its content along lines that privileged one group over the other. With the growing numbers of women online, and the fact that women comprise 50 percent of the cable TV audience, Oxygen's inclusive, audience-driven programming strategy was not only politically astute and timely but, at that time, apparently it was an economically sound business strategy.[17] Given these notable shifts in cultural and market forces, it is not surprising that media analysts were interested in Oxygen's expression of the emerging synergy between the web and TV, especially since it was positioned in direct competition for Lifetime's audience share. But popular press analysts were not the only ones speaking out.

At its cable TV launch in 2000, the press reported Laybourne (who oversaw Lifetime when she worked at Disney) as saying that Lifetime "appeals 'to a woman who is exhausted and wants to sit there and be entertained in a passive voice.'"[18] In contrast, she "calls Oxygen's programming 'very contemporary, very in-your-face, as opposed to passive.'"[19] Leaving aside the debatable issue of passive television viewing, the fact that Oxygen would "rely more heavily on its Web sites than anyone has ever before,"[20] and use the web as its programming backbone does distinguish Oxygen from Lifetime, MSNBC, CNN, and other cable television (and broadcast TV) networks. In addition, Oxygen TV's overall look was different from Lifetime and others. From the beginning, Oxygen's televisual flow consisted of strikingly visual montages including, for example, its show-length animation programs about the joys and pain of women's lives (X-*Chromosome* and *Pond Life*); its interstitial animation shorts; Moms Online (featuring helpful parenting hints); its short promotional spots featuring paintings and celebrity endorsements; and even its prowomen and protechnology commercial advertisements. Arguably, there has not been this level of experimentation with the look, tone, pace, and structure of television since *The Ernie Kovacks Show* and *Your Show of Shows* in the early 1950s, and later, *Pee-wee's Playhouse* and the stylistic innovations of early MTV. All this combines with its anchor programming of more familiar TV fare combined with web content to bear out Laybourne's assertion that Oxygen was "doing everything we can to make this look like a different experience. The (on-air stripe) says to people that this is more than just TV."[21]

With these factors in mind, it became apparent to us that indeed Oxygen's television programming was marked by decidedly feminist-friendly content and a sort of neoformalist and postmodernist experimental structure rarely found on television designed for a female viewership. With this focus in mind, some aspects of film studies' obvious and not so obvious critical approaches were useful for thinking about and making evaluations of Oxygen's programming beyond a simplistic reduction of its myriad complexities to a mere commodity culture fetish tainted because of its founders' willing participation in America's ever-expanding culture industries. (This is especially true for studying Oxygen's programming during its formative and more experimental stages, which is the focus of the present discussion.)

Elements of classical film theory, then, enable us to contextualize Oxygen's innovative visual styles and feminist-friendly themes within a historical tradition of subversive media practices and political agendas developed by some of the cinema's early, revolutionary filmmakers. The recent work of theorists such as Lev Manovich, Peter Lunenfeld, and others also considers new media practices' indebtedness to classical media influences.[22] In Oxygen's case, what classical theory reminds us of is the fact that innovative codes of media signification can inspire spectators to accept new ideas, imagine new realities, and thereby effect transformations of repressive social structures and ideologies. Thinking about Oxygen's programming in this way allows us to recognize how Oxygen's disruptions of dominant media's codifications of, say, gender roles might function to interpellate and hail female viewers into Oxygen's routine portrayals of women and girls as technology masters in regular shows and in commercials (see figs. 15.3–15.5). Also, Oxygen's barrage of images presenting women succeeding in non-traditional as well as traditional careers and activities, many produced by women documentary filmmakers, certainly helps to disrupt television's male dominance, if only temporarily. Similarly, contemporary theorists of

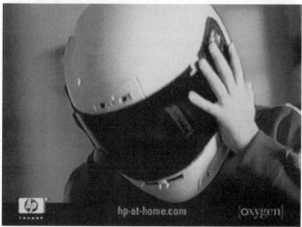

Figures 15.3–15.5. Hewlett-Packard commercials for Oxygen featuring young computer user, presumed to be a boy until the helmet is removed to reveal a computer-savvy young girl. Courtesy of Oxygen Media, LLC.

media equip us with important conceptual frameworks for interrogating Oxygen's programming (both online and on TV) in terms of fan culture, resistant and subversive spectatorship, new-media literacy, cyberfeminism, computer image manipulation, and new-media information flows, or what Nancy Fraser might call "counter publics."

much ado about the stripe

In addition to its spirited women's empowerment discourse across different media platforms (cable TV, the Internet, print newsletters) and genres, and its imaginative formal uses of animation, Oxygen makes another key contribution to new media practice. Oxygen has repurposed the cinema's familiar letter-box feature, and its TV counterpart (the ticker), renaming it the "stripe," that ubiquitious, information-rich black space appearing at the bottom of all its television programming. In addition to transmitting a SAP function (second audio program for the hearing impaired), foreign language dialogue translations, or preserving important visual information usually lost when film texts are exhibited on television, Oxygen uses its stripe to transmit additional textual information about its programs and the products advertised on the network. Interestingly, this is one of Oxygen's specific programming features that was singled out for negative criticism in the popular press's coverage. The complaint was that the stripe was an unnecessary distraction that especially detracted from advertisers' messages. One advertiser put the case thus: "I want to know that viewers are going to stay with the network long enough to see my commercial run . . . I sell for TV, not for the Internet."[23]

So, too, the words on the stripe often interact ironically and parodically with the image on the screen in the manner of VH1's *Pop-Up Video* or *Mystery Science Theater 3000*, encouraging and following the viewer in her own activity of "talking back" to television, to borrow bell hooks's popularization of the phrase. As we note above, Oxygen did not invent the televisual practice of using the space at the bottom of the TV image to convey supplemental information, as television news organizations transmit important news flashes in this manner, and business shows such as those on CNBC and Bloomberg use it to convey streaming, up-to-the-minute stock information to its viewers. But Oxygen was the first to design this feature as a value-added informational enhancement for the entirety of its programming flow, including its advertisements. Moreover, Oxygen used its stripe function to brand all of its programming visually with the ever-present Oxygen logo. In effect, Oxygen used its televisual stripe to transfer a popular Internet practice of placeholding ("bookmarking" a site for easy website navigation) to the medium of TV, whereby television surfers could easily know when they happened upon the Oxygen network.

The stripe not only served as a placeholder for its viewers, and as means of providing value-added information about shows and ads; another central element of Oxygen's stripe function was its literal enacting of television and Internet convergence. Through its stripe, Oxygen routinely directed television viewers to go to its family of websites for interactive participation in both its TV shows and online content development and transmedia programming strategies. This strategic practice represented Oxygen's stated goal of making its female viewers programming partners in the organization's bold experiment with new media convergence. Although it is too early to tell if recent mainstream media reports that "The Oxygen TV Channel Is Bowing to Tastes" reflect Oxygen's capitulation to market forces or to its audience's demand for less-adventurous programming, it is not too early to note Oxygen's impact on its rival media organizations.

Far from accepting the view that Oxygen's informational stripe represented an untenable match for advertising's traditional practice of product promotion, in the two years since Oxygen began that controversial practice we have observed its appropriation by many television shows and commercial TV advertisers on network and cable broadcasts alike. Among those entities presently featuring the stripe are: Progressive.com, ABC's daytime programs (i.e. *General Hospital*), ESPN's *Women and Sports*, and MSNBC's show promos. Tellingly, American Movie Classics (AMC) has begun what it calls "Much More Movie+" (MMM+), using the strip for what it terms "Instant interactive information included that doesn't pop-up and ruin the video." Here AMC is using the stripe exactly the way Oxygen does for its *Girl in the Picture* movies. Even more important, it has become quite evident that Oxygen's alternative strategy of programming shows and complementary websites designed to address the special needs of women has engendered a new bout of television's famous copycat syndrome.

Despite the popular press's incessant predictions of Oxygen's imminent demise, the struggling network is still around, at least at the time of this writing. And during its first two years of operation it has inspired two of its chief rivals to refashion their own women's television networks or launch new network franchises targeted at women.[24] Included in the Oxygen emulation club are the American Movie Classics, who have overhauled their Romance Channel as the new WE network, and Lifetime's own cable TV and website redesigns, and its new spin-off network entitled Real Women.

watching oxygen in 2002—and beyond

As Oxygen embarked upon its third year of operation, Alessandra Stanley wrote what amounts simultaneously to its epitaph and rebirth announcement. Amid widely reported news of Oxygen's staff reductions and its cancellation of unpopular shows such as *Pajama Party* and *Trackers*, among others, and the disquieting realization that its "biggest draw is *Xena, Warrior Princess*, a campy syndicated fantasy program it shows in reruns three times a day, and which has a huge cult following among women, teenagers and gays," it is clear that Oxygen is restructuring. (Most recently, the website's name and URL have changed to reflect Oxygen's next stage—the current name is "New Oxygen Media," and its new web address is: <http://www. newoxygenmedia.com>.) Stanley reports that Karen Ramspacher, who oversees Oxygen's focus-group research, admitted their miscalculation of what smart women want from media, at least at this moment. Conceding the disconnect between Oxygen's vision of smart media and smart women's apparent preference for dumb TV, Ramspacher conveys Oxygen's determination to not give up the vision entirely, "We still have a strong advocacy stance. . . . What we learned after the launch was to balance it with more fun."[25] What we, the members of the Oxygen Media Research Project, have learned in all this is that our collection of the massive mainstream press reports about Oxygen, and our videotape archives of its first two years of television and website programming, constitute an important historical record of the changing role of women in powerful media industries.

If history is any indication—and given other television media's appropriation of Oxygen's key programming strategies, and the organization's apparent forced move toward more standard media practices—the early years of Oxygen's innovations and promise to help democratize the new media environment may well be eclipsed and hidden from public view. However, as we continue to follow Oxygen's progress, we are pleased to have amassed an extensive archive of documentation to set the historical record straight, and to provide a reservoir of data for our ongoing research and analyses. Like the New Oxygen Media enterprise itself, our research project is only beginning.

the oxygen media research team

At the University of California, Santa Barbara, in the United States: Primary Research Investigators: Constance Penley, Professor of Film Studies; Anna Everett, Associate Professor of Film Studies; Lisa Parks, Associate Professor of Film; Graduate Student Researchers: Karl Bryant in Sociology, Sara Mason in Sociology, and Molly Maloney in Sociology; Undergraduate Student Intern: Amy Pocha in Film Studies.

At the University of Utrecht, in the Netherlands: Primary Research Investigators: Rosi Braidotti, Professor of Philosophy and Women's Studies; Berteke Waaldijk, Assistant Professor of History and Women's Studies; Mischa Peters, PhD Candidate in History and Women's Studies.

At the University of Nijmegan, in the Netherlands: Primary Research Investigator: Anneke Smelik, Lecturer in Film and Digital Media.

See our website <http://www.hydrogenmedia.ucsb.edu> for fuller biographies of the Oxygen Media Research Project team.

notes

1. Geraldine Laybourne, quoted in Alessandra Stanley, "The Oxygen Media Channel Is Bowing to Tastes," *New York Times*, February 25, 2002, C1.
2. Karen Ramspacher, quoted in Stanley, "The Oxygen Media Channel Is Bowing to Tastes."
3. Berteke Waaldijk, "When the Woman Citizen Meets the Woman Consumer," paper for panel on New Feminist Practices: The Oxygen Media Research Project and Digital Media Texts, at the Console-ing Passions: Television, Video, Feminism conference, Bristol, England, July 2001.
4. Anneke Smelik, "Considering State Feminism: The Missing Links and State Reform Measures of Dutch TV in Comparison to Oxygen Media," paper for panel on New Feminist Practices: The Oxygen Media Research Project and Digital Media Texts, at the Console-ing Passions: Television, Video, Feminism conference, Bristol, England, July 2001.
5. Laybourne, quoted in Stanley, "The Oxygen Media Channel Is Bowing to Tastes."
6. This part of our research is indebted to projects such as Janice Radway's *Reading the Romance: Women, Patriarchy and Popular Literature* (Chapel Hill: University of North Carolina Press, 1984); Annette Kuhn, "Women's Genres," *Screen* 25:1 (1984), 18–28; Ien Ang, *Watching Dallas: Soap Opera and the Melodramatic Imagination* (London and New York: Methuen, 1985); Jane Shattuc, *The Talking Cure: TV Talk Shows and Women* (New York: Routledge, 1996); *Lifetime: A Cable Network 'For Women'*, (Special Issue), *Camera Obscura* 33–34 (1994–95); Charlotte Brunsdon, Julie D'acci, Lynn Spigel, eds. *Feminist Television Criticism* (Oxford: Oxford University Press, 1997).
7. For more information about the importance of interviewing those who work in the television industry see Kathleen Rowe's essay in *Feminist Cultural Theory: Process and Production*, ed. Beverley Skeggs (Manchester: Manchester University Press, 1995).
8. For further discussion of these practices see Lisa Parks, "Flexible Microcasting: Gender, Generation and Television and Internet Convergence," in *The Persistence of Television: From Console to Computer*, ed. Lynn Spigel (Durham, N.C.: Duke University Press, forthcoming 2003).
9. Martha Stewart was the first to coin this term, but such practices are also used by Oprah Winfrey and others.
10. Roberta Pearson and William Uricchio, eds. *The Many Lives of Batman: Critical Approaches to a Superhero and his Media*, (London: Routledge, 1991); and Tony Bennett and Jane Woollacott, *Bond and Beyond: The Political Career of a Popular Hero* (London: Macmillan, 1987).
11. See Courtney Macavinta's 1999 CNET News essay, "Oxygen: Women at center of convergence," for useful information about the expectations for Oxygen from both its promoters and detractors just prior to the launching of Oxygen's cable television efforts, at <http://www.news.com/SpecialFeatures/ 05.35693.00.html>. The article is particularly important as a measure of the early thinking about PC-TV convergence by individuals helping to shape its commercial foundations.

12. For a revealing look at Oxygen's special relationship with AOL, see Saul Hansell's September 16, 1998 article "The Media Business: Advertising," for *The New York Times on the Web*, <http://oxygen.com/corporate/html/me_cli_2.htm>.

13. Shortly after Oxygen initiated its cable TV programming, *Hoover's Online* posted the story "RealNetworks to Deliver Oxygen Media's Programming to Internet Audiences . . ." credited to *PR Newswire*, February 23, 2000, at <http://www.hoovershbn.hoovers.com/bin>. This material was available online at the time of this writing; unfortunately, however, this URL is now defunct. It is this reality of disappearing websites that prompts those of us conducting research on the Web to download online content for future reference and preservation.

14. This quote is taken from Jefferson Graham's article "Today's the day that much-hyped Oxygen hits the air," posted online on February 2, 2000 at <http://www.USA TODAY.com>.

15. Courtney Macavinta, "Oxygen: Women at center of convergence," <http://www.news.com/SpecialFeatures/05.35693.00.html>.

16. Tom Werner, quoted in Tom Post's, "The Convergence Gamble," in *Forbes*, February 22, 1999, <http://oxygen.com/corporate/html/me_cli_7.htm>.

17. Graham, "Today's the day."

18. Ibid.

19. Ibid.

20. Ibid.

21. Ibid.

22. See for example Lev Manovich, *The Language of New Media* (Cambridge, Mass.: MIT Press, 2001).

23. Chris Geraci, quoted in Paula Bernstein, "Waiting to Exhale," for Yahoo! News, February 2, 2000, <http://dailynews.yahoo.com/htx/nm/20000202/re/television_oxygen_1.html>.

24. See Bernstein, "Waiting to Exhale."

25. Stanley, "The Oxygen TV Channel Is Bowing to Tastes."

from barbie to

mortal kombat

further reflections

h e n r y   j e n k i n s

It is early summer, 2001. I am walking through the great exhibition hall at the Electronic Entertainment Expo (E3), the most important trade show in the games industry. It is hard to imagine many activities that would pack in so many men per square foot of exhibition space and so few women. Many of the women we see here are dressed in scant clothing—leather-bound Valkyries, bikini-clad space bunnies, or women in tight jumpsuits prepared for motion-capture demonstrations. In what is the loudest, most visually oversaturated place I have ever been—with the possible exception of the streets of Hong Kong—women are used as bait to lure dazed buyers into the booths. One understands instantly why most of the games on the market look and sound the way they do. It has little to do with consumer tastes and everything to do with the competition for attention at the floor show. In this environment, subtle games—nuanced games—disappear without a trace. The Sims or Black & White, for example, commanded far less space at the Electronic Arts booth than the more action-packed games, and Majestic debuted off the main floor altogether in a corporate suite.

One booth captures my attention. A female gamer is taking on all challengers. There is a long line of male gamers, game designers, and game executives, each pumping each other up, in the expectation of "whipping her sweet little butt," as I overhear one man to say. And one by one they return from the encounter with their tails between their legs, their masculinity in tatters. She is *that good!* She is one with the machine—the closest thing to a cyborg I've ever encountered—with absolute economy and precision of movement. She knows the game so well that she anticipates every move and compensates for it. And she slaughters all of the best gamers.

Later that same summer, I am walking down the streets of downtown Melbourne and stumble past the window to a game arcade. In the window of the arcade, there are two teenage Moslem women—dressed in flowing robes, headdresses, and veils—and they are dancing barefoot in front of Dance Dance Revolution. They seem absolutely free of all inhibitions, totally in touch with the rhythms of the machine. And people along the streets, like myself, are stopping and gaping at the spectacular dance performance unfolding before us.

I could be optimistic and suggest that these two chance encounters suggest the increased visibility of female gamers. After all, the Interactive Digital Software Association is reporting dramatic increases in the number of women playing games in the United States (43 percent overall, with women constituting the majority of online gamers). The same research shows that, while the female Quake clans get lots of publicity for breaking across the gender barriers in gaming, more women play traditional card games such as bridge, board games such as chess, or trivia games such as Jeopardy, and only a small number play the kinds of games most often produced by the IDSA's member companies.

I fear that what these stories really suggest is that the sight of a female gamer remains a remarkable spectacle within a commercial and cultural space still dominated by male designers and male consumers.

From Barbie to Mortal Kombat: Gender and Computer Games was conceived and coedited with Justine Cassell in the midst of an era of limited but very real optimism about the ability of female-run startup companies to transform the game market, creating new kinds of games that might appeal to a broader range of female consumers.[1] Barbie Fashion Designer had been a top seller for the Christmas season, 1996, and had continued throughout the year to outsell industry standards, such as Quake or Myst, establishing that there was potentially a rather large market for female-centered software titles. Brenda Laurel, who was one of the most respected women in the computer industry, had established Purple Moon games with the explicit goal of designing products that reflected her sociological and ethnographic research into young girls' play patterns. And a number of other companies—Girl Games, Her Interactive—were producing girl-targeted titles; independent artists, such as Theresa Duncan (Chop Suey), were designing playful interactive works with a distinctly feminine sensibility; the major games companies were being forced to reconsider their marketing and design decisions to factor in female consumers more fully; and the introduction of Tomb Raider's Lara Croft character represented a significant new era for the female action hero in games.

The girl's game movement took shape around a series of competing goals and expectations:

1. *Economic.* The platform game market had entered into an age of heightened competition at a time when, in fact, 90 percent of American boys were already playing computer games. To survive, these game companies understood that they would need to expand their market and thus, then as now, there were three major targets—casual gamers, older gamers, and women. Any product that could succeed in attracting one or more of those prized demographics might hold the key for the company's long-term viability.

2. *Political.* The plight of preteen girls had become a central focus of feminist concern, following the publication of a series of books that suggested serious self-esteem issues that were impacting their ability to learn and grow within the classroom. Further research suggested that the gender gap in technological fields was growing rather than shrinking despite decades of feminist intervention, and the computer was more and more being coded as a "masculine" technology within the culture. Some felt that computer games might hold a key to getting girls engaged with computers at an earlier age, a head-start program for technological literacy. By the time they encountered computers in the classroom, boys had spent many more hours playing games than girls and often shoved them off the hardware to show them how it should be used.

3. *Technological.* The introduction of the CD-ROM as a staple of the home computer opened up a new opportunity for female-centered games to find their market. As long as platform games ruled the roust, there was little chance of building up a girls market because consumers would have to buy the hardware before they could play games at a time when there was not going to be a critical mass of relevant product available. Once the home computer became the locus of game play—either through CD-ROM games or web-based games—then people who had bought the computer for other purposes could take a chance on buying software for girls or playing an online game. Moreover, while three major companies determined

what products would be available for their platforms, the CD-ROM and web game markets were open to competition. Technological changes had lowered the barriers of entry into the market place.

4. *Entrepreneurial.* A growing number of women had tried working within the mainstream industry, enjoyed some degree of success, but had wanted to develop independence so they could create products that more fully reflected their perspectives and experiences. The girl's game movement caught the rising tide of female entrepreneurship in American culture at a time when women were starting new businesses at a rate significantly higher than men and in doing so were introducing new kinds of products, opening new kinds of markets, and developing new forms of business management and new kinds of customer relationships.

5. *Aesthetic.* The girl's game movement promised new kinds of content, new models of play and interactivity, new visual aesthetics, and new approaches to the soundtrack. The movement set a goal of making games radically different from those on the market, so that they could attract new kinds of consumers. This made the movement a hotbed for innovation and experimentation, with a strong push toward more psychologically nuanced characters, softer color palettes, more richly-layered soundtracks, new interface designs (including those, such as Barbie Fashion Designer, that helped bridge between the computer and real-world play), and more complex stories.

Our book tried to document the complex interweaving of ideological idealism and market calculations that shaped the development of the girl's game movement. We were interested in the ways that the girls game movement brought together feminist academics and female CEOs in a collective effort to transform the current state and the future direction of a sector of the entertainment industry which is drawing in an annual income roughly equivalent to the gross domestic box office returns for Hollywood movies.

In that context, the book's focus shifted from whether there was going to be software for girls (which seemed almost a given) to *what kinds* of software for *what kinds* of girls. We asked, for example, whether games should be designed to reflect girl's existing tastes and interests or to transform them, and whether this question represented a contradiction within feminist entrepreurship. Feminism has always sought to critique and reinvent gender roles, whereas entrepreneurship has had to start where the market was. We pointed, for example, to a controversial statement that Brenda Laurel had made, "I agreed that whatever solution the research suggested, I'd go along with. Even if it meant shipping products in pink boxes."[2] In many ways, this was a challenge that feminist critics had never had to confront before—how to write about cultural production in a context where women now exercised a considerable degree of power. If women were heading up the games company, their efforts could no longer be called marginal, but at the same time they were now forced to respond to the same economic realities which shaped corporate decision making in what remained a largely patriarchal society. Earlier generations of feminists had celebrated filmmakers like Dorothy Arzner who produced films from the margins of the studio system as engaged in a kind of "countercinema." Yet, a game company executive like Laurel had control over (and thus was forced to take responsibility for) the products she shipped under the Purple Moon logo.

In hindsight, it is troubling how quickly Laurel found herself caught in a feminist backlash against the reproduction of feminine stereotypes in her work when so little attention was being given to her explicit goal of using popular culture to empower young girls. We might compare the feminist backlash against Purple Moon to, say, the much more friendly reception given to *Buffy the Vampire Slayer*, *Xena: Warrior Princess*, or *The Power Puff Girls*. As Laurel writes in her new book, *Utopian Entrepreneur*, "By trying to do anything socially positive at all, the utopian entrepreneur opens herself up to the endless critique that she is in fact not doing enough. . . . I am reminded of the old saw: the one who attacks you is likely to be the one closest to you on the road. . . . I wondered, did anyone notice that this wasn't Barbie—that Rocket struggled mightily to be ethical and self-defined? . . . Our characters exhibited loyalty, honor, love, and courage. They also struggled with gossip, jealousy, cheating, lipstick, smoking, exclusion, racism, poverty, materialism, and broken homes. When we had to choose, we sacrificed political correctness in order to meet the girls where they were, in the realities of their own lives."[3]

What bothers me even more, however, is the degree to which Purple Moon has been treated not only within the industry but also within academia as a "failed experiment," as if the importance of a political and cultural intervention could be or should be measured only by market standards. As *Utopian Enterepreneur* makes clear, however, even by market standards, the company could scarcely be viewed as a failure, simply because it couldn't compete effectively for the girl's market against Barbie, the most successful girls franchise of all time, or American Girl, another successful franchise with brand loyalties arranged well before it sought to introduce its software line. Purple Moon sought to use a new set of characters and a new set of stories in order to introduce a new kind of product to a new kind of market. In doing so, it had notable success on the web, where it became the third most popular site for children, though its success came at a time when the business models for turning a revenue stream from the web still had not jelled (and—guess what, folks—they still haven't, several years later). As

Laurel explains, "Here's one of the perversities of dot-capitalism: if Purple Moon had not actually produced any real products, I'd probably be 'post-economic' today. Just as the dot-economy started spinning straw into gold, Purple Moon was spending real money to make real products to go into real shelves in real stores. In investment terms, this was a big mistake. Even though we had an extremely popular Website, the embarrassing detail of real goods prevented us from passing for a dot-company in the venture community. And so, instead of the wild valuations that made some of our younger friends multimillionaires, the valuation of Purple Moon could never exceed some small multiple of our revenues—because we actually had revenues."[4]

What killed Purple Moon wasn't the lack of a girl's market for games or the invalidity of her core model about what a girl's game might look like, but rather the impatience of the company's core investors to make the kinds of turnaround that they were seeing elsewhere in the digital economy. In the end, Purple Moon suffered the fate that befalls most startups—it was acquired by a larger and more firmly established company, an old-economy company—in this case, Mattel. In trying to break into a market, startups are often forced to try riskier new methods or to test alternative approaches or to innovate new kinds of products, whereas established companies tend to be more conservative, taking a wait-and-see attitude toward innovation since they can afford to make adjustments down the line. Larger companies absorb startups for two reasons—to kill competition, and to absorb the innovation back into the mainstream of the industry. Mattel apparently absorbed Purple Moon with an eye toward killing off competition to Barbie with the result that it made only a halfhearted attempt to extend the Rocket franchise beyond those products that Laurel's company had produced. Mattel never understood what it had acquired. Rocket's ultimate disappearance from the marketplace, then, may have less to do with the viability of its model and more to do with the serious corporate forces that Purple Moon was challenging.

One of the most frequently asked questions when our book first appeared was whether it made sense to gender segregate—that is, to create a girls' market rather than expanding the existing boys' market to include more gender-neutral material. We were told, for example, that no one designed games specifically for boys. I would suggest that the release of a major piece of hardware known as the Gameboy suggests that the industry *did* identify its products along gender lines. Many felt that it was time to consciously signal to girls that there might be some forms of digital entertainment that reflected their tastes and interests. Without such a gesture, a gender-neutral play space would remain simply a de facto masculine space. The argument for more "feminine" content lay in the recognition that a significant number of girls were playing games—those who were already comfortable searching for and finding common ground with boys—whereas those girls most apt to be left behind were those whose tastes were the most traditionally feminine.

Suppose we take at face value the claim that game designers aren't designing for boys, that they are simply designing games they would like to play. The existing employee pool for the games industry is overwhelmingly male, so the games designed appeal overwhelmingly to men. One important step would be to significantly expand the number of women working in the industry and give them enough room to develop products that would reflect their tastes and sensibilities. Another would be to make a conscious effort to broaden the range of game content—based on research, if not firsthand experience—in order to expand the number of women who get excited about the medium and thus help to develop the next generation of game designers. What this situation doesn't justify is complacency on the part of the games industry.

The decline of the girl's game companies has taken some of the pressure off the major games companies to respond to this gender gap, buying them time to take a more conservative approach. We are not seeing what we might have anticipated five years ago—a growing "pink" aisle at the software stores. Instead, we are seeing the major companies absorb those lessons that they can from girl games companies' experimentation and apply them to existing franchises that have already proven successful with their predominantly male consumers. So, for example, Barbie Fashion Designer enables girls to design Barbie's clothes, style her hair, select her theme music, choreograph her movements, and have her walk down the fashion runway. The new World Wrestling Federation games would then enable boys to design the wrestlers' clothes, style their hair, select their theme music, choreograph their movements, and then have them walk down the aisle into the ring, where they beat the crap out of each other. Is this new focus on designing your own characters at least partially a product of the success of the Barbie franchise? Hard to tell, given the fact that hardcore gamers have long traded in "skins," but the parallels between the two interface designs are striking.

Ironically, this more conservative strategy of integrating selected traits from girl's game models into existing boy's game genres and franchises may be leading us toward something approaching the "gender-neutral" play spaces some of us were advocating. (Let's bracket for the moment the nagging question of whether any of us really knows what it would look like to live in a *gender-neutral* society and thus whether gender-neutral doesn't still mean second-class citizenship for girls.)

It is interesting to look at The Sims, one of the most successful games in recent years, in light of the distinctions that Brenda Laurel mapped between the classic boy game and her vision for the ideal girl game:

> GIRLS—Leading characters are everyday people that
> girls can easily relate to, and are as real to girls as their
> best friends.
> BOYS—Leading characters are fantasy-based action
> heroes with "superpower" abilities.[5]

In the case of The Sims, the default set of characters are, indeed, "every-day people," the setting is domestic, and the challenges confronted are familiar ones. Because The Sims supports the development and sharing of "skins," artifacts, and architecture, some players have developed larger-than-life protagonists and spaces that can be retrofit into the game universe—including the kinds of superhero or wrestler characters found in more traditional games. What is striking, however, is the degree to which boys are forced to adjust the game to accommodate their interests, whereas so often in our culture, women are expected to read their interests from the margins of popular culture texts that center on male interests.

> GIRLS—Goal is to explore and have new experiences,
> with degrees of success and varying outcomes.
> BOYS—Goal is to win, and the play is linear. Outcome
> is black and white; die and start over; one "right" solu-
> tion.

The Sims lends itself to a broad array of different goals and outcomes. Often, players use the game to do psychological experiments. Friends have told me that they have used the game to see if they are compatible with a proposed set of roommates or learn what adjustments they would need to make in order to move in with their girlfriends. A single mother described the different ways that she and her son used the game to work through the issues surrounding the recent divorce—the son to create a perfect nuclear family, the divorced mother to imagine what it would be like to reenter the dating world. The features of the game are familiar and evocative, encouraging us to use them to simulate our own experiences and thus test different social strategies, much as the design of the Purple Moon games was designed to allow pre-adolescent girls to rehearse social strategies for responding to the challenges of high school life.

> GIRLS—Play focuses on multi-sensory immersion, dis-
> covery, and strong story lines.
> BOYS—Speed and action are key.

The exploratory nature of The Sims differs dramatically from the fixed goals and rapid fire action associated with traditional boy's games. The pace of this game is slower, dealing more with gradual processes and repeated routines, rather than rapid-fire challenges and conflicts. The Sims almost immediately developed a fan culture surrounding the production of scrapbooks documenting the experiences of the Sims characters and over time, these scrapbooks became more and more narrativized. To read those scrapbooks is to learn more and more about the emotional lives and motives of these characters. Indeed, while the scrapbooks were intended to record game actions, many players report that they play the game to get the images they need to complete narratives they want to tell. The Sims has thus found a way to encourage players to create more narratively compelling experiences. While Purple Moon authored stories within its games (while providing a web space in which girls could expand upon their understanding of those characters), The Sims was designed as a "sandbox" or "dollhouse" where players could play out their own narratives.

> GIRLS—Feature everyday "real life" settings as well as new places to explore.
> BOYS—Features non-realistic, larger-than-life settings.

In *From Barbie to Mortal Kombat*, I contrasted Sim City with the "play town" that Harriet constructed for her imaginary life in the classic children's book, *Harriet the Spy*: "Sim City embraces stock themes from boys' play, such as building forts, shaping earth with toy trucks, or damming creeks, playing them out on a much larger scale. For Harriet, the mapping of the space was only the first step in preparing the ground for a rich saga of life and death, joy and sorrow, and those are the elements that are totally lacking in most simulation games." The Sims, however, is Harriet's "play town." The shift in the scale of the game from Sim City's objectifying top-down view of urban renewal to The Sims' subjective, eye-level perspective on individual characters, reflects this openness to new kinds of narratives, which center around characters and their emotional lives. The interface is designed to foreground emotional responses—rendered all the more powerfully when abstracted from the specific verbal content of their speech. The characters weep when other characters die; they make passionate love; they flirt; they get depressed and mope; they get tired and cranky. As The Sims moves from a stand-alone game to a multiplayer online game, the universe of spaces and characters expands enormously, creating many more opportunities for both spatial and social exploration.

> GIRLS—Success comes through development of friendships.
> BOYS—Success comes through the elimination of competitors.

Consider Laurel's descriptions of the different ways that girls and boys compete: "Girls and boys are equally competitive—they are just different kinds of competition. Girls assert social influence and structure relationships while boys seek to dominate and defeat." Girl's competition, she asserts, reflects a "desire to establish relationships/friendships," to extend their "social status" through processes of affiliation and exclusion, and to "figure out" opponents. The Sims can be seen as a game that rewards precisely these kinds of social and cultural competition, including the development of a rewards system based on the player's ability to establish strong social bonds with a broad array of other players and characters. Much of the game play consists of social interactions within the family or with friends, and the expansion packs offer more options for hosting parties and thus expanding the circle of one's social contacts. The game excludes almost altogether those forms of competition that are traditionally associated with boy's games, where "social status tends to be by achievement and physical domination" and where the goal is to "outwit" opponents. Indeed, in the absence of pre-structured goals or pre-determined competition, the element of direct physical combat is excluded from The Sims almost altogether.

I have spoken to Will Wright and others at Maxis and I am reasonably convinced that they were not directly modeling The Sims on girl's game–movement products. Rather, the decisions they made came out of a context where there were more female designers and more highly ranked female designers than I have seen at any other mainstream game studio. In such a context, even if there is no conscious goal of expanding the female market, the unconscious decisions made by men and women working together is likely to produce a product that is very different from one where the intuitive decisions were made by an all or predominantly male team of designers. Not surprisingly, then, The Sims has proven to be highly successful in attracting female players while at the same time expanding the range of play experiences available to boys.

I concluded my essay in *From Barbie to Mortal Kombat* with these words of caution:

> [Sociologist Barrie] Thorne finds that aggressive 'border-work' is more likely to occur when children are forced together by adults than when they find themselves interacting more spontaneously, more likely to occur in prestructured institutional settings like the school yard than in the informal settings of the subdivisions and apartment complexes. All of this suggests that our fantasy of designing games that will provide common play spaces for girls and boys may be illusive and as full of its

own complications and challenges as creating a 'girls only' space or encouraging girls to venture into traditional male turf. We are not yet sure what a gender-neutral space will look like. Creating such a space would mean redesigning not only the nature of computer games but also the nature of society. The danger may be that in such a space, gender differences are going to be more acutely felt, as boys and girls will be repelled from each other rather than drawn together.

There are reasons why this is a place where neither the feminist entrepreneurs nor the makers of boys' games are ready to go, yet as the girls' market is secured, the challenge must be to find a way to move beyond our existing categories and to once again invent new kinds of virtual play spaces.

The Sims is an important step in that process—one that shares many of the traits associated with the girl's game movement without calling attention to them as such, and embeds them within a successful preexisting franchise with a known appeal to male consumers. The Sims, of course, in reproducing domestic space, reproduces many of the ideological assumptions that currently shape the contemporary family, yet it also gives us the tools to rescript and restage those relationships in new terms. As such, it would seem to me to represent the logical culmination of the girl's game movement and the beginning of the process of developing a more "gender neutral" play space. As we move in that direction, however, we need to be aware of the kind of "border work" that demarks places where boys and girls can and cannot play together and try to understand what it really means to provide a common ground for both genders.

notes

1. Justine Cassell and Henry Jenkins, eds., *From Barbie to Mortal Kombat: Gender and Computer Games* (Cambridge: MIT Press, 1998). This essay was originally presented at Playing by the Rules: The Cultural Policy Challenges of Video Games Conference, hosted by the Cultural Policy Center, University of Chicago, October 26–27, 2001.
2. Brenda Laurel, as quoted in G. Beato, "Girls Games: Computer Games for Girls Is No Longer an Oxymoron," *Wired*, April 1997.
3. Brenda Laurel, *Utopian Enterpreneur* (Cambridge: MIT Press, 2001).
4. Ibid., 3.
5. This formulation of the differences between girls and games, which run throughout the rest of this essay, was formulated by Brenda Laurel. It was widely reproduced in internal documents and press releases from Purple Moon in the late 1990s. She discusses these ideas in detail with Jennifer Glos and Shari Goldin, "An Interview with Brenda Laurel (Purple Moon)," in Cassell and Jenkins, eds., *From Barbie to Mortal Kombat*, 118–135.

endnotes for a

theory of

seventeen **convergence**

j o e   a m a t o

1. For a brilliant analysis of the "restorative disabling," or what he
   terms "indigence," inherent to encyclopedic narrative/discourse, see Jed
   Rasula, "Textual Indigence in the Archive," *Postmodern Culture* 9, no. 3 (1999),
   <muse.jhu.edu/journals/pmc/v009/9.3rasula.html>. Through trenchant
   readings of Thomas Pynchon, Don DeLillo, Thomas Mann, Herman
   Melville, and James Joyce, Rasula conjectures that the (narrative) impulse
   to thematize the All (formerly the universal) brings with it a "thicken[ing]"
   agent (paragraph 37) that complicates reductive notions of knowledge, of
   our capacity to know (there may be a trace here of what anthropologist
   Clifford Geertz, after Gilbert Ryle, called "thick description"). Despite the
   rosier epistemological proclamations associated with our digital era, "the
   issue is not strictly technological," for more "organic visions" are equally
   culpable on the count of presuming "faith in the beneficence of a higher
   power" (paragraph 38; Rasula cites, among others, James Lovelock's Gaia
   hypothesis, C. G. Jung's collective unconscious, and "utopian affirmations
   of our multi-media 'infosphere'" as a sort of "global nervous system"). It is
   precisely against such cosmic convictions that indigence, as theorized ana-
   logically by Rasula, may augur an "apparently aimless circularity" that
   serves to offset "the new dromocracy [sic]—the world of entitlements to

speed," thus instructing us as to "the scope and limits of 'learning' as such" (paragraph 39). As for "thick description," see Clifford Geertz, *The Interpretation of Cultures* (New York: Basic Books, 1973).

2. In *The Poetics of the Common Knowledge* (Albany: State University of New York Press, 1994), Don Byrd mounts a poetic revaluation of "the postmodern assumption . . . that all of the possibilities—all of the infinite possibilities—are accounted for" (348). Hardly opposed to postmodernism as a field of artistic endeavor, Byrd queries the Lyotardian condition of postmodernity to mount a damning (and often exhilarating) polemic directed against a "statistical world" in which the All that "is already accounted for" (348) militates against public apprehension of the finite and singular nature of our planet (not to say our cosmos). The burgeoning digital information complex may be precisely (a version of) that whole which passes today for All—and as Byrd has it, building on the work of Alfread North Whitehead and Charles Olson, the "philosophic" truth of such a "non-statistical" All "does not satisfy the creative eros" (348–49). Indeed, it cannot—at least philosophically (!), to the extent that the creative prevails as that "investigatory" moment imagined by Olson à la Byrd (357) wherein the (North American) poet-creator (-historian) articulates the requisite interworkings of information, knowledge, and uncertainty (this is a prime feature of what Byrd intuits and limns as "the common knowledge"). One may debate the type and merits of poetic inquiry so conceived, but Byrd's exhortation has the effect of placing the creative act squarely in the midst of all-too-singularly-human, aspiringly communal, technologically informed, and unremittingly social embarkations of desire. See also Ed Sanders, *Investigative Poetry* (San Francisco: City Lights, 1976).

3. This is Charles Bernstein's point in his provocative essay "Provisional Institutions: Alternative Presses and Poetic Innovation." "One of the clichés of the intellectual- and artist-bashing so fashionable in our leading journals," Bernstein writes, "is that there are no more 'public intellectuals'" (146). "The truth of the matter," he continues, "is that writing of great breadth and depth, and of enormous significance for the public, flourishes, but that the dominant media institutions—commercial television and radio, the trade presses, and the nationally circulated magazines (including the culturally upscale periodicals)—have blacklisted this material." For Bernstein, the "crime" of the artists and intellectuals to which he refers "is not a lack of accessibility but a refusal to submit to marketplace agendas" (146). In *My Way: Speeches and Poems* (Chicago: University of Chicago Press 1999), 145–54. For more on the publishing marketplace and its once-and-future conglomerations, see André Schiffrin, *The Business of Books* (New York: Verso, 2000), and Jason E. Epstein, *Book Business* (New York: Norton, 2001).

4. Genealogy evidently ranks second only to pornography in generating web traffic, as reported by Peter T. Kilborn, "In Libraries and Cemeteries, Vacationing with Ancestors," *New York Times*, August 19, 2001, late national ed., sec. 1, 1+. "The Internet's message boards, family news groups and genealogical services," writes Kilborn, "are its second-busiest destinations after the sexually-oriented sites" (24).[1] (The hunt for descendants and the hunt for sexual gratification [that might, on the off-chance, beget descendants] thus take place side-by-side.) The development of sophisticated online databases and search engines, most notably of late at <www.ellisislandrecords.com>, helps to explain public

access to, if not public fascination with, family immigration records and the like. Good middle-class citizens may now conceivably clear up long-standing confusion resulting from faulty, or competing, memories; family secrets may be outed; family myths may be put to rest. (I speak here from personal experience, having recently perused "original" [digitized] ship manifests using the Ellis Island archives to learn the actual dates of immigration of my Sicilian grandparents; the names and destinations of several heretofore obscure relatives; and the timing of those to-and-fro ocean journeys that brought my kin to the states. And this online glimpse of what C. L. R. James, while imprisoned on Ellis Island, wrote of as a "miniature" of the world's nations and societies is brought to me in the terra firma comfort of my loft office.) If one considers this form of electronic recuperation alongside the more biologically anchored, if correspondingly computational, realities of DNA forensics (I have in mind here the Thomas Jefferson–Sally Hemings affair), we may be witnessing a collective, participatory reconstruction of the thus abstracted, singularized, and pixeled past (person or polis). History may begin to resemble those dinosaurs in *Jurassic Park*—reanimated, alive, with teeth. See C. L. R. James, *Mariners, Renegades, and Castaways: The Story of Herman Melville and the World We Live In* (London: Allison and Busby/Schocken, 1985; originally published 1953).

5. "The web is now a place of quantity in [Charles] Olson's sense," observes Michael Joyce, "and its quantity here too is increasingly termed an environment or a society." Proposing that we treat the web as a "ritual space," Joyce asserts that this space "encourages us to seek some sense of [Cara] Armstrong and [Karen] Nelson's 'revised history and broader framework'" (412). Joyce is wary, however, of the ease with which we take such "ritual action" as a guarantor of a more profound spiritual cartography. See Michael Joyce, "Beyond Next Before You Once Again: Repossessing and Renewing Electronic Culture," in *Passions, Pedagogies and Twenty-First-Century Technologies*, ed. Gail E. Hawisher and Cynthia L. Selfe, (Logan: Utah State University Press, 1999), 399–417. As many have commented, one casualty of "multiclick" search and save missions is likely to be a certain trivializing of our public infosphere (think of DVD "Easter egg" hunts), for Euro-rootedness or not, we frequent flyers are hence ultimately bound to our presumed origins via a retrospective accumulation of raw data capital—no doubt to be merchandised along the lines of the Ellis Island endeavor (see note 4, above), "to give a truly meaningful gift [hard copies of ship manifests etc.] to your loved ones" (promotional e-mail received August 9, 2001 from <News@ellisisland.org>). And such armchair memory processing may constitute a false grasp, again, of what it means to know, given the ineluctably pixilated erotics of assemblage and communication.

6. Similarly, the Electronic Literature Directory, launched in September of 2000 (<www.eliterature.org>), served to authorize and focus the international multimedia field as such by providing a user-friendly database of that field's productions and authors. Among the many benefits of listing oneself in the database, according to the Electronic Literature Organization: "Having your biographical information and work listed in the Directory will increase your readership and visibility. The Directory will be unequalled as a reference source for electronic literature and is bound to become a significant portal for readers. It will serve as a valuable tool for event organizers looking for readers and lecturers. It will help teachers find

works to assign for class study and will aid scholars and journalists who write about the field" (e-mail received August 25, 2000 from <directory@eliterature.org>). I certainly do not wish to derogate or dispute any of these solicitations (especially as some have already proved accurate, and especially as I am myself a participant in the ELO enterprise!), but I do wish to highlight the more direct (if subtly stated) appeal of such a listing: that it imagines a community of readers, event organizers, lecturers, teachers (and by implication, students), scholars, and journalists; in short, that it imagines an entire public intellectual sphere, however geopolitically reconceived or redistributed, that pretty much parallels existing print networks and functions (and with regard to publishing, see note 3, above). Such functions are in fact no doubt undergoing rapid deformation—to judge by all but the most stodgily recalcitrant rear guard—yet I would surmise that more thought needs to be given to the nature of our marketplace transactions; specifically, urgencies surrounding royalties, copyrights, and so on. (Marketing and advertising concerns are not necessarily paramount here, as print-on-demand distribution mechanics, for instance, have been rapidly absorbed into the Bertelsmann et al. entertainment complex.) An apt place to begin retheorizing might be with that vexed term, *editor*, for the editorial function invokes at once the practical necessity for limiting (via simple selection) seemingly unlimited web capacities, and the desire for some more conscious form of aesthetic-ideological discrimination. (Preferably of the "Ask not what your cultural practice can do for you" variety. And let's be clear: It's not that popular culture is so banal—and much of it is, sure—it's just that it's getting tougher and tougher to find a small press distributor.) We mustn't let such discriminatory apparatuses get in the way of real change, either. Even a quick survey of multimedia work will reveal that animated graphics often obscure moribund ideas, that clumsy imaging often foregrounds verbal eloquence. Much the same situation characterized twentieth-century developments in cinema. As Wheeler Winston Dixon makes the case for the "B" film: "In a very real sense, 'B' films were forced to be trailblazers, simply because they inherently could not compete in the area of spectacle; they had too little money for anything beyond the bare physical necessities of production" (76); Dixon, *The Second Century of Cinema: The Past and Future of the Moving Image* (Albany: State University of New York Press, 2000). As for "imagined communities," see Benedict Anderson, *Imagined Communities: Reflections on the Origin and Spread of Nationalism*, rev. and extended ed. (London: New York, Verso, 1991). John Perry Barlow's "The Economy of Ideas," published during the initial clamor over Internet incursions, remains an eminently useful document. See *Wired* 2.03 (March 1994), 84–90, 126–29, or <www.wired.com/wired/archive/2.03/economy.ideas.html>. Finally (and if I may): English Studies (or whatever we eventually call it) could profit in general from a renewed discussion of aesthetic convergence (per se). Marjorie Perloff's (characteristically controversial) investigation of Ludwig Wittgenstein's diverse philosophical (-aesthetic-ethical) platform in the context of various twentieth-century arts strikes this reader as an appropriate place to start; see Perloff, *Wittgenstein's Ladder: Poetic Language and the Strangeness of the Ordinary* (Chicago: University of Chicago Press, 1996). See also Brian Kim Stefans's lively poetry and poetics site, <www.geocities.com/arras_online/>.

7. Privacy issues are another matter. That privacy is gradually coming to be seen—by the corporate sector—as a commodity should give us pause. See Toby Lester, "The Reinvention of Privacy," *Atlantic Monthly* 287, no. 3 (2001), 27–39; see also Philip E. Agre and Marc Rotenberg, eds., *Technology and Privacy: The New Landscape* (Cambridge, Mass.: MIT Press, 1997.) For an important early government document detailing First Amendment issues, see U.S. Congress, Office of Technology Assessment, Science, Technology, and the First Amendment, OTA-CIT-369 (Washington, D.C.: US Government Printing Office, 1988). K. Eric Drexler's discussion of hypertext in the context of nanotechnology is pertinent here; his speculative remarks circa mid-1980s, drawing from the work of Vannevar Bush and Theodor Holm (and, it would seem, Marshall McLuhan), distinguished him as being among the first to associate, directly, advancements in information access (hypertext in particular) with the entire spectrum of emerging (nano)technologies; and Drexler was careful to consider the dangers posed by these new information technologies in terms of government surveillance and the like. See Drexler, *Engines of Creation: The Coming Era of Nanotechnology* (New York: Anchor Press/Doubleday, 1987), esp. 217–30.

8. I agree fully with Michelle Kendrick's assessment when she writes, "In this respect, any subjectivity or identity—any sense of a pretechnological reality or a reality distinct from or prior to technological intervention—can only be imaginary. The technological real, therefore, describes the inextricability of embodied identity and technology in the construction of working fictions of subjectivity" (144–45). See Kendrick, "Cyberspace and the Technological Real," in *Virtual Realities and Their Discontents*, ed. Robert Markley (Baltimore: Johns Hopkins University Press, 1996), 143–60. OK then. But if you assume, as almost every media scholar these days does, that writing is itself a technology—well, Kendrick's articulation (like the one you're reading) must be at least vulnerable to the (writerly) charge that it too works to create a fiction of subjectivity. Rather than debate here the merits of scholarly vs._____discourse, I would simply point to the liability of operating without due consideration of related . . . effects. It's rather like László Moholy-Nagy's belief that "[g]roup activity of the future must be more consciously aware of the mechanics of its own operation as well as of its results" (358). See Moholy-Nagy, *Vision in Motion* (Chicago: Paul Theobald, 1965 [originally published 1947]; I can't get behind the sociobiological drift of Moholy-Nagy's speculative postwar [and Bauhaus-derived] remarks, but his book is nonetheless one helluva read from a media perspective).

9. H. Kassia Fleisher has made this case a bit more forcibly: "To inhabit passively another novel that tugs you along (machinery silenced) with seductive readability . . . this also is to sell your agency. To write, to compose, to order, to organize a world passively in lined story form; to fail to expose, to yourself if not to your reader, the mechanisms by which you tug, seduce; to fail to value your reader's intentions and resistance . . . this also is to sell your agency—as well as the agency of your readers. It is to contribute to the building of more little [publishing] Celebrations all over the land." See Fleisher, "Fucked by the Master's Plot: Miss Collins and Mr. Sawyer Celebrate the American Dream," *Electronic Book Review* 9 (1998), <www.altx.com/ebr/ebr9/index.html>.

10. At the very least, our tools themselves are at stake as we surf the web, plumb the archives, navigate the constructed world. "The activity of navigation," argues M. A. Syverson in a more cognitive vein, "is a process of thinking through the tools, charts, records, and social structures, not a simple question of applying them" (174). See Syverson, "Thinking through Worlds Fair: Evolutionary Rhetoric," *Computers and Composition* 18, no. 2 (2001): 163–76. For Syverson, the "major challenge" of "incorporat[ing] visual rhetoric into . . . composition courses" is a matter of "thinking with," rather than "representing . . . in," such media (174). And on this note, I would argue that literary and composition practitioners alike could benefit from greater exposure to more artistic (including visual) products and processes. Jim Andrews has compiled a stellar archive of "webartery" at <vispo.com/misc/links.htm>. And Steve Tomasula's *VAS: An Opera in Flatland* (Barrytown, NY: Station Hill Press, 2002; graphic design by Stephen Farrell) is likely to become one of the seminal print works to explore conjunctions of (fictional and nonfictional) narrative and image. Tomasula's dance through the minefields of intelligence testing, genetic research, and bleeding-edge body technologies (while chewing gum and walking his dog) amounts to a collision between scientific discourse and fictive meditation; the frissons that result signify a new twist on what is in reality an ancient word/image poetic, a poetic sublimated in the past century by inexpensive paperback production. In fact, Jay David Bolter and Richard Grusin's recent work on remediation is apt to provide a more bracing account of Tomasula's achievement than might be had using current literary-theoretical models. As reviewer Nancy Allen has it, remediation posits a "reciprocal relationship" between "the logic of immediacy"—that "which produces the sense of a lived experience"—and "the logic of hypermediacy," or that "which makes us aware of the technology used to create such an experience" (192). Hence Tomasula's *VAS* may be understood as remediating the print book in response to the onslaught of web-based imagery (courtesy of a recombination of digital graphic arts with word processing). Whether in fact the primary aim of (Tomasula's) hypermediacy is to effect immediacy will perhaps be the occasion for future disquisition. See Bolter and Grusin, *Remediation: Understanding New Media* (Cambridge, Mass.: MIT Press, 1999); and Allen, "Telling Our Stories in New Ways," book review, *Computers and Composition* 18, no. 2 (2001): 187–94. For book as artifact, see Johanna Drucker, *The Century of Artists' Books* (New York: Granary Books, 1995).

11. Whatever you make of it, Alan Sondheim's remarkably expansive (and expanding) oeuvre gives the lie to the notion that alphabetic technologies can be understood as independent of, not simply the materialities, but more specifically the protocols and devices of contemporary communication networks and practices; see <www.anu.edu.au/english/internet_txt/>. Moreover, in reading/browsing Sondheim's works and days, one gets the distinct impression that the digital world circulates a (healthy?) measure of despair (indigence redux?), upsetting, or offsetting, all dreams of a common lingo even as "Englishes" becomes a commonplace. For a helpful overview of Sondheim and others' reprogramming of textuality, see McKenzie Wark, "Codework," *American Book Review* 22, no. 6 (2001): 1, 5.

12. To clarify: those monthly posts from Subcommandante Marcos hardly allayed my desire for a good spicy bean burrito. (Here in Lafayette, Colorado, La Familia turns out to be the place.) The problem is not one of conspicuous consumption, exactly (I am, after all, talking burritos), or the way commodity culture infiltrates and undermines the better angels of our nature. The problem has more to do with whether the vast relatively well-to-do of the online world are willing to channel their appetites in constructive, ecologically sound, politically responsible (and responsive) directions; and once willing to do so, whether they're aware of their participation in an oppressive global arrangement that—though apparently thriving on smaller, dispersed collectives, everything from terrorist cell to chat room—is as harsh as ever on have-nots. I want my burrito; I want to eat my burrito, too, and I'm probably doing more for local Latino populations (not to mention my nutritional well-being) if I stay the hell out of Taco Bell. But spending one's money here, not there, is like learning Spanish on the campaign trail: you talk, money talks, and customers listen. Awareness comes at a price, finally—more awareness, burrito or not.

13. Neologisms abound today [my current favorites: *Netwar*, coined by Rand consultant David Ronfeldt, with *biometeorology* running a close second], not necessarily because things are so new that they require new words, but possibly because we of the information age value novelty. (Or at least, we who are hacker-minded.) The *New Hacker's Dictionary* (now a decade old) defines *neophilia* as "[t]he trait of being excited and pleased by novelty" (256), and assigns this "trait" to all manner of technophile. See Eric Raymond, ed., *The New Hacker's Dictionary* (Cambridge, Mass.: MIT Press, 1991). Neologisms have been greeted by the poet set with mixed reception. The *New Princeton Encyclopedia of Poetry and Poetics* reports that "[n]eologisms (new-coined words), tend now to be associated with novelty more than freshness, and sometimes with strained effects" (690); further, that "computer terms" would seem to be "expanding" the English language lexis, "though they have yet to be entered in general poetic" lexis (on this latter point, however, see note 11, above). See Alex Preminger and T. V. F. Brogan, eds., *The New Princeton Encyclopedia of Poetry and Poetics* (New York: MJF Books, 1993). Perhaps some poets resist the neologism simply because one can never be sure who was the first to coin a given word, throwing into doubt questions of originality and longevity (not to say authenticity). Not surprisingly, e.g., *digitext* is also the name of a (Canadian) website design firm (see <www.digitext.on.ca/>). The poet and publisher Miekal And (alias, The Avant-Garde Museum of Temporary Art) compiles an unusual *International Dictionary of Neologisms* at <net22.com/neologisms>. Happy click trails! And for more on *Netwar*, see Thomas A. Stewart, "America's Secret Weapon," *Business 2.0 2/10* (2001), 58–68.

14. There's probably a literacy issue, which is to say a political issue, embedded someplace here, as well. Richard A. Lanham's early foray into things digital kick-started subsequent (progressivist) educational theorizing. See Lanham, *The Electronic Word: Democracy, Technology, and the Arts* (Chicago: University of Chicago Press, 1993). And Stuart Moulthrop has offered sage commentary as well regarding those incipient (legalistic, and personally impassioned) battles over copyright and appropriation that are bound to punctuate the electronic era. "The fault line between expression and commodity cuts deeply across the technological landscape," he writes,

and this "may in fact be the channel that carries the muddy waters of literacy and electronic culture" (424). See Moulthrop, "Everybody's Elegies," in Hawisher and Selfe, eds., *Passions*, 418–24.

15. Steven Spielberg's (Stanley Kubrick's) alternately praised and buried *A.I.: Artificial Intelligence* (written by Spielberg and Ian Watson, and based on Brian Aldiss's "Super-toys Last All Summer Long") seems at first viewing to slide by the (posthuman) figure of the cyborg by exploring the dialectic of "mecha"—mechanical, robotic (and note the homophone)—and "orga," or us organic types. Jonathan Rosenbaum's laudatory *Chicago Reader* review (July 13, 2001) does a nice job of exploring the film's various intertextual-metacinematic nods, and his searching explication of the film's strengths benefits from his refusal to "succumb . . . to media typecasting of both filmmakers." See Rosenbaum, "The Best of Both Worlds," *Chicago Reader Online*, September 4, 2001, <www.chireader.com/movies/archive.html>. Rosenbaum deems it "logical that *A.I.* should turn out to be an allegory about cinema . . . because the prime issue for the modern world may be our willingness to treat nonliving matter as if it were alive and living people as if they were objects." And of course this is what cinema consistently portends, especially cinema of such complex (if in this case, racially narrow) ambitions; as Rosenbaum has it (echoing perhaps Jean Cocteau's "Registration of Death at Work"), film is "a form of bringing the appearance of life to nonliving matter." But Rosenbaum registers a near miss in his efforts to tender filmic allegory as a preemptive variation on posthuman-biotech traumas (which may be said in some sense of all fictive work). Of those otherwordly "future beings" at the conclusion of *A.I.*, he writes that they "resemble the aliens in *Close Encounters of the Third Kind* (except that they appear either to combine the categories orga and mecha or make them both irrelevant)." Or make them both irrelevant: the dystopic residue of *A.I.* is owing not simply to David's (as played by Haley Joel Osment) programmed and irreversible desire for unconditional love, for the "artificial" in "artificial intelligence," like the figure of the cyborg, marks (as so many have observed) the imminent collapse of the artificial-natural binary. The film's titular wordplay—implying, ironically, the possibility of "real" intelligence, like "real" love—also suggests that the real is only as "real" as we might imagine it, not least because the fictive is often the first stop on *Homo faber*'s way to (re?)making the world in his/her/its own image. (Social prophecy is, to be sure, one measure of science fiction's claim to legitimacy, and one sense in which scifi, it could be argued, transcends the plain vanilla plots and syntactic complacencies of so much pulp fiction.) Thus *A.I.* is less an "allegory about cinema" than a treatise on human nature, for if it "speaks otherwise" (as the etymology of "allegory" would suggest), it does so only to remind us that we are who, and what, we would aspire to be; those worldly others at film's end, however telepathic or televisual, constitute self-consciously poor projections of our long lost humanity (i.e., this is not a Spielbergian regress into sentimentality, as Rosenbaum would have us believe). David's final lapse into "that place where dreams are born" suggests that the meaning of life (and death), whatever it is, turns on our capacity (and willingness) to desire, and to imagine dèsire—even at the risk of self-negation (there is at least an

intertextual hint here of Rutger Hauer's existential angst as "replicant" Roy Batty in *Blade Runner*). Hence David's evocative death-sleep is, paradoxically, a projection of . . . the artist. With regard to which enigmatic grasp of creative consciousness, Bhanu Kapil Rider projects a correspondingly perplexed cyborg interiority grappling with the meaning of (everyday) posthuman circumstance: "When I walk amongst thy/When I tryst with/Eat with/These are not my kind. (In marrying, I will make a cyborg offspring: ach. I fear for my children's children. Not even when eating my breakfast of black coffee and fried okra am I steadfast. Listen, I tell my bridegroom, I want to have it in a hospital. I do not want a natural birth.)" (8–9). Bhanu Kapil Rider, *Autobiography of a Cyborg* (San Francisco: Leroy chapbook series, 2000).

16. Leigh Shoemaker's crisp reading of Henry Rollins's writing, lyrics, and stage persona unveils a somewhat-less-than-appealing aspect of Rollins's "part animal part machine" boast. Using Kurt Theweleit's work on National Socialist male fantasies, Shoemaker demonstrates Rollins's equally problematic "literary fascism" (108). Under Shoemaker's scrutiny, Rollins's boast becomes less "a statement of cyborg allegiance" than "testimony to the fact that the fascist . . . is under construction and is incomplete as long as the animal is allowed to exist in conjunction with the machine" (108–9). See Shoemaker, "Part Animal, Part Machine: Self-Definition, Rollins Style," in *Third Wave Agenda: Being Feminist, Doing Feminism*, ed. Leslie Heywood and Jennifer Drake (Minneapolis: University of Minnesota Press, 1997), 103–21. Most of us have heard too much already of the cyberpunk-tive desire to transcend the body (or "meat") via uploading consciousness, but what remains intriguing about this fraught vector of disembodiment is that it should persist as a form of liberatory wish fulfillment when it is precisely the "meat body" (to borrow from Michael McClure) that served as the locus of liberation three or four decades ago (aided by numerous discourses whose purpose was to situate the body at the center of repressive forces). Either the digital world is perceived as the only place left to flee to, or the ostensibly "free," yet obediently industrialized body (à la Michel Foucault) must be strengthened to suffer its status as a center of repressive forces. My hunch is that the cyborg serves in effect as something of a transhistorical go-between, modulating (while figuring) the presumed raptures of the successively escaping former and the inescapable realities of the professional-managerial latter. As Shoemaker concludes (with regard to Rollins), the cyborg-inclined thereby hazard a fascism of the machine, neopostfuturists that they (we) are. See McClure, "Phi Upsilon Kappa" (1962), in *The Poetics of the New American Poetry*, ed. Donald Allen and Warren Tallman (New York: Grove, 1979), 416–29; and Michel Foucault, *Discipline and Punish: The Birth of the Prison* (1975), trans. Alan Sheridan, 2d ed. (New York: Vintage, 1995). For more on the masculinist proportions of technological development, see Roger Horowitz, ed., *Boys and Their Toys: Masculinity, Class and Technology in America* (New York: Routledge, 2001).

17. For poetry per se, see Joe Amato, "Let me tell you all about myself," unpublished manuscript dated November 8, 1997: "A necessary loss of presence/in our failure to swap epidermal layers/to see and feel who we really are/ought to/have been, be: /No I'm not really here/in this [millennial] romp (having to write/uninspired handling of "uninspired handling/of original

footage")/not really here/in these words/nevertheless/incumbent starters
all/my race is killing me and/yours is/probably killing you too/little matter
whether it's less/ murderous/66 low Earth-orbit satellites or/1 office for every
300 Fortune 500 workers or/3000 IP addresses for each/atom on the surface of
the planet the news today/yesterday Chicago Trib 17 August oh boy" (4).

18. In contrast to which, John Cage's use of mesostics in (e.g.) *Composition in
Retrospect* (Cambridge, Mass.: Exact Change, 1993) creates a network of
associations that, as the result of its chance-determinate roots, seems both
more and less contingent on local knowledge. See also Steven Johnson,
Emergence: The Connected Lives of Ants, Brains, Cities, and Software (New York:
Scribners, 2001). Depending on your critical druthers, connectedness can
signal either sheer ecological bliss or Pynchonesque paranoia.

10:19² As of this writing, we are so many things. It's in the nature of the
exchange.

ending notes

1. The events of September 11, 2001 reduced porno traffic substantially, but
only momentarily.

2. Military "hoist and fly" (width-to-length) ratio of the U.S. flag (only by
executive order). (Thanks to Jeffrey Jullich for alerting me to same.) Final
facts to include finding the cost of freedom through the electrification of
history.

notes on

contributors

Joe Amato is an assistant professor of English at the University of Colorado at Boulder, where he teaches creative writing and literature. He's the author of *Symptoms of a Finer Age* (1994), *Bookend: Anatomies of a Virtual Self* (1997), and *Under Virga* (forthcoming).

Bertolt Brecht, perhaps best known internationally as a poet and a playwright, has also been recognized as a significant contributor to Marxist-inflected literary and aesthetic theory. Among his major dramatic works are *Mother Courage*, *The Caucasian Chalk Circle*, and *Galileo Galilei*. Following a wartime period of exile in the United States, Brecht returned to Germany where he founded the Berlin Ensemble. Opposing himself to Lucaks's influential theories of literary realism, Brecht outlined crucial critical categories of "epic" (or "dialectical") theater using distancing modes of staging and composition evolved during his years of work toward creating a theater for "the scientific age." These techniques were designed to create a *verfremdungseffekt* (alienation effect) that would foster a more critical detachment on the part of the audience. Brecht died in Berlin in 1956.

Karen S. F. Buzzard is a professor and department head in the Department of Media, Journalism, and Film at Southwest Missouri State University in Springfield. She writes in the areas of media audiences and interpersonal relationships and her books include *Chains of Gold: Marketing the Ratings and Rating the Markets* (1990), *Electronic Media Ratings, Turning Audiences into Dollars and Sense* (1992), and *Holding Pattern: How Communication Prevents Intimacy in Adults* (2001). Her work has been published in the *Journal of Radio Studies*, the *Journal of Popular Culture*, and the *Journal of Media Economics*, as well as in encyclopedia entries and book chapters.

John T. Caldwell teaches television and media studies in the Department of Film, Television, and Digital Media at UCLA. His books include *Televisuality: Style, Crisis, and Authority in American Television* (1995) and *Electronic Media and Technoculture* (2000). His essays have been published in *Cinema Journal*; *Media, Culture, and Society*; and *Television and New Media*. He is the producer/director of the award-winning documentary films *Freak Street to Goa: Immigrants on the Rajpath* (1989) and *Rancho California (por favor)* (2002). He has had numerous grants from the National Endowment for the Arts, regional fellowships, and state arts councils. His films have been featured in festivals in Berlin, Sundance, Paris, Amsterdam, Chicago, Toulouse, and Hawaii, and broadcast on television in the United States and Australia.

Anna Everett is an associate professor of film and TV history and theory and new media studies at the University of California, Santa Barbara. She is the author of several books and articles, including "The Revolution Will be Digitized: Afrocentricity and the Digital Public Sphere," and "Returning the Gaze: A Genealogy of Black Film Criticism, 1909–1949." She is completing two other manuscripts: *Digital Diasporas: A Race for Cyberspace*, and *Inside the Dark Museum: Black Film Criticism from 1909 to 1959*. Her essays have been published in *Cinema Journal*, *The Denver Law Review*, *Film Criticism*, and encyclopedias and book chapters. She is also the founding editor of *Screening Noir: A Newsletter of Film and Video Culture*.

Tarleton Gillespie is an assistant professor of science and technology at Cornell University. His current work considers recent legal disputes about digital copyright and the implications for the character of Internet technology and the social arrangements of culture. His interests, however, are nomadic; his most recent publication is "Recognizable Ambiguity: Cartoon Imagery and American Childhood in *Animaniacs*," coauthored with Chandra Mukerji, in *Symbolic Childhood*, edited by Dan Cook (forthcoming).

Henry Jenkins is director of the MIT Program in Comparative Media Studies. His books include *From Barbie to Mortal Kombat: Gender and Computer Games* (1999), *The Children's Cultural Reader* (1998), *What Made Pistachio Nuts: Early Sound Comedy and the Vaudeville Aesthetic* (1993), *Classical Hollywood Comedy* (1994), *Poachers: Television Fans and Participatory Culture* (1992), and the forthcoming *The Politics and Pleasures of Popular Culture*. Jenkins testified before the U.S. Senate during hearings on media violence that followed the Columbine High School shootings.

George E. Lewis is professor of music in the critical studies/experimental practices area at the University of California-San Diego. An improvisor and trombonist, composer, and computer/installation artist, Lewis's work in electronic and computer-music, computer-based multimedia installations, text-sound works, free improvisation, and notated forms has been documented on more than 120 recordings. A member of the Association for the Advancement of Creative Musicians since 1971, his scholarly writing on music has appeared in such journals as *Contemporary Music Review*, *Black Music Research Journal*, *Lenox Avenue*, and *Leonardo Music Journal*. He has recently been awarded the McArthur Genius Grant.

Peter Lunenfeld is director of the Institute for Technology and Aesthetics and teaches in the Graduate Media Design Program at the Art

Center College of Design in Pasadena. He is the author of *Snap to Grid: A User's Guide to Digital Arts, Media and Cultures* (2000) and editor of the *The Digital Dialectic: New Essays in New Media* (1999). Recent publications include "The Myths of Interactive Cinema" for *The New Media Book*, edited by Dan Harries (2002) and "Moiré Eels," a catalog essay about the digital artworks of ChanShatz. From 1998 to 2002, he wrote the "User" column for the international journal *artext*. He is editorial director of the highly regarded Mediawork pamphlet series for the MIT Press. These "theoretical fetish objects" cover the intersections of art, design, technology, and market culture; <mitpress.mit.edu/mediawork>.

Stephen Mamber is a professor in the Critical Studies Program of the UCLA Department of Film, Television, and Digital Media. He is the author of *Cinema Verité in America* (1974) and several web-based projects. He is a former visiting research scientist at the IBM T. J. Watson Research Center and has done work on three-dimensional modeling and visual databases under a grant from the Intel Corporation.

Lev Manovich (www.manovich.net) is an associate professor in the Visual Arts Department, University of California, San Diego, where he teaches new-media art and theory. He is the author of *The Language of New Media* (2001), *Tekstura: Russian Essays on Visual Culture* (1993) as well as many articles that have been published in over twenty countries. *The Language of New Media* has recieved over thirty reviews and is being translated into Italian, Korean, and Chinese. His awards include a Guggenheim Fellowship, a Mellon Fellowship from Cal Arts, a 2002 Digital Cultures Fellowship from University of California, Santa Barbara, and a 2002 fellowship from the Zentrum für Literaturforschung in Berlin.

Laura U. Marks is associate professor in the School for Studies in Art and Culture at Carleton University, Ottawa. She is the author of *The Skin of the Film: Intercultural Cinema, Embodiment, and the Senses* (2000) and *Touch: Sensuous Theory, Multisensory Media* (forthcoming). A theorist and programmer of artists' media, she is especially interested in low and obsolete technologies, intercultural histories of media technologies, and the representation of sensory experience.

Lisa Parks is associate professor of film studies at the University of California, Santa Barbara. She is the author of *Cultures in Orbit: Satellites and Television* (2003), and coeditor of *Planet TV: A Global Television Reader* (2002) and *Red Noise: Buffy the Vampire Slayer and Television Studies* (2003). She has also published articles in *Screen, Television and New Media, Convergence,* and *Social Identities*. Parks is working on a new book, *Kinetic Screens: Movements at the Interface,* and teaches courses in global media, television history, video art and activism, advanced film analysis, war and media, and women and film.

Constance Penley is professor of film studies and director of the Center for Film, Television, and New Media at the University of California, Santa Barbara. She is a founding editor of *Camera Obscura*. Penley has written and lectured widely on feminist media and cultural studies and science and technology studies. Her most recent books include *NASA/TREK: Popular Science and Sex in America* and *The Visible Woman: Imaging Technologies, Science, and Medicine* (coedited with Paula Treichler and Lisa Cartwright).

Mischa Peters is a Ph.D. candidate at Utrecht University, in the Research Institute for History and Culture and the Department of Women's Studies. Her dissertation is on the representation of new technologies such as cloning, brain implants, and xeno-implants in popular science and cyberpunk fiction.

Katherine Sarafian is an eight-year veteran of Pixar Animation Studios. Most recently, she served as production supervisor of Disney/Pixar's *Monsters, Inc.* Her other feature-film credits include *Toy Story* (1995), *A Bug's Life* (1998), and *Toy Story 2* (1999); and she has produced or served as production manager on Pixar short projects, film trailers, and commercials for such clients as Levi-Strauss and Hershey. Currently, she is the production manager for *The Incredibles*, an upcoming Pixar feature film. Sarafian formerly coordinated the marketing and publicity efforts of Sanctuary Woods Multimedia, an educational and entertainment CD-ROM production company, and has worked in the development department at Castle Rock Entertainment and in video and television studios in Los Angeles, Washington, D.C., and the San Francisco Bay Area.

Jeffrey Sconce is an associate professor in the Department of Radio/Television/Film at Northwestern University. He has written extensively on television, electronic media, culture, and the politics of taste, and has published in the *International Journal of Cultural Studies* and in *The Revolution Wasn't Televised*. He is the author of the influential book *Haunted Media: Electronic Presence from Telegraphy to Television* (2000), which examines "electronic presence" and American culture's persistent linkage of new electronic media forms (from the invention of the telegraph to the introduction of television and computers) with paranormal or spiritual phenomena.

268

Mark Williams is associate professor and chair of the Department of Film and Television Studies at Dartmouth College, where he teaches courses on film, television, and new-media history and theory. He is the coeditor of a new book series at Univesity Press of New England titled Interfaces: Studies in Visual Culture. His book on early Los Angeles television history, *Remote Possibilities*, is forthcoming.

index

A. C. Nielsen, NetRatings, 198–199, 201–204
Aesthetics for aliens, 63–64, 69–70
African/Afro-American music making, 95–96
Africobra art movement, 95, 100
Agre, Phil, 115
A.I.: Artificial Intelligence (film), 160, 164, 168–171, 262n.15
Aitken, Doug, 85
Alberti, Leon Battista, 84
Aliens and Anorexia (Kraus), 70
Althusser, Louis, 13, 191
Amato, Joe, 255, 263n.17
AOL-TimeWarner, 13, 141–142
Apparatus theory, 160–161, 164, 166–167, 172, 191
Architecture; *see also* Augmented space
    augmented architecture, 80–82
    as communication, 86
    information surface of, 87
    Koolhaas's Prada store, 89–90
    retail industry designs, 89–90
    Venturi vision of, 86–88
Arnheim, Rudolf, 21–22, 24–25
Art
    moving images in space, 83–84
    video art, 85
    white cube as cellspace, 82
Artifacts, politics of, 108–109
Artist
    animation/digital artists, 213–214, 222
    as entertainer, 71
    as researcher, 70–72
    triangulation strategy, 72
Association for the Advancement of Creative
    Musicians (AACM), 98–99
Atlas of the European Novel: 1800–1900 (Moretti), 150–151
Audio walks, 81–83
Augmented architecture, 80–82
Augmented reality (AR), 78
Augmented space, 75
    2-D/3-D space, 82–84
    architecture and, 80–82
    audio walks example, 81–83
    computer culture and, 79
    electronic displays, 84
    realistic virtual space, 80
    research of, 80–81
    use of term, 78
    video installations, 83–85
    white cube vs. black box, 84–85
    white cube as cellspace, 82
Augmented-space research, 80–81
Ayler, Albert, 100

Bagdikian, Ben, 226
Balsamo, Anne, 48, 52
Bazin, André, 21–22, 24–25

Bear, Greg, 51
Bebey, Francis, 101
Bentham, Jeremy, 109
Bernstein, Charles, 256n.3
Bey, Hakim, 4, 34, 38, 42
Bijker, Wiebe, 108
Birds, The (film), 151–152
Black box, 84–85
Bohm, David, 34
Bolter, Jay David, 7, 117
Bordwell, David, 188
Borges, Jorge Luis, 83
Born, Georgina, 94
Bourdieu, Pierre, 186
Braidotti, Rosi, 57n, 240
Brain-computer interfaces, 48, 52, 57, 69; *see also*
    Posthuman condition
    alternatives for, 48–49
Branding, 137–139, 141
Brandscaping, 89
Braxton, Anthony, 99
Brecht, Bertold, 29
Breer, Robert, 85
Browne, Nick, 133
Bryant, Karl, 240
Bug's Life, A (film), 216–220
Bulletin boards, 12
Bush, Vannevar, 79
Buzzard, Karen S. F., 197
Byrd, Don, 256n.2

Cable industry, 3; *see also* Oxygen Media
    gender equity in, 234
Cadigan, Pat, 51–52, 56
Caldwell, John T., 5, 8, 127, 184, 187, 190, 192
Cameron, Bailey, 94
Cameron, Catherine M., 94
Capitalism, 66, 68
    as computer-mediated, 36
Cardiff, Janet, 81–83, 90
Carsey, Marcy, 225, 233
Carsey-Werner-Mandabach Productions, 225
Cassell, Justine, 244
Cellspace technologies, 76
Chomsky, Noam, 226
Cinema, 85; *see also* Computer animation
    Arnheim's complete file, 22, 24
    Barzin's myth of total cinema, 21–22
    computer animation and, 209–211
    Delluc's *photogenie*, 23–24
    digital cinema, 22–24
    digitextuality and, 9–10
Click theory, 7, 14–25
    aesthetics of digital texts, 19
    as "click fetish," 14–16

Click theory (continued)
  complete film/total cinema and, 23–24
  digitextual "remediations" and, 21–25
  hyperlinks and rhizoplane structures, 16
  interactive/passive media, 17–19
  new media limitations, 20
  sensory plenitude functions, 21, 24
Coffey, Steve, 199–200
Coltrane, John, 100
Communications
  as implicate/explicate, 34
  invisible media and, 33–34
  self-interpretation and, 112–113
"Complete Film" (Arnheim), 22, 24
Complexity and Contradiction in Architecture and Learning from
    Las Vegas, 86
Computer, as dynamic nonconsciousness, 69
Computer animation, 209–211
  aesthetic of, 218–219
  animation artists, 213–214
  challenges/possibilities of, 214–215
  computer models, 215–216
  filmmakers and, 219–220
  process of, 212–213
  storytelling, 210–212
  technology/special effects, 216–218
  tools of, 214
  use of term, 213
  video/DVD audience, 220–222
Computer games industry, 80, 243–244
  aesthetics of, 246
  entrepreneurial challenges of, 246
  feminist stereotypes, 247
  girl's game movement, 245–249
  "pink" aisle decline, 249
  The Sims, classic boy/girl version, 249–253
  women's involvement in, 244–247
  young girls' play patterns, 245
Computer music, 94, 96; see also Voyager musical
    environment
  aesthetics of multidominance, 95–96
  interactive languages for, 97
  trans-African formalism and, 96–100
Computer/video displays (public), 76–77
Conceptual mapping, 149
Conjectural mapping, 149
Contemporary urban architecture, 86
Content-aware computing, 78
Corporate feminism, 226, 228, 234–238
Critical visualization, 145
Cruz, Jon, 95
Cultural institutions, augmented space and, 90
Cultural Revolution, 67
Cultural theories
  events of 1968, 67
  post-1968, 66–69
  post-1989, 66–69, 71
Culture of theory, 186–192
Cyberbody, 53
Cybernetic tools, 21–22
Cybernetics, 57
Cyberpunk literature, 51–57
Cyborgs, 50, 64

Data piracy, 4
Database art/artists, 40
Davis, Erik, 189

De Gaulle, Charles, 67
Delluc, Jean, 23
DeMuccio, Ralph, 199
Descartes, René, 192
Design
  artifacts and politics, 108–111
  author in authoring software, 117–129
  interface metaphors, 115–117
  politics of, 113–117
  self-interpretation and, 111–113
Desktop computing, 80
Diallo shooting, 154
Digital, 5
Digital cinema, 22
Digital culture, 180, 186–192, 255
  Haraway's vision of, 213
  study of, 190
Digital divide, 191–192
Digital image
  for filmmakers, 219–220
  for video/DVD audience, 220–222
Digital media, 183
  academe impact of, 185–186
  artist as researcher, 70–72
  author in, 118
  as avant-garde, 70
  culture of theory, 186–192
  narrative mapping, 145
  second-shift aesthetics of, 132–135
  seriality vs. simultaneity, 142
  time vs. space, 142
Digital media production, 70–72, 117
Digital Millennium Copyright Act (DMCA), 13
Digital moviemakers. see Computer animation
Digital revolution, 5
  media culture and, 3
  new technologies of, 3–4
Digitextuality, 5; see also Click theory
  aesthetics, ethics, and rhetorics of, 7
  defined, 5–7
  digital media's remediation, 7
  experience of, 12–14
  film and, 9–10
  hyperattentive theory, 8
  ontologies of, 8–9
  television and, 10–12
  über-real/grand construction of, 9
Discipline and Punish (Focault), 83
Dispositif analysis, 162, 164
Dixon, Wheeler Winston, 9
Donaldson, Jeff, 95, 100
Dot-com economy, 179–180, 248
Douglas, Robert L., 95–96, 100
Dreamworks SKG, 227
Druckrey, Timothy, 189
Dulac, Germaine, 21, 23–25
DVD, 3

e-commerce, 200
e-ink, 78
e-marketing, 200
e-paper, 78
Eisenstein, Sergei, 21
Electronic displays, 84, 86
Electronic Entertainment Expo (E3), 243
Electronic Literature Directory, 258n.6
Electronic Media and Technoculture (Caldwell), 190

Electronic suburb, 76
Electronic vernacular, 86–88
Engelbardt, Douglas, 79
Epstein, Jean, 21, 23–25
Everett, Anna, 3, 225, 240
Ewart, Douglas, 96, 99
Experience, 36, 38
Extraordinary Popular Delusions and the Madness of Crowds (Mackay), 179

Fairy Tale: A True Story (film), 160, 164–167, 171
Federal Communication Commission (FCC), 13
First-mover advantage, 198
Fleisher, H. Kassia, 259n.9
Fontana, Tom, 129
Foucault, Michel, 83, 110, 114, 190
Freenet, 4
Freshwater Pavilion, 88
Friedberg, Anne, 162
From Barbie to Mortal Kombat: Gender and Computer Games (Cassell and Jenkins), 244, 251–252
Fukuyama, Francis, 65
Fundamentalism, 67

Gambrell, Jamey, 65
Garcia, Jerry, 99
Gates, Bill, 13
Generation X television, 12
Geographic mapping, 148–149
Gibson, William, 51–52, 56, 181
Gilder, George, 69
Gillespie, Tarleton, 107
Gingrich, Newt, 192
Glance theory, 8
Global capital, 13, 37
Global positioning systems (GPSs), 76, 83
Global village, 142
Godard, Jean-Luc, 3, 21, 37
Google, 205–206
Gordon, Andrew, 215
Gorky, Maxim, 64
Graham, Jefferson, 233
Gray, Herman, 134
Grazing, 141
Greenberg, Clement, 71
Greyson, John, 35
Grosz, Elisabeth, 54
Grusin, Richard, 7, 117
Guzman, Onel de, 42

Halberstam, Judith, 50
Haraway, Donna, 48, 50, 213
Hardware manufacturers, 80
Hayles, Katherine, 48, 50–51, 54, 56
Heidegger, Martin, 21
Hickey, Dave, 71
High-definition television (HDTV), 10
Hill, Gary, 85
Hitchcock, Alfred, 151–152
Hoberman, Perry, 85
Hockenberry, John, 47, 49, 52, 54–56
Hollinger, Veronica, 51
Holzer, Jenny, 89
Home page, 206
"Homicide.com," 128–129, 131
How We Became Posthuman? (Hayles), 48
Hutchins, Edwin, 110

Hydrogen website, 228–229
Hyperattentive theory, 8

Ideological corporate apparatus (ICA), 13
Ideological state apparatus (ISA), 13
Image, 36–39
Information/capital, 36, 39–42
Information capitalism, 42
Information retailers, 19
Information space, 147–148
Infotainment, 71
Inhuman, The (Lyotard), 14–15
Intelligent buildings/architecture, 78
Intelligent spaces, 78
Interactive Digital Software Association, 244
Interactivity, 13
Interface metaphors, 115
Internet, 3–4, 12
    business model for, 205
    consumer behavior and, 200–201
    home page, 206–207
    as information retailers, 19
    interactivity on, 13
    pink content market, 232
    portal business, 206–207
    portals, 198
    portalopoly, 198
    ratings marketplace, 198–199
    sampling process, 202–203
    search engine vs. portal, 205–206
    tracking services history, 199–202
    traffic measurements on, 198
    web metrics, 202
    web tracking methods, 199–203
Internet relay chat (IRC), 12
Intertextuality (Kristeva), 5–7
Invisible media, 33–34, 42
    enfolding/unfolding, 34–35
    experience: information/capital: image, 36–38
    Gulf War and, 34–35
    temporary autonomous zone (TAZ) media, 34, 36–38
It Looks at You: The Returned Gaze of Cinema (Dixon), 9

Jam Packed and Jelly Tight (Donaldson), 100
Jarman, Joseph, 99
Jenkins, Henry, 243–244
Jewish Museum of Berlin, 81–83
Johnson, Mark, 116
Johnson, Todd, 199, 201–202
Joshi virus, 42
Joyce, Michael, 257n.5
Jupiter Media Metrix (JMM), 198–205

Kant, Immanuel, 16
Kay, Alan, 85
Keane, Patrick, 206
Kendrick, Michelle, 259n.8
Kennedy, Robert F., 67
Kilborn, Peter T., 256n.4
Killing, The, 147, 153
Kinder, Bill, 222
King, Martin Luther, Jr., 67
Kitsch, 71
Klein, Norman, 76
Koolhaas, Rem, 86, 89
Kraus, Chris, 70

index

Kristeva, Julia, 5–7
Kubrick, Stanley, 147, 153, 168

Lacan, Jacques, 69, 190–191
Lakoff, George, 116
Lamotte, Emmanuel, 40
Language of New Media, The, (Manovich), 5
Lasseter, John, 209, 212–213, 217–8
Lateef, Yusef, 100
Latour, Bruno, 109–111
Laurel, Brenda, 244, 247–249, 252
Law of Enclosures (film), 36
Laybourne, Geraldine, 225, 227, 232–233, 235–236
Lessig, Lawrence, 110
Lester, Toby, 259n.7
Levin, Gerald, 142
Levinson, Barry, 129
Levy, Pierre, 69, 135
Lewis, George E., 93
Liberskind, Daniel, 81, 83, 90
Licklider, J. C. R., 79
Life on the Screen (Turkle), 13, 190
Lifetime network, 227, 234–235
Lindstrom, Martin, 141
Lissitzky, El, 82
Lister, Ardele, 41
Listservs, 12
Litman, Barry, 197
Livingston, Ira, 50
Loos, Adolf, 88
Lotman, Jeffrey, 10
Lovink, Geert, 68
Lozano-Hemmer, Raffael, 87
Lunenfeld, Peter, 5, 21–22, 63, 236
Lyotard, Jean-François, 14–20

McBeath, Dale, 217
McChesney, Robert, 226
McCormick, Matt, 37
McFarland, Doug, 198
Mackay, Charles, 179–180
McLuhan, Marshall, 33, 135, 142
Macromedia Director, 116, 118
Macromedia Dreamweaver, 112–113, 118, 120
Maghostut, Malachi Favors, 101
Making Meaning (Bordwell), 188
Malone, Molly, 240
Mamber, Stephen, 145
Man with a Movie Camera, The (Vertov), 211
Mandabach, Caryn, 225, 233
Manovich, Lev, 5, 9, 75, 117, 219–220, 236
Marey, Etienne-Jules, 152
Markle Foundation, 226
Markley, Robert, 180
Marks, Laura U., 33
Mason, Sara, 240
Mass audience, 4, 137–141
  aggregating, tiering and branding, 137–141
Mass media, virtual reality (VR) and, 79
Mattel, 248
Media; *see also* Invisible media
  apparatus theory and, 160–161, 164, 166–167, 177, 191
  convergence theory and, 255–264
  electronic culture *dispositif*, 162, 164
  grazing, herding, navigation, 141–143
  mass audience, 137–1141

new vs. traditional media, 130, 182–186
news reconstructions, 153–155
passive/interactive consumption of, 17
real time, 163, 171
second-shift aesthetics of, 132–135
TV/dot-com sites, 127–131
Media corporations, 3–4, 13, 137, 234
  convergence of, 229–231
Media culture
  digital revolution and, 3
  mass audience fragmentation and, 4
  new-media colonization, 4
  new technologies and, 4
  posttelevision age, 3
Media Metrix, 198
Meehan, Eileen, 199
Methode Graphique, La, 152
Michelson, Annette, 211
Microsoft, 13, 129–130
Mitchell, Roscoe, 96, 99
Miyake, Haruna, 96
Mobile computing, 80
Moore, Charles, 97
MOOs (multiuser object-oriented environments), 12
Moretti, Franco, 150–151
Morse, Margaret, 5, 10
Moser, Mary Ann, 189
Moses, Robert, 109
MP3, 4
MSN TV Service, 4
MUDs (multiuser domains), 12, 191
Multi-instrumentalism, 98
Multimedia applications, 118
"Myth of Total Cinema, The" (Bazin), 21

Nagy, Peter, 71
Napster case, 3
Narrative mapping, 145
  analysis, 147
  conceptual mapping, 149
  conjectural mapping, 149
  examples of, 150–156
  geographic, 148–149
  information space, 147–148
  interface, 148
  popular types of, 148–150
  purposes of, 148
  representation, 146–147
  temporal units, 149
  thematic or structural mapping, 149
NASDAQ/dot.com market, 179–180, 248
National Endowment for the Arts (NEA), 71
Negroponte, Nicholas, 135
Nelson, Ted, 85
Neologisms, 261n.13
NetRatings (Neilsen), 198–199, 201–204
Neuman, W. Russell, 4
Neuromancer (Gibson), 52–53, 56, 181
News reconstructions, 153–155
"Next Brianiacs, The" (Hockenberry), 52, 54, 56
Nickelodeon, 225
NPD Group, 199–200

Olson, Charles, 256n.2
Oxygen Media
  advertising women's media, 231–232
  audiences/fans of, 231

272

cable, on line, in print, 231–234, 238
corporate feminism and, 226, 234–238
feminist public sphere, 227
media convergence and, 229–231, 233
organization culture of, 230
programming strategies 2002 and beyond, 239–240
"stripe"/SAP function, 238–239
textual/ideological analysis of, 230
Oxygen Media Research Project, 225, 227–228, 240

Paik, Nam June, 85
Panopticon, 3, 109–110, 114
Parker, Charlie, 100
Parker, Evan, 96
Parks, Lisa, 225, 240
Parran, J. D., 96
Penley, Constance, 225, 240
Peters, Mischa, 47, 240
Photogenie, 23
"Pink" aisle, 249
Pink content market, 232
Pixar Animation Studios, 210, 213, 215–219, 221
Pocha, Amy, 240
Pogue, David, 14
Political economy
digital media production and, 70–72
post-1989, 64–66
VDNX/Sears Pico Store contrasts, 64–66
Pop art, 71
Portal, 198, 205–206
Portal business, 206
Posthuman Bodies (Halberstam and Livingston), 50
Posthuman condition, 48, 50, 170
cyber body, 56–57
in cyberpunk novels, 51–57
enhanced body, 54–56
modified body, 53–54
natural body vs., 52
technological body mapping, 51–52
Prada store, 89–90
Prague Spring, 67
Privacy issues, 259n.7
Purple Moon, 244, 247–248, 251

Radio, as communication apparatus, 29–31
Ramspacher, Karen, 240
Rasula, Jed, 255n.1
Relevant Knowledge, 198, 200
Replay, 4
Retail environments/industry, 86, 89
Revolution in Poetic Language (Kristeva), 6
Riewoldt, Otto, 89–89
Rodchenko, Alexander, 82
Rodowick, David, 172
Rollins, Tim, 71
Rose, Jon, 96
Ross, Andrew, 185
Rowe, Robert, 97

Sarafian, Katherine, 209
Satellite TV, 3
Scherer, F. M., 199
Schwartz, Ineke, 88
Sconce, Jeffrey, 179
Search engine, 19, 205–206
Sears Pico Store, 65–66
Sela, Ayelet, 129

Self-interpretation, 111–113
Sensor networks, 78
Shiner, Lewis, 51
Shoemaker, Leigh, 263n.16
Sissako, Abderrahmane, 39
Smart objects, 78
Smelik, Anneke, 240
Smith, Wadada, 99
Snap to Grid: A User's Guide to Digital Arts, Media, and Cultures (Lunenfeld), 5
Sobchack, Vivian, 21, 57
Software design, 115
author in authoring software, 117–129
interface metaphors, 115–117
Sondheim, Alan, 260n.11
Spielberg, Steven, 168
Spigel, Lynn, 183
Spuybroek, Lars, 88
Stanley, Alessandra, 239
Stentz, Zach, 10
Stephenson, Neal, 51
Sterling, Bruce, 51
Stone, Allucquere Rosanne, 189
Sturridge, Charles, 164
Susilo, Hardja, 101
Synners (Cadigan), 52, 56
Syverson, M. A., 260n.10

Tangible interfaces, 78
Tatlin, Vladimir, 82
Taylor, Paul, 100
Technologies of the Gendered Body (Balsamo), 52
Technology; *see also* Posthuman condition
augmented reality, 78
Brecht on radio, 29–31
causality and, 111
cellspace technologies, 76
content-aware computing, 78
e-paper, 78
human applications/interfaces of, 47–49, 52, 55, 69
as incorporated/lived, 21
intelligent buildings/architecture/spaces, 78
political properties and, 108–109
public computer/video displays, 76
sensor networks, 78
smart objects, 78
social matrix/relations and, 108–110
social problems and, 107
tangible interfaces, 78
ubiquitous computing, 77
video surveillance, 76
visual media and, 33
wearable computers, 78
wireless location services, 78
Telecommunications Act (1996), 10, 13
Telephobia, 189
Teletopia, 189
Television
aggregating, tiering, branding, 137–141
content convergence, 139
digitextuality and, 10–12
glance theory, 8
grazing, herding and navigation, 141–142
Internet convergence and, 239
liveness of, 163, 171
programming strategies of, 133–134
ratings measurements, 198

Television *(continued)*
    second-shift aesthetics of, 132–136
    TV/dot-com sites, 127–131
*Televisuality: Style, Crisis, and Authority in American
    Television* (Caldwell), 5, 8
Temporary autonomous zone (TAZ), 34, 36–38, 41–42
Textualism, 132
Thater, Diana, 85
Thematic/structural mapping, 149
Thomas, Peter, 52, 56
Thompson, Robert Farris, 93, 96
"Thought Control" (Thomas), 52
Threadgill, Henry, 99
3-D interactive virtual spaces, 80
TiVo, 4, 181
Toy Story (film), 212, 218–19
Trans-African culture, 95
Triangulation strategy of artists, 72
Tribalism, 67
Tufte, Edward, 152
Tulipomania, 179–180, 189
Turkle, Sherry, 13, 190–191

Usenets, 12
Utopian Entrepreneur (Laurel), 247

Van Dijck, José, 48
VanderBeck, Stan, 85
VDNX exhibit, 64–66
Vectorial Elevation, Relational Architecture #4 (Lozano-
    Hemmer), 87
Venturi, Robert, 86–88
Vertov, Dziga, 21, 24, 211
Video art/artists, 85
Video displays, 86
Video installations, 83–85
Video recorders, 3
Video surveillance, 76–77
Virilio, Paul, 34, 135
Virtual communities, 12
Virtual reality (VR), 3, 48, 75, 78–79
Virtual reality modeling language (MRML), 76
Virtual spaces, 75–76
Virtualities: Television, Media Arts, and Cyberculture
    (Morse), 5
Viruses and worms, 41–42
Visual artists; *see also* Computer animation
    electronic vernacular, 86–88

Visual media, 33
Volti, Rudi, 120
Voyager musical environment, 93–97
    aesthetic of variation/difference, 99
    African/Afro-American music making, 95–96,
        100
    composed vs. improvised, 103
    construction of, 101
    improvising orchestra, 101–102
    multi-instrumentalism of, 98
    setphrasebehavior subroutine, 97–98
    structure and freedom of, 102–103

Waaldijk, Berteke, 240
Walczak, Marek, 40
Warner, Marina, 166
Wattenberg, Martin, 40
Wearable computers, 78
Web metrics, 202
Web property, 203
Web ratings
    business model and, 205
    NetRatings, 198–199
Web-tracking services, 203
Web traffic, 256n.4
Weinberg, Alvin, 107
Werner, Tom, 234
"What Is Digital Cinema" (Manovich), 22
White cube vs. black box, 84–85
White, Mimi, 163
Whitehead, Alfread North, 256n.2
Williams, Mark, 159
Williams, Raymond, 133, 187
Wilson, Olly, 96, 100
Winfrey, Oprah, 225, 233–234
Winner, Langdon, 108–109
Winter, Tex, 102
Wireless communication, 3
Wireless location services, 78
Wolf, Mark, 164
Woolgar, Steve, 111, 113
Wright, Will, 252

Xerox Palo Alto Research Center (PARC), 77, 79

Yahoo, 205–206

ZKM building (Karlsruhe), 86